# TO HELL IN A HANDBASKET

# to *Hell in a Handbasket*

# H. ALLEN SMITH

1962

DOUBLEDAY & COMPANY, INC.

GARDEN CITY, NEW YORK

Library of Congress Catalog Card Number 62–7680

Copyright © 1962 by H. Allen Smith

First Edition

*I'd welcome a return to loud damnation in our literature. Our writers are becoming all too timid.*

—JOHN CIARDI

*I would sooner a writer were vulgar than mincing; for life is vulgar, and it is life he seeks.*

—SOMERSET MAUGHAM

Some anecdotes connected with the author's disgraceful boyhood were first published in *Sports Illustrated* in July 1957, and appeared later in the author's spirited but non-commercial book, *Let the Crabgrass Grow*, issued by Bernard Geis Associates in 1960.

Some of the elegant details (missed by the society reporters) which attended the author's wedding to Miss Nelle Simpson in Tulsa, Oklahoma, were set forth in the February 1960 issue of the *Detroit Athletic Club News*. Rather weird place to have your wedding reported.

The author's unparalleled account of the Culbertson-Lenz match as set down in this book was paralleled in a longer version in *Sports Illustrated*, issue of December 20, 1954.

# table of contents

TO HELL IN A HANDBASKET

# Exordium

The reason people write autobiographies is that they read the autobiographies written by other people and decide, with considerable justification, that they can do a better job.

This is partly true in my case. I have read a great many autobiographies. I have even read the life story of Raymond Poincare, not because of any great interest in his years as President of France, but because he wrote every word of it in the bathroom, sitting down. Not long ago I had a second whirl at Irvin S. Cobb's fat book of memoirs, *Exit Laughing*. It is my custom to keep a scratch pad at hand whenever I'm reading so that I can jot down felicitous anecdotes and things of a moral nature I want to remember. In all those pages of Cobb's autobiography I made no more than two or three notes. One of them was concerned with his regret over the fact that his family was going to name him after his father . . . but, no, even that is a dull story now that I give it a second look.

Recently I read Mark Van Doren's autobiography. I had no thought of picking up some of his literary grace. I have enough of that. I was interested in Mr. Van Doren's boyhood, for he came from my part of the country—downstate Illinois. He has long been established as a man of great talent and achievement in the world of letters, yet when he sat down to write his memoirs, his windshield fogged up and a hair got in his butter. It seemed clear to me that he was writing solely for the edification of other Van Dorens; there were long, dull passages about his kinfolks whose drab and serious doings could be of interest to no one but Cousin Claude and Aunt Min. This sort of thing seems to happen to so many people when they belly up to the job of writing their memoirs. I think I have made a step toward solving this problem—at least for myself.

Twelve or fifteen years ago a New York newspaperman of my acquaintance said to me, "You've developed a pretty good racket for yourself, haven't you?" I do not like being called a racketeer so I asked for an explanation, and he said, "You sit down and write your autobiography and it climbs onto the best-seller lists, so you sit down and write your autobiography again, and after that you write your memoirs, and then another autobiography." He was exaggerating, of course. Yet it is true that many of my early books contained autobiographical segments, some long and some short. So I have hit upon the device of pulling those sections out of the books and organizing them into a framework on which I can weave the chromatic tapestry of my fabulous life. I have subtracted from this early stuff, added to it, rewritten it, bridged it. I am now at that point in life where, like John Barrymore, I can remember every detail of an incident that took place forty years back, but I can't recall what I had for breakfast two hours ago. More and more things have been coming back, and I have gone to my friends and my kinfolks for additional enlightenment.

Nobody—no publisher, no editor, no friend, no enemy—suggested that I put together an autobiography. If the idea had come from someone other than myself, I think I would have backed away from it. In the paste-up job called *The Autobiography of Will Rogers*, that widely venerated gum-chewer stands revealed as a man who was not really very funny. (I will have more to say about this Rogers character later on.) Irvin Cobb's book shows him to be an uncivilized and bellicose man, and, at least in his later years, a miserable writer. For a long time I have been a worshiper of Mark Twain, yet his autobiography impresses me as being one of the worst pieces of writing turned out since twelve hundred years before Christ, when the Chinese invented ink.

If, then, I have fallen into the trap that has snatched so many others, it is a trap of my own making.

In the event anybody suggests that I am not ancient enough to produce an autobiography, let me hasten to advise him that one book is not big enough to hold the story of my life. This is only Volume I of my memoirs; Volume II will follow, maybe three or four years from now. It will be fully as charming as this one. I am going at the job now because I want to get a lot of stuff on paper before my wits shrivel. The plasma is beginning to set in the periganglionic spaces of my gray cortex. I am fast losing my sense of humor because of the idiot world in which I live. It becomes increasingly painful to laugh at the human race and the incredible situation it has got itself into in the Glorious Year of Advanced Civilization, 1962.

I have heard it said many times that a person cannot tell the whole truth about himself in a book. I honestly think that I can come closer to it than most authors of autobiographies. Gypsy Rose Lee and George Bernard Shaw have said that all men past forty are scoundrels. I am past forty and I have all the instincts of a scoundrel. Even in this time of pressures and compulsions, I tend to speak my mind.

In the first supplement to *Twentieth Century Authors* (1955) I am quoted as follows:

> I believe that the human race will soon blow itself up and I am already at work weaving the handbasket which shall serve as my transportation into the afterworld.

Scholarly investigators in the field of roughneck linguistics say that a person who is going to hell in a handbasket is going to hell because of amateur sinning, such as playing the horses, social drinking to excess, striking a lady real hard, gossiping, indulging in sex orgies, and other small misdemeanors. Such a person has not murdered anyone, he has not robbed any widows or widowers and he has not been a member of Congress. His sins have been the sins of pleasurable dissipation and I understand, from high authority, that when he arrives in hell they may even turn him away from the gate, telling him that his credentials show he belongs in the Other Place.

In this connection I take pleasure in quoting William Dean Howells. "Great literature," said Mr. Howells, "is the creation, for the most part, of disreputable characters, many of whom looked rather seedy, some of whom were drunken blackguards, a few of whom were swindlers or perpetual borrowers, rowdies, gamblers or slaves to a drug."

This is the first time that anybody has ever accused me of creating great literature.

Almost all of the friends I have had have been rowdy and intemperate rebels, and all but a couple of them are dead. Many of those who worked alongside me in newspaper jobs, who were approximately my own age and who led the same kind of undisciplined life as I, are now gone traveling in their own handbaskets. I admired them for reasons of intellect as well as for companionship. The fact that they are gone gives me a vague feeling that I am living on borrowed time. I really don't believe that they are in heaven or hell—neither place would have been able to cope with them. I have no religion, unless you consider agnosticism to be a religion. *I do not know.* That is all. *I do not know* as passionately as Bishop Sheen and Billy Graham and Norman Vincent Peale say that they *do know.* I have a strong suspicion that there is no such creature as an angel, but *I do not know* because I have no evidence. I can't place any reliance on the substance of things hoped for, the evidence of things not seen. I think that there are miracles but that they are not wrought in heaven. I have seen miracles. I have seen a miracle in which three ballplayers executed a double play, but prayer had nothing to do with it and the Holy Ghost was in the dugout.

Almost everybody I know is in trouble one way or another. Tragedy seems to prevail, and pain far outweighs pleasure in this world. Look around you—take a census of your friends and neighbors. Count up the broken marriages, and the unbroken ones where husband and wife live together in mutual bitterness and hatred. Listen to these last ones, trying to put on a gay and deceptive front about it in polite company: "Oh, we have our little scraps like everybody else—all part of the game!" By this they mean that they go for weeks without speaking and clout each other to the carpet with iron skillets.

Look at your neighbors who have broken and crippled children—innocent kids who suffer from all manner of frightful and often incurable diseases and disfigurements. This, I think, is perhaps the ultimate in human unhappiness. It would be for me.

Look at the neurotic ones, the secret drinkers, the gulpers of tranquilizers, the ones who sit alone and weep, and all of these benighted people citizens of that GREAT BIG WONDERFUL WORLD WE LIVE IN—as the songwriters have it.

I am generally classified as a humorist, but I don't particularly care for the designation. I prefer to think of myself as a reporter, a reporter with a humorous slant. I am funny only in the sense that the world is funny. Once on a television show, where a panel of literary hopheads was trying to arrive at a definition of humor, I made the remark that a humorist must have a disorderly mind. I have a disorderly mind, Grade A, but I do not intend to write a disorderly book if I can avoid it. That awful autobiography of Mark Twain's was a disorderly book—he admitted as much and said he did it on purpose, and that all autobiographies ought to be written that way. I think he was old and tired and lazy and didn't feel up to the job of organizing the book.

I intend to begin at the beginning, in that lovely land of Little Egypt, and keep as close to a chronological pace as is possible. There will be some flashbacks or, more probably, some flash-aheads. And out of the whole will emerge the vivid portrait of a fine and heroic man, the stirring saga of an exemplary life, a model for the young people of America. My one major regret is that I am unable to come up with an opening paragraph as nice as Billie Holiday's. Her autobiography began:

> Mom and Pop were just a couple of kids when they got married. He was 19, she was 16 and I was three.

If some of the opinions in this book seem rude and waspish, a part of the blame can be placed on Thornton Wilder. When Mr. Wilder arrived at the age of sixty he told an interviewer that the time had come for him to take a stand; he no longer intended to be considerate of bores and the multitudes of others who make life miserable for writers. I read the Wilder interview at the time I had reached my fiftieth birthday, and I made a quick decision. Why wait till the age of sixty to wallop the lunatic center? I began at fifty, and that's why my wife says of me today: "In a very few years you will be the undisputed meanest old man in the Western Hemisphere."

# tribute to Egypt

Egypt is the popular name given to the southern part of Illinois. Take a map of the state and draw a line from St. Louis across to Vincennes and all of the triangular Illinois land to the south will be Egypt. Its boundaries are the Wabash, the Ohio, and the Mississippi.

It is a strange and wondrous country and in the spring of 1961 it came into the national spotlight twice. The Department of Commerce in Washington concluded that the nation's center of population had shifted to a spot on Fred Kleiboeker's farm near the town of Centralia, which is in northern Egypt. My birthplace, McLeansboro, is about sixty miles southeast of the new center of population. It is an important thing to have the center of population in or near your town, a thing to brag about. The people of Centralia were represented as "overjoyed at the distinction that has come to them." No mention was made of the town of Olney, which had been deprived of the same distinction. I have studied a map of the Western Hemisphere, trying to figure out a way of shifting the center of population from Centralia to McLeansboro. It could possibly be done if we conquered and annexed Cuba and Venezuela and possibly a chunk of Brazil. Seems a lot of trouble to go to.

The other distinction, which applies to Centralia and seven other towns in Egypt, came from the Kennedy Administration. Eight communities in Egypt were designated as "distressed" and "depressed" areas. This would seem to be a somewhat negative distinction, yet I'm sure the people of those eight towns were overjoyed; it meant that they would be getting a lot of federal money. I was quite disappointed that my home town was not included in the list—it is a *deserving* town if nothing else—but I can take some satisfaction that it is almost completely surrounded by distress and depression.

There is dispute about why the southern part of Illinois is called Egypt. Certain authorities say the name came from the valley of the Kaskaskia which the first white settlers likened to the valley of the Nile. That sounds like hogwash to me. The first white settlers of the valley of the Kaskaskia were probably hoary and horny-handed and ugly as sin behind their whiskers and it's almost a certainty that they stunk. They may have heard of the valley of the Nile but they had no idea of how it looked. Other historians say Egypt was originally called "Little Mesopotamia" and that the first white settlers of the valley of the Kaskaskia somehow got their geography bollixed up and switched to Egypt. Mesopotamia stems from the Greek and means "between rivers." Cairo (pronounced like canned syrup) is a slightly depraved town at the confluence of the Ohio and the Mississippi with a name that comes out of Egypt. Old Egypt, that is. There is a Thebes in the region, and a Dongola, and a Delta, and a Karnak. My own theory is based on the condition of my native heath and its people down through the years. Biblical Egypt was a land of cruelty, slavery, violence, great darkness, and a thing called the "Egyptian disposition"—meaning a disposition to thievery. I have heard it said that these things have long been characteristic of the region where I was born.

It used to be called *Little* Egypt but the people and their leaders rebelled against the adjective. There was a moral issue involved, as well as a matter of civic egocentricity. In 1904 at the St. Louis Exposition there was a sensational hootchy-kootchy dancer named Little Egypt. She became world famous for rotating her pelvis and twitching her backside and this, of course, was horrifying to the church people of that era. Preachers and their flocks have always been a power in Egypt and they bristled whenever they heard their homeland called by the same name as a wanton backside-twitcher. Meanwhile civic groups protested against the adjective "little" and their cause was taken up by a magazine called the *Egyptian Key*, published in Carbondale. This sterling periodical spoke as follows:

> The area is not small geographically, industrially, nor intellectually . . . Egypt is here to be a mighty force in Illinois. It is not little.

I am a fair man and I must state that there is another side to the question. Some people have described Egypt as the sorriest piece of real estate in the United States, nurturing a miserable tribe of human beings whose equal for depravity and ignorance has not been seen in the whole history of the world. Now, I ask you. That's carrying things just a little too far. These same people laugh at the *Egyptian Key* and say that Egypt will be a mighty force in Illinois just as chiggers are a mighty force in Illinois. Geographers have a special name for the area; they call it The American Bottom.

The opinions of the *Egyptian Key* are not to be taken lightly. It is shrewdly and brilliantly edited and its contributors all write like angels. From time to time the *Key* has reviewed my books, warming my heart with their tributes to me—a native son who went forth into the world and made his mark. Here are a few of the more perceptive things the *Key* has had to say about my work:

> Filled with coarse comments and low stories of the near great . . . we are unable to decide whether he writes for the financial remuneration or whether he is a new form of Crusader.

> Our personal feeling in the matter is that Smith writes the type of rot that he does because he knows a certain large class of present-day Americans will buy it, thereby earning him royalties. The latest in this category of low-brow, coarse, crude reminiscences is published by Doubleday.

> The book holds no attraction for the literary reader. It is overrun with obscene passages, lurid details, and sex. It reeks with poor taste, sarcasm, and vulgarity.

Honor in my own country! Cuts straight to the heart of the matter, doesn't it? I tell you, I cherish every word of those *Key* notices because the magazine, I understand, is the only publication in all of Little Egypt that carries book reviews.

So, if they are still around, I would like to pause in the day's occupation and bestow my fondest blessings on the entire staff of the *Egyptian Key*. They are serving as watchdogs against the invasion of their lovely land by furrin critics. I remember when an Englishman named Graham Hutton wrote a book about the Midwest a few years ago. It was a serious, sociological study of the region and Egypt was not treated too well. Mr. Hutton didn't think southern Illinois could rank as a modern Utopia; nor did he find the Egyptians themselves to be the most progressive and cultured people of the Western Hemisphere. The *Egyptian Key* simply blasted that Englishman to shreds; I imagine he crawled off into some corner of Hants and killed himself. And I agreed with the magazine. An Englishman couldn't possibly understand the most basic things about Egypt. The language itself would baffle him. When my family lived in Egypt the end slice of a loaf of bread, sometimes called the heel, was known as the oppsott. I'll wager you could travel all over the world and never find an Englishman who could define the word oppsott. I always understood it came from the German, but I have German neighbors and *they* never heard of it. And one other thing. There is an old saying among the farmers of Egypt which goes: "Between the rabbits and the crows, I don't know whether to puke or go blind." How could a Britisher ever comprehend the despairing beauty that lies behind that eloquent sentence?

Down through the years Egypt has always been a proud land, and eternally contemptuous of northern Illinois. Egypt was settled and (some say) civilized long before there was any hint of a settlement in the northern part of the state. The first settlers, in fact, arrived by way of the Wilderness Road and the Ohio River and settled. Almost all of them were Southerners and remain so, in their talk and their customs, to this day. To all intents and purposes, whatever that means, I am a Southerner.

I have read that the first settlers of southern Illinois were of Celtic and Anglo-Saxon strain; they were well established in Egypt when some people from the East made their way to northern Illinois and tried to establish a civilization up there. Some of these people got up a fort on Lake Michigan and called it Fort Dearborn. In order to do this it was necessary that they get the Indians so drunk they wouldn't know a scalp from a breechclout, and then they decided it was about time they started a town called Chicago.

Now comes a thing that causes me and every other native Egyptian to swell with pride. Those people up north got a village started but something was wrong with it—they couldn't attract any heavy industry, the river seemed to be running in the wrong direction, and they didn't have a single keg of nails for building a Haymarket to have a riot in. Enviously they looked to the south where, on the banks of the Beautiful Ohio, stood the thriving little city of Shawneetown. A committee was appointed and its members rode horseback more than three hundred miles and, arriving in Shawneetown, went to the local bank. They described their attempts to make a town on the shore of Lake Michigan and the hardships they were encountering, and said they would like to borrow (pronounced borry) some money to tide them over. The Shawneetown banker was dubious about the whole thing, but promised to investigate, and he did. He sent a shrewd Egyptian up to have a look at the village on the lake, and when he came back he shook his head from side to side. "Nawp," he said. "It's too fur from Shawneetown to ever amount to nothin'."

The fact that the Shawneetown investigator was in error and that Chicago got along without Egyptian aid cannot be attributed to any progressiveness on the part of the early Chicagoans. The whole thing came about by accident, and the accident was called the Erie Canal. As soon as the canal was completed, great tides of immigrants began moving upon northern Illinois. They came in swarms and built sheds and shacks and shanties and the next thing anybody knew they had a big Chicago, a fitting backdrop for the fire and the riot and the *Tribune* and the Loeb-Leopold case. Downstate the once-dominant Egyptians tried to make the best of a bad break. They scoffed and cocked a big snook northward and pointed out that they, the Egyptians, were Celtic and Anglo-Saxon, whereas northern Illinois was populated by *immigrants*. The argument, unhappily, lacks relevance. Personally I'd just as soon they had all been Indians.

But let us concern ourselves no more with the Illini of the north and confine our attention to Egypt. After all, only about ninety per cent of the state's population is in the north.

Many paragraphs have been written about Egypt by great men ere I came along. Dickens, for example. He looked at Egypt from two directions when he was traveling in America. First he passed the southern boundary by boat, and the gladsome shore of Egypt caused him to write:

> The trees were stunted in their growth; the banks were low and flat; the settlements and log cabins fewer in number; their inhabitants more wan and wretched than any we had encountered yet. No songs of birds were in the air, no pleasant scents, no moving lights and shadows from swift passing clouds. Hour after hour, the changeless glare of the hot, unwinking sky, shone upon the same monotonous objects. Hour after hour, the river rolled along, as wearily and slowly as the time itself.

> At length . . . we arrived at a spot so much more desolate
> than any we had yet beheld, that the forlornest places we
> had passed were, in comparison with it, full of interest. At the
> junction of the two rivers, on ground so flat and low and
> marshy, that at certain seasons of the year it is inundated to
> the housetops, lies a breeding-place of fever, ague, and death . . .
> A dismal swamp, on which the half-built houses rot away . . .
> teeming, then, with rank unwholesome vegetation, in whose
> baleful shade the wretched wanderers who are tempted hither,
> droop, and die, and lay their bones . . . a place without one
> single quality, in earth or air or water, to commend it.

It is shocking to say so but I do believe that Mr. Dickens mis-
used the comma several times in the passages cited above. At least
I would have left some of the commas out where he put them in, and
put in a few where he left them out. Oh well, every man to his own
style.

Mr. Dickens went on to St. Louis, where in time he announced
that he would enjoy having a look at a prairie. Nothing was too good
for him, so they hauled him across the river into Illinois where they
had some prairies. He wrote extensively about that side trip. For
example:

> We had a pair of very strong horses but travelled at the rate
> of little more than a couple of miles an hour, through one un-
> broken slough of black mud and water. It had no variety but in
> depth. Now it was only half over the wheels, now it hid the
> axletree, and now the coach sank down in it almost to the
> windows. The air resounded in all directions with the loud
> chirping of the frogs, who, with the pigs, (a coarse, ugly breed,
> as unwholesome-looking as though they were the spontaneous
> growth of the country), had the whole scene to themselves.
> Here and there, we passed a log hut; but the wretched cabins
> were wide apart and thinly scattered, for though the soil is
> very rich in this place few people can exist in such deadly
> atmosphere. On either side of the track, if it deserves the name,
> was the thick bush; and everywhere was stagnant, slimy, rotten,
> filthy water.

God *damn* a man who would foul up his commas so often! And I
used to think he was one of the greatest writers who ever lived! He
turns out to be just another Englishman, looking at Egypt and failing
to see anything much because of all those commas swimming before

his eyes. He speaks of stagnant, slimy, rotten, filthy water. What did he expect, brandy?

Let us turn to the writings of William Cowper Brann, who was known as Brann the Iconoclast. He was born in Coles County, some distance north of Egypt, spent his boyhood in those parts, and knew the functions of the comma. In recalling the way things were in his native state, he once wrote:

> To call a man a "son of Egypt" was considered an unforgivable affront to his family, and meant a fight or a footrace. It is a popular idea that, south of Centralia, the employment of the people consists in catching bullheads and crawfish, frying out rattlesnake oil as an antidote for rheumatism, shaking with "buck-ager," drinking "sasafrack" tea, chawin natural leaf, and expectorating the juice at a knothole. The "Egyptians" are generally thought to be immoral, but lacking sufficient vigor to break the Seventh Commandment; hungry, but too lazy to work and too cowardly to steal; lousy, yet lacking sufficient intelligence to scratch for relief. And, truth to tell, this portrait of Southern Illinois was no caricature a third of a century ago.

Somehow the observations of Mr. Dickens and Mr. Brann don't appear to be a bit complimentary to the sod from which I sprang. Let us try a man named Dr. John Merritte Driver, who wrote a book called *Purple Peaks Remote*. This gentleman chose to evaluate my people as follows:

> The society in Southern Illinois is loud, conceited, sometimes coarse and vulgar. It is given to display and vanity. It is sometimes what we call "raw." The best literature is not in vogue, except in isolated instances, and the music that calls forth the most vociferous applause is of the "coon" and ragtime order. The young lady who can make the most noise on the piano and execute the most difficult composition with the greatest rapidity, regardless of expression, or the thought or purpose of the composer, is hailed as the greatest pianist.
> On the streets, they bawl at each other; in the home they shout across the room, and when they laugh one is reminded of Balaam's faithful beast.

The robust authorities I have quoted up to now were describing an Egypt of many years ago. The land of my birth has improved, but not much. In the late 1950s a professor by the name of Baker

Brownell accepted an assignment to do an *American Folkways* book called *The Other Illinois*. This appears to be one of the few books written about Egypt and Professor Brownell, a native of the Chicago area, does his level best to find something good to write about. He gets to going on the beauty of the scenery in certain portions of Egypt and then he begins to feel guilty, and he stays with the facts, and tells the truth. He says the Egyptians are proud "without much of anything to be proud of." He says they have a stubborn, recalcitrant, unresponsive reticence. He dwells on their poverty and their indifference toward education. They'd rather fish or hunt squirrels than work. They live in a land of imaginative cussers, of howling revivalists, of river pirates and cave-dwelling cutthroats. Their history is a history of incredible violence. Professor Brownell speaks often of the cliques and cults of villainy, of "a culture era of common and de-luxe murder, robbery, piracy, brigandage, beginning in the Revolutionary period or before, after the Flatheads, the Vigilantes and their murderous decadence, the Regulators and their equally murderous decay, after the copperheads, the informers, bushwhackers, the local killers on one side or the other, or on no side, of the Civil War period, after the big, bloody vendetta and the lesser feuds, after the blood-soaked coal wars and massacres over a period of fifty years . . . after Klan killings and gang killings of one kind or another, or private, fashionable killings in a gambling house, a whorehouse, or a night club . . ."

Professor Brownell tries again to get away from such unpleasant things; I can almost see him pacing the floor and pulling at his hair, searching his mind for something nice about Egyptian folklore, and then he returns to the scenery, and . . .

> It is a tired land. The people are silent. In many of the things that count southern Illinois is far behind the rest of the state. Her wealth is less, her income lower. Her educational level is lower and so also are the levels of employment and wages. Her services are relatively poor, her buildings and plants often decrepit. Her fields rarely smile; her soil is unresponsive to the ancient demands of those who till it.

Pretty soon he is talking of the hills and the forest and the lakes, and how they attract visitors from the big cities, and then he has to tell what happens to those visitors:

The restaurants are poor, the hotels terrible, the stores and shops run down. The plant for human operations, the residences, the workshops, and often the churches and schools, the stores, the small factories, the production and service centers are more than likely unkempt and close to worn out. The service itself is often sour and slow. The soup, specked with soot and other debris, is served with a stony look, a bump, and a somewhat greasy spoon.

When I was a kid in Illinois the only presidential election that lingers in my memory is the one in which Woodrow Wilson and Charles Evans Hughes were opponents. There was a campaign jingle which the children loved to sing and which went:

> Hughes! Hughes! Settin' on the fence,
> Tryin' to make a dollar outa fifteen cents!

That, I think, is what Professor Brownell was trying to do with Egypt. Mr. Hughes *almost* made it, but as Florian Slappey used to say, "Almost ain't is."

Egypt has produced some great men and attracted others to its sod. Remember old Pontiac? After stirring up all that trouble, old Pontiac decided to get drunk for a while and, looking around for a likely place for such ignoble behavior, he chose Egypt and took up residence at a place called Cahokia (sounds like someone clearing his throat).

Pontiac had a granddaughter named Elizabeth who lived with him at Cahokia and this Elizabeth, when she wasn't busy feeding Alka-Seltzers to her grandfather, found time to get involved with an Englishman named Williamson. Emotionally involved—that's what they call it nowadays. This Williamson must have been getting to Elizabeth because Pontiac began threatening to scalp him clear down to his sternum. The Englishman took fright and went out and hired a Peoria Indian to eliminate Pontiac. So one night Pontiac went out in the woods to practice walking pigeon-toed or some such thing, being clobbered at the time, and the Peoria Indian crept up behind him and knocked him in the head. Thus, in Egypt, the glorious career of a great chieftain came to an end.

William Jennings Bryan was a product of Egypt. He was a great man although he had a shockingly low opinion of apes and believed them to be inferior to man. William E. Borah grew up on a farm near

Fairfield. He was against tobacco and liquor and never learned to drive an automobile. Burl Ives was born in an Illinois town called Hunt. It doesn't appear in any of my reference works but I suspect it is, or was, in Egypt because Mr. Ives talks and acts like an Egyptian. He was once a member of the Hoboes of America, Inc., but that organization, in emergency session, expelled him on the grounds that he had been "charged with and found guilty of steady work."

What an assemblage of brilliant individuals has come out of my own, my native Egypt! Frank Willard, creator of Moon Mullins, was born in Anna. Elzie Crisler Segar, creator of Popeye, came out of Chester. Consider the town of Cobden. Agnes Ayres, who once played opposite Rudolph Valentino, was born in Cobden, and a man named Parker Earl of that town is said to have invented a thing which allegedly inspired somebody else to invent the refrigerator car.

Egypt can even lay claim to Robert G. Ingersoll and, in fact, does. This is a thing that passeth my understanding inasmuch as organized religion is powerful throughout the length and narrowness of Egypt, as it is elsewhere in the land. Yet the Egyptians boast of the fact that the great agnostic lived five years in their midst. He was around eighteen when he arrived in the company of his father, who was an itinerant preacher. He lived for a while in Mount Vernon, not far from my birthplace, and he sang the glories of his new home by describing it as "a very miserable part of the world." He spoke feelingly of the texture of the Egyptian countryside, made up chiefly of mud. Eventually he went to Metropolis, a town on the Ohio River, to teach school. One evening he was sitting around with some of the townspeople when the discussion turned on baptism. This has always been a topic for lively disputation in Egypt. It is not, however, a question of whether one is for or against baptism; the arguments develop over methods and techniques. Men have had their teeth loosened for contending in favor of triple immersion as against a single ducking; people have quit speaking to each other because one argued that baptismal water has curative powers while the other said that it ain't got no sitch of a thing; bitter feuds that have lasted for generations have been started by controversy over whether it is proper for a person being baptized to hold his nose. Even the quantity of water employed in a standard-gauge baptism has at times brought on conflict. In my prowlings through the confused history of McLeansboro, I found that my native town once harbored a group of worshipers called the Forty Gallon Baptists.

Robert Ingersoll sat that night in Metropolis listening to the wise old people of the community argue about baptism. He remained discreetly silent until someone turned to him and asked him what *he* thought of baptism.

"Baptism?" he repeated, as though he hadn't been listening. "I think baptism is a good thing—with soap."

As of that moment he was no longer the local teacher, no longer a local resident. The suddenness of his dismissal caught him so short that he had to walk all the way to the home of his parents in Marion, fifty miles to the north. His experience in Metropolis reminds me of a man named Leete True in New England, who was asked if he believed in infant baptism. "God yes," he said, "I've seen it done."

Let it not be said that the people of Egypt are dull-witted and lacking in ingenuity. They invented Memorial Day; at least they claim they invented it. There are people in Georgia who will give them an argument; the *Egyptian Key* has said over and over again that the first Memorial Day was celebrated at Carbondale in 1866. After the graves in Woodlawn Cemetery had been decorated, everyone adjourned to a grove west of town and had a sort of barbecue— hogs furnished by the Dillinger family, bread by John Borger.

Not long ago I had a letter from Major General E. B. Sebree of Carmel, California, who came from Egypt and who likes to remember the region as a place where something was always going on. General Sebree remembers how his Uncle Will, a doctor, was accorded the honor of being the first local citizen to use a new-fangled electric cigar lighter which had been installed in the town cigar store. Uncle Will lifted the lighter cord into position and then got the full charge straight in his teeth. It blew out the lights in the store and a ball of fire as big as a grapefruit leaped from Uncle Will's face to a spot on the opposite side of the room, where it vanished. Uncle Will dropped to the floor and when they tried to pick him up, his body gave off quite violent shocks. He said later that enough electricity went through his teeth to run a sawmill for a week.

# CHAPTER 3

# McLeansboro, I love you!

Now and then we hear of a writer described as "a legend in his own lifetime." Gene Fowler was so described and so were Richard Harding Davis and David Graham Phillips.

Just recently, in the course of digging up information for this book, I learned that I have become a legend in my own lifetime. Not as a newspaperman, not as a writer, but as a connoisseur of woolly worms.

All my life, up to the age of about forty, I was compelled to sit and listen to various relatives tell about "the time Bud ate the woolly worm." (I was called Bud when I was a kid but I have renounced the name for fear people will think I am Bud Smith, the former lightweight boxing champion.) I have heard sisters and brothers and cousins and aunts and uncles say that *they* caught me at it—that they walked out of the house and there I sat on the greensward, calmly eating the woolly worm.

Then when I reached middle age I began to hear stories from other people, both male and female and usually Midwesterners, to the effect that when *they* were infants *they* had been caught eating a woolly worm. So, every time I encountered a Midwesterner I asked a question.

"When you were a kid," I'd say, "were you ever caught eating a woolly worm?"

"God yes," they'd respond and then, usually, "Hey! How on earth did you find out about *that*?"

I suspect that word got around among my relatives that eating a single woolly worm was an achievement of little consequence; everybody had eaten at least one woolly worm. So they began piling up woolly worms and the living legend began to build. I didn't know about it until 1961 when I called a meeting with three of my sisters.

We were going along real nicely with stories about Pop and Mom and McLeansboro and Decatur and Defiance and Huntington and then one sister addressed a question to me. "Has anybody ever figured out," she asked, "just how many woolly worms you ate when you were a kid?"

My wife was present and she almost cried out in protest, saying, "What do you mean, how many? He only ate ONE!" And I added, "That's right, and I have reason to doubt that I ever ate that one."

Those sisters of mine tossed their heads and laughed and accused Nelle and me of trying to conceal the true facts. They made it appear that I subsisted on a diet of woolly worms when I was a child; that I spent most of my waking hours crawling around the property, over the grass and through the bushes, *scouting* for my furry delicacies.

Amidst continuing roars of laughter, one sister said: "Why, every time anybody looked up, there you sat—eating another woolly worm."

I decided to make a joke out of it. I said that I had a confession to make. I said I had never got over my craving for woolly worms, that the habit had stayed with me into manhood and, in fact, had grown into a raging hunger. I said that it reached the point where I had to have a woolly worm or two immediately on getting out of bed in the morning. I said that my obsession over woolly worms had caused me to neglect my work and to say nasty things to my wife and children. And now, I said, my doctor had taken me off woolly worms for good. I told my sisters that if they knew anybody who needed a good woolly worm trapper, the best one in the country was now available. He had been in my employ for years and kept one corner of my basement stacked with shoe boxes full of woolly worms. I said that he was so upset by my swearing off woolly worms that he had taken to drink.

For myself I must say that I have no memory of ever eating a woolly worm. If I did have, I wouldn't ever dwell on it. My memories of McLeansboro are confined to a few random incidents and impressions. Thomas Wolfe, who was a legend in his own lifetime, did some phenomenal remembering in *Look Homeward, Woolly Worm* . . . pardon me . . . *Look Homeward, Angel.* He remembered many things that happened around the house when he was three years old, and even younger; he even recorded the thoughts and sensations that came to him as he lay in his crib. Then there was Theodore Dreiser, who wrote a book of 589 pages about his infancy and adolescence. Among other things he remembered that as a baby he crawled across the floor to his mother and found that her shoes had holes in them, whereupon a great sorrow came over him. The suggestion is that from that moment on, Dreiser was on the side of the poor people. It is my opinion that the literary license gimmick can be overdone. I've never been able to understand, for example, how one man writing a biography about another man who is dead can set down the thoughts the dead man had when he was a child. I can't even do it about myself, because I can't remember what I thought about, if anything. I have a vague recollection of sitting on the front steps of our house in McLeansboro when a man came up the walk and told my mother that the *Titanic* had sunk. I didn't know what a Titanic was so I asked my mother and she said it was a ship. I didn't know what a ship was so I let the whole matter slide. At that time I refused to think about anything I didn't know, and I didn't know anything, so I didn't think.

The opening sentence in the first successful book I ever wrote went this way: "When I was five years old I fell head downward into an empty cistern and was not found until six hours later, at which time I was quietly eating dirt." Several years after that book was published I went back to McLeansboro and found that I had become a minor sort of celebrity in my home town. The telephones jangled in the homes of my relatives and some of the callers were men, who addressed me by my first name, with great affection, and when I said I couldn't quite place them, they'd cry out: "Hell's farr, pal, you oughta remember *me!* I'm the one pulled you outa that cistern you fell in." Later on I told my father about this and he said that all of them were liars to who-laid-the-chunk, that he himself pulled me out. Subsequently I published a book about my investigations in the Midwest and especially in McLeansboro. The people of my home town were enraged because I described them and their town as they actually were. It is not fitten for a person to ever say anything un-favorable about his home town; his birthplace must always be spoken of with solemnity and reverence. How dear to this heart are the scenes of my childhood. That's the way the poets do it, but that's not the way I do it. I told the plain truth and the people of McLeansboro came close to burning my birth certificate in the public square. There-after, no man ever said that he had pulled me out of that cistern.

In fact, many said it was a dern shame I hadn't been left in it, and
some even said I should have been covered over. With, as they call it,
see-ment.

As for the history of my family, I hesitate to tackle it in the
ordinary manner. Once a female relative who was paying me a visit
in New York gave me her version. She was a talking woman. When
she got to going real nicely she created wind swells. Isotherms and
isobars and high pressure areas all took cover. I did my best to get it
all into a notebook and so I am able to present the following Family
History:

> There was Caleb that was your grandfather you remember
> him used to have that brickyard in McLeansboro well he came,
> let me see now, he came from Baden around the Black Forest
> and he had some brothers, I think it was two, Dicker and
> Valentine, but first Caleb, his father brought him to a town
> called Mowequa Illi-noise and then somehow they got to
> Decatur and that's where he met your grandmother Maria Fitz-
> patrick, you remember all those Fitzpatricks in Decatur, lived on
> Eldorado Street I believe, you used to go over there when you
> were a youngun and mash down their bushes and tromp their
> vegetables and one day, I remember that was maybe in . . . All
> those Fitzpatricks were Irish, come from Kentucky, but I
> think Maria's mother, that is . . . I mean . . . that would be
> your great grandmother, I think she was English, at least I've
> always *heard* she was, though I myself never heard of any Irish
> people bragging about having any English people in the family,
> but as I remember it, and I'm more Irish than anything else,
> they always said that Maria's mother—that would be a Mrs.
> Fitzpatrick—she would be an Englishwoman, at least they always
> *said* she was, but anyway Caleb your grandfather he married her
> and after that Dicker and Valentine . . . Valentine got his
> name from *his* grandfather, and Dicker, that's a funny name,
> I've always thought it was a funny name, but Dicker wasn't his
> real name, but Henry, and I suppose they called him Dicker be-
> cause he liked to dicker with people except that as I remember
> him all he liked to do was sit in the front yard and spit. But you
> should be real interested in Dicker because his real name was
> Henry and that's what your own father was baptized. Henry
> Arthur, I don't know where the Arthur came from—*he'd* probly
> say from King Arthur—but the Henry was from Dicker, except
> that they never called him Henry but Harry, I mean your father,
> he was Harry all his life so when it came to naming you they

didn't name you Henry but Harry, and anyway it all goes back
to Dicker and that's the reason you happen to have the name
Harry.

Now, as I said, Dicker and Valentine they came to Mc-
Leansboro and started the brickyard and there were a couple
of other brothers that were farmers around Springer, Illi-noise,
and they came down to Haw Creek Bottoms, but that has
nothing to do with it, because Caleb is the important one, and
he was back in Decatur, making cigars I think, and finally he
came down to McLeansboro and bought the brickyard from
Dicker and Valentine. Dicker! I simply can't get over that
name, Dicker! Caleb and Maria, you always called him Grandpa
but your grandmother you called Gran, and they had four
children, three besides Harry, and they were Vieve, she's a
widow, and Roy, he went up to Decatur and got into the insurance and real estate business, and Nellie, your Aunt Nellie,
and that's the Smith side.

Your mother's people date back to the Moores of South
Carolina, very important family I've heard, and your great
grandmother was a Hull, daughter of a Henry Hull, up around
Carlisle, Illi-noise, near East Sant Louis and she married Joseph
Allen, he come from Memphis, and she brought him a lot of
money, he was a real estate speculator, and that's how they
happened to land in McLeansboro, he had a grocery store and
then a drugstore and he owned a lot of property and gave the
land for the public school, your own flesh and blood, you
might say. They had four children and one of them was your
mother's father, C. J. Allen, but everybody called him Cad,
that's your other grandfather, he was mechanically inclined and
finally he had a sawmill up around Aiken, Illi-noise, and that's
where he met Almeda Lane, that's your grandmother, she was an
orphan girl and the old lady postmistress at Aiken adopted her
and that's where Cad met her when he had his sawmill up there.
He married her when she was fourteen years old. Tyrrell was
the youngest of the kids, named after that old postmistress, and
your mother was the oldest, and your grandmother was only
fifteen years old when your mother was born, and then there was
Willie and Sam and then Tyrrell. That was all in McLeansboro
and Cad had a machine shop there and after that a flour mill,
it was quite a town in those days, very lively, with stock shows
in tents and there was the Grand Opera House, it was a town
of retired farmers with two flour mills and a barrel-stave factory,
and that's where you was born.

A most adequate Family History, though confusing in spots even to me. On the surface it doesn't reflect much in the way of antiquity, though I'd like to note the presence of Fitzpatricks in my line. There's a paragraph by Horace Walpole in a book of quotations which says: "The Fitzpatricks are so ancient that the best Irish antiquaries affirm that they reckoned many generations before the first man was created."

There are other points that need clarification. I can remember Caleb Smith. He was a spry little German with white whiskers and in his later years he developed a passion for playing tennis, which he called "dennis." I have been told that he was a kindly man, so kindly in fact that he never got angry. That's hard to believe. I sometimes tell people that I am an amalgam of the two meanest breeds on earth—the two nations that have caused the greatest amount of trouble and strife and misery down through the centuries—namely, Ireland and Germany. This description of my ancestry amuses everyone, except Irish people and German people. *They* resent it bitterly, insisting that their people have *never* been difficult, and almost invariably they want to take me out in the alley and beat my god damn ignorant head off.

Caleb's father, who was Valentine Smith and who brought the tribe to America, needs a bit more in the way of mention. He fought in the Civil War or, rather, he was a soldier in it and was present at many of the principal battles. When it was over the government offered him a pension but he turned it down, saying that in all those four years he had never shot one single Confederate. Thus he made a living legend of himself in his own lifetime. He makes me think of Bill Arp, the Georgia humorist, who was once asked to summarize his career as a Confederate soldier. "Well," said Mr. Arp, "I reckon I killed as many of them as they did of me."

Cleveland Amory said not long ago that the desire to brag about ancestry is an almost universal trait; that a person who sneers at the pretensions of society often takes great pride in tracing his own family tree back to the attorney general in James Madison's cabinet. I've always been mildly astonished at the way people talk about their ancestors in their autobiographies. Almost always those ancestors have been distinguished and good to look at. Irvin S. Cobb made it clear that all of his forebears back to Noah were men of achievement, famous, kindly, strong, handsome, wise, witty, servants of God, dedicated to the welfare and happiness of their fellow man. Cobb was not being comical. He even told of one ancestor who vanished from West Point and was never seen again although, according to Cobb, many people believe that he made his way to Mexico and in time became the famous General Santa Ana.

This same sort of business—trying to make a dollar out of fifteen cents—goes on to a certain extent in my own family. There isn't really much to work on in the way of ancestors. Yet all of my kinfolks hasten to tell me about Henry Clay's gardener. Henry Clay was in England in the 1820s and there met a landscape gardener from Lancastershire. Mr. Clay hired the man and took him with his family back to America where he spent the rest of his life working on the Clay estate near Versailles, Kentucky. He was the grandfather of my grandmother. Hodamighty! Stand aside, boys, and let a *man* pass!

Then there was the Clarence Saunders heritage. Saunders was the Memphis man who grew rich and famous as the founder of the Piggly Wiggly stores. He went broke during The Depression; later he tried to make a comeback with a store called the Kedoozle, and that failed, and then he came up with an idea for a chain of Zizz-Buzz stores—"you zizz right in and you buzz right out." Another failure.

In the time when he was rich and famous the name of Clarence Saunders was often spoken around the Smith household and he is still talked about in the family. We have a strong connection with Saunders; there are two versions of how it came about and I have never been able to determine which is the truth, if either of them is the truth.

Version One: Before he got rich Clarence Saunders drifted in to McLeansboro and did odd jobs around town for a while. My mother, then in her teens, attracted his eye and he began paying court to her. She spurned him and he went on his way and never came back. In this version my father is represented as bragging to the other town sports: "I took 'er away from Clarence Saunders."

Version Two: A girl named Walker, a beauty, lived in McLeansboro and "took a shine" to my father. They went around together but finally Miss Walker left town and somewhere ran into Clarence Saunders and married him. After Saunders became rich she returned to McLeansboro for a visit, and Pop called on her and reported that she was "very friendly disposed." In fact, he said, "the way she acted tords me, it was plain as the nose on your face that she realized her mistake and she ought to of married me instead of Clarence Saunders."

I have been told that when my mother and father had quarrels— the little scraps that every married couple have—they were always throwing the Clarence Saunders thing at each other. What I can't figure out is who threw what? I have two sisters who are older than me. One says it was Pop and the Walker girl; the other says it was Mom and Clarence Saunders. Me . . . well, I'm inclined to just zizz right in and buzz right out.

My mother has always been described to me as having been the most beautiful, the most vivacious, the most charming girl who ever slapped shoe leather against the granatoid sidewalks of Mc-Leansboro. I have never read an autobiography in which the subject's mother was anything less than that. I have seen pictures of my mother when she was a young woman, wearing wagon-wheel hats. She was a good-looking gal but from those pictures I would not have called her a ravishing beauty. It may be that I have a blind spot as concerns photographs of beautiful women of the late-Victorian period. I have looked at pictures of Lillian Russell and Maxine Elliott and Lily Langtry and some of those other great beauties of the time. Most of them have the appearance of sickly sheep.

Now, as to Dicker Smith, whose real name was Henry. My garrulous female relative speculated on the origin of Dicker's nickname, suggesting that he enjoyed dickering. I now have the matter straightened out. My Aunt Nellie, who is in her nineties and does beautiful water-color paintings at the rate of about one a week, says that when Dicker was a child he was pudgy and he was called "Der Dicker" which is German for "the little fat one." To me Dicker was one of the great men of his time. When the first automobile arrived in McLeansboro, he looked upon it with deep suspicion, though he didn't say anything. He seldom said anything. The second horseless carriage arrived. Then the third. And now Dicker Smith spoke up. "Mottomobiles," he said, "is ruinin' the country." *There* was a man with vision!

As for the "Willie" mentioned down toward the conclusion of the Family History, that would be Willie Allen, my mother's brother, the only member of the family on either side who ever distinguished himself *physically*. He was once the top steeplechase rider in the country and lived at Laurel, Maryland. He made big money at his trade and was always sending packages of things back to my mother in Illinois, chiefly his castoff clothes. I spent a large part of my boyhood in his britches and jackets. Apparently he never wore a pair of jockey's boots in more than half a dozen races, after which he'd send them back to Illinois and I would wear them. They were usually two-tone jobs and often had patent leather tops. I wore them with great pride even though it was the custom among my friends to sneak up and stamp on them. Almost all of my adult life my feet have been troublesome, and I attribute this difficulty to the jockey's boots—either the boots warped my feet, or my metatarsals were all knocked out of shape by those stompings. My sister Lou tells me that during her days as a schoolgirl, she almost always wore skirts and blouses made from the jockey silks of the leading racing stables of the land. And just because credit is due him, I want to mention Uncle Sam—Mom's other brother. He was a traveling salesman for the Del Monte line and somehow he managed to ship us a case of canned peaches every week. There were times when we didn't have meat, but we had canned peaches to give away.

Willie Allen committed suicide back about 1918 and once in New York City I met an ex-jockey who used to ride with him. This fellow, Jimmy Collins, said he was Willie's best friend and roommate for a number of years.

"So you're Butch Allen's nephew!" Mr. Collins exclaimed. "Well, I'll be god damned. You don't look anything like him. Killed himself, Butch did. Some say he killed himself over a horse, and I believe it. Horse name of River Shannon, a great horse, great jumper. Butch always rode him. Well, sir, River Shannon died and right after that Butch Allen took a gun and shot himself. Killed himself over a horse."

Have I yet mentioned the fact that I was born? The date was December 19, 1907, and I did not learn that it has a special significance until I had passed the age of thirty. I know now that December 19 is a fine day for a man of my instincts and inclinations to be born. The Romans had a god of seed corn called Saturn, and December 19 was his day, the day of the Saturnalia. On this great festival day all business was closed down, executions and military operations were called off, and slaves were freed and allowed to say anything they thought needed saying (just for that one day). The Romans greeted one another by saying, "io Saturnalio!" and expensive presents were exchanged. Gambling was against the law but on this day everybody shot craps and played *morra*. There was much drunkenness and a lot of sleeping around, both in public and in private, and men in togas stretched themselves out on the streets and let beautiful girls dangle grapes and other things over them. That's my day.

My father's name was Henry Arthur but he was always called Harry and that was the name my mother wanted for me. She reckoned without my Grandmother Smith, a woman of backbone. *She* felt that I should be named Henry Arthur Smith, the same as my father and the same as The Little Fat One. There was a small argument about it and Grandmother Smith—always called "Gran" for short—let it appear that she had lost. But she had her way. The doctor who brought me into the world was her son-in-law, husband to Aunt Nellie, and Gran saw to it that he put my name into the records as Henry Arthur. And a while later she came to the house and carried me off to St. Clement's Church and had me baptized the way she wanted me baptized. Meanwhile my parents knew nothing of her cloak-and-dagger activities and they brought me up as Harry Allen Smith. Eventually I had to make a decision. I could be Henry Arthur or Harry Allen. I chose to continue through life as myself. That is, as myself was, or had been, or thought I was all along, regardless of error. The county clerk in McLeansboro proclaimed my legal name to be Harry Allen Smith. Esquire.

There are certain things I know about the way life was in the McLeansboro of my first six years. I know that we had an outdoor privy and that we actually kept the old mail order catalogues in it. I date back to the era when nobody ever mentioned toilet tissue— even if they knew about it. Today it is much different. Recently I was on a train riding through a town in Pennsylvania when I saw a water tower shaped and decorated and labeled the same as a roll of the famous toilet paper manufactured in the factory below. There it was, looming against the eastern sky, visible from every section of the town. And toilet paper has become a star performer on television. Irregularity does pretty well, and underarm effluvium, but toilet paper is real big and fraught with dramatic implications in this great, miraculous medium of twentieth-century communications. Sweet-faced little children are shown holding a wad of it against their velvet cheeks, expressions of ecstasy on their angelic faces. They look up ever so sweetly and meet the gaze of their mothers, and their mothers say, "Yes, my sweet, it's *very* soft." By god, it's enough to make a man break down and cry!

One of my sisters denies with heat that we ever had an outhouse. She insists that we were always "quality" in whatever town we inhabited. This is pure dreaming. We had privies. When I went back to McLeansboro in the middle 1940s I found that many families still used outdoor facilities and that morning glories still grew upon them. The word "modern" was used to describe people who were blessed by fortune and had indoor toilets. I can't remember if McLeansboro had a honeydipper wagon, but I assume there was one around somewhere. A cousin wrote to me once about a lady living in a town near McLeansboro. She had an outdoor structure and one day the honey-dippers came to clean it. When they were finished the lady called out to the boss dipper, "Would you mind picking up that little bit of trash there by the corner of the house?" The man gave her a scornful look and said, "Please, lady! We don't handle *garbage!*"

I have always been told that Mom and Pop flew in the upper echelons of McLeansboro society, and that life was an unending round of parties and that every hostess was required by social law to hang Japanese lanterns in the yard and serve Welsh rabbit out of a chafing dish. Those were the Chafing Dish Years in McLeansboro —some people even fried chicken and cooked pork chops over an alcohol flame. And everyone tried to be just as genteel and polite as the people they heard about in New York—the Astors and the Vanderbilts and the Bradley-Martins and the James Hazen Hydes.

Rigid adherence to the traditional forms of etiquette are required of people who live in small Midwestern communities, more so than of those who live in the cities. In the small town this particular idiocy borders on superstition; it begins with the banker and the people to whom he nods, and then filters down to the lower divisions of the population, often with unhappy consequences.

I have had a long letter from a woman describing a family of Smiths in Egypt and suggesting that those Smiths may be relatives of mine. It could be—they sound a bit like my people. They had no drawing room but they had their social traditions and those traditions were strong. They lived in the country, beside a crick, and there were fourteen children in the family. There was also a feud with a neighboring clan, the Bents. The Smiths said the Bents were white trash, and the Bents said the Smiths were so low that hogs wouldn't stay on their place, and the Smiths replied that the Bents weren't fit to tote guts to a bear, and there was considerable shooting and knifing back and forth in the classical American tradition.

Among the Smith girls was Effie, described by my correspondent as "a young lady of exceptional character who could outdrink and outcuss any human being I ever knew." Came the inevitable time when Effie fell in love with one of the Bent boys and, after a brief and sodbusting courtship in the woods, an elopement was plotted. On the appointed afternoon Effie was to creep out of the Smith house and meet her lover at the edge of the wood, where he would be waiting with a mule. Then off they would go into wild and distant lands—the adjoining county—to live in happiness ever after.

As the hour for her departing approached, Effie began to worry about violating a social tradition. In those parts when a girl married it was traditional for her family to give her a feather bed, and the gift had come to have a special meaning—it would insure lasting bliss for the newlyweds. So Effie sat in an upstairs room fretting about a feather bed until at last she heard her lover's whistle from the woods. She started to leave the room, then stopped and said: "By god, I ain't a-gonna go without my feather bed!" Quickly she seized the one that belonged to her mother, then hurried to a window and threw it out. It landed on a chicken and the chicken screeched an awful screech. This so alarmed the romantic young man in the woods that he yanked out a revolver and fired a wild shot at the barn and within a few seconds shotguns were roaring and the whole plot was laid bare and Effie Smith remained Effie Smith the rest of her life.

Many of the citizens of Egypt are of the type who don't believe in showing family affection in public, who are never emotionally demonstrative when other people are around. They simply can't bring themselves to kissing and hugging in front of strangers or even in front of friends. Members of my family were this way in former times, although today we have unbent a little and I always greet my sisters with a kiss in the modern manner—as close to the ear as I can get so as not to foul the make-up. The best illustration of this hinterland reticence is contained in a story Fran Allison tells. Her grandparents lived not too far from Egypt when they were first married and they rode a train to St. Louis on their honeymoon. The train stopped at every village along the way and after a while Grandma hinted that she was getting hungry. So at the next stop Grandpa got off and trotted over to a grocery store near the depot to get some crackers and cheese. When he came back the train had gone, carrying his beloved into the wild and terrifying unknown. He was frantic. He appealed to the station agent who said he would telegraph ahead and have Grandma get off at the next station and wait; then Grandpa could catch the next train and join her there. That's the way it worked.

"Grandpa got off the train," said Fran, "and there stood Grandma on the platform. They were so happy to see each other they shook hands."

It is my intention to tell about my return to McLeansboro in another chapter, coming up soon. During the time I was there and after I had done sufficient research to get an adequate picture of its history, I took to wondering why the town existed at all. The McLeansboro Chamber of Commerce is not going to admire me for having such thoughts but I had them, and if my writing is to live through the ages, I must report them.

The town was founded before railroads had opened up the Midwest. The only sensible settlements were those established on waterways. There was no beaten track anywhere near McLeansboro. Certainly there was no water, other than a little crick that passes through the old Caleb Smith property and runs on through the town and is called the Rhine.

What on earth had ever led the founders to pick McLeansboro as the site for McLeansboro? Were they running from somebody, trying to hide? They couldn't possibly have known that the railroads would eventually penetrate to Egypt. It happened, of course, and that was the making of McLeansboro—such as it is. If the railroad hadn't come the town would likely have withered away, and I would never have been born, unless by some quirk I happened to become the son of Clarence Saunders down in Memphis. In that event I might have gone roaring through life like another Tommy Manville, and the bannerlines would have screamed: *HEIR TO ZIZZ-BUZZ MILLIONS IN JAM AGAIN*.

People used to say that McLeansboro hadn't changed a bit in a hundred years and would never change in another hundred. That of course is not so. I have word that progressive things are happening in my home town. When I was there a dozen years ago the place looked pretty much the same as it did at the close of the Civil War. Now many of the business buildings around the square have modern fronts. The rococo bank building, which is the town's chief landmark and which was constructed of handmade bricks from Caleb Smith's place, has been given a cleaning exteriorwise. A new bank building has gone up next door but the old structure is being retained for vaults and storage. Thus those wonderful bricks—Caleb Smith's second greatest gift to the world—will survive. There is, I am informed, a new golf course and a new airfield and a new shirt factory and a new park and a new high school. McLeansboro is the county seat and Hamilton County is gushing oil as if it were part of Texas; I suppose all these improvements may be attributed to petroleum. Maybe not. I've heard that oil people like to keep their money and don't even enjoy paying taxes the way the rest of us do. I doubt if such things are true.

The people of my home town remain God-fearing. I have a clipping from the McLeansboro newspaper about a recent visitor, one Harvey N. Miller, described as the author of *Good Cheer*, a book of essays and poems. Mr. Miller said that from 1906 to 1910 he was a salesman and made frequent calls in McLeansboro.

"He told us," said the newspaper, "that he writes from inspiration and that to do so he must be among spiritual people if he is to get spiritual inspiration." Ole Harve added that it was his intention to set up shop in McLeansboro on account of the many spiritual people living in the town, but he said he couldn't find adequate rooming accommodations. So he took his sad departure and later on sent word that he had found what he was seeking in the Missouri Ozarks.

# *introduction to Pop*

At various times I have written little essays and stories about my father. He was a real primitive. He could cut hair, make cigars, half-sole shoes, build a houseful of mission furniture, cure disease in chickens, grow navy beans, cook, fell trees, sew on buttons that Charles Atlas couldn't pull off, harness a horse, make an automobile run on kerosene, sharpen skates, rewind an armature, play the harmonica, skin a rabbit, clean a catfish, and shave himself with a straight razor while suffering from a severe hangover.

Pop knew how to extract amusement out of simple equipment. He had a pair of beef bones which he cut and polished himself and which he employed, in minstrel show style, to clatter out the rhythm while he sang *Old Dan Tucker* and *Goodbye, My Lover, Goodbye*. He could take a comb and a piece of tissue paper and play such sad and throbbing music that strong men wept, especially when they were full of beer.

In spite of all these talents and an apparent zest for living, Pop was just about the most worthless man who ever came down the pike. It is my own theory that he woke up one day and found himself in an enormous trap—the father of *nine* children. He didn't really have the temperament to be the father of *one* child. He lacked many of the qualifications for parenthood but most of all he lacked the prime quality of patience. And so one day he just walked away from it all. He expressed his irascibility with great resounding periods of profanity. If he had no eminence in any other field, it could be said that he was a truly great cusser. I have inherited that talent from him, along with a double-ended nose. Sometimes I am criticized quite severely for cussing as much as I do, by word of mouth as well as in my books. The critics say that cussing denotes a lack of imagination, that the English language, properly handled, is adequate in any contingency without resort to cussing. Oh, fiddlesticks and shuckins! What about Mark Twain?

In his later years Pop was visiting one of his daughters in Maryland when he got his first real look at television. He spent a couple of days looking at the screen, then he got up, flipped the switch and delivered his verdict.

"That," he said, "ain't the way people are."

Thereafter he seldom looked at it except for baseball, which he loved, or political conventions, which brought from him bursts of loud profanity, violent snortings, and threats to leave the god damn country.

During that visit with his daughter she said to him, "Pop, I've often wondered what you people did back in the days when you were a teen-ager. I mean what you did for fun, back when there wasn't any TV, and no radio, and no movies. What on earth did you do for entertainment?"

"Oh, we found plenty to do," he said defensively.

"What, for example?"

Pop cast his thoughts back to his years in McLeansboro.

"Well," he said, "I remember one day the lady lived next door she come home with a new spool a thread. I happened to be over there and picked up the spool and it said on the end, '120 yards.' So the whole family, me included, we took 'er out in the alley and unwound 'er and measured 'er. She was a yard and a half short."

One of his sisters once told me that when Pop was about twelve years old he was unreasonable about bananas. He could never get enough of them. In those days bananas were as rare as rotolactors in southern Illinois, but young Harry continued to plead and whine for them and this passionate yearning for them became a source of irritation to his parents.

One afternoon Caleb Smith summoned his boy to the front yard of the Smith homestead. Hanging from a lower limb of a mulberry tree was a full stalk of bananas.

"Yonder's some bananas for you," said Caleb.

The entire family, augmented by half a dozen neighbors, gathered in the front yard to watch Pop eat bananas. His sister said that he didn't stir from the spot until he had consumed them all. He never ate another banana during all the remaining years of his life. It nauseated him to be in the same room with a banana.

Whenever I have written about Pop I have always made an effort to quote him accurately, for he spoke the language that is common to Egypt—a fusion of Midwest twang and Southern drawl. Some of my relatives have been displeased over "the way you make Pop talk," contending that I make him sound ignorant, which he was not.

I used to draw him out on his life in McLeansboro and I continued to quote him as he actually talked, with the full Ozarkian flavor. I have been able to do this because I have strong remnants of the Egyptian dialect in my own speech. For some years I have been howling against the insane pressures that are being brought to bear against writers who quote Negroes and Jews and even Irishers in their true manner of speech. Right now I can only make one small addition to the argument: it is a fact that a writer today is forbidden to quote a Negro as speaking in Negro dialect, although it is all right to quote a Southern white man as speaking in Negro dialect.

Here is Pop on the subject of one of McLeansboro's citizens: "Acey Todd was a little crazy. He was born in McLeansburr and lived there all his life, but he believed he really come from Shawneetown. He'd have spells where he'd go a round tellin' everbody he come from Shawneetown and sayin' he was the toughest son-of-a-bitch on earth, and he might near *was*. This went on for years and then finely Acey *did* go to Shawneetown. I guess he decided he had talked so much about it that he better try to make it true. Anyways, he went to Shawneetown and somewhere down there he got a holt of a horse. He rode that horse back to McLeansburr and come into town in the early evenin'. He had a pistol and he started racin' that horse up and down the streets and all around the square and across the courthouse lawn. Ever time he saw a street light he'd shoot 'er out, and then he'd yell about how by god he come from Shawneetown and about how tough he was. It took might near all night to get Acey roped up and put in jail."

Pop also enjoyed telling about the time when a portion of Coxey's Army came through McLeansboro. The people were warned a couple of weeks ahead of time that the "Army" was planning to camp overnight in a field on the outskirts of town. The citizens didn't quite understand what Coxey's Army was all about. To them "Army" meant only one thing—fightin'. The women of the town were especially alarmed, and under their worrisome goading the men got out their shotguns and rifles and spent a week at intensive target practice. All this shooting had a sort of hypnotic effect on the men-folks and before long *they* were believing that an armed enemy force was marching against their town and it was up to them to repel the invaders. Business houses made plans to close down and some people began putting up barricades and laying in supplies against the possibility of a long siege.

At last the Coxey followers arrived, piling off freight trains outside the town, armed with nothing more lethal than corncob pipes and buttonhooks. For a few hours the town lay quiet, its citizens awaiting the first awful assault, hiding themselves in basements and attics. At last a scout from Coxey's Army got together with a sentry from the defending force and convinced the sentry that nobody was going to invade anything. The Army merely planned to camp overnight and then move on toward Washington. Some of the more venturesome of the townspeople, including Pop, went out to see the camp; the others stuck to their houses with blinds drawn until all danger was past. The next day the Coxey men went out south of town and rubbed soap on the rails of the L.&N. Along came a freight train; the locomotive wheels hit the soaped rails and started spinning. By the time the engine could get across the stretch of soaped track, the Coxey warriors were all on board and the Great Invasion was over.

After Pop told me that story I challenged his veracity in a gentle sort of way. I told him that it just couldn't have happened that way—it was too much like a work of fiction. "Admit it, now," I said to him, "that story's a lie." And he replied, "No, by god, ever god damn word of it is true." So there you are. We've got to believe it.

The most famous incident in McLeansboro history, according to my father, was not Coxey's Invasion. It was Th' Hangin'. A farmer at Piopolis named Fred Behme got into an argument with his wife about religion. I have no information on the exact nature of the argument, though it might have been about the quantity of water needed in a christening in order for the baptism to "take." The Piopolis farmer disagreed with his wife and got so riled up that he knocked her in the head with a chunk of firewood; then he took their youngest child, a boy, out to the barn and lynched him between two mules. Never argue about religion.

Fred Behme was hanged amid great ceremony on the courthouse lawn in McLeansboro and it has been said that every able-bodied

person in a hundred miles of the town, plus eighty-three dogs, attended the execution. Statement in error. There were three missing
from the throng—boys of an age when, you would think, no power
on earth could keep them away from a hanging. One of these boys
was Pop. A couple of days before the hanging he and two of his
pals had a conference. They knew that every farmer and every farmer's wife and every hired hand in the whole county would be in
McLeansboro to witness the spiritual spectacle of a man standing
on nothing, as they used to say in Texas, and kicking at the United
States of America. What an opportunity to get some rabbits! All the
farmers for miles around had forbidden rabbit shooting on their
land and the sport of killing rabbits was all but dying out in the
county. Pop and his two friends waited until midmorning of Fred
Behme's last day and then took their guns and started out. Everywhere they went they found deserted farms and before they were
finished they had killed a hundred and twenty-six rabbits (so Pop
said) which they carried back to town strung on long poles.

"In them days," Pop told me, "I'd rather shoot a rabbit than see
a hangin'. Now days I know of quite a few hangin's I would like
to look at."

It is my own opinion that, when he spurned Th' Hangin', he
was acting his ordained role in life—a hardshell non-conformist.
Thank goodness that's the *one* thing I didn't inherit from him.

In the summer before we got into World War II, Pop was living
in a fishing camp on the banks of the Potomac twenty miles above
Washington. He was employed there, renting boats and tackle to
the customers, keeping the cabins in repair and looking after the
vegetable garden. It was a pleasant setup, far from any main highway.

I found Pop among his cronies. One of these was a gentleman
employed as an assistant plumber in an insane asylum. God's fact!
I could call him a plumber's *helper* in an insane asylum and it
would be funnier; but he actually *was* an assistant plumber in an
insane asylum. Another of Pop's associates was a stiff-backed old
man, around seventy, wearing a drooping mustache and inhabiting
a cabin back in the woods some distance from the camp. This old
guy's name was Mose. He was the final remnant of an old Virginia
family.

Mose often walked eight miles to a crossroads store to get some
beer and many times Pop made the sixteen-mile hike with him.

Mose always bought a case of beer and then he'd start off for home with the box on his shoulder. He'd walk maybe two miles and then he'd remark that his cargo was getting intolerably heavy and maybe he ought to drink a bottle or two to lighten the load. He'd stop and knock off two bottles, walk another half mile, sit down under a tree, drink three more, walk another half mile, and so on—reaching his cabin at last with an empty case.

One day Mose drank a dozen bottles of beer at the store before taking up his full case and starting the long journey home. When he got into the woods he soon grew thirsty. He drank half a dozen more beers, moved on, and then tried to drink some more, but he had lost his opener and couldn't get the caps off the bottles. His condition was such that he was unable to use a fence rail or a rock to get them off. He couldn't even bite them off. He had to weave all the way home before he could get another drink and, once in his cabin, he resolved loudly that this dilemma should never be put upon him again.

Mose got busy the next day acquiring bottle openers and when he had about fifty he went into the woods with a hammer and a pocketful of nails. He hung beer bottle openers on trees all along the eight-mile trail to the store and thereafter he never got home with anything but an empty case.

Living in the neighborhood was a lady who wrote novels, and she had long taken an interest in the welfare of Mose and Pop. One day she came down to the camp to see Pop.

"Mose has lice on him," she said. "I found it out today. Now, Mr. Smith, I want you to get him down here and give him a good scrubbing and get some food into him."

Pop went up and got Mose, who was full of beer, and led him down to the camp. He heated some water and put it in a galvanized washtub. Mose sat and mumbled. He was ashamed of himself, but he swore that the man didn't live who could give him a bath, like as effen he was a little goddam baby. Pop gentled him and told him that if he submitted and behaved himself, they would have a nice mess of black-eyed peas after the bath. Mose had a great passion for black-eyed peas.

Mose began to chant:

"Drunk and lousy and black-eyed peas! Drunk and lousy and black-eyed peas!"

He kept it up all during the bathing operation and finally, cleansed and depopulated and fed, went back up the hill to his cabin. The next afternoon he came into the camp again. He had been to the store. He was chanting:

"Drunk and lousy and black-eyed peas! Drunk and lousy and black-eyed peas!"

"Mose," said Pop, "you're drunk all right, but I garrantee you, you ain't lousy."

Mose laid a forefinger against his nose and studied this intelligence for a while. Then he began a new chant:

"Drunk and *crazy* and black-eyed peas! Drunk and *crazy* and black-eyed peas!"

Pop was then in his early sixties and I hadn't seen him in a long time. When I decided to visit him I approached the thing a little sadly. I figured I would probably find an old man, spiritless and debilitated. When I first came upon him there in the camp he was working in the garden with his shirt off. He looked a good deal like Harry Carey of the movies. His arms and shoulders and chest were muscular and smooth, with the look of strength. His biceps were as hard as mahogany. There was little gray in his black hair and he had his own teeth. He could take a rifle and without glasses out-shoot anyone in the neighborhood. And though work was the thing he hated most in life, he had a reputation for being the handiest man in forty square miles.

He always spoke his mind and when I asked him why he had always been so impatient with his fellow creatures he worked the conversation around to a story.

"You was the first boy," he said, "and I suppose I felt a little like other men about it. Maybe you don't remember this but when you was about four or five years old I made you a kite. Be god damn if I didn't work half a day at it. Made the best damn kite I ever saw in my life. Then I took you out to a field alongside the brick-yard and give you the string, and stretched 'er out, and I held the kite up. Then I hollered at you to run like hell. Well, you run a little ways and the kite started goin' up and got up about fifty foot and you stopped and turned around and looked at it. It started comin' down and I hollered at you to run, and you run a little piece and then you turned around and looked at it again. I was cussin' you and tellin' you to keep runnin', but you'd only run a little ways and then you'd stop and turn around to look. Finely the kite come down and I was so god damn mad I walked up to it and stomped it to pieces and went on home and cussed ever step of the way."

Up until I was about ten years old Pop always cut my hair. It was always pure torture—surely one of the most horrible memories of my childhood.

I would be jammed into the baby's high chair (there was always a baby). A sheet would be tied around my neck so tightly that it is a wonder to me I didn't die of strangulation. Then Pop, who enjoyed the business no more than I, would begin.

It always took him an unreasonably long time, or so it seemed to me, and he kept up a running commentary throughout the operation—a flow of bitter, acid language that kept my scalp free of parasites. He made disparaging remarks about my hair. He objected to its texture and somehow blamed *me* for it. His speech, as I've said before, had a strong Ozarkian flavor. The syllable "ire" became "arr" in his dialect. Thus he spoke of a thing being "hard as arrn" and of "buildin' a farr" and so on. During those harrowing haircuts he'd keep growling:

"Hair jist like warr!"

The actual cutting of the hair was akin to being broken on the rack, yet it was as child's play compared to the torture that came with the conclusion of the transaction. Throughout the snipping (he never managed to acquire clippers) I must admit that I had a certain amount of compensating enjoyment from my sire's unorthodox use of the nine parts of speech. But the climax of a haircut at home was unleavened horror.

Having finished the actual scissorwork, Pop would stand off and sight at me with one eye and then the other, cursing a bad job badly done. Then he'd unfasten the sheet and I'd bend my head for the furious assault. This was the job of removing particles of hair from my neck and its environs. He would clap his left hand down over my skull, lean forward, and begin blowing and puffing. As he blew he would flail my neck with the flat of his right hand—full, vigorous blows they were too—huffing and cuffing for what seemed like an hour. My pleasure was not enhanced by the fact that he was a cigar smoker and his breath usually smelled like the corner of Twenty-second and Cary in Richmond, Virginia. When at last it was over I would get out of the high chair, stagger into the back yard, collapse on the grass beneath the cherry tree, and just lie there. If a wasp stung me I wouldn't even notice it.

I wish my memory of other things was as sharp as the memory of those haircuts. I do know that in those days Pop became a sort of unassociated socialist. He didn't belong to any political party but, being a have-not and being a man who did more reading than most of his neighbors, the time came when he took to thinking about the creed of socialism. It has been remarked in the family that his socialism dated from the day he saw a photograph of the original, the nonpareil John D. Rockefeller, playing at golf. That was back in an era when the common man snorted at golf and cigarettes and wrist watches and mixed drinks. Pop saw this golfing picture of Rockefeller in a newspaper. He sat and stared at it a long time, growling and cussing. From then on, for a period of several years, it was not unusual for us to hear him burst out with:

"God damn Rockafella!"

He clipped the picture from the paper and, making some paste out of flour and water, mounted it alongside the mirror where he shaved. It somehow symbolized his discovery of a new political creed and he wanted to have it in a place where he could look at it every day. Gradually he expanded his philosophy. "Rockafella" was a symbol of a world that was all wrong, and that included his own crazy world.

I have mentioned his inventiveness, his talent for extracting amusement from simple equipment. Once during a Christmas shopping season I was in the most famous toy store in America and I found myself marveling at the ingenuity of the men who fashion our modern playthings. They had dolls that would do everything human except live together as man and wife. There were mechanical contrivances much more intricate than the insides of a cow. Watching these things whirr and whizz and click and clack, I got to thinking about a straight pin. The toy makers were clever, but never so clever as Pop.

At Christmas time when I was a kid we always managed to get a few toys, some purchased out of Pop's pay envelope and some contributed by relatives. These toys were never of an enduring quality and by mid-January we had broken them beyond hope of repair, or traded them off, or thrown them at a cat. The rest of the year we had to depend on our own ingenuity for playthings.

Pop was a man who enjoyed reading his newspapers and magazines in peace each evening—those evenings when he didn't have shoes to repair or younguns needing haircuts or furniture to fix.

Peace and quiet, in a house containing eight or nine children and a dog is well-nigh unthinkable. He tried yelling at us, but you can't quiet a zoo by yelling. Maybe for a few minutes, but then the leap-frog and the pillow fights and the quarreling and the slugging would start all over again.

One evening six or seven of us were creating the usual bedlam and Pop was trying to read his newspaper. At last he had an idea. He took a penny out of his pocket, got down on the floor, and began to rub the coin vigorously back and forth on the rug. All of us gathered about him, wondering if he had suddenly been stricken daft. He rubbed the penny for a minute or two, then held it up for us to see. One side of it glistened as it hadn't glistened since it left the mint.

Pop then handed us each a penny and set us to work. We rubbed those pennies until they shone like bright gold, and we were quiet doing it, too. When we had given a glitter to both sides of our coins we took them proudly to Pop. He received each one, examined it on either side, and in each case grinned and said:

"Hm-m-m-m. Bee-yootiful!"

Then he put the shiny pennies back in his pocket.

For a time after that, whenever the tumult grew large in the house, Pop would summon us to his chair, give us each a penny and say:

"Go shine."

This assured him at least a half-hour of quiet. He always took the pennies back and when we began asking if we could keep them, he came up with a new game. Once again he got down on the floor, this time with a magazine cover and a straight pin. On the magazine cover was an illustration of a girl's head, in the Gibson style, and Pop placed it flat on the rug, face up. Then, with the pin, he began sticking holes around the outline of the head. He made the pinholes as close together as possible and covered almost every line of the illustration—eyes, nose, mouth, chin, hairline. It took him a long while and when he had finished he got up, went to the lamp, and held the paper up to the light. To us it was undiluted beauty—a beautiful girl's head in sparkling pinpoints of light.

Thereafter Pop's evenings were once again quiet. When the hub-bub started, he'd call us around, hand us each a pin, and say:

"Go stick."

We'd lie on the floor and stick by the hour. We got magazine covers from the neighbors and Pop brought home all he could find. We'd spend a whole evening sticking a single cover, and when we were finished we'd take the result to Pop. He'd put down his paper, take the magazine cover, hold it up to the light, and say:

"Hm-m-m-m. Bee-yootiful!"

My sister Lou reminds me that when we were of pre-school age Pop worked his own brand of psychology on us. One night he told us he would give us each a nickel if we would follow his directions. He blew out the lamps and then had us feel our way around the house in the blackness, saying over and over, "I'm not afraid of the dark. I'm not afraid of the dark." On another occasion he gave us each a nickel to stand at the window, during a violent electrical storm, repeating the words, "I'm not afraid of thunder. I'm not afraid of lightning." To this day not a one of his children has ever been frightened of the dark, or of thunderstorms.

At that camp on the Potomac I had hoped to mine a lot of good stories out of Pop. I told my brother Sam in advance but suggested that he keep quiet about my intentions. I figured that if Pop knew I was planning on writing about him, he'd likely clam up. In typical brotherly fashion Sam went at once to Pop and told him I was coming and that I wanted to talk to him about his early life. I heard later that Pop made the eight-mile hike that day but not for beer. He came back from the store with a handful of writing tablets. He shut himself up in his cabin and wrote for a week and a half, neglecting his work around the camp and telling no one what he was doing. Sam knew he was writing, but never made mention of it. Then one day Pop returned to his regular work. A few days passed and Sam finally asked him about it.

"Did you get finished writing your life story, Pop?" Sam asked.

"Who told you I was writin' anything?" Pop demanded.

"Ah, I knew it," said Sam. "Where is it?"

"I threw the god damn thing in the stove and burnt it up," said Pop.

"Why?"

"Because I couldn't get no good endin' for it."

After my arrival Pop didn't mention the manuscript he had destroyed, nor did I say anything about it. Once while we were sitting on the porch of the cabin, looking out at the Potomac, I thought he was coming to it, for he said:

"Heard you wrote a book."

I confessed the rumor to be true.

"Does a fella make any jack outa writin' a book?"

I said that some fellas do and some fellas don't and that I had made a nice piece of jack out of the book I wrote.

"Well," he said, getting to his feet, "in that case I'll leave you buy me a beer."

It being midsummer the eight-mile trip to the crossroads was not necessary because bottled beer was sold at the next camp, less than a mile down the river. To reach this place it was necessary to enter the woods by way of a trail filled with deep mudholes. We made that trip half a dozen times, twice in the dead of night, and Pop did some talking along the way. He knew that trail through the woods like a storybook Indian and in the dark avoided every mudhole while I, stumbling along behind him, managed to cover myself to my knees with mire. Thus there wasn't much chance for conversation during the night expeditions but when we went beer-hunting by day Pop talked of many things. He told stories about Mose and the assistant plumber in the insane asylum. And he talked about how he almost came to be a rich man.

When his father died the will gave Pop two acres of land on the edge of McLeansboro. He told me that in recent times oil had been discovered all over Hamilton County.

"For all I know," said Pop, "there may be oil wells right this minute on my property. I been afraid to ask. I'm damn near certain about it, though, because it's not my property any more. I kept worryin' about it and worryin' about it and finely I just got on a train and went to McLeansburr and sold the two acres. I took the money and bought me an old Ford and went drivin' off. I'm like anybody else when they get money, I like to gallavant, and so off I went in this old Ford. Did I ever tell you about that trip? Had the god damndest time I ever had in my life drivin' down in Tennessee, right in the mountains where they have all these genu-wine hillbillies, real comical talkers."

He talked some more about his travels, about the years he spent as a hobo, about the social customs that prevail in the hobo jungles, and then he got off on the subject of women. Pop was always a misogynist. From all I've heard he was a highly moral man in matters of sex. His magnificent cussing was usually blasphemous in character, seldom lewd.

He got started on women by condemning the widespread use of

the expression, "Like mother used to make." He himself was an expert cook at campfire or kitchen stove and he wouldn't concede that women had any talent in the same direction.

"You hear people talk," he said, "about how good their mothers could cook, but it ain't true. Kids will eat anything and think it tastes good. Almost all kids are that way. A growin' kid will eat the bark off a tree and say it's better'n cherry pie. So when kids grow up and start losin' their appetites, they remember back when they used to eat their mothers' cookin' and how good it used to taste and they say their mothers were wonderful cooks. Probly nine-tenths of them couldn't cook as good as old Mose can, and he don't even know how to fry a fish."

From that point he went into a rather novel discussion of feminine beauty.

"It's all in the way you look at them," he said. "If you give some thought to it you won't decide that women are so damn beautiful. Men are always talkin' about how beautiful a woman's breasts are. Go look at one. I mean a breast. Suppose women were built different from what they are today. Suppose all the women in the world had only one breast apiece and it was right in the middle and had tits on it like a cow. You know what the men would say? Bee-yootiful! They'd go around grabbin' at that ugly thing and talkin' about how lovely and round it was and how pink-titted and so on. All right. Suppose that's the way it was. A world full of single-titted women. Now, along comes a woman with two breasts on her, like they got now. My God! That woman would be a circus freak and men wouldn't be able to look at her without getting sick to the stummick. So, if you look at it from that point of view, it is easy to see that a woman's breasts are unbeautiful."

I never looked at it from that point of view. Too late to start now.

CHAPTER 5

*return to Egypt*

My family took me away from McLeansboro when I was about six and I was nudging forty when I finally got back to Egypt. O. O. McIntyre used to preach in his column that a person should never return to the scenes of his childhood. It was a sure thing, said McIntyre, that such a person would be terribly disillusioned. What he was saying, in effect, was this: people should not face up to reality; they should never let their minds dwell on the cold fact that there is much unpleasantness and dirt and evil in the world; they should try to live always in a world of roseate dreams.

In 1946 my wife and I set out for a tour of the Midwest, taking in some of the scenes of my childhood. It gave me a strange sort of feeling to return to McLeansboro but it was not disillusioning. I had read everything I could lay my hands on concerning the town and its surroundings; I knew about what to expect.

On the last lap, driving down from Mount Vernon, I tried to remember things about McLeansboro. A few incidents came back to me. I recalled being taken quite often to the Home Place—the house where Caleb and Maria Smith lived, 'way out in the country, so it seemed. I would soon learn that the Home Place was less than a mile from the house where I had lived.

We drove into McLeansboro from the west, past highway billboards most of which were advertising God, and arrived at the courthouse square. Traffic around the square was one-way and my first act was to violate this regulation. I drove against the grain no more than fifty feet when a policeman yelled at me and came bounding into the street. The very first words spoken to the far-wandering son upon his return to his birthplace were: "Fer god sake cain't you read?" I apologized and said I was a stranger in town and he let me go. A minute later I was heading into an angle-parking place. An old guy in dirty overalls was sitting on the curb at the spot where I was trying to park, his legs sprawled out, a newspaper in his hands. I eased the car in, figuring he would see me coming, and finally I gave the horn a gentle tap. He bounced a yard or two off the curb, glared at me, started mumbling some indecencies and then resumed his seat. Be-danged if he was gonna move! For a moment I thought of making an issue of it, but then I remembered that I was a complete stranger to the town and its people—that this foul curb-sitter might be the Mayor or the Sheriff or the County Judge or even a relative; so I backed out and went on around and parked in front of a movie house where a double bill was playing, both Westerns.

After that I made the complete circuit of the square on foot, admiring the new courthouse standing where the old brick one had been. Most of the stores, facing the square, had shed roofs extending out over the sidewalk. These unlovely awnings were constructed of wood or galvanized iron and supported by iron poles and they reflected the Southern traditions of the town. Subsequently I remarked to a McLeansboro merchant that I considered them to be unsightly and he agreed with me, and I asked why they were not torn down.

"When it rains here," he said, "it rains cats and dogs. And when it comes on summer, you never see the like of such heat. If we was to tear down them roofs, we'd have a revolution on our hands. Where could people loaf if they didn't have that protection from the weather?"

I had an assortment of aunts and cousins in McLeansboro but we stuck to our resolve never to stay in the homes of relatives when we could possibly avoid it. The little hotel had no space for us and so we rented sleeping quarters at the residence of Orlin Davis, a retired merchant. Mr. Davis was an old-timer in McLeansboro and his house was built in the year I was born and, at that time, was considered a real showplace. He was a widower and lived alone in the big house and had plenty of room. Before we moved in one of my aunts gave me a little talk on what a nice man he was. "Orlin," she said, "used to give readings. He was a James Whitcomb Riley reader, one of the best, and in his day he was quite a flat-foot waltzer." I had few dealings with Mr. Davis but I do recall the time he pulled me off into a corner, looked in all directions to see if we were alone, winked broadly a couple of times, dug me in the ribs with his elbow, and then said, "I hear you write books that are a little on the risky side." I'm surprised I didn't take offense.

The prodigal son spent a couple of days going through the old files of the local newspaper. I wanted to find out what else was going on in McLeansboro during its most splendid moment—the time of my birth—so I concentrated on the files for 1905, 1906, and 1907. From those old papers and from talks with McLeansboro people I was able to accumulate quite a bit of history.

The first settlers of Hamilton County came up from the South about 1815, built themselves dirt-floor cabins, and settled down to a life of eating hominy. By 1818 there were enough of them to get up prayer meetings, and it is recorded that at one of these meetings an old Negro walked in, a complete stranger, and preached a sermon. His appearance made such an impression that he was put to work teaching a little school. Thus the first sermon ever preached in the county was preached by a Negro, and he taught the first school. I never saw a Negro in McLeansboro, nor did my folks, and the last I heard there are none there today.

The first people of Hamilton County had no town. Along came a certain Dr. William McLean and some of his friends. They acquired a large tract of land and in 1821 Dr. McLean himself decided he would contribute twenty acres toward a townsite. In that same year the settlement was platted and my fate was sealed.

For a while they didn't know what name to give to their town. There was talk of calling it Rector, after a surveyor named John Rector who did the original survey of the county. There is a Rector Creek named for this man, but I bring him into the story solely because of his obituary notice. In an old history of Illinois I found mention of the fact that he had been killed by Indians while at work on his survey. His obituary, as reported in that history, was singularly appropriate for a surveyor. It said:

> John Rector died May 25, 1805, at the section corner of
> Sections 21, 22, 23 and 28; buried from this corner, south 62
> degrees west 72 poles, small stone monument, stone quarry
> northwest 150 yards.

Sounds almost as if old John Rector wrote his own obit. They didn't name the town after him. They toyed with some names out of Greek mythology, such as Penelope and Hector and Agamemnon and Argus and Bellerophon. Then along came an old geezer who, as the historian puts it, had "partaken too freely of tanglefoot." I don't think that the historian meant that the old guy had been eating flypaper. He listened a bit to the discussion and then spoke up. "By god, boys," he said, "less name 'er after Ole Doc McLean there." And so they did.

In later years John B. Kinnear attempted a historical sketch of the town, telling how it had grown from "the darkest and vilest pit, where the slime of the serpents would pour, to a thriving temperance town of two thousand." McLeansboro, given its name by a drunk, has been a dry town throughout most of its history.

I found in the newspaper that Pinkney McNabb was the first mayor, the first typewriter in town was owned by Ottis McNabb, and "Lena Powell owned the first piano, a Steinway brought to Cincinnati by boat and to McLeansboro by ox team." When I told my father about these matters he exploded. That note about McLeansboro's first piano was the thing that set him to cussing. He said that Lena Powell was *not* the owner of the first piano. The first piano belonged to the Joe Allen family—my own ancestors. Pop said there was no question about it. Once when he was bumming around in Arkansas he got into conversation with a hobo who, it turned out, also came originally from southern Illinois. This hobo told Pop that he was not a bum by nature, that he came from good stock, that his people were important in the history and culture of southern Illinois.

"My people," he said, "hauled the first piano into southern Illinois and delivered it to the Joe Allen family in McLeansboro."

"Why, Jesus Christ!" my father exclaimed. "I married into that family!"

Joe Allen, my great-grandfather, must have fallen on evil days in the end because his name figures in a saying that is still heard in McLeansboro. One of my relatives told me that "Old Joe Allen liked to . . . well, he liked to rest. He would sit all day on his porch, almost every day. Once a friend of his came along and asked him what he was doing these days. He said, 'I'm helpin' Joe Allen.' That remark went all over town, and ever since then whenever a man is out of work and loafing or just plain no-good lazy, he says he's helpin' Joe Allen."

I enjoyed reading the country correspondence in those newspapers of forty years back—items from such places as Dogtown and Opossum

Creek and Piopolis. Most of the country correspondents seemed to be temperance people and the demon rum was roughed up in almost every column of crossroads chitchat. There were items such as this:

> Ernest Bode was seen Saturday night riding his horse in Craw Lane. Drunk as usual.

Or this one:

> The neighbors of Mrs. Katie Gregg saved her from being murdered last week when they found her husband beating her with a piece of stovewood. He has been drunk for three years.

Along about the time of my birth Mrs. Martha Gullic inserted an ad in the *Times*. It was strongly worded. Her husband had just died and she wanted to deny the malicious gossip that he passed away in consequence of drinking wood alcohol. He died, said his widow, of nothing more serious than cramps of the stomach and bowels. Her notice was headed: Card of Thanks.

At the very moment of my birth Professor Oldreive, a sort of a nut, was walking on water not many miles to the south of McLeansboro. The news dispatches said that the professor got into an argument with a steamboat captain in Cincinnati, heaping abuse on the captain's romantic profession and making the statement that he could *walk* on water all the way from Cincinnati to New Orleans. The steamboat captain bet the professor five thousand dollars that he couldn't do it. Before long the professor was on his way, and he was walking on the surface of the Ohio River, going past Egypt, at the time I was born.

The story in the McLeansboro paper said that Professor Oldreive wore shoes shaped like little boats. They were four feet long, six inches wide and six inches deep. "At the bottom of each shoe," said the dispatch, "are duck flaps to aid the professor in moving forward."

Accompanying the professor on his long liquid walk were his wife and his manager, who traveled alongside him in a skiff. He walked with "a twisting motion" and progress was very slow because even the duck flaps wouldn't hold the shoes steady in the water. The *Times* correspondent reported that there was much talk among the riverfront Egyptians to the effect that the professor was a fake and that there was some kind of crooked business involved in his adventure. There was even gossip that he walked on water only when he was passing a town and that he rode in the skiff between towns. When this allegation was relayed to the professor he slapped water real hard and issued an angry denial.

I have spent hours trying to find out if the professor ever made it. There was no later word in the *Times* and I found no reference to him in the books I've examined. I doubt very much that he ever got to New Orleans, or even to Memphis. If, at any time in our history, a man walked on water from Cincinnati to New Orleans, then he would surely be in the history books, and there would be a statue of him, duck flaps and all, somewhere along the way.

It is required by law that any person who undertakes a reminiscence of childhood in the Midwest shall write at least one chapter about food. It is not necessary that he deal with the taste of it, the smell of it being the important thing. Unfortunately, I can remember only one fact about food as it touched my consciousness during the first six years of my life. Bacon rind was always saved and put aside in our house and my father used it to rub on his handsaw.

Eating habits have not changed much in McLeansboro down through the years. They stack it high, and anything that can be fried, they fry it. That is probably why, in this enlightened age, I often defy my wife, who is a broiler, and fry stuff for myself. She believes, with a great many other people, that fried foods are all but lethal.

At the home of the Cooneys, my cousins, we had a magnificent meal one noontime—fried chicken, fried potatoes, fried lettuce, fried peas, fried lemon chiffon pie, and coffee that was first put through the percolator and then, I think, fried. Most of my McLeansboro relatives were present for this banquet and, while we sopped gravy with oppsotts, I brought up the matter of the house in which I was born.

Aunt Nellie, the oldest and wisest of all those present, said I was born in the little cottage on Hancock Street. Her daughter, Eula Cooney, said she didn't think so; that she seemed to remember that the Smiths moved to another little house near the Catholic church just before I was born. Aunt Vieve was under the impression that we already lived in the house on East Main Street, next door to the Goodrich family. Aunt Nellie insisted that she ought to know the circumstances of the mighty event—her husband was the attending physician, and they lived catty-cornered from the house on Hancock Street. Veronica Hassett said she was too young to remember, but that she was willing to instigate an inquiry around town. As soon as she found out which house was the correct one, she said, she would get some film and take some pictures of me in front of my birthplace.

Aunt Nellie (I always think of a baseball pitcher whenever I write her name) talked about Dicker and Valentine and how they seldom went into the business district of town unless their brother Caleb was going. Caleb was just a trifle over five feet tall; Dicker was a little taller, and Valentine was the tallest of the three. It was their custom always to walk in single file wherever they went—Caleb in front, then Dicker, and Valentine bringing up the rear. That was the way they "went in to town" and as the small parade moved toward the square they rarely spoke a word to each other. It was common among the townspeople, when they saw the Smith men approaching, to say: "Here comes rag, tag and bobtail." I am a grandson of Rag.

None of my relatives remembered anything about the matter of me and the comet pills. This was an incident my father told me about, saying that he had kept it a secret for years because he had certain apprehensions about it.

Back about 1910 on a Saturday afternoon Pop and some of his friends took what he called a kag of beer into the woods. They set the kag on a hillside and went to work on it. When they returned to town they found a pitchman from St. Louis at work in the court-house square. This man had come into McLeansboro with a barrel (or kag) full of pills.

Halley's comet was in the sky at that time and the pitchman preached that the comet was giving off lethal gases, that a mere whiff of these fumes would be sufficient to kill a person, and that the only way to gain immunity was to swallow one of his pills. They were twenty-five cents each and the man was selling them as fast as he could hand them out. Word of his presence and of his lifesaving pills spread swiftly over the county and those farmers not already in town were hitching up their sandy-land mules and hurrying across the dusty roads, watching the sky, hoping the comet gas wouldn't get them before they reached the square.

My father said he listened to the pitchman's spiel and, becoming smitten with beery foreboding, got to worrying about me, his only son, and the likelihood of my being carried off by comet fumes before I'd even had a good start in life; so he stepped up and bought one of the pills and hurried home with it, and when nobody was looking, poked it down my gullet.

"I never told anybody about it," he said, "because I figured that maybe the pill had some kind of a permanent effect on you."

I don't think it did. *Something* had a permanent effect on me, but I don't think it was the comet pill. I think it may have been the nux-you-ated iron . . . but that comes a little later.

After the Cooney fry I went over to Aunt Vieve's house and she got out some family albums. They were filled with ancient photographs, mostly of men with long beards and a belligerent fear of God reflected in their eyes; they all looked as though they hated the photographer who was taking their pictures and would shortly assault him. Most of them were my kin but I had never heard of them and was just as happy that I hadn't. Those fierce-looking old baboons were inhabitants of Egypt and other parts of Illinois and I can't understand why William Jennings Bryan, who grew up in the same region, ever went to Dayton, Tennessee, and took the side he did. The tintypes of my ancestors argue more for the theory of evolution than all the writings of Darwin.

Aunt Vieve also had scrapbooks and these contained fragments of minor family history—newspaper clippings of births and marriages and who went to visit for a week in East St. Louis or Decatur. There were occasional items relating that Miss Genevieve Smith had gone to Decatur to visit relatives.

"Oh, yes," said Aunt Vieve, "I used to be on the go all the time. I always went up to Decatur to visit the Skellys, but every time I came back to McLeansboro, I'd swear I'd never do it again. In those days I thought the Skelly girls led an awful fast life. It was just go, go, go, go, from morning to night."

"Where did you go?" I asked her.

"Down to the drugstore," said Aunt Vieve. The memory of those days of helling around in a drugstore reminded her of some girls who were her friends in McLeansboro and whose father was a stern and righteous man. He was forever complaining about the corrupt ways of his girls. "All my daughters ever do," he would say, "is put tal-sum on their faces and go down to the depot."

The telephone seemed to ring all the time. Word had got around and people wanted to be helpful. A lady called to report an incident which she said occurred when I was about four years old. She was, at that time, a neighbor of ours, and she said I turned up at her house one afternoon and said:

"Odie, give me some tobacco."

"What on earth do *you* want with tobacco?" she demanded.

"I'm gonna put it in my mouth," I said, "and I'm gonna chew, and then I'm gonna *SPIT!*"

Then Doc Tevis called and said he had been a pal of my father's when they were young men and he would greatly enjoy having a talk with me. He was a dentist so I arranged to have him clean my teeth while he told stories of old times in McLeansboro. He had machinery going inside my mouth most of the time and I couldn't take notes, but I remember some of the things he talked about.

During one of the brief periods when McLeansboro tolerated saloons, a man named Earl Something kept a bar on the square. His best customer was a middle-aged citizen, a retired farmer, who was a sort of marathon drinker. This man was always waiting at the door each morning when Earl arrived to open the saloon. The customer began his day with breakfast—three quick ones. Then he walked out and took his place at the curb, leaning against one of the iron posts which supported the shed roof over the sidewalk. He would lean there motionless for perhaps an hour, then march back into the saloon, have another drink, and return to his pole. This procedure was repeated during all the hours the saloon was open. I sometimes think that man had figured out the ideal way to live.

One morning he must have had an upset stomach; either that or he took on more than his customary load. At any rate, he was leaning against his pole along about noontime when his legs collapsed and he slumped to the curb and just lay there. A few moments later a prominent merchant came down the street. He took one look at the fallen man, stepped over to the door of the saloon, stuck his head inside, and yelled:

"Hey, Earl! Yer sign's down!"

I asked Doc Tevis if the town had a village atheist, which is standard equipment for small communities, and he said he didn't believe so at the moment; but at one time there was an old guy who went around talking socialism and atheism and, as regards the latter creed, he had a convincer which he used on anybody who would hear him out. After enumerating all the standard proofs, McLeansboro's village atheist would deliver this convincer as follows:

"You think they's a God? You think they's a God that's always good to his chuldern? Well, *I'll* show you how good he is. You ever look at a hog real close? How many hams has he got on him? Right. Two hams. On the back. Now—*WHY AIN'T HE ALSO GOT HAMS ON THE FRONT?* If they was a God, that space on the front of a hog wouldn't of been wasted, would it? They ain't no reason on earth why a hog shouldn't pervide a man with four hams insteada two, and if they was a God and he was takin' proper care a his chuldern, then by god he'd a put them extra hams on."

Doc Tevis finished working on my teeth, hung up his drill, then stood back and looked at me as I lay in his chair. Finally he grinned a broad grin and then he started whacking me across the nose with his index finger, roaring: "Right by god on the end of your nose you look exactly like your old man!"

I have already remarked that I inherited a double-ended nose from my father. Once I decided I would seek out an eye-ear-nose-and-throat man and have him look at it and tell me something about it. My wife said that would be a silly thing to do, that I would look like a fool. I answered this haggle with customary reason and aplomb, saying, "What the hell good is an eye-ear-nose-and-throat doctor if he can't tell you the reason for a double-ended nose?" But I never went to find out.

Later that same day a telephone call came from a Mrs. Green. She said that her departed husband had been a friend of Grandpa Cad Allen and that Grandpa Allen had once presented Mr. Green with a very famous meerschaum pipe. Now that Mr. Green was gone, I could have that famous pipe if I wanted it. I am not a smoker of pipes nor a collector of antiques but I hurried over to Mrs. Green's house. I asked her what was famous about the pipe and she said that it had once belonged to Captain Longworth and that Captain Longworth had been an admirer of my grandfather and had given it to him, and my grandfather had been an admirer of Mr. Green, and had given it to *him*. She went into another room and got out the pipe, which looked somewhat like a small saxophone.

My main interest was in the historical significance of this pipe and I asked Mrs. Green about the Captain Longworth who had given it to Cad Allen.

"You mean to sit there and say you never heard of Captain Longworth?" she said. "Why, sakes alive, he was famous around here."

"What was he famous for?"

"Well, I couldn't say for sure, but anybody in McLeansboro will tell you he was famous. I think he must have been in some war or other. You look up about him and you'll find that his pipe is about as famous a pipe as there is in the country."

I went back to the house where I was rooming and cross-examined Orlin Davis about Captain Longworth.

"Yes," said Mr. Davis, "I remember him. I think he clerked in a grocery store. He wasn't around here very long."

"What was he famous for?"

"He wasn't famous for anything that I ever heard about. He just worked in a grocery store."

"Why was he called 'Captain?' "

"Because he was a private in the Civil War."

Grandpa Cad Allen was famous for more things than that, at least in McLeansboro. He was celebrated for the sage observations he made about life, such as: "Generally speakin', ugly people are nicer people than good-lookin' people." He was a member of the volunteer fire department although he didn't occupy the eminence of my other grandfather, Caleb Smith, who was First Plugman of Hose Company No. 1. I have heard it said that nobody enjoyed a good fire so much as Cad Allen. One summer night the alarm sounded and Cad leaped out of bed and began throwing on some clothes. He was all ready to rush out of the house when one of his young daughters began wailing in another room, saying she wanted a drink of water. Cad went to the kitchen and got it and took it to her and had to stand by until she had finished it. Again he started for the door, but my grandmother called him back and asked him to turn down the wick in the lamp near her bed. He came back and turned it down and for the third time started for the door, but halfway there he stopped and announced loudly: "Now, if they's *anything else* anybody wants, just speak up, because I ain't in no goddam hurry a-tall!"

When Cad Allen was on his deathbed his next-door neighbor, Mrs. Vada Johnson, would stop in to visit with him. One day she baked a mince pie and as was her custom she put two cups of whisky in it. When the pie was done she took a large piece of it next door and offered it to Cad. He thanked her but said he couldn't eat anything, that it wouldn't stay down. "But Uncle Cad," she said, "this pie has almost a pint of whisky cooked into it." He struggled up on one elbow and stared at the pie and then he said he thought he might give it a try. He wolfed it down, and it stayed there, and he said to Mrs. Johnson: "I bleeve that's the best damn pie I ever ate!"

In the course of my rambling around McLeansboro I met a middle-aged woman who was famous for her piety. She was the wife of a well-to-do businessman and she was actively against drinking, smoking, cussing, gambling, and other pleasant things. One day she told me a story—such a story as I would never permit within the pages of a book bearing my name, except for the incredible fact that it came from the lips of such a devout and dedicated person. We happened to meet down at the square and were standing and talking when the subject of our conversation sent me off on a story which I realized, too late, was slightly off color. I had to go on with it, and I did, and arrived at the "risky" tagline. I wouldn't have been surprised if that lady had turned her back on me, but instead she tittered, and then she asked me if I ever knew Ferd Clemming. I said I didn't.

"Ferd," she said, "was a fellow worked as a clerk in the —— hardware store. He was a little short and skinny man, bald-headed and very bashful. One day there was a trashy peroxide blonde came to town. I can't remember what she came here for but, anyway, she walked into the hardware store and Ferd Clemming waited on her. She said she wanted a doorknob, and Ferd went and got it for her, and laid it down on the counter in front of her. Then he looked at her and said, 'You wanna screw for this doorknob?' And that peroxide blonde said, 'It's all right with me if it's all right with you.' "

Isn't that awful? You never know what to expect in McLeansboro.

The discussions over the location of my birthplace were now growing hotter. Aunt Nellie said she had talked to a woman who had been in the house when I was born, and the house was the one on Hancock Street. Aunt Vieve stuck to her guns and Cousin Veronica continued combing the town for further evidence.

On our last day in town the matter was settled; it was Hancock Street and when I arose that morning I spoke feelingly about it, and Nelle said: "I wish you would control yourself about that crummy cottage. Who do you think you are—Voltaire?" I don't believe in wrangling. Compromise is the thing. I simply said to her, "Shut up." Then I regretted saying it. Up to that moment she had taken McLeansboro without complaining, but I knew that portions of it had been rough on her. The dust, for one thing. In Egypt we had not seen any of that mud which Dickens and Ingersoll had found to be the chief characteristic of the region. I don't believe, however, that I was ever in a dustier place. The stuff seemed to hang suspended in the air and moved around only when it wanted to get into the houses or into my nostrils. I hated it as much as my wife hated it but I think it's a small quibble and if I had lived all of my years in McLeansboro I might possibly have become accustomed to it by this time, and I would have been uncomfortable and asthmatic without it.

Veronica came to get me and the two of us, with camera, set out for Christian Hill. This is the name given the eastern residential section of the town as opposed to Dogtown on the west. If I had been given my choice I think I would have chosen Dogtown as my favorite place to be born, just so I could talk about it, but it was Christian Hill and Hancock Street. We pulled up in front of a small white house and Veronica said: "There she is."

"Bow your head," I said. "Always be reverent in front of this house."

"Okay," said Veronica. "Now get over there in the yard and pose."

I suggested that the people who lived there wouldn't like it but she felt certain nobody would object. I got out of the car and walked across the scraggy lawn, deep in thought, searching my soul for a tingle, a stab of pain. Veronica began taking pictures from various angles and distances and was trying to balance herself on top of a fireplug when I heard a rustling noise behind me. An elderly woman had come out on the porch and I could see from her face that she was alarmed.

"What is it?" she asked in a quavering voice. "Are we losing it? Oh, please don't take it away from us!"

"Pardon me, madam," I said. "I was born in this house."

"Right out from under us!" she wailed. "That's what you're going to do! I can tell! You don't need to try to fool me!"

"I was born right here in this house," I insisted, "and we just wanted to take some pictures, and I hope you don't mind."

She considered my words for a while and then got it straight.

"Oh," she said. "Then you're not going to rent it right out from under us?"

I assured her we were not. I wanted to tell her that the house in which she lived would very likely some day be a sort of historical edifice, a museum, a shrine, but Veronica interrupted, complaining about my inadequacy as a photographic subject. She felt that I ought to look like an author instead of what I looked like; that there was little point in a picture of me the way I was posing. I told her that to look like an author I would have to stick a pipe in my face, or roach up my hair, or pose beside a fireplace with my hand on a large dog, or hanging in the rigging of a schooner with a yachting cap on my head, or holding my chin in my hand with my forefinger laid up against my nose, or correcting galley proofs with a studious frown, or wearing a black beard. None of these poses appeared to fit the situation so I just went ahead looking like the guy who was delivering the laundry to the little house on Hancock Street.

I asked that extra prints be ordered and that Aunt Nellie use them, together with her memory of how the house looked in former years, to do me a nice painting of my birthplace.

A month or so later, back in New York, the water color arrived. It was a beautiful job and I made plans to have it put in a nice frame and hung on the wall of my office. Then my mother came to visit me and I got out the painting, eager for her to see the reverence in which I held the house where she bore me.

She looked at it and said:

"Why, son, *that's* not the house you were born in. You were born in a little house a couple of blocks from this place. I ought to know."

A darkling cloud came over me, and a great sadness took me in its grip; but only for a moment. Then I said a bad word, a word containing more than three letters and less than five, and preceded by "Oh." I said it right in front of my own mother, and she didn't speak a word of protest. I think maybe she understood.

# into the Land of Lincoln

Along about 1913 the Panic of 1907 penetrated to Mc-Leansboro and the brick business went into a decline. Pop had been working at his father's brickyard since his marriage but now he had to look around for something else. Out at the Home Place my grandfather kept a little shed next to the house and in the shed he made cigars up to the time of his death. Possibly for security reasons he taught each of his children, including his daughters, to make cigars.

Pop took off for Decatur, where he soon got a job as a cigar maker and sent for his family. For the next dozen years we were a traipsin' family. My older sisters have stronger memories of it than I, although I can remember the exciting train trips from town to town. There was always that pungent smoke, and cinders enough to load the eyes of all the children, and flies galore, and dirty, whining, squalling, runny-nosed kids, and fragments of food scattered up and down the aisle, and dirty diapers and many other lovely and nostalgic things. We moved from town to town but also in each town we moved from house to house. On our first jump to Decatur we went into Abe Lincoln country and I think of a story that Abe used to tell about his own family. The Lincolns went from Kentucky to Illinois by short stages; Tom Lincoln was always looking for a better cabin a bit farther up the trail. Abe said that the Lincoln chickens got so they knew when moving day had come round again. Those chickens would take note of certain activities in and around the cabin; then they'd all go over to the wagon, lie down on their backs and stick their legs up, ready to be tied.

We lived in two or three houses in Decatur but finally settled on a big rambling place on West King Street. All of my boyhood—in the sense of storybook boyhood—was compressed into the few years we spent on West King Street. These were my Tom Sawyer and Penrod days, and I can remember a great deal about them.

For a brief period I was a boy scout but I never progressed beyond the tenderfoot class. In Fairview Park stood a structure known as the "Lincoln Log Cabin Courthouse." It was the patriotic custom of Decatur scoutmasters to take small groups of boys out to this cabin and sleep them overnight. I went on one such expedition. The cabin, as I remember it, was a one-room affair and after we had all disposed ourselves around the rough floor, our scoutmaster gave us a solemn lecture. He said that the walls and the floor and the ceiling were hallowed by the spirit of Abraham Lincoln, that Abe used to pace back and forth on these very planks when he was arguing a case. It was a great and beautiful thing that we should have the privilege of sleeping in such a sanctified place and we should try to remember every moment of it, and every sensation, so we could tell our grandchildren about it.

Also in Fairview Park I once participated in a wand drill.

I lived in a land where the influence of McGuffey's Readers was still a power, as it is to this day. I can't remember that I ever saw one of his Readers during my childhood and I'm quite happy that I didn't. I've read a lot about McGuffey and his miserable schoolbooks and I'm quite sure that he was one of the ten most *evil* influences ever let loose on the American people. Because of McGuffey and others of his kind I grew up in an atmosphere of moral lunacy and witless chauvinism. Thus there were certain sentimental matters connected with my boyhood, but not many. I worked at various boy-jobs because that was the only way we had of getting pocket money. The word "allowance" hadn't been invented yet.

The first paying job I ever had was driving a cow. This was not an uncommon employment for boys in our section of Decatur. The town had its share of retired farmers and some of them were unable to exist in this roaring metropolis without certain comforts and conveniences out of their old way of life, such as milk cows. In order to keep cows they had to graze them in the fields outside the town limits and this is where my friend Donnie Etherton and I came in. We were hired by the proprietor of a cow to take his animal from his home to the pasture, a couple of miles distant, at daybreak each morning; then in the evenings we would drive the cow from the pasture to the farmer's house. For this service we divided twenty cents a week. I remember the first day we had the job. There was some fear that I wouldn't awaken in time. Before I went to bed I poked a small hole in the middle of the window screen, ran a fishline through it to the ground, and then tied the end of the line around my big toe. Donnie was to come along about daybreak and give the line a few jerks, and we'd be on our way. During that night a storm came up and my mother came in and closed the window. When Donnie arrived he jerked and tugged on the line and ripped the screen clear down to the bottom of the sash. When my father found out about it he whipped me till I almost bled. That was another thing he was good at—he knew how to whip a kid. He had never heard of George Bernard Shaw but he believed in one of the Shavian precepts: never strike a child except in anger, for a blow delivered in cold blood will never be forgiven.

I delivered groceries for a man who ran a small store a mile or so from our house. I learned one valuable lesson in human relations from that grocer. A Mrs. Tompkins always got her order delivered before any of the other customers because she complained the loudest; she hollered and belly-ached constantly about prices and quality and delays, and she got service. My instructions were to always give this female squeaking wheel prompt attention, putting her ahead of everyone else. The moral: nastiness pays off.

I was a newsboy for a while, selling the Decatur *Review* on the downtown streets. I carried my papers in the regulation canvas bag and one bitterly cold day I was huddled in a doorway, shivering, when a man saw me and walked over to me. He asked me why I didn't go somewhere and get warm and I told him I had to sell the rest of my papers first. He asked me how many I had left and I said three. He then pulled a dollar out of his pocket and handed it to me and said, "Go on home and get warm." He didn't even take a paper, and I don't think I'll ever forget him. There was another man who made just as big an impression with a smaller capital outlay. I was in a barber shop waiting to get a haircut when this well-dressed, brisk-moving gentleman entered. He asked the barber how long he'd have to wait. The barber said I was the only person ahead of him. The man turned to me. "Tell you what I'll do, son," he said. "You trade places with me and let me be next and I'll pay for your haircut." I stammered out an agreement, all but overwhelmed by the kingly gesture. I think that I thought: "What a wonderful world

I live in! If you got enough money, you can buy anything you want! It is probly a good idea to have money!"

This was the period, too, when I experienced religious ecstasy. As I have noted, when I was an infant I was baptized in the Roman Catholic Church. In my Decatur days I was devout at those times when I was supposed to be devout. You might think that strict adherence to the rules and regulations of the Catholic Church would be enough to occupy the time and energies of one small boy. Not me. I had to have more.

The Dunkards had a church in Decatur and my closest friend, Eddie Abbott, was a member of it. His parents were strict about religion and life and various other matters; for example, his mother always removed her little black bonnet before whipping him. Eddie took his religion quite seriously and had enormous affection and respect for his parents.

When I first found out about the facts of life, with particular reference to the manner in which babies are come by, I hurried to Eddie to let him in on the discovery. An older boy had furnished me with the information and I had it correct as to fundamentals, though a bit confused as to details.

I told Eddie about it and he sat and glared at me for a long time, and then he began to blubber. Suddenly he turned on me fiercely and cried:

"That's a dern lie!"

I didn't know what was going on in his head, but I defended myself just as other scientists have defended themselves down through the ages.

"You mean," he demanded, "that my mother and father did that?"

"They sure did," I said.

Whereupon he beat hell out of me.

Our friendship was interrupted for several months, but after a while his anger cooled and we became pals again, though we never mentioned the hateful thing.

I can't remember the details of how Eddie converted me to the Dunkard Church. It was not exactly a conversion, because I didn't convert *from* anything, most especially the Catholic Church. But I was secretly a member of both churches for a while. On Sunday mornings I would go to early mass at St. Patrick's and then scurry over to the Dunkard church for services there.

Came the Sunday when the Dunkards were having a baptismal

ceremony and damned if I didn't hit the sawdust trail. I was taken
into a little room where I was stripped. They gave me a white night-
gown which I put on. Then they led me out, with half a dozen others,
to the rostrum. Some sliding doors had been shoved back, revealing
a small concrete pool full of water. Somebody took hold of me and
lowered me into the pool. I can't recall whether the water was warm
or cold, or if I held my nose. I suppose I was whooping and praising
the Lord and otherwise carrying on. They gave me my dunking and
I became a certified Protestant Catholic, practicing both religions
simultaneously and to the best of my ability.

This confusing double allegiance continued for weeks. I kept my
Dunkard affiliation secret because I was then attending the Catholic
school. Eventually the situation began to bother me and I decided
that I ought to make up my mind and abandon one or the other
religion. I needed advice and I searched around until I found the
person I thought I could question safely.

This was Old Joe, sexton of St. Patrick's Church. Old Joe had one
eye and a facial tic. I came upon him one winter day sitting on the
basement steps of the school, picking his teeth with his pocket knife.
I sat down beside him and talked aimlessly for a while, and then I
got down to business.

"Joe," I said, "I was just wondering—could a fella belong to the
Protestant church and the Catholic church at the same time?"

Old Joe turned and twitched at me and I had a strange feeling
that he was reading my thoughts. He didn't say a word, but got up
and started away, and then beckoned for me to follow. I was at a
crisis in my life and I was trembling. To me it seemed that Old Joe
was acting in a most mysterious manner. I felt that he had divined my
ecclesiastical duplicity and that he was going to take me to Father
Murphy. I pictured myself being knocked cat-west-and-crooked and
then undergoing excommunication.

Old Joe led me to the rear of the big church and we entered the
furnace room. Using an iron hook, he opened one of the massive
furnace doors. Then he seized me roughly by the arm and shoved me
to a spot directly in front of the door.

"Look in yonder," said Old Joe.

I looked in yonder. It was an inferno—solid fire—and the heat
came beating out at me in waves that left me gasping for breath.

"You see it?" chortled Old Joe. "Now, lemmy tell you sumpen.
That there is ice cold. That there is *ice cold* alongside the hell

you would go to if you so much as set foot in a Protisan church. That there is *ice cold* alongside the hell the Protisans go to. Don't never go in no Protisan church."

Old Joe's illustrated lecture did the trick. I never went back to the Dunkards. I had never fully appreciated the high warmth of hell before.

Next door to us on King Street lived a retired preacher who was called "Reverent Branch." He wore baggy clothes and a handlebar mustache that made him look like Chester Conklin of the Mack Sennett movies. He had a son, Johnnie, who was about a year older than me, and two daughters in their early teens. Reverent Branch got up every morning at dawn, fell to his knees beside his bed, and prayed in a loud voice for an hour. He had a cast-iron larynx and as he prayed his voice increased in power and volume until, during the last ten minutes of his beseechments and supplications, he was roaring like a God-fearing lion. This was all right in the wintertime but in the hot summer months, when bedroom windows were wide open, he made quite a disturbance. His bellowings awakened everybody in the neighborhood and while people had great respect for his faith, they felt that he should address his Creator in more subdued tones. Finally someone wrote an anonymous letter and left it on his front porch, telling him of the unhappiness of his neighbors, and saying, "You don't have to holler at the Good Lord to get his attention." Reverent Branch was furious. For a week or two after that he knelt at his bedroom window and howled his prayers at the entire neighborhood. After that he packed up his family and moved away. His son Johnnie, an interesting case, was known as the meanest kid in the neighborhood and was looked upon with awe by the rest of us because of his constant boast about "jazzing" his two sisters. He told us he did it all the time; I can't remember that we were greatly shocked—possibly because we knew so little about what was involved.

At home I complained so bitterly about the distance I had to walk each day to parochial school that I was finally allowed to enter a public school. Its name was Pugh and it was a tribulation to be a pupil there because of the foul behavior of kids from other schools. Whenever they saw us on the street they'd grasp their nasty little noses and chant, "Pugh! Pugh! Pugh!"

There is a small legend about my career in Pugh School, and my brief association with Miss Nighswonger, who was my teacher in the third or fourth grade. I can remember vaguely that Miss Nighswonger prophesied before the whole class that I would probably grow up to be a writer. There was a war on in Europe and we grew vegetables at school and one day I whipped out a "composition" entitled "My Garden." Miss Nighswonger read it aloud to the class and then made her prognostication. Many years later she wrote to me and reminded me of it. She said she felt sure her prophecy was the catalyst which stirred literary ambition in me and led eventually to my becoming an author. It did no such thing. I became a writer by accident, by sheer dumb luck. I do believe, however, that I had more than a passing interest in words when I was a boy. I remember the time I picked up a can of condensed milk and grew fascinated by a long word that was on it. I learned to say it. I pronounced it eva–pore–rated. Accent on the pore. I was very proud of being able to pronounce such a whopper of a word and spoke it so often that it still has the look of eva–pore–rated to me.

I cannot recall ever having had a real serious ambition to become a policeman, a cowboy, a doctor, a writer, or anything else. But my mother decided it was time to guide me into a career. She chose it for me—I would be a telegraph operator. She sent away to a mail order house for a sounder, a key, some batteries and a manual of the Morse code. She made me practice every day for a while, but I never really learned telegraphy. In after years I sometimes caught myself wishing she had succeeded. I have known a lot of telegraph operators in my time. They have all but vanished from the scene but in my early newspaper days there were plenty of them and, with a few exceptions, they were a noble and profligate breed. They got drunk and gambled and kicked hell out of their wives and were always in debt. They had an ingenious code which they employed in calling each other obscene names across great distances. They always seemed to have a good time.

In after years my father told me about his career as a cigar maker in Decatur. He worked in a big room with sixteen other men, and they produced a cigar called the Little Rose—the same brand my grandfather made in the same shop forty years earlier. These men had no "reader" to entertain them during their labors. In Cuba and Tampa and other localities where the cigar makers were Latins, a man was paid by the workers to sit in the room and read aloud.

"We never had a reader," Pop told me, "but we had a system of talkin'. We had one guy named Benny and ever' morning after we got into the swing of the work, somebody would yell out, 'Start somethin', Benny.' That meant Benny was to think up a good subject to talk about. In a little while Benny would say, maybe, 'Airplanes.' Then the guy on the end next to the door would start to talk. He'd talk about airplanes. Maybe he'd say that by god they'd never get *him* up in one a them things. When he got through it moved on to the next man and he would talk as long as he could about airplanes and he would say that if God meant for us to fly he'd a put feathers on us.

"I remember once when Benny give us the subject about plantin' crops in the light a the moon or the dark a the moon. Everbody had a strong opinion; me and one other fella, we were the only ones that said we didn't believe in that crap. It almost ended in a fight. Finely everbody decided they would appoint me to write a letter to the State Agriculture Department in Springfield and get a scientific answer to it. So I wrote to the head guy of the Department and in about a week I got my answer. Course the son-of-a-bitch was a politician and he hedged on me. He wrote this letter and he said in it, 'I have no official data on this matter. Some people say the moon affects plantings and other people say it don't. It is my personal opinion that there may be something to it, although it might be that there is nothing to it.' I could tell in a minute that he was gettin' ready to run for governor or somethin' and he wasn't gonna take a chance on losin' any votes by comin' out one way or another about the moon. I'm glad it happened the way it did because it woke me up to these politicians. Why couldn't he come right out and take a stand on the moon? He knew damn well that the moon's got nothin' to do with plantin' reddishes or corn or when you should put shingles on your house. But would he say so? No! The bastards are all the same."

The thought occurs to me that maybe I have another important heritage from my father, in addition to impatience and a double-ended nose. I hold myself to be among the fortunate few of the world who have not a single superstition. Yet when I was a child in the Midwest I was exposed to many superstitious beliefs and practices and for a long time I swallowed them whole.

In our Decatur years my adolescent friends and I had no television and no radio to enlarge our perspectives so we spent a lot of time sitting on the grass and exchanging philosophical views. We all carried buckeyes with us night and day, for it was an accepted fact that no man was ever found dead with a buckeye in his pocket. I believed that if a turtle ever got hold of me he would never let go until he heard a clap of thunder. If I lost a ball or a marble or a penny I would spit in the palm of my hand and strike the spit with my forefinger and the spit would fly off in the direction of the lost article. We were really wise—far beyond our years. I can remember a disturbing belief that was common among kids as well as many grownups in Illinois. It was concerned with the art of the undertaker —the process we called "imbombing." There was a widespread notion that many persons, thought to be dead, were buried alive. We used to discuss this matter at great length, shuddering at the horror of it and saying fervently, "Boy, I hope they imbomb me good when I die!" Constant speculation led, of course, to the belief that almost everybody was buried alive. Stories were always in circulation to the effect that so-and-so's coffin had been dug up and there he was, or there she was, all twisted around inside it. Civilized man, we believed, had invented "imbombing" to make certain that people wouldn't have to go through such a horrible experience.

Our conversations dealt with many mysterious things. We talked about "morphadites" so often that, to this day, I have no use for the true and accurate word. One boy once told of a farm where they had a morphadite cow . . . I mean bull . . . I mean . . . I don't know what I mean. I try not to think about it.

We didn't live completely in the Dark Ages. Mechanical things were beginning to intrude upon us. Some of us had "talking machines" at home. We got our recording kicks from those old Edison gramophones with the morning-glory horns and the cylindrical records. Nobody seemed to care much about the nature of the sounds that came out. Yet our parents were always complaining about our choice of records. We went for "Cohen on the Telephone" and "Uncle Josh at Punkin Center"—the standup comics of the time— and the old folks would keep reminding us that there were beautiful records by Caruso and Galli-Curci and John McCormack.

Gene Austin and Rudy Vallee were not too far in the future, and neither was Lindbergh. It was on West King Street, in fact, that I saw my first airplane up close. One weekend a couple of men with their caps on backward brought a flying machine to a pasture out in the direction of the crick where we swam and fished. Everybody in that section of Decatur went out to see the plane. It looked a good deal like that thing the Wrights flew at Kitty Hawk. This one took to the air about once every hour or so. One of the men got into the seat, fiddled a bit with the broomstick controls and then signified that he was ready. The ship was always kept tied to a tree and as it strained against the hawser, the second man unhooked it and off it went. It rumbled and bumped across the field, lifted into the sky, arrived at an altitude of perhaps three hundred feet, and then circled the pasture twice before coming back down. After that the two men passed their caps through the crowd. I still don't see how they even paid for their gas with the nickels and dimes they collected.

There were twenty-five or thirty boys in the two blocks that comprised our realm on West King Street and each of us, in order to participate in our games, had to develop the skills and instincts of the hawk, the beaver, and the pack rat. We probably spent more time in searching for and manufacturing sports equipment than we spent in our actual games. No matter where we went, no matter what important errand we were performing, our eyes were constantly alert for certain articles that were almost essential to existence. Sports for us began at the junk pile.

An old discarded shoe was a prize beyond valuation. The tongue was the most valuable part of the shoe, furnishing material for at least two sling-shot pouches. String was as important to us as candy. Lumber scraps and old nails were hoarded as if they were ebony and silver, and to find a wheel of any kind—even the iron band off the hubcap of a farm wagon—was to find bliss.

We had few "boughten" things. Everybody had a pocketknife, which he usually got for Christmas, and every boy had a bag of marbles, including an aggie, a steelie, and a lot of commies. (In my time I've had association with a lot of commies, but they've always been under my thumb.) This wealth was kept in fairly equitable distribution through trading. Negotiations over the swap of, say, one knife with a busted handle for one steelie and ten commies would sometimes last an entire week and might even require outside arbitration. It was a more obdurate and unsentimental form of commerce than you'll find even in Manhattan's midtown diamond market. I've long since lost track of the King Street boys, but I feel certain that some of them grew up to become either merchant princes or highly successful confidence men.

So far as the sporting life was concerned, we really lived off the land. We seldom went out deliberately to hunt for equipment—we were forever on the prowl for it. Out toward the crick, in the neighborhood where the plane had been tethered, were wooded areas where we went hickory-nutting, and fields where we occasionally passed an hour or two snatching grasshoppers. Snatching grasshoppers can be a more beneficial sport than badminton and serves to develop both the *latissimus dorsi* and the *pectoralis* muscles. There is the same amount of purpose in catching a grasshopper as there is in mountain-climbing. After a grasshopper is caught, you close your fist over him, leaving his head sticking out and, squeezing him gently, you say, "Spit tuhbacca juice er you die!" The grasshopper obliges by spitting tobacco juice and you let him go.

Whenever we were in the woods we occasionally cut prongs for sling-shots. Our sling-shots were made from a tree-fork, two lengths of rubber cut from an old inner tube, bits of string and the pouch fashioned from the tongue of the old shoe.

Quite frankly we used our sling-shots to kill birds. Usually we only shot at sparrows, which we called spriggies and which we understood to be anti-social varmints. We fancied ourselves as marksmen but to be candid about it, something over two-and-a-half tons of stone were shot at spriggies for every spriggie hit.

I belonged to a gang that ruled the roost in our block, and there was a rival gang in charge of affairs in the next block. We fought, and I mean we fought with guns. Well . . . I don't want to go overboard here . . . in the whole theatre of war there were only about three BB guns and two of them were busted and the other one was employed in battle only when its owner could afford ammunition, which was seldom. Usually we battled with our homemade slingshots, or we simply threw rocks by hand. In the winter our primeval ferocity led us to make snowballs and pour water on them and set them outdoors overnight so they'd freeze and might nigh kill a kid if you hit him good. I had a pair of brass knucks (only one, really, but if you had one it was called a pair) and I daydreamed of the time when I'd be able to use them (it) on an enemy—meaning when I got big enough for the instrument to fit my hand.

Actually we didn't need weapons because our wars were fought with our fists. If I could get all my black eyes assembled into one big bunch of black, it would look like two and a half tons of coal.

One of our most common pastimes was hoop-rolling. Not the brand they practice at Wellesley. Our hoop-rolling was a boy-sport that seems to have been indigenous to the Midwest. The "handle" was usually made of lath—a long piece with a short piece nailed crosswise at the bottom, forming an inverted T. This handle was employed to keep a small wheel upright and moving, and the best wheels were the spoked and rubber-tired variety taken off old go-carts. The game may sound dull but it wasn't. We could keep a wheel going as fast as we could run, uphill or down, or we could keep it in an upright position while walking very slowly behind it. There were periods when we never took a step outside the house without our hoops traveling ahead of us, even going to church.

Nowadays whenever I see a kid whirling a Yo-yo, which may have cost a dollar and a half, I think of the shining hours I spent swinging buckeyes. We'd fasten a buckeye to either end of a string about three feet long. Then we'd grasp the string at the middle point and set the buckeyes to whirling in opposite directions. Now and then we'd engage in contests to determine which boy could keep his buckeyes whirling for the longest time. I can remember that Donnie Etherton one day kept his going for two hours and fifteen minutes and for a week afterward was unable to use his right hand for scratching himself. There were some boys who could perform intricate maneuvers with their hoops, using one hand, while keeping their buckeyes whirling with the other. I think such boys were freaks of nature, kin to that man in the circus who can stand on his index finger.

Of course we made our own kites—three thin strips of wood which we covered with newspaper, using a paste made of flour and water, and a tail of varicolored rags tied tastefully together. A real sporty kid was one who covered his kite with the Sunday funny paper. Kite flying, to be sure, involved the use of lots of string and each of us spent the entire winter gathering it. We always wound it on a stick, using a figure-eight motion, and a single stick of kite string might consist of more than fifty pieces knotted together. A boy who had a ball of boughten string with no knots was most fortunate because he could send "messages" and little paper parachutes up the string to his kite.

String was most useful, too, in the fabrication of our baseballs. We'd simply wind the string into a tight ball and then cover it with two or three layers of bicycle tape. Our pitchers seldom threw anything but "drops." Major league baseball has never been altogether satisfactory to me for the reason that the pitchers never throw a drop. I suppose the sinker is the same as a drop, but it doesn't sound the same to me.

We built scooters, using old roller-skate wheels, and most of us made our own sleds, employing for runners the metal strips that came off wagon bodies. We played mumbly-peg (not mumblety-peg) by the hour. We played shinny with clubs cut from trees and a Karo syrup can for a puck. The shinny games grew more interesting and more lethal as, from constant walloping, the can shrank in size until it was a dangerous metal projectile, not much bigger than a hen's egg.

Many of our sporting pursuits were, in fact, quite hazardous. Each tree and each telephone pole in our neighborhood had been climbed more times than the Matterhorn. It seems to me, on reflection, that I spent more time in trees than Tarzan. We played follow-the-leader which usually involved climbing up on things, such as sheds and embankments and poles and trees, and then jumping off. No paratrooper ever took ground-shocks greater than came to us in follow-the-leader.

Sometimes in the evenings we played crack-the-whip, a simple exercise in erosion of the human body. I can only remember the times when I was end-man on a line of ten or fifteen boys, and how the whip would be cracked and I'd be sent flying across the fields as if I'd been shot from a cannon. I'm reasonably convinced that I broke through the sound barrier years before anybody dreamed of the jet age.

Also in the evenings we played a multitude of other games, such as chalk-the-rabbit, duck-on-a-rock, run-sheepie-run, and Indian wrestling—games known to the kids of other sections of the country but often known under different names. All in all, we kept in fine physical trim. We watched our diet, subsisting on such things as green apples dipped in salt, and the pungent tops of certain pasture weeds. We never needed rubdowns; every boy in our group was bound to get a licking at home once or twice a week and these, as I've suggested, were not tame affairs. They kept the muscles toned up.

And then after a while the King Street boys grew older and our thoughts turned to the profound mystery of girls and we grew corrupt and decadent and seemed to prefer playing post office to swinging buckeyes and chalking the rabbit and jumping off sheds. I've always thought that, in the glow of nostalgia, those were splendid and memorable days on West King Street. I mean the days when we gave up sling-shots in favor of girls.

# sex and God in Ohio

Shortly after the conclusion of World War I we moved to Defiance, an Ohio town perched above the confluence of the Maumee and Auglaize rivers. It is about sixty miles southwest of Toledo and it was named by Mad Anthony Wayne who built a fort on the site and defied people. Later the ramparts were occupied by troops under a tough officer named Winchester. This Winchester believed in discipline and one day when a private was found asleep at his post he was sentenced to "ten cobs on his posterior, well laid on, with a paddle four inches wide and one half inch thick, bored full of holes." Thus it would seem that Defiance's contribution to civilized living includes a form of sport widely practiced by members of fraternal organizations who band themselves together in a spirit of undying love and bang each other across the butts with paddles much like the one described here. I shall report on fraternal prat-flogging, as it affected me, a bit later in these pages.

When I was a mere smidgen of a human being there was a document in wide circulation throughout the Midwest, warning boys of the terrible dangers involved in the act of thinking about girls. In order to acquire this warning a boy had to send ten cents to a doctor in Buffalo and in time the document would arrive in the mail. It proclaimed the fact that thinking about girls could bring on nervousness, sexual debility, languor, tiresome feelings, forgetfulness, gloomy forebodings, lack of energy, despondency, unfitness for business, unsociability, cowardice, bashfulness, irritable temper, lack of confidence, unfixedness of purpose, broken sleep, trembling, dizziness, staggering, soft muscles, weak back, scanty beard, pasty skin, hollow eyes, blunted senses, and eruptions.

I must have done a lot of thinking about girls in my lifetime; I don't think I've bypassed a single one of those symptoms. I began to think about girls in Defiance and I've thought about them ever since but what I think I keep to myself—I'm not the kind that thinks and tells. I don't talk about sex and I don't write about it, except of course from a pathological point of view.

I do believe, however, that it is necessary for me to mention Mr. Ed. This was a man I met in Defiance when I was eleven or twelve years old. For a brief period I was an errand boy for a shoe store and Mr. Ed was a customer there. The first time I met him he invited me to have a chocolate soda with him, and I did. He was a short man with a yellow mustache, a carpenter by trade and he lived alone in quarters above a store. He began "running into me" almost daily and before long I was going to his rooms with him. He was an *extremely* friendly man, full of stories and jokes and laughter, and he seemed to think a lot of me because he enjoyed rubbing his hand over my shoulders and back when he was talking to me. I felt real flattered that he should choose me as his friend. One evening he told me that he had quite a bit of money in the bank and that I was the only true friend he had in the world and that he was making a will and leaving that money to me.

I may have suggested, some distance back, that I was never very strong on sentiment but I tell you I was real touched by Mr. Ed. I would have given him the shirt off my back, though I'm glad I didn't. One day my mother questioned me at great length about Mr. Ed and told me it was wrong for me to be hanging around with him, and I protested angrily, saying cripes a-mighty, what the dang dickens was wrong with it? I said that Mr. Ed was gonna leave me a lot of money and he was very nice to me in other ways and patted me on the back a lot and smoothed my hair down which was a dang lot more than I ever got around *this* house, and I might even just pack up my dod dern things and run away from home and go live with him. So my mother went downtown to see somebody and a day or two later when I called at Mr. Ed's place they said he had moved out of town.

Folks, I've lived!

Going back to that Buffalo doctor and his warning, I think it is possible that I got my soft muscles and broken sleep and gloomy forebodings and hollow eyes from thinking about girls, but some of the aches and pains must stem from other sources. I am thinking about Jack Dempsey's pills. He had become heavyweight champion and I considered him to be the greatest man in the world. There were ads in the newspapers in which Dempsey said that he got strong and tough from taking a sort of tonic which we kids always called nux-you-ated iron (arrn). So I saved and scrimped and spent all the money I could get on it. For months I scarcely ate anything but nux-you-ated arrn, that I might grow up to be like Dempsey. I never did, and I feel today that overindulgence in the stuff may have been responsible for my being cowardly, unfit for business, bashful, irritable, weak-backed, and all those other things.

Before I have done with sex, I think I ought to report on the fact that I was the alert pupil at St. Mary's School who discovered the presence of shocking language in Webster's Dictionary. The big book was on a stand at the front of the classroom and it was permissible for the pupils to look up a word or words whenever they felt like it. One day I was at the book, looking up *why* or *who* or *wholesome*, when I fell victim to serendipity. I hurried back to my desk and scribbled a note to the boy next to me, saying, "Whore is in the dictionary honest to god." He sneered in disbelief but went up and had a look and his eyes were bright and sparkling when he returned to his desk. He told me later he had sneered at me because he thought it was spelled "hore." Before long all the kids in the room, including the girls, were trying to get to the big book. A certain amount of self-discipline was necessary, plus some convincing histrionics. If the sister had ever found out what was going on, we'd all have been thrown in oubliettes. So we were careful. I would saunter up to the dictionary and look up "bitch" or "bastard" and frown thoughtfully all the while; then I'd pass the word on "bitch" or "bastard" and someone else would go through the same routine and our teacher was real pleased at our sudden great interest in lexicology.

Our school day began with mass and there was additional praying from time to time in the classrooms. It seems an odd thing, but when we prayed we seldom had any notion of what we were saying. We recited the Apostles' Creed in unison with a singsong rhythm, so that it went: "I . . . bleeven . . . God—th'—fah—ther allmidey . . . crater uv . . . hevn . . . n . . . nerth." The delivery was much the same as that of a mynah bird, or a three-year-old child reciting Mare-ree had uh litt-tull lamb. During this same period I became an altar boy and a choir singer. I never knew what I was saying in the

Latin responses when I was serving mass, nor did I know what most of the words meant when I was singing in the same language. Even today, when I see the words "Adeste fideles," I think of a dog I once heard about. The dog's name was Dusty, which was short for Dusty fideles—he was born on Christmas Day. They never got through to me when it came to identifying the Holy Ghost. In this respect I am like Washington Duke, the man who started that tobacco fortune in North Carolina. He once said: "There are three things I cain't understand—*ee*lectricity, the Holy Ghost and mah son Buck." Not long ago one of my grandsons, a boy who believes that I know everything, came up to me and asked me the straightforward question: "What is the Holy Ghost?" I struggled with it manfully for a bit and then gave up. I simply didn't know. I had a hazy notion that the Holy Ghost was a pigeon, but that wouldn't do under the circumstances, so I excused myself quickly on the grounds that water was running out of a hose somewhere.

My sisters tell me that in our Defiance home I organized a game in which I played the part of a bishop celebrating mass. I built an altar and devised sacerdotal vestments for myself. I wore a small rug hanging down my back (the fiddleback chasuble) and for a mitre I wore a tin sauce pan on my head with the handle turned to the back. My congregation, consisting of my two younger brothers and one sister, knelt behind me with hands clasped. I told them that while I was going through the ritual of the mass, they were to keep murmuring all the time as if they were praying. Sometimes they would become so fascinated by my maneuverings before the altar that they would forget the murmuring. Once I whirled around, took off my tin mitre and banged my sister Martha on the head with it, yelling, "*I SAID KEEP PRAYIN'!*"

One of my close friends at St. Mary's was a boy with a marvelous name, better even than Pinkney McNabb (the first mayor of Mc-Leansboro). This boy's true name was Theodore Kahout, but his nickname was "Tater" and his last name was pronounced "Cahoot." Tater Cahoot! In recent years I had a letter from him saying he was in the insurance business in Defiance. He ought to sell a lot of insurance on the strength of his name alone. There was another boy named Floyd Moody, a strapping athletic kid bigger than the rest of us. He was an "A" student in two subjects—fist-fighting and jaw-grinding. I was always trying to ape the personal mannerisms of people I admired and I admired Floyd Moody. The place where he made the biggest impression on me was at worship.

Floyd always sat in the pew ahead of me at morning mass. He was blond and handsome and square-jawed and his manner in church was that of an angry bull. Whether standing, kneeling, or sitting, his head was always tipped forward, and he glared straight ahead, looking out from beneath heavy eyebrows. And he constantly worked his jaws so that the muscles in his cheek went in and out. I was always doing it too, with my head lowered, hoping that I would look as masculine and heroic as Floyd Moody.

The Mother Superior in our school was a thin-faced little woman who, as they used to say of Ray Robinson, was pound-for-pound the best belter of her time. She could knock a boy bowlegged with the flat of her hand, and she frequently did. She weighed perhaps ninety-seven and was sallow-skinned and it was her custom to say, "Why, you impertinent young whippersnapper!" just before clouting a boy to the turf. How I'd love to find her like today! Imagine a nun fighting in Madison Square Garden for the championship of the world!

We marched in double file from church to school each morning and the law said that we were not to talk or giggle or caper about during the procession. Floyd Moody, however, was always contemptuous of such regulations. He defied authority whenever he felt like it; consequently he got more judo chops from the Mother Superior than the rest of us. And then came the morning when he crossed the Rubicon. We were marching along the sidewalk and Floyd was talking and gesticulating when Mother Superior appeared out of nowhere. She got him twice across the face before he could get his guard up. I was close by and I sensed that real trouble was coming because Floyd lowered his head, bull-fashion, and glared at her. Then his hands shot forward and seized the starched white collar which extended from her neck to the middle of her chest. Floyd gave that collar a mighty jerk, ripping it off and hurling it to the ground. Then he grabbed her headdress and tore it off. Now her head was uncovered and we could all see how her hair had been shaved or clipped. She was screaming bloody murder and she clapped her hands over her scalp and started running toward the house where the nuns lived. Now we all turned to look at Floyd. It was almost a sure thing that God would strike him dead on the spot, maybe even burn him to a crisp right before our eyes. He glared back at us and then a sardonic little grin flickered over his mouth and he said, "Go learn your lessons." After which he calmly walked away and disappeared. He was reported to be around town for a few days and then he vanished for good. I assume he is in a penitentiary somewhere, although he may be a corporation lawyer.

Our main sporting activity at St. Mary's was a game called burnball, which was a variation of baseball. It was played with a rubber ball slightly smaller than a tennis ball. The pitcher delivered with an underhand swing and the batter used his fist, knuckles forward, for striking. It was permissible to pull the sleeve of the shirt or sweater down over the fist, or wrap a handkerchief around it, to take out the sting. After the batter hit the ball he pursued the usual course toward first base, though it wasn't necessary for the fielders to throw to the first baseman. All they had to do was hit the runner with the ball. At the age of fifty-three I hurt all over just thinking about it. Nobody ever *tossed* the ball at the runner. It was thrown with maniacal force and the most capable fielders were those who could hit a runner in the face. Getting hit in the cheek, or even on the arm or leg, was as painful as anything on earth. If you were ever stung on the cheek by a wasp, or hit in the leg by a shotgun blast, you have some idea of what it meant to be put out in the game of burn-ball.

Once or twice a week Father John, our parish priest, was accustomed to play burn-ball with us. He was a man in his forties, a stern, frightening figure to most of us. Though we didn't know the word tyrant, we considered him to be one, and he knew that we did. I am aware of the fact now that he was a good man and a reasonable one. He proved it by casting aside old scores and coming out regularly to join in that brutal pastime of ours. He'd come out of his house and wander into the schoolyard, reading his office, pretending he wasn't aware of the burn-ball game. After a while he'd close his book and stand and watch us a bit. Then he'd ask if he could get in, and we would joyfully welcome him into the contest. He'd shuck himself down to his shirt, even removing his collar, and he'd play until he could no longer stand the punishment.

How we gave it to him! At all other times Father John was in the driver's seat, but in burn-ball we had him where we wanted him. Meaning no disrespect, I am impelled to say that Father John was overly sensitive where he sat. He was inclined toward pudginess in that direction and his black britches had little slack at the hips. It was a glorious experience to get a square shot at that bottom, and an ignominious thing to miss it. Father John rarely hit the ball out of the infield and the fielder who got it almost always ran forward a few steps so he could get a good bead on Father's sensitive area. We rarely missed, and I can see him now, scampering toward first base and, on coming within a few feet of it, hunching his shoulders against the awful stab that he knew was coming. He was well aware of our sadistic intentions but he never complained and I don't think he ever padded himself against those painful assaults. Nonetheless, he couldn't stand up under them for more than four or five direct hits at which point he'd make his excuses, pick up his clothes, and head for the house, never giving us the satisfaction of rubbing the sore places while in our view.

It was great sport to have him in the game for a while, but it was a relief when he departed because we could never take the name of the Lord in vain while he was around. There was only one proper remark for a boy to make when, running the bases, he was stung with a full-bodied hit. That was "Jee-zuss Kay-ryst!"

Father John's presence placed us under severe restraints.

The first great unquenchable love of my life was Helen Weisenburger, who was in my class at St. Mary's. I worshiped her, although she didn't know it. She was the star pupil in the school and the only one who could ever put me down in a spelling bee. It was always an intense and palpitating pleasure to me whenever Helen outspelled me, as I admired her no little. I had to tell somebody about this love and so one day I told my sister Lou. "The thing to do," she said, "is to grab hold of her and kiss her right on the mouth." I came close to slapping my own sister for even suggesting such a caddish procedure.

Helen and I transferred from the main school and enrolled for a business course which was taught in a little one-story frame house that stood between the church and the parish house. We studied shorthand and typing and bookkeeping and things of that nature. We were required to keep a complete set of books for a mythical commercial establishment which, as I remember, dealt largely in oats, and I think that if it hadn't been for Helen Weisenburger's superb scholarship I would have been drummed out of the course before ever taking in my first imaginary peck of oats. Helen's bookkeeping was perfection, with trial balances balancing and credits and debits behaving themselves and accounts receivable and payroll in their proper places. Mine, on the other hand, was a botch and I always seemed to be far behind the rest of the class . . . until I discovered the unlocked window. It became a practice for me to go to the little frame building at night, a couple of times a week, raise the unlocked window, climb in, draw the shades, get Helen's books out of her desk, thrill to the touch of them for a few seconds, cast off thoughts of love for the moment, and copy her figures into my own books with the aid of a small flashlight. O youth! O impetuous, cribbing youth! I've often wondered what might have happened if I had gone on to become a bookkeeper in a real business. Would I have crept down to the office at night and jimmied a window in order to keep my accounts in order? Or would I have been content with payroll kickbacks and dishonest competitive bidding and payoffs to police as an outlet for my business acumen?

I'm afraid that I was a real sneak and a cheat in those days. I even indulged in an act of blackmail. Up the street from us lived a family named Summers. There was a boy in the family, Paul, a fat and insolent kid who was about fifteen. They had an old Dodge touring car and Paul was allowed to drive it whenever he felt like it. I had ridden with him many times and studied the operational procedures closely and I was always pleading with Paul to let me try it. He never would, saying I was too dern young. One afternoon I went over to his house to ask him to go swimming with me (the Auglaize was just behind the Summers residence). I walked around the corner of a chicken shed and there stood Paul—grasping a hen with both hands. The thing that he was doing with that hen . . . well, I've all but given up telling it to people because they call me a liar, and say I must have dreamed it, and that it couldn't have happened—but *it did happen*. I saw it. Who could ever forget such a thing? My God, I don't think they put on that kind of a performance even in Peyton Place. Paul looked up and saw me and quickly flung the chicken to the ground. I turned my head away and tried to pretend that I hadn't noticed anything unusual. But Paul knew I had seen it all. Neither of us spoke for a while and then I broke the silence. I said, "Hi-yah, Paul. How 'bout lettin' me drive the car?" He all but shouted his answer: "Sure! Go right ahead! Drive it any time you wanna!" And so I went around and got in the old Dodge and started off and drove it across a few sidewalks and through some front yards, but I didn't hit anything and in the next few days I was jockeying that car all over the Ohio countryside.

I hope that if I'm ever on a television panel show and I'm asked to describe how I learned to drive an automobile, that I'm able to restrain myself. And if anybody asks me if I ever blackmailed anybody, I think I can truthfully answer: "Yes, but it was a *distinctive type* of blackmail."

It was required of me as an All-American Boy that I play hookey from school and I always tried to arrange the crime so I could disappear into the darkness of the local movie house on those afternoons when an Eddie Polo serial was playing. For me the movies have never produced another red-blooded, stout-hearted he-man to compare with Eddie Polo. I recall one afternoon when I crept into the little theater and found a seat directly behind Old Man Hocker. He was a town character who apparently spent every afternoon of his life at the picture show.

On the screen that day Eddie Polo got himself into a frightening dilemma. The villain had Eddie in a cabin and I knew that the dirty rat was getting ready to torture and kill and otherwise humiliate my hero. He lugged Eddie over to the cabin door and spread-eagled him against it with some rope. Then the big whiskered sheepherder picked up a blacksnake whip, let go with a few demoniacal cackles, and made ready to lay it on.

At this point Old Man Hocker turned around and hung his ancient chin over the back of his chair, facing the rear of the theater, and facing me.

"I ain't gonna look," he said. "I jist ain't gonna look. Don't *need* to look. Not a bit. That dirty bastard ain't gonna hurt ole Eddie. I *know* it. I know it so well I ain't even gonna bother lookin' at it. I'm jist a-restin'."

"Turn around!" I yelled at him. "Eddie's gettin' loose!"

Old Man Hocker whipped his head back around to face the screen. Sure enough, Eddie Polo was down off that door. Wham! Down went the villain. In no time at all Eddie had *him* tied to that door and *Eddie* had picked up the blacksnake whip. It was just too beautiful for Old Man Hocker. He stood up and waved his arms excitedly and hollered:

"Give it to 'im, Eddie! Give 'im some of his own medicine! Beat the son-of-a-bitch to death!"

Old Man Hocker was the first person I ever encountered who was deeply unhappy over the fact that his dog was a dog. I have known several since then, including a prosperous advertising man who lives in Westchester. He and his wife say, in all gravity, that they do not want their beloved dog to ever find out that he is a dog. So they ask all guests not to use the word "dog" in the dog's presence. The first time I was in their house, their pet came bounding into the room and I said, "What kind of a dog is he?" They almost blew me out of the room with their shushes. They actually believe that if their dog ever finds out he is a dog he will become a compulsive neurotic with the unending fidgets. Like humans. Old Man Hocker didn't go quite as far as that. He lived alone in a small house and had a venerable hound named Jeff. On Saturday nights the old man would get loaded on home brew and then he'd take to grieving over the plight of his dog in merely being a dog. He'd sit and weep and talk to Jeff, wailing, "You're nothin' but a dog . . . jist a dog . . . you won't never be nothin' else but a dog . . . I'd do somethin' about it if I could but I cain't . . . Oh God how I woosht I could do somethin' about it!"

In order to recapture other glorious memories of Defiance it was necessary for me to return to the town. So my wife and I drove out from New York and wandered around looking at various scenes of my boyhood. Something about the atmosphere of the main street aroused an urge for a banana split and I headed for the soda fountain where I had not only eaten banana splits but, as a jerk, had learned to construct them. I entered the place and took a seat at the fountain. A young man and a girl were at work cleaning and polishing things and a small radio was going on the back bar and next to it I noted, with satisfaction, a plate containing three bananas.

In my day the architecture of a banana split was, as the saying goes, frozen music. When I took up jerking soda my boss spent at least an hour, at that very fountain, instructing me in the finer points of building this single heavenly dish. The split banana had to be placed just right in the boatlike dish. Then the three dippers of ice cream—called "scoops" nowadays but always "dippers" to me— and after that the chocolate, plus an application of liquid marsh-mallow, and maybe a couple of chunks of pineapple and a cherry placed on the middle gob of ice cream. Over that a liberal sprinkling of crushed nuts. All done with extreme care under the critical eye of the customer, and no hurrying about it.

The girl slapped a paper napkin at me and said whadull-ut-be?

"I'd like to have a banana split," I said.

She looked at me and I thought I detected resentment.

"Did you say a banana split?"

"That's right."

Her attitude suggested that she'd like to split my skull. Here was a girl who didn't enjoy her work. Assembly-line thinking. Remembering the pride with which we, in the old days, put together a banana split, I grew impatient.

"Look," I said to her, "you have some bananas over there in that dish. What're *they* for?"

"Cereal," she snapped at me.

"Well, I don't want any cereal. I want a banana split. Know how to make one?"

I was hoping she'd say she didn't, and that I could invite myself back of the fountain and build my own. But she knew how, and she went to work on it, and it was the sleaziest job I've ever seen. She simply threw it together, starting with only two dippers of ice cream, squirting some sheep-dip and argyrol on it and then sprinkling coarse sawdust over the whole. Only then did she get to the banana. Know what she did? She didn't split that banana. She *sliced* it. That dame was right out of a snake pit. She performed the entire operation in something like a minute and a half and when she put it in front of me I sat and looked at it a long while.

I put two-bits on the counter, got off the stool, and hurried away from that place. I wouldn't be surprised if they're still talking about it—the goofy-lookin' creep that come in and orders up, of all things, a bananner split, and don't touch it but runs for the street like a black widder had bit him. I don't care. I don't care what they say. All I do know is that anybody who would slice bananas onto a banana split—that person's grandmother sucks eggs.

So I moved on down the street and after a while came abreast of the bank where I had opened my first account and where I had met my first bank president—on a close personal basis. Once when I was working as a nailer in a box factory I walked into that bank and opened a savings account with a deposit of four dollars. It was a thrilling sort of experience and it remained thrilling until the next day when the romantic aspects began to fade a bit. I went back to the bank and drew out two of the four dollars. After I had frivoled away one of the two dollars, remorse set in and the following morning I redeposited the remaining dollar, giving me a new balance of three dollars. Two days later I drew out two dollars. The day after that I got paid at the box factory so I went back and deposited three dollars, fetching me up to my original holdings of four dollars. Then I let two whole days go by before I returned and drew out three dollars. This was the end. The teller told me to wait just a moment. He went backstage somewhere and pretty soon I was called into an enclosure where sat the man who was president of the bank. He was straightforward and aboveboard with me. He said:

"Young man, you have just withdrawn three dollars from our bank. You have a dollar balance. The teller is now withdrawing that dollar for you. I want you to take it and get the hell out of here and stay out."

Many years later I wrote an account of some of my misadventures in Defiance and I got a letter from an officer of that bank. He was hurt over what I had written. He said I had made it appear that the people of Defiance were "country jakes." He concluded by writing: "We may be hicks but we would much rather live here than in Jew York." That's what you get for throwing your business to a bank.

Driving along a street I once traversed on my way to school, I remembered another thing.

"Every morning," I said to my wife, "I'd come walking along this street and every morning I'd meet the Miller brothers, coming toward me, running at top speed, on their way to the high school. Don Miller, you know."

"Who?" she said.

"Don Miller. And his brother Jerry. Doesn't the name Don Miller mean anything to you?"

"You couldn't mean that carpenter from Yorktown?"

"Jesus God," I said and then lapsed into quiet disgust. No use to tell her that Don Miller went on from Defiance High to become a member of Notre Dame's Four Horsemen, and to become a great hero to me. If *he* had endorsed nux-you-ated arrn, I'd have killed myself eating it. No use to tell my wife that I was once on speaking terms with him. He and his brother, also a fine football player, used to start late and run all the way to school each morning. Part of their self-imposed training schedule. They'd come ripping down the sidewalk and as they whipped past me they'd both yell out, "Hi!" And I'd yell out, "Hi!" That's how I was on speaking terms with one-fourth of a famous backfield before it got famous. Before it even *was*.

We drove to the south end of town, out near the Auglaize River, and I talked about the time I tried to ice skate all the way to Toledo. And about the time Pop surprised us all by putting on skates and cutting some fancy didoes on the ice. In the end he shot into the air and landed on his back, and a deep, thunderous rumbling followed as the ice tried to adjust itself to the situation. Pop crawled and slithered to the shore, got the skates off, flung them across the ice, then stood up and cussed that river from its source to its confluence with the Maumee. The Auglaize will never forget the words that were spoken to it that winter's day.

I found the house we lived in, a block from the river. It was a box-like frame house painted an unmentionable brindle color. This whole trip through the Midwest was a sentimental expedition, so I parked the car and stared at the house a while, trying to think of something connected with it that would tug at my heartstrings. I remembered an incident involving my brother Bill. In this very house Bill spent one entire morning and part of an afternoon sitting moodily, then getting up to pace the floor, brooding over something, and when my mother would ask him what on earth ailed him, he'd tell her to leave him alone, that he was wrestling with a problem. Finally in midafternoon he let out a triumphant cry.

"Got it!" he yelled. "Finally figured it out!"

He then told my mother that he had been wondering where the word "pickaninny" had its origin. And finally he had puzzled out the answer. He said that a long time ago there was a Negro mammy who had a lazy child. One day she ordered this lazy child to get out of the house and into the fields and pick some cotton. Whereupon the lazy child said: "No, mammy, I ain't pickin' inny."

That's all I could remember about the house and I was about ready to drive away when my eye fell on a residence across the street. This had been the home of a Mrs. Milligan. She had once caught me smoking a cigarette down by the river and told my folks about it and I got a licking for it—such a licking that I told myself I'd get even with the old woman. A day or so later I saw her and threw a brickbat at her. Missed her. But she called the cops and there was a big neighborhood uproar.

Pop didn't whip me again. He decided on more drastic measures. He had my mother put an ad in the paper saying: "Wanted—place for Catholic boy, age 12, to work on farm during summer vacation." A few days after that a buggy pulled up in front of our house and out stepped a big rawboned farmer whose name, as I remember, was Heffner. Actually he was not rawboned; how the hell can anybody be rawboned, short of a compound fracture? But he was big and when his buggy rolled away from the house I was sitting beside him.

What followed was my first and last personal experience with the glories of farm life.

This Heffner had a farm as big as Idaho and no hired help. His wife did most of the minor chores while he worked in the fields. I don't ever want anybody to say I never did a hard day's work in my life. That guy got me out of bed before daybreak, raced me through breakfast, and worked me steadily until sundown. Even then he wasn't satisfied. We'd come in from the fields and wash up and eat supper and then maybe the two of us would wander into the yard. Mr. Heffner, the dirty hind, would glance at the sky.

"Be dog-gone," he'd say. "Lookit that moon! Purty as a picture! Might near bright as day!"

"Yeh," I'd say dispiritedly, knowing what was coming.

"That moon," he'd go on, "is easy bright nuff fer us to go out and bring in that hay. C'm on, boy, le's horness up. Makes a body feel good t' work by moonlight."

I couldn't argue with him. I was indentured. I couldn't tell him that it didn't make *me* feel good to work by moonlight. Many times I wanted to tell him the difference between him and me; I wanted to point out that farm work gave him pleasure because he owned the farm, whereas I hated it and would take pleasure out of seeing it sink to China.

I did almost everything that's to be done on a farm and hated every moment of it. By the time September came and I got my release, I hated Heffner himself and all other agricultural people in the land. To this day I still get enormous pleasure out of reading the long essay called *The Husbandman*, by H. L. Mencken. It is the most lacerating indictment of the farmer ever put on paper. Some day I'm going to read it when the moon is might near bright as day.

# the shoeshine heard
# round the world

The county seat town of Huntington, where the Smith family arrived at the beginning of 1922, is in the northeastern part of Indiana about midway between Peru (which gave Cole Porter to the world) and Fort Wayne (which produced Carole Lombard and George Jean Nathan). Huntington's population has lingered around fifteen to sixteen thousand as long as I can remember and the town is somewhat grass rootsey and crawling with churches.

My esteemed job-losing father became a foreman at Ditzler's poultry house in Huntington and I transferred from St. Mary's School in Ohio to St. Mary's School in Indiana and in the process acquired another Father Murphy for overseer. I don't think I ever absorbed any real book-learning in any school I ever attended. If I had known what the future held for me I think I might have applied myself to the study of grammar, but I didn't. To this day I know less English grammar than the crow that comes up near my house on summer mornings and calls me dirty names. I think my lack of grammar must have been in my mind when I titled the book preceding this one: *How to Write Without Knowing Nothing*. And as I am writing these paragraphs about my syntactical shortcomings, a letter arrives from a little girl in Rye, New York, who has just read one of my books. Here is what she says:

"You aren't very good on punctuation. After adverb clauses at the beginning of sentences, you are supposed to have a comma (,). You didn't. How can you write a book when you can't write right yourself?"

Not knowing about adverb clauses, and not caring about them, I decided to answer her by saying, "Dear Helene: You are a little snot." But I changed my mind and simply quoted Mark Twain, who said that every man ought to be entitled to his own punctuation.

I may have been an inferior animal in the schoolroom but I was sharp and efficient as an altar boy. It was the custom there at St. Mary's for the acolytes to receive cash gratuities after serving at a wedding or a funeral. A wedding was usually worth a dollar and a half to each boy, whereas a funeral brought two dollars and a half. In those days two dollars and a half was almost enough money to put a kid through college. I can remember that the serious illness of a prominent member of the parish always filled me with anxiety—a fear that he would get well—and on more than one occasion I prayed for death to strike swiftly because I needed the money.

The behavior pattern of altar boys in the Midwest is traditional. Almost every man who ever served mass will admit that when the service was over it was customary for the acolytes to sneak back of the altar and drain off the wine which the priest may have left in the cruet. A good many altar boys will confess, too, that at one time or another they snitched money from the collection basket after it had been brought into the sacristy. I did these things but they got me into no trouble (what the hell *is* an adverb clause at the beginning of a sentence?) and when I told about them in confession I was simply given my penance and told to go and sin no more. My trouble came when I undertook to revitalize the serving of the mass.

A boy named Ted was usually my partner on the altar and we were assigned to the seven-thirty mass on Sunday mornings. We were good, and we knew it. One day the thought occurred to me that the ancient ceremony needed brightening up, that altar boys had been serving mass in the same old way for hundreds of years and the ritual had grown stuffy with age. I sounded out my partner, Ted, and convinced him that we could do something about it. For two or three days we worked together in secret, inventing and practicing new techniques. Then one Sunday morning, without warning, we popped it on the parish.

From the very beginning of the mass Ted and I ran counter to tradition. We executed double genuflections when we came together in front of the altar—quick, precise bobbings instead of the old, more dignified single genuflections. One moment we'd be doing a sort of goose-step, then we'd be moving like toy soldiers, and after that we'd swing into rhythmic, flowing motion, like a pair of halfbacks sweeping left end. When we stood together at the side of the altar with the cruets containing water and wine, we were not content to pass them along to Father Murphy's hands as he indicated his wants. We had little crisscrossings of arms, and sometimes we writhed a little like Balinese dancers and made the cruets clink together musically. The whole business was fancied up and the congregation sat bug-eyed as Ted and I caracoled and swooped and tangoed around the altar. At first Father Murphy tried to pretend that he didn't notice how we had improved the service. Then he began casting quick, apprehensive glances backward, as if the Ku-Kluxers were creeping upon him with knives and ropes. He must have felt that Ted and I had become mentally ill for he didn't take action for quite a while; then at last he stopped the proceedings, called us to one side, and spoke to us in firm tones. So we finished the mass in the old-fashioned way and then took off cassock and surplice for the last time. Our names were stricken from the rolls. Thus it was with Galileo.

I made it through the eighth grade at St. Mary's and the following autumn enrolled in the freshman class at the public high school. For some reason there had always been open warfare between the boys of the little Catholic school and the boys of the nearby public high. For another reason that I can't understand, one Catholic boy could usually lick two Protestant boys. There was fighting all the time, and rock-throwing, and club-swinging, and name-calling. And some of the Catholic boys who went into the public high school took on the colors of the Protestant majority, and joined in the war against St. Mary's. The high school warriors used to yell nasty taunts at us about the priests and the nuns and we in turn attributed horrible habits to the principal of the high school—a gentleman known to us as "Stubby."

I was already a cigarette smoker when I entered high school and on my second day as a freshman I left a classroom where French was taught and went to the boys' toilet for a smoke. There was one other kid in the big room and as I leaned against a window sill, puffing my cigarette, he began making idiotic motions and crazy faces at me.

"What's the matter with you?" I demanded.

He kept up the wild gesticulations and I concluded that he was upset about my infraction of the rules.

"Listen," I said to him, "if that son-of-a-bitch Stubby Sellers ever says a word to me I'll yank his ass clean out of his britches."

The other boy was now pointing frantically at one of the toilets. I leaned over and looked. I saw a pair of shoes—men's shoes. Stubby Sellers was in that cubicle. I crushed out my cigarette and walked out of the place, rapidly. I walked out of Huntington High. And that was the end of my school days.

My father was boss of the top floor at Ditzler's poultry house and supervised the feeding of a buttermilk porridge to thousands of chickens in metal cages which were called "batteries." I got a job on the floor below, helping pick the chickens that Pop had fattened. In the East this process is known as "plucking" and it confuses a New Yorker for me to say that I was once a chicken-picker. He thinks I went around *selecting* poultry.

Chicken-picking is to my way of thinking the most god-awful job in the whole category of employment. It involves wallowing in blood and feathers and worse, and the personal accumulation of chicken lice. At the end of the day all of us in the picking room looked like prehistoric beasts, vaguely related to the pterodactyl though more horrible to contemplate. Our work clothes accumulated blood and then the feathers built up in layers and I suppose the multitudes of lice that crawled over us thought that we were big chickens. Yet I loved every moment of it. I loved it because of a girl named Eunice, one of the twenty-odd men and women employed in the room (I was the only minor allowed to participate; my father had influence and this is the only time in my life I ever benefited from nepotism). In my inexperienced eye, Eunice was a most beautiful young woman. I loved her dearly and whenever I looked at her there were stirrings within me. She labored at a chicken line not far from my own, and my work suffered from my inability to concentrate on pin feathers in her presence. I used to gaze cow-eyed at her, standing there so sweet and virginal in her blood-caked, feather-encrusted old apron, scratching gracefully wherever the lice might be crawling (how I envied them!) and I used to vow that some day I'd clean her up and marry her. There was a "ruffer" named Bill Tudd, a villainous roughneck whose job was to kill chickens with a flick of his knife and then rip off the outer feathers. As this monster plied his gory trade he sometimes addressed himself to Eunice in a loud voice, asking her to go out with him at night, telling her he had a bottle of mule, and once he said, "AH'll bet the inside uh your thighs are smoother than a duck's belly!" For days I wanted to kill that nasty beast with his own chicken knife.

One season of this profession was enough. I grew tired of chicken lice and there were stories that the foul Tudd was "making out" with Eunice. I had not yet reached my sixteenth birthday when I went to work in Neil Ashley's barber shop on Market Street. My job was to shine shoes, sweep up used hair and operate a machine which sharpened old safety razor blades. Mr. Ashley had this contrivance set up in the front window of his shop. It looked something like a lathe. Eight or ten blades were clamped into metal arms and these arms flicked back and forth, pressing the blades against little wheels. There wasn't much professional entertainment around in those days outside of the movies, so little knots of people gathered in front of the window and watched me and the machine sharpen blades. This was, in a sense, my first public appearance as an entertainer and I was nervous at the beginning and cut my hands to ribbons changing blades. But soon I grew more composed and was able to hold my audience through an entire cycle of blade-sharpening. And I was ambitious, for Mr. Ashley himself had given me a solemn lecture at the time he hired me, saying that some day I might become a master barber like he was, and own my own home, and have an auto. This sounded great to me. It was the first time, in my recollection, that I ever gave any thought to the future. Sometimes I catch myself wishing that Mr. Ashley had been right.

One afternoon I was feeding blades to the machine and enjoying my position there in the window for all the world to see . . . when Fate stepped in for a once-over-lightly. A young man named Donnelly Sullivan wanted a shine while he was waiting for a barber to shave him. I switched off the machine and hurried back to the shoeshine chair and went to work.

I knew Mr. Sullivan because he was courting my sister. He and I were now in a classic stance—I was his true love's kid brother and it was required of him that he make a favorable impression on me so I would go home and say that he was *some punkins*. While I shined his shoes I asked him where he was working.

"Haven't you heard?" he said. "I'm a reporter now over at the *Press*."

I must have read something somewhere that had given me the notion that newspaper reporters were something special, engaged in a romantic, swashbuckling, derring-do sort of business. I got a small tingle from the knowledge that I was shining the shoes of a real reporter and that, moreover, this real reporter was in love with my own sister. Mr. Sullivan may have read my thoughts, for he said: "How would you like to be a reporter?"

That prospect was more remote than the presidency of Guatemala but I hadn't reckoned on how much Mr. Sullivan adored my sister. He told me that I would hear from him later and within a week I was summoned to the offices of the Huntington *Press,* a morning daily. I was hired as a proofreader at a wage of three dollars a week, with the understanding that greater things lay ahead.

Within a month I was being sent around to feed stores to collect personal items about the doings of farmers. In Huntington a novice started out on country jakes and worked his way up to writing about town people. My first piece of professional writing was nothing that would likely stir the souls of future generations; it told how a man named Ed Ramsey of Bippus was in town for the day, buying harness. I mention this item not because of the clean, graceful flow of its writing, but because of Bippus. Bippus is a small community a few miles northwest of Huntington. I am continually hearing mention of Bippus in, of all places, the borough of Manhattan. Recently I became acquainted with a lady who is an executive at one of New York's biggest department stores. She is from Bippus. Once I fell into conversation with the TV sportscaster, Chris Schenkel, and I asked him where he came from and he said Indiana and I said where in Indiana and he said a place you never heard of and I said name it and he said Bippus and we mygodded all over the place for fifteen minutes.

Personally I don't see anything screechingly funny about the word "Bippus" but other people do. Once I happened to mention the town in the presence of a friend named Ben Serkowich and when I had convinced him that there actually was a town with such a name, he laughed for ten minutes and talked about it for a month afterward. I met the lady from the department store at the home of neighbors. Her real name is Martha but these neighbors think her home town has such a funny name that they always refer to her as "Bippus." So I got to talking around about Bippus, and told Ginny Street about it, and she said there was a fellow named Bippus worked for the Rockefeller Brothers at Williamsburg. I wrote to him, and he said he knew about Bippus the town and that it was his impression that it was named for a family of Bippuses, and that there were a lot of Bippuses, or Bippi, around Evansville, but he recommended that I refrain from approaching anybody named Bippus for information. "It's my impression," he wrote, "that every Bippus I ever knew was a little on the crazy side."

The above seems to be a digression.

After I had mastered the two-line item about people from Bippus I took another great step up the ladder that would lead to fame and fortune: they gave me the job of covering undertakers.

There were three undertaking parlors in Huntington and I had to visit each of them twice daily. The composition of obituary notices and funeral reports was a simple matter, all done by formula, and the important part of the assignment was to spell all names correctly. Hell hath no fury like that of an honorary pallbearer whose name has been misspelled in the newspaper.

Late one afternoon I walked into one of the undertaking parlors and found the front office deserted. By this time my identity was known around the place, so I poked about and finally saw a light shining through the crack of a door in the rear of the building. I walked back through two rows of caskets and pushed open the door of the little room where the light was burning.

I saw Joe Poore, the old embalmer, bending over the naked corpse of a little old man, a man with chin whiskers, a body that seemed extraordinarily white below his leathery face, and clothed in nothing save socks and heavy work shoes.

"Come on in," said Joe Poore. I swallowed a couple of times and moved into the room.

Joe was a big man whose face was always flushed and who wheezed noisily whenever he moved about. He was wheezing and puffing now as he made his way to the foot of the embalming bier.

"Charlie Miller," he said, gesturing at the body. "Farmer out near Markle. Knowed him since he was a boy. Went to school with him. Out ridin' a hay tedder this mornin'. God damn horse run away with him. Wheel hit a rock. Threw Charlie off and broke his neck."

Throughout this disconnected narrative Joe busied himself removing Charlie Miller's shoes. As he pulled off the first sock he straightened up and glowered in the direction of the little farmer's head. Then he said:

"Charlie, you old son-of-a-bitch, why didn't you warsh your feet?"

True enough, Charlie Miller's feet were dirty, but he had been working in the fields and his dirty feet didn't shock me nearly so much as did Joe's behavior. But old Joe had to wash those feet and he was angry. While he cursed and sponged I edged toward the door and escaped to the street. I was feeling green.

This little experience made me ashamed of myself. After all, I was a reporter and I was supposed to be hard and unflinching. I decided that the best way to cure myself of this squeamishness would be to see Joe Poore at work more often. Before long I had become a sort of assistant "im-bomber" under the coaching of Old Joe, running the pump, handing him his tools and listening to his conversations with the dead. He knew everybody in the county and he loved to talk to his customers as he prepared them for the tomb.

"Bill," he would say to a corpse, "you never got it, did you? Never got all that money. That dirty son-of-a-bitch wife of yourn, she'll get it now, won't she Bill?"

I learned a lot about people in that little room.

Almost everyone employed by the Huntington *Press* was slightly off balance. There was Zip Mason, the circulation manager, a man with flashing gold teeth who loved to startle the farmers when they came to the business office to renew their subscriptions. Zip would stride up and down, calling on God to strike all women dead in their tracks, pretending that a woman he loved and trusted had stolen his life savings and then tried to kill him with an ax. Occasionally during this flamboyant discourse Zip would confront the cash register, press a key to open the drawer, spit emphatically into the penny compartment, then slam it shut.

After that he would approach the customer, glare at him a moment and then demand:

"How's your Uncle Bill?"

Almost everyone had an Uncle Bill and those who didn't would usually say, "Oh, you must mean my Uncle Ed."

Zip would listen to a long exposition of Uncle Bill's troubles, meanwhile cocking his head from side to side, studying the farmer from different angles. Then he would interrupt:

"Pardon me for taking the liberty of mentioning it, but you've got the makin's of an ugly old man."

Our printers' devil actually bore the nickname "Scoop" and was egregiously goosey. It always somehow gets around that a goosey person is goosey with the consequence that that person gets goosed. Thus it was with Scoop. He was secretly in love with the society editor, the lovely Gertrude Walters. He wore a square hat fashioned out of a newspaper, in the time-honored manner of pressmen, and he was usually smeared with ink. One evening he came into the newsroom to pick up some copy. Turning back toward the composing room, he stood for a moment beside Gertrude's desk, mooning inside himself. As he gazed at the one he loved his mouth dropped open and he grew limp all over; he had achieved, in the jargon of goosers, "perfect pitch." The city editor was Sam Ballard, now a top advertising man on Madison Avenue. Sam had a foot ruler in his hand. The target was tempting. He reached over and gave Scoop a gentle goose with the ruler. Scoop shrieked, copy paper flew in all directions and he leaped forward, landing right on top of the society editor and her typewriter. Things were quite noisy for a while and Scoop tried to kill Sam Ballard with a telephone. Mr. Ballard was understandably astonished at this turn of events and while fighting off his assailant, kept yelling, "For Christ's sake, all I did was *goose* you!"

The makeup man in the composing room was Old Eck. He was in his seventies, small and frail and bent and deaf and wore a mustache and always chewed on a cigar stub. The business manager of the paper was Jack Wilhelm, a stout dressy man who was looked upon by all hands as a tyrant. Much is made of the fact nowadays that the business office has no authority in the editorial end of newspapering. I sometimes suspect that this is, in Dave Apollon's phrase, a lotta poppely cock. Jack Wilhelm was boss. He was loud and forceful and penny-saving and all of us shuddered slightly when he frowned. At the time of which I write, there had been a series of boneheads in the composing room and one morning the paper came out with Sowerwine's Department Store ad upside down. That afternoon Jack Wilhelm strode into the composing room. Everyone knew that Old Eck was going to get his hide removed. The old makeup man was puttering at the forms, chewing on his cigar. Jack started slowly, but along about Paragraph Three of his oration his organ tones began to swell and soon he was yelling at the top of his voice, god damning and Jesus Christing and threatening to fire everybody in sight, and especially Old Eck. But Old Eck went calmly about his work under this rain of violent language, shuffling type from stone to form and back to stone, and finally he took his cigar stub out of his mouth and spoke in his high, cracked, old-man's voice: "Jaccccck . . . do . . . you . . . like . . . paw paws?" The question stunned Mr. Wilhelm. He stood there and sputtered for a moment, then turned and headed for his office. On the stairway someone heard him say, "I am trapped in a looney bin."

Fred Hammes was an aging Linotype operator with a big vocabulary and a pair of bleary eyes. He was always slightly drunk when he arrived for work in the afternoon and each day he brought with him a pint of white mule, which had the fragrance of a load of manure. Jack Wilhelm spent many hours trying to find where Fred kept his bottle hidden, but he never succeeded. I did. I caught Fred in the act of removing it from the flush box in the men's toilet. He pretended this was not a hiding place, saying, "It keeps nice and cool in there." He always put a dozen aspirin tablets into the bottle of mule before taking the first drink out of it. He said the aspirin made it the equivalent of three bottles of rotgut. Fred knew that Jack Wilhelm was after his hiding place and he also knew that Jack had formerly worked in Arnold's Department Store. He usually referred to the business manager as "that pusillanimous ribbon clerk." Fred knew words and he knew spelling and whenever he found an error in the copy he was setting, he would walk grimly into the newsroom and say, "Who wrote the story about the Legion circus?" When the proud author spoke up Fred would address him in a scornful voice: "Why don't you learn to spell, you god damn ignoramus!"

The truth is Fred Hammes was a more efficient Linotype operator while drunk than the others were sober. He was the only man in the shop who could and would set in type the livestock reports and the curtailed stock market averages and similar cabalistic stuff that was hated by other operators. And Fred Hammes was responsible for a traditional cry that usually went up among *Press* employees at the sound of a certain vulgar noise. One evening Fred gave a fellow printer a couple of belts from his bottle of medicated mule. Shortly thereafter the man dropped a stick of type, making a great clatter on the sheet-iron floor, and Fred Hammes shouted, "Let 'er went, Cleavely, never even touched me!" Nobody ever figured out what it meant. Nobody ever heard of anyone named Cleavely. But for a while whenever any loud noise was heard in the place, someone would cry out, "Let 'er went, Cleavely, never even touched me!" And then one evening Scoop, the printers' devil, broke wind noisily beside the city desk and Don Sullivan uttered the Cleavely cry. From that day on it was employed exclusively in connection with the breaking of wind. Not, however, by me. I considered the whole matter to be vulgar, and still do.

A redhead named John Moynihan, from nearby Bluffton, joined us as a reporter and he and I became close friends. He had been to college and knew about somebody named Mencken and somebody else named Joseph Conrad and an Englishman named Max Beerbohm. He talked about these people but he also talked about batting averages and the uses of girls and Gerald Chapman and George Gipp and ten thousand other things. He was to remain my friend until his death a few years ago in California.

The publisher of the *Press* was a distinguished-looking man named Homer Ormsby, who wrote miles of editorials which nobody ever read. He usually thought out these editorials while pacing back and forth in the newsroom, clinking a handful of quarters. He was a pleasant and soft-spoken man and in later years he moved to California where he became the mayor of Arcadia. One day he and I were alone in the newsroom and he was pacing and clinking quarters when the phone rang. He answered it and was told that there had been a frightful interurban wreck at Roanoke, ten miles up the line in the direction of Fort Wayne. Everyone else being out of the office, Mr. Ormsby told me to high-tail it for Roanoke. I high-tailed it for the interurban station, thinking there might be a wrecking car going out. Then along came Don Sullivan in his car and picked me up and the two of us drove to Roanoke. Two interurban cars had crashed head-on right in the center of the little town. Seventeen or eighteen people had been killed and it was a wild and crazy scene we found when we arrived. Don and I climbed through one of the wrecked cars, looking for papers that would help identify some of the victims. The new county coroner arrived and asked me to help him make up the list of names. After a while Don and I telephoned our office and Homer Ormsby and Jack Wilhelm and Zip Mason did a rare thing for Huntington—they put out an extra. It was my first big story, the first extra I ever worked on, and out of it came a reward. The coroner was a young druggist who ran a store around the corner from the newspaper office. He asked me if I would serve as his clerk at a fee of five dollars per case. Whenever there was a death by violence in the county he would call me and I would go with him to the scene and make notes of what the witnesses said and then type out the full report later on. We sometimes had two and three cases a week—auto accidents or murders or farmers being thrown headlong off of hay tedders. It was the first time I ever held public office but I didn't mind it because I was never called upon to speak.

My being the only staff member in the office when the Roanoke story broke reminded some of the old-timers of a similar occurrence a few years earlier. A local politician who had a financial interest in the paper also had a twelve-year-old son who yearned to be a reporter. Nepotism set in, but I can't complain about it in view of my own experience as a nepotistic chicken-picker. The kid was allowed to hang around the newsroom when he wasn't in school, and then came the day when he was the only available person to send on a big story. Three workmen had been killed in a sewer explosion and the boy was dispatched to the scene. He was gone a long time but finally he came dashing into the office, out of breath. He plopped down at a typewriter and went to work. It seemed fully an hour before he got his big story written the way he wanted it. Then he walked forward and placed it on the city editor's desk. He had written the big local story of the decade as follows:

> Three men were killed in a dynamite explosion today in the new sewer. An explosion is about the worst thing that can happen to a man.

There was one other assignment I remember with a touch of emotion. Two young men named Jacobstein ran a men's clothing store on Market Street and were fun to horse around with and one day they told me that I could get a good story for the *Press* if I went to a certain number on South Jefferson Street at eight o'clock that night. I did so. The number was on a door at the side of a two-story building. I knocked and nobody answered and so I opened the door and saw a long, steep, narrow flight of steps. At the top was a small landing with a single light bulb hanging over it. I started up the stairs, feeling lonely and a little nervous, and then I froze in my tracks. A figure had materialized on the landing—a Ku-Kluxer in full regalia. From where I stood he looked like a menacing giant. I wanted to turn and run but something made me continue slowly up the stairway. The Kluxer said not a word, and I said nothing. When I reached the landing I could hear the rumble of male voices from behind a door, and then the hooded man spoke.

"Whadda *you* want?" he demanded.

"I'm a reporter from the *Press*," I said, trying to be brave. These were the big years for the Ku-Klux-Klan in Indiana. Its leaders were running the state and if you got in trouble with the Kluxers they might haul you out to a sylvan dell and ruin your virility with a paring knife. So there I stood, a quaking kid from a Catholic family sent to the scene by a couple of Jewish haberdashers.

"Who tole you to come here?" said the Kluxer.

"N-n-n-nobody tole me," I stammered. "I mean my boss tole me."

"You can't come in here," he said. "This here is a private meeting." He took hold of my arm to turn me around and head me back down the steps. "Why, boy," he said, his whole tone changing, "you're shakin' like a leaf! You're scared to death. Why, boy, you got nothin' to be scared about from us. What we are is good hunnert per cent Americans. We wouldn't do you no harm. Now, you just go on home and forget about this whole thing."

I gulped and nodded, grateful for being spared both my life and my virility. Like Norman Vincent Peale says, there is good in everyone. I went on down the stairs and the next day I offered to write a story about my little adventure, but the paper didn't want it. Not that the paper was afraid. Oh, no. They just didn't want it. Said forget about it. Didn't want it. No.

Donnelly Sullivan, my future brother-in-law, took to writing occasional feature stories under the by-line of "Miss Ann Other." His pitch was that of the dumb female trying to cope with men, and mechanical things, and sports, and men, and politics, and men. The word to describe these stories is "cute." At the local level, as they say, the gimmick was quite successful and popular with the readers, and so I decided to play the copycat. I began writing features under the name, "Miss Ella Vator." The first of the Ella Vator columns was a sober essay on how to build a birdhouse that would attract a bird called a martin. Later on Miss Vator grew cocky and began dabbling in personalities.

One of my sisters was proud of my work as Miss Ella Vator. She acquired a small catalogue put out by the Diem & Wing Paper Company of Cincinnati and using this for a scrapbook, began saving my brilliant essays as they appeared during parts of 1922 and 1923. She has presented me with that little book and from it I have extracted some of the sparkling metaphors and graceful figures of speech that came from my typewriter. You may readily detect the spark that later ignited the literary world in the following examples:

"That gang sure takes the embroidered hot water bottle."

"I answered the Whoozit."

"Steaming poodle!"

"Vice Versa and Versa Vice."

"I'll tell both hemispheres!"

"Radiated canine!"

"Pete is a baker by trade and he sure makes the dough and has got the crust. He is a well bred boy."

"Perspiring pup!"

"I think he is the nicest and best-looking cookie-duster I have focused mine eyes on in manys the day."

"Tropical airedale!"

It would have been a criminal offense for me to have written "hot dog!" in those days. A sports writer of the period would have been committed if he ever called a baseball a baseball. A man was never held in jail; he was always "languishing in durance vile." Nobody ever danced—they tripped the light fantastic. And a baby boy wasn't legal unless it bounced. Every boy child born in Huntington was a "bouncing baby boy." I myself gave up writing it that way when a vision came to me—a vision of a woman on her way home from the hospital, dribbling her baby like a basketball.

A few weeks after she came into being, Miss Ella Vator was in trouble. A merchant named Till Priddy was hopping mad at me for having disputed his claim to being champion mushroom hunter of the county. I never suspected that hunting mushrooms could become a thing of such dedicated seriousness. Yet Mr. Priddy's anger was as nothing. In one of my stories I made mention of a local hotel proprietor and his wife. Owing to the circumstance that his wife was a blonde, I referred to her as "Blondie." I didn't know it, but in the Huntington of forty years ago to call a woman "Blondie" was tantamount to calling her a whorelady. The enraged hotelman telephoned Homer Ormsby, canceled his advertising contract, announced that he was going to sue, and said that if he ever caught me on the street he'd stomp me to death.

I was ordered to go to the man's hotel and face him in his own lobby and apologize to him. "But," I told Mr. Ormsby, "he said he'd stomp me to death." Mr. Ormsby gave me a gentle reply. "Of course," he said. "That's the chance you have to take."

The apology was accepted in good grace and I didn't get stomped, but that ended the career of Miss Ella Vator.

# the difference between boys and girls

Whenever I returned to Huntington in later years my feelings should have followed the normal course as set down in autobiographies and the novels of nostalgia. By all the rules of the American Dream it was required of me that I think of this as the town where I got my start in the newspaper profession, the wood-burning incubator in which my God-given literary talent was nursed and nurtured. That rickety green building where the *Press* was published had served me as a training ground for great and heroic exploits. These were the sensations I should have had when I went back, but somehow my mind fastened on other things. Girls, for example.

Once in the middle 1940s I stood in front of the decaying structure that had housed the *Press*. I closed my eyes and reflected on the many days and nights I had spent on the second floor of that building, and then a strange memory came back to me. I was sitting in the newsroom one slow evening reading a magazine containing "true" confessions of people who had been guilty of wrongdoing, usually with their clothes off. I was not reading this magazine with the intention of writing an exposé of its contents. I was reading it because it pleasured me to do so and even made me squirm a little. I had not fallen for John Moynihan's man Mencken, or his Conrad, or any of the others he talked about. So I sat there and turned a page and looked at the heading over an article: "*HER HUSBAND LOVED HER BUT . . .*" In my own perverse way I thought there was something funny about that headline; I felt that the man who had written it was a true literary artist, with creative imagination. I still think so.

And then, standing there on the pavement in front of the old building, my thoughts switched to a letter I got from a soldier during the recently ended war. He wrote:

"I wonder if you would be able to tell me what part of a woman is her yet. We have been puzzled about it out here in the Philippines. We know that a woman has got a yet. The reason we know it is that we heard an officer talking the other day. He said there was a girl in Manila who had been shot recently and the bullet was in her yet. Please tell us what it is."

I wasn't able to oblige them. No more than I would have been able to tell what that husband loved when he loved her but . . . I do remember that I took the matter of a woman's yet to my literary agent. He is a man who knows everything and he wasn't stopped this time.

"Yes," he said, after a few moments of reflection, "I know what a woman's yet is. It's the same as her now."

"And what is her now?"

"Oh, you know," he said. "Don't you remember? I Wonder Who's Kissing Her Now?"

I wrote of these confusions some years back and recently a letter came from a reader in Australia. He said there was a story in a Sydney newspaper about a man who had been married thirty-eight years and then one day his wife disappeared. Said the newspaper: "He never saw her more." My Australian reader said that it seemed like a long time, thirty-eight years, but I still don't know what is indicated, no more than I know what is meant in the story of the lady who suffered a fall which bruised her somewhat.

Furthermore, I don't see much in the way of nostalgic warmth in these musings.

Possibly because I was a genuine newspaper reporter, I was accepted by the *haut monde* of Huntington. The girls I dated were the girls from the best families. I was invited to their homes and their fathers some times talked to me, asking what I thought about business conditions. I didn't know there were any. These families formed a tight-knit group and there was a certain amount of snobbery among them; they were inclined to be uppity toward the lower orders but their daughters all seemed to be beautiful and smelled nice and were good dancers and had marvelous yets and mores and nows and somewhats.

Years later when I came back to town, I saw but few of these people. What I found in Huntington was what I found in other towns I had known. A quarter of a century can effect some wondrous social adjustments. In many cases the aristocrats of my youth had gone to the dogs, lost their money and lost their fine homes. Some of the mighty who had fallen had turned to sinful pursuits and I heard of a few who were sodden drunks and even drug addicts. When their day of glory had vanished, some had gone to work— the barons become vassals. One man who had been rich and powerful in the community when I had dated his daughter was now wearing overalls and working in a filling station. On the other hand, this leveling process worked in two directions and I heard of people who were impecunious and raffish in my day who now sat at shiny desks and bellowed orders at the hired help.

Only a few of the "society" girls were permitted to go with us to Idle Hour. This was a resort a couple of miles east of town. A dance pavilion stood near the lip of an old quarry, and the quarry was filled with nice clean water and was so deep in places that the best divers had never found bottom. There were diving towers and floats and a few rowboats. At night the big attraction was the dance hall, which brought people from as far away as Fort Wayne (twenty-six miles). Good orchestras, by the standards of the day, played fast jazz tunes which fitted the current style of dancing. To dance ballroom style in those days usually meant to bob up and down at a rapid rate while the band played "Chicago, Chicago, that toddlin' town!" If you have read the tender story of Studs Lonigan by James T. Farrell you will likely recall the kind of dancing Old Studs and his pals went in for in that toddlin' town. I think the expression Studs and his friends used was "sockin' it in." We went in for that sort of thing at Idle Hour. We always knew which girls liked it and would put up with it and which girls liked it and wouldn't put up with it.

Inasmuch as it had been my custom to spend a lot of my spare time at Idle Hour, either swimming or dancing, I had strong nostalgic feelings about it and once I drove out to have a sentimental look at it. My wife was with me and on the way I told her of the glorious golden days and nights I had spent at Idle Hour and of the things I did there, not mentioning the Studs Lonigan business. We had gone about five miles when I realized that I was too far out, so I turned the car and started back and after a while I saw it, off to the right of the road. The banks of the old quarry were grown thick

with brush and weeds and the water, which in years gone by had affected me the way the water of the Mediterranean affects others,
was scarcely visible from the highway. The dance pavilion was gone
—everything was gone (how fleeting is time and life and sockin' it
in!) but there was a rectangular clearing where the dance hall had
been, and a few remnants of the foundations, and in the middle of
that rectangle, lying on that sacred ground and chewing a vulgar
cud, was an old nanny goat. A great sadness descended upon me, but
it lifted when I heard my good wife's voice: "Well," she said, "I see
one of your old girl friends is left."

None of us in the crowd that I ran with had a car of his own but
there were a few who could sometimes get the family bus for an
evening. In the summertime on Saturday nights we would load up
with five or six boys and head for the glamorous lake resorts of
Winona and Wawasee far to the north (thirty miles). These were
splendidly iniquitous expeditions; someone usually had a package of
tailor-mades, meaning store-boughten cigarettes, and there were even
times when a pint of panther sweat was brought along, the same
being a colorless beverage tasting like the stuff poured off a keg of
rusty nails. It was the same nectar as Fred Hammes's mule, minus
the aspirin tablets. Those of us who were gallant enough to take a
few swigs of it had spells of throwing up for the next three or four
hours, but it was worth it.

I can remember how Rome Brading or Joe Renner or whoever
happened to be driving would come to a straight stretch of gravel
and yell out, "Hang on, you god-dern cake-eaters, I'm a-gonna open
'er up!" He'd bend low over the wheel, at the same time turning
his cap around backward in the manner of Ralph DePalma or Dario
Resta, and we'd all crouch forward tensely, jaws tight and eyes squinting as he edged the gas lever downward, and soon we'd be roaring
precipitantly through the night—I'm not exaggerating when I say
there were times when we hit thirty-five.

Up at the lake resorts our dancing was slightly more civilized
than at Idle Hour. We danced to a smoother and dreamier type of
music called syncopation and we gripped the girl in a bear hug
that sometimes shut off her breathing and turned her features a
fascinating and passionate purple.

By this time records had flattened out and Cohen and his telephone were one with Tyre and Nineveh. In the homes of our girl
friends we turned the crank and changed the bamboo needle and

toddled to the rhythms of Henry Santry and His Jazz Musicians, or we played "Ma—He's Making Eyes at Me!" holding the right hand with the palm outward and making circular motions in time with the lovely beat. It was the living, screeching end. Madsville. We went ape on four feet for "Wang, Wang Blues," and "Lena, She's the Queen of Palestrina," and "Indian Love Call," and "She's Got Hot Lips," and "Tuck Me to Sleep in My Old 'Tucky Home." And if the kids of today believe that their clatter-and-grunt-and-bang is the most important musical innovation in the recorded history of mankind, let them consider that we had wild songs like "Barney Google, With His Goo-Goo-Googly Eyes" and "Oogie-Oogie-Wa-Wa."

Then along came radio and some of us had crystal sets and we got numb ears and narrow heads from sitting long hours with those headphones clamped on. Yet it was much the same with radio as it was with the old Edison talking machine—we didn't care so much about what programs we heard; the idea was to strive for distance and when you picked up Kansas City or Pittsburgh, well . . . hot cat! (The kids of today have no monopoly on the word "cat." We always said that a thing was the cat's pajamas, which was much the same as saying it was the bee's knees, and we were constantly using the exclamatory expression, "Hot cat!" I think, however, that we may be dealing with two different kinds of cat. Today's cat, as I get it, is a sort of human. Our cat was a cat.)

Naturally we went to the movies a lot. I had outgrown Eddie Polo and switched to the dazzling ladies; I can remember sitting in movie theaters and going limp over Alice Terry. We all fell desperately in love with Alice, and with Clara Bow, the girl who had "It" and was billed as "The Hottest Jazz Baby in Films"—not to mention Pola Negri and that same Agnes Ayres who came out of Little Egypt to have Rudolph Valentino snatch her off a horse and say, "Quit struggling, you little fool!" (She quit.) And Theda Bara —lands! She would give any boy the clammydamps. One of the three-sheets announcing a Theda Bara picture of the time said: "As this man has done to me, so shall I do to all men. From now on my heart is ice, my passion consuming fire. Let men beware." We were deeply stirred by this statement of determined principle; we thought it meant that whenever Theda encountered a man she was going to sock him one right in the mush. Some of the teen-age girls in our crowd used to try to imitate Theda and Pola and Clara in their manners and movements and sometimes even in their dress, but their mothers stepped in at this point—they weren't going to let *their* daughters go around "showing too much throat."

There was one period in Huntington when most of us boys of high school age wore corduroy pants, flared at the ankles with triangular insets of red flannel, and these insets were bordered with little jingle bells. In retrospect I'll admit that a rhinoceros might have gagged at the sight of us coming down the street but *we* knew we were on the ball. And there was another time when it became fashionable in the winter to wear our galoshes wide open and winging, so that the buckles and hooks struck together when we walked. It was not uncommon for a boy to come striding down Jefferson Street in full view of half the town and have his buckles hook together, throwing him forward onto his face. Such headers were most unfortunate (though our elders viewed them with profound satisfaction) and highly embarrassing and productive of cuts and abrasions, but fashion is fashion and we were willing to accept all risks.

Huntington had two Greek letter fraternities when I lived there. These groups were not connected with any colleges or schools; as near as I can make out at this distance in time, they were somewhat on the order of young Elks, immature Odd Fellows. Each fraternity had its clubrooms and the principal function of the membership seemed to be the giving of dances, and the flailing of pledges across the britches with heavy paddles. Cobs, as such body blows were called in Old Fort Defiance.

If you were a young fellow in Huntington and didn't achieve membership in one or the other of these fraternities you were scum, and your entire future was certain; to-wit, nothing. Probably because of my standing with the "society" crowd, plus my powerful posture in the realm of journalism, I was pledged to one of the clubs. I never achieved full knighthood in spite of the sorest prat in the whole Northwest Territory.

Every time I walked into those clubrooms one of the older guys would say, "All right, half-wit, over the chair!" I had to obey or lose my franchise. I had to lay myself over a big leather chair in a posture that would make my pants tight across the seat, and then I would be whaled and whacked on that selfsame seat until I felt that my spinal column was coming out the top of my head. Jesus God but it hurt! Slowly it dawned on me that this was injustice. They didn't necessarily flog a pledge because he had done something wrong; they whaled away at him simply because he was a pledge. They beat

my butt ragged in spite of the fact that I performed every errand
and chore assigned to me and said "sir" to every son-of-a-bitch in
sight.

There came a time when the current pledges were to be initiated,
the night on which they would be awarded full membership and the
privilege of beating later pledges across the pants. The first thing
they gave me to do was a window-counting job. I had to go to the
extreme north end of Jefferson Street. I had to count every window,
every pane of glass, that faced on the town's main thoroughfare
whether it be in a house or a store. The street was at least a couple of
miles long but I went at the job with assiduity. A badly chosen word.
I had been warned that the initiation committee knew the exact
number of windows on the street and that if I made an error I would
not get into the fraternity. When I finally arrived at the clubrooms
and announced my findings, there was considerable argument as to
the accuracy of my count. Two men supported me and one was
against me (my sister had thrown this varmint over for another guy)
and the one who was against me grudgingly settled for the privilege
of assaulting my buttocks with twenty cobs. Ten more than that
sleeping sentry got in Defiance.

Having passed the window test by the skin of my . . . well, teeth
. . . they gave me a new assignment. A coonskin cap was placed on
my head and an alarm clock was hung around my neck by a heavy
cord. I was escorted to the town's chief intersection, Market and
Jefferson. All this touching ceremony, I should explain, took place
on a Saturday afternoon and evening and the town was crowded
with farmers and citizens from such outlying villages as Markle and
Roanoke and Bippus. At the intersection a tall lamppost was pointed
out to me and I was told to shinny up this post once every five
minutes and, on reaching a point where I could touch the light
globe, I was to cry out in a stentorian voice, "Coo-koo!" ten times.
I was to keep this up until I had been up the pole twenty-five times
and cried "Coo-koo!" two hundred and fifty times. With all her
great patience and forbearance, I doubt that Eleanor Roosevelt
would have done it.

My feet and legs were killing me from that window-counting job
and the paddle whacks had been delivered with such hateful vigor
that every blood vessel in my behind ached, but I went at that lamppost manfully. In ten minutes a large crowd had gathered. Most of
the onlookers had no comprehension of what was going on and,

being rural-routers, wouldn't have understood the shining symbolism even if they had been told. Many of them spoke to each other in confidential tones; they seemed to be under the impression that, as the British say, my head wanted seeing to.

The crowd was overflowing onto the pavement by the time a half-hour of coo-kooing had passed, and then John Johnson, the cop, arrived. He began shooing people on their way, but most of them refused to budge, never having seen anything quite like this before. Then Officer Johnson stood off and watched me climb the post and perform my ritual. He was waiting for me when I came down.

"I might of known it would be you," he said. "Where'd you get it?"

"Get what?"

"The booze. C'm on, where'd you get it?"

I denied that I had been drinking and told him what I was doing.

"Oh," he said with that fine sarcasm that most policemen employ in the presence of untruth, "Oh, so you're being initiated. That's all right with me, except that if you go up that pole one more time I run you in. Go somewheres out in the country and climb a tree like a goddam nut if you want to, but don't go up that pole no more."

Dejectedly I made my way to the clubrooms and reported what had happened.

"Get the hell back there," the committee ordered, "and climb that pole and finish the assignment."

"But what about John Johnson?"

"Defy him."

"He said he'd run me in."

"You been run in before. Get going."

I returned to the corner to find that the crowd had dispersed but John Johnson was still there. He remained obdurate. If I shinnied up that pole just one more time, I'd spend the night in jail. Again I went back to the clubrooms and again I found no sympathetic ear. The man who had given me the twenty cobs began yelling for my blood. Sore of body, weak of limb, hoarse of voice, I now got a little hysterical and did some yelling on my own and worked some profanity into it. I saw my enemy start for the corner of the room to get the heavy paddle and he was shouting that this time he was going to beat my ass clean off of me. Such as it was, I preferred retaining it and at that moment all the yearning for blessed brotherhood with burial benefits went out of me. I took off the coonskin

(1) This is Pop, a man almost as baffled by life as is his oldest son.

(2) My mother, who hoped I would be another Arthur Brisbane.

(3) A McLeansboro candid shot of my sister Mary and me. Note the innate wisdom shining from that young face. I mean Mary's.

(4) In Defiance we played tennis in our street pants and I had a bank account.

(5) Newsroom of *Huntington Press*,
1923. Left is Sam Ballard. I am next
to him, pretending to read proof, sitting
in the approximate spot where "Scoop"
got goosed. The society editor is
Gertrude Walters. Then Ross Hurd,
sports editor, and Abe Andrews,
managing editor. At far right is Don
Sullivan, the guy who got me into all
this.

(6) Don Sullivan as he looked at the
time he coaxed me away from the
honorable profession of shining shoes.
He was a sport. He is now my
brother-in-law. No longer a sport.

(7) Taken in Huntington soon after I became a reporter.

(8) Character at left looks drunk. Is. Seated is John Moynihan and at right Frank Rager. Taken in Jeffersonville after a long night of river-front roadhousing.

(9) Nelle tries always to pose with tongue out. Here she is in Sebring with Margaret Moynihan and Lake Jackson.

(10) This is Nelle as she looked when she was stupidly shouldering me aside in Sebring.

(11) The $75 adenoidal Lake Wales portrait, which evoked a perceptive remark from Nelle's father. (PHOTO BY ALEXANDER)

(12) Joe Alex Morris ponders an Imponderable Object.

(13) Morris Watson, who had a way of using God in his daily work.

(14) Frederick G. Bonfils, unretouched, as he looked when I knew him. (PHOTO BY ROCKY MOUNTAIN NEWS)

(15) A cultural center in the Rockies—the celebrated Denver Press Club. (PHOTO BY ROCKY MOUNTAIN NEWS)

(16) With son and daughter at our South Denver recreation hall.

(17) Lee Taylor Casey, Denver's leading columnist, shown in one of his occasional playful moments.
(PHOTO BY ROCKY MOUNTAIN NEWS)

(18) In the Cheyenne press box shortly after Will Rogers met a man he didn't like.

(19) Sidney B. Whipple, friend of Mister Nowatney.

cap and threw it at him. I took off the alarm clock and dashed it against the wall. I announced in a loud voice that every accredited member of the fraternity was closely related to a female dog, unwed, and then I turned and ran out of the place before they could seize me and kill me.

Those guys never did like me after that and I think it was a good thing that within a few months I left Huntington under more clouds than the United States Weather Bureau has in its handbook for beginners. Before I left, however, I indulged myself in a small bit of satirical writing. I went to a Greek friend who ran a candy store and soda fountain and asked him to give me the Greek words for a vulgar expression which describes a physical impossibility. This vulgar expression is in common usage throughout the United States and contains three words, the first of which is "go." My friend gave me his translation in Greek, and it too consisted of three words. Then I went to the office and wrote a story about the organization of a new club, the ———— ———— ———— Society. I described its aims and purposes, all noble. I listed its members—all the young men of my crowd, plus myself. I handed this story over to the society editor, who was simply tickled to death to get it. If she'd only known!

Subsequently I wrote additional stories, reporting on meetings of the ———— ———— ———— Society, and each meeting became a sort of burlesque of the doings of the fraternity I had failed to make. The Greek gentleman who had given me the words was vastly amused at seeing them in print, but then he grew nervous and one day called me aside. He pointed out that there were probably some people in Huntington other than himself and his brother who knew Greek. Maybe a teacher, maybe some of the town lawyers. I said yes, but they wouldn't likely know *that* kind of Greek. And he said, you be a supprize whadda some pipples knows. So I began to get nervous about it and in my final story killed off the Society, explaining that its officers had not been able to find suitable clubrooms.

I have often heard girls and women make the following flat-footed statement:

"Men are beasts."

I am under the impression that in making this statement they have reference to the male animal's sexual appetites. It may be that they are right but they ought to take a good long look at themselves before attributing beasthood exclusively to men. It took me many years but I finally discovered that girls are beasts. And I, too, have reference to the sex urge. In order to prove my point I must tell a fairly long and difficult story. I shall proceed with all the delicacy at my command.

During one of my return visits to Huntington I ran into Christopher Camp, who had been one of my closest friends when we were in our middle teens. Chris had become a successful businessman in Ohio and he too was back for a visit. Both of us had our wives with us and during dinner together at a Huntington restaurant, we talked of the golden days of yore. I remembered that Chris Camp was a great hand with the girls when we were young—at least he had that reputation. He always managed to be so suave and gentlemanly when he was around them.

I decided that evening in the restaurant to tell the truth about my own career as a lover. I recalled the time a girl named Betty Stover came to town. She was one of several girls who tried out for the job of society editor of the *Press* after Gertrude Walters resigned. Betty Stover came from North Manchester and was a real beauty. It took a while for me to get up the courage but I finally asked to walk her home one evening. After that I walked her home every night, her home being a room she rented in a private house. There came a period of two weeks when the family was away and Betty and I had the house to ourselves. I was then sixteen or seventeen; I have never heard of a boy that age who couldn't boast of conquests by the dozen. I could boast of none. And here was this lovely, shapely, vivacious Betty Stover flopping herself down and all but shrieking at me to take her. I won't go into the details of all the hours we spent in the darkness of that big house. I'm too overcome with shame about it. I can remember that Betty, during a heavy necking session, would often swoon dead away (she was an accomplished actress) and then after a while, when she recovered her senses, she'd moan and gasp and blink her eyes and say, with a strange note of eagerness in her voice, "Did you *do* anything?" And I'd say, "Betty! Of course not!" Jesus! When I think of how it happened, time after time, I could go out and hang myself.

And so I told this story in the presence of my veteran wife, and in the presence of my old friend Chris Camp, the lover boy of yesteryear. There was much laughter and then Chris gave me a long, amused look and grinned and said, "Well, I guess I'd better tell *mine*."

He asked me if I remembered Priscilla Moon. Remember her! She was merely the loveliest, most ravishing creature in town, a couple of years older than Chris and me, member of a well-to-do and socially prominent family and as proper as proper could be.

Chris said he had always admired Priscilla from afar and never even dreamed of fox-trotting with her. So far as he was concerned, she was an unattainable creature. Yet one soft summer evening Chris and some of the other boys were loafing at that same corner where I had climbed the lamppost when a car drew up at the curb and Priscilla Moon poked her lovely head out of it.

"Chris!" she called out. "Chris Camp! Will you come over here a moment, please?"

"Yes, ma'am," Chris responded, hurrying to her side.

"I'm in a terrible fix, Chris," she said. "I'm frightened. My folks have gone out of town for a few days and I'm up at the house all alone and I think somebody has been prowling around the place. It's all right when I get in the house and the doors all locked, but when I have to put the car away—it's so awful dark in the garage and I get so darn nervous. If you'd have the time to ride up with me and help me put the car away and . . ."

"Happy to do it," said Chris and climbed into the seat beside her. In a little while they were turning into the Moon driveway and, sure enough, it was quite dark. Priscilla shot the car into the garage with an expert hand, and they got out and Chris closed the garage door.

"My goodness, Chris," she said to him, "but it was real sweet of you. I always did say that you were one of the *nicest* boys in this town."

"Gee, thanks," said Chris. "It wasn't anything. I was proud to—"

"Now," she went on, "now that you've been so nice—I know it's not really proper and all that, but as I said, my folks are away and if you'd care to come in for a few minutes—"

"Oh, no. Thank you very much. Wasn't doing a thing. Glad to help you out."

"Now, Chris," she coaxed, "come on in. The least I could do is show my appreciation, maybe fix up a few sandwiches."

He had never been in the big Moon house and suddenly the urge was on him to see it. He had heard so much about it, heard they even had a billiard table in it. He'd like to see that. "Well," he finally said, "I'm not really very hungry, but—all right, just for a few minutes."

In the living room Priscilla walked straight to a big divan and flopped onto it in a semi-reclining position. Chris sat down in a chair opposite her, gazing uncomfortably at the splendors all about him.

"Why don't you come over here?" Priscilla said, patting a spot beside her.

"Thank you," said Chris, wondering where the billiard table was, "but I'm very comfortable."

"Oh, Chris," she pouted, "is that any way to act? There's nobody home. Not a soul here but just we two. My goodness, don't you think we ought to get a little better acquainted? After all, living in the same town and . . . here, you come right over here! Right this minute!"

Chris said a sickly grin came on his face and he was amazed to find himself getting to his feet and walking uncertainly across the room and sitting down on the divan. He perched on the edge of the cushion as if prepared to spring away. Miss Moon fluttered her eyelids and then gazed at him in a manner meant to suggest that carnality was in order but which he interpreted as an indication that she might be coming down with the measles. He could not make himself believe that a girl of Priscilla's social standing would ever even *think* of sex. Chris had grown up in the same atmosphere as me—girls from the better families never *did* anything until after they were married. They were just, well . . . just . . . god dern it, they were just *pure.* He had no trouble at all reaching the conclusion that the antics of Priscilla Moon were the antics of a person taken suddenly ill. She was lying back with one shoulder on the arm of the divan and now she wriggled her body sensuously and he thought: "She sure has been upset about something . . ."

"About these prowlers . . ." he began.

She interrupted him. "Don't you think it's *warm* in here, Chris?" She accompanied the words by a tugging at the front of her dress.

"I'm quite comfortable," he said, fixing his gaze on a painting of some sheep on the opposite wall. There was a long pause and then Priscilla moaned and stretched her arms back over her head and flexed her body several times in a most provocative way and then she threw her left leg upward and onto the back of the divan. Her right foot remained on the floor. This whole posture gave her what might be called a *friendly* appearance. Chris swallowed hard.

"This is a real nice place you got here," he said.

Priscilla's left leg came down. She sat up straight on the divan and bit her lip. The sudden change in position startled Chris.

"Did you hear something?" he asked. "Something outside?"

"No!" she snapped at him and he could tell from the tone of her voice that she was emotionally disturbed. Suddenly she flung herself on him and little whinnies and moose calls began issuing from her throat.

"*Miss Moon!*" he cried. "*Priscilla!* For heaven's sake! You're sick!"

She had him down on the divan, her arms wrapped around him, and now she kissed him on the lips. He was trying to talk but all that came out was a gurgling noise. The moment she lifted her lips he quickly twisted his head away and now she pounced on him again, and this time bit him on the ear.

"*Miss Moon!*" he howled.

It was obvious to him that Priscilla Moon was having a seizure, known locally as a fit; her face was down now in the curve of his neck and her hot breath was beating against his flesh. He was sure she was running a temperature. A person as sick as that shouldn't be left alone in such a big house. Might die in the night. She had relaxed her grip on him and now, abruptly, he freed himself and got up. She lay sprawled on the divan, looking up at him, a strange brightness in her eyes.

"Miss Moon," he said, "I got to go now. I think you better call the doctor. And keep the doors locked. Thank you for inviting me in. It's been a real pleasure and I . . . well, I hope you get to feeling better."

She said nothing, and he left the house.

"All the way home I kicked myself," he said, "because I didn't get to see that billiard table."

That's the way he told the story of his adventure with Priscilla Moon and I believed every word of it in the light of what had happened to me with Betty Stover. At that time I was working on a novel about a Midwestern boy who was as dumb as three fenceposts and who grew up to become a famous cowboy star in movies. As a device for illustrating my hero's stupidity, especially about girls, I took the story of Chris and Priscilla Moon and used it as a sort of prologue

in my book. I told it in much the same way it is told above. There
were complaints from many readers about that prologue. They said
that such a thing could not have happened. All who complained
were men. There were no objections from the female customers.

# my brief career in crime

There was only one bootlegger in Huntington. I had never been in his house but I was told that he kept his supply of white mule in a fifty-gallon tank that was sealed inside the living room wall. There was a gas jet coming out of this wall, with a mantle on it. When a customer arrived the bootlegger would remove the mantle, twist the brass pipe and the rich, heady rotgut would flow into a bottle.

My friends and I dealt with this bootlegger through a middleman, a taxi driver, who took a two-bit commission on each pint. It was against the law to sell illegal whisky to boys of our tender years. One night I drank half a bottle of the stuff and along about four in the morning found myself in a somewhat tiddley state. I was cockeyed, and in this condition I had the misfortune to encounter Emmet Bickel, an enormous policeman with a walrus mustache who, in other circumstances, was a friend of mine. He tried to turn his back on me but he couldn't escape. I spoke harsh words to him, calling him names and assuring him that I was going to have him canned off the force the next morning. He still tried to get away from me but, well . . . liquor is such a wonderful thing, instilling a certain grit and determination and stick-to-itiveness of the kind preached by McGuffey and Horatio Alger, Jr. So I spent the rest of the night in a cold jail cell. When I finally got out of that mess I felt truly ashamed until I learned that most of my friends looked upon me as a sort of hero.

That episode was soon forgotten but my criminal career in Huntington was just beginning. Ahead lay the celebrated "Stranded on a Davenport" case.

At this time my best friend was Rome Brading, who attended high school and who had a sardonic turn of mind that appealed to me. The *Press* was not published on Monday mornings, so the office was closed on Sundays. One summer Sunday night Rome and I wandered into the deserted newsroom. He sat down at a typewriter and began pecking out a special-delivery letter to his girl friend (who lived a block and a half from him). Having nothing better to do, I went to work on one of the old Oliver machines and in about thirty minutes knocked out the bawdy screed that was to send me forth into the world, a disgrace to heaven, home, and mother.

I titled it "Stranded on a Davenport" and in length it ran, I should say, between a thousand and two thousand words. It was in the first person, told supposedly by a young woman with swivel hips and animal appetites. It described in luxuriant detail the inception, progress, and conclusion of an amorous adventure. It was one of those things—well, as Mart O'Malley told the jury: "I'll venture to say, gentlemen, that there's not a man among you who never has had such a piece of literature in his possession."

I pasted the sheets together and tossed the completed essay over to Rome Brading. He read it and as he read he giggled and guffawed and slapped his lean thighs in the traditional manner of prurient youth. After that we adjourned to Tommy Ellis's all-night restaurant for coffee.

By the next day I had forgotten it. Not so Rome Brading. He took "Stranded on a Davenport" to school Monday morning. Somehow it got into the hands of his girl friend, who was studying typing. She made half a dozen copies and distributed them among her female friends, and they made copies, and typewriters were humming and clattering all over town and by the end of the week the thing had snowballed into a circulation approaching that of *The Saturday Evening Post*. All this while I was blithely going around town in pursuit of little news items, oblivious of the terrible storm soon to break.

It was said that every teacher in high school had her personal copy of "Stranded on a Davenport" before two weeks had gone by, but the explosion didn't come until Stubby Sellers, the principal, got hold of it.

Phil Baker, the chief of police, walked into the *Press* office one

afternoon and had a talk with Publisher Ormsby. Then they called
me in. Chief Baker questioned me about the odious story and I told
him that I didn't know what he was talking about. He reminded
me that he was my friend, that the school authorities were putting
heavy pressure on him, that he had to clear things up, that he *knew*
I wrote it. He knew I wrote it because the original copy had been
traced to my crony, Rome Brading, because it was written on newspaper copy paper, and because it had been written on an Oliver
typewriter, an instrument as rare in Indiana as the barracuda. The
chief promised nothing unpleasant would happen to me if I'd just
be a man and own up and under this unctuous goading, I finally
confessed. He slapped me on the back, told me not to worry, and
walked out. Never trust a cop.

The next day a crippled marshal thumped up the stairs to the
second floor of the *Press* building and served a warrant which ordered
me to appear three days later before Justice of the Peace Stults to
answer a charge of "authorship and circulation of lewd, licentious,
obscene and lascivious literature." A half-hour later Rome Brading
received a similar invitation, though he was charged only with circulation of said literature.

We were both frightened, and two things were obvious: we had to
see a lawyer and we needed some money. I managed to borrow ten
dollars against my wages and we took ourselves into the presence of
Martin J. O'Malley, a young lawyer with a commanding presence
and a reputation as a courtroom orator. We surrendered our destinies into his hands and when he had finished laughing he said
he'd take the case.

The Huntington *Herald* seized upon the story of my troubles
and went to work with laudable malice. Without putting it in those
precise words, the evening paper informed the pious citizens of Huntington that this was the type of scoundrel hired to produce the
drivel they read in the *Press*. Further than that, the story got Page
One play in both of the Fort Wayne papers.

As for the *Press*, Mr. Ormsby was surprisingly understanding and,
I think, secretly amused. He lectured me on the sin of indiscretion
but he didn't fire me.

On the appointed morning Brading and I were in O'Malley's
office at eight-thirty, due to appear before Squire Stults at nine. We
walked across the public square behind our lawyer to the office
building where the Squire had his musty tribunal. It was all we

could do to push our way up the rickety stairs and into this habita-
tion of Hoosier justice. The crowd overflowed the gloomy little
room, packed the stairway and extended across the sidewalk to the
curb. Women of all ages were predominant in the crowd and I felt
embarrassed when I saw my mother, who told me at breakfast that
morning that she wouldn't believe I had written IT . . . that she
knew I was protecting some older person.

Squire Stults was a little old man straight out of a Keystone comedy. He was skinny, bald, and wore white chin whiskers which
fanned the air when he talked in precisely the manner of a rube
comic. He had a habit of spitting tobacco juice over his right shoulder, in the general direction of a cuspidor, just before speaking and
especially before delivering an emphatic "Over-r-r-ruled!"

Inside the railing, which was verging on collapse beneath the
press of the crowd, stood the county prosecutor and his assistant, the
crippled marshal, a desk and several additional cuspidors. The prosecutor, Wilbur Branyan, was tall and hard of hearing with a pronounced clerical look. Cato Hurd, his assistant, was short and broad,
with the carriage and pugnacity of a football linesman.

Prosecutor Branyan announced himself ready for trial and then
O'Malley asked that the defendants be tried separately and that
Brading be first to face a jury. Agreed. Then the prosecutor called
the court's attention to the size of the crowd, suggesting that if a
larger room could not be found the building would likely collapse
with great loss of life. Squire Stults said nothing, picked up the
telephone, spat fiercely and called someone at the county courthouse
across the street. He explained the circumstances and was given
permission to use the facilities of the Superior Court for, no doubt,
the most sensational case of his entire juridical career.

The Superior courtroom was soon jammed and the audience was
eighty per cent female. The jury was selected by the simple demo-
cratic process of sending the marshal out in front of the courthouse
to round up the needed men, all of whom loafed around the square
awaiting just such a summons to sovereign duty.

It was not a long trial. Several high school girls squirmed and
blushed their way through admissions that they had received copies
of the contaminating document. Each admitted that she had read
it, volunteering the information that she had no idea of what it
meant. Chief Baker told of Brading's confession. Then Cato Hurd
picked up a paper from the table where he sat.

"If the Court please," he addressed Squire Stults, "I would now like to read this—this article—this 'Stranded on a Davenport'—to the jury. May I ask that all women be excluded from the courtroom?"

The Squire leaned forward, eying Cato Hurd balefully.

"This," he wagged out with his whiskers, "is a public court of law. Them that wants to go can go. Them that wants to stay can stay. Over-r-r-ruled!"

I thought he was going to jerk his head off when he spat.

Not a woman, not a girl, stirred from her seat.

Cato Hurd did then and there read "Stranded on a Davenport" to the jury. I had been sitting at the defense table and, though my name had never once been mentioned during the proceedings, this was too ignominious. My face was flushed as I hurried to a side door. I waited outside in a corridor, bouncing a golf ball against the stone floor, until the case was given into the hands of the courthouse loafers about ten minutes later. I was relieved to learn that the assistant prosecutor read the "lewd, licentious, obscene and lascivious litera-ture" in a low voice and that it was impossible to distinguish his words (meaning my words) a dozen feet away.

Mart O'Malley put in no defense and the oratory was brief. Cato Hurd summed up for the prosecution. He denounced Brading and "the author" as corruptors of maidenhood, sin-sodden wolves bent on sullying the fair name of Huntington before the world. As for O'Malley, he narrowed the issue to a single point—every man had had such a thing in his possession at one time or another.

After about fifteen minutes of weighing that issue the jury con-cluded that Brading was not guilty. The defendant, on advice of counsel, ran up and shook hands with each of the jurors, who grinned suggestively at him and winked lasciviously and wisecracked in lewd and licentious undertones. With this touching ceremony out of the way, Squire Stults set my trial for a week later.

There was no holding us back that week. The verdict stifled any fears Brading and I may have entertained before. For seven days we were celebrities of a sort. People in the town who had never noticed us before now pointed us out and whispered to one another. The young blades of the community developed an almost respectful attitude to-ward us. Men we had barely known by name came to us pleading for copies of IT.

At the *Press* I continued with my work, wrote the story of the

Brading trial and with overweening cockiness typed out an account of my own forthcoming ordeal at bar.

Then came the day. I found that I had to go it alone, that Brading's father had ordered him to school. But I was in high spirits when I reached Mart O'Malley's office.

"Well," I asked, "are we all set?"

"Sure."

"How long do you think it will take?"

"Five minutes," said Mart O'Malley.

"I mean the trial."

He looked at me and grinned. "There's not going to be any trial," he said. "You're going to plead guilty."

I couldn't speak for a moment. Then I demanded things. I *wanted* to have a trial. I insisted on it. But he shook his head. Brading had merely circulated the thing. I was the *author* of it. I couldn't afford to take a chance with a jury. The plea that had won for Brading wouldn't apply in my case. At last I had to surrender.

We pushed again through the crowd on the sidewalk, up the stairs and into the little room. The setting was the same, but the proceedings were brief. Squire Stults took my plea, looked in a book, fined me twenty-two dollars and fifty cents, spat, looked at me, and added that I could have ninety days in which to pay. It was the first time I had ever heard of installment plan justice.

On the ninetieth day I delivered the money to the Squire, who chuckled as he counted the bills. On the ninety-first day the city attorney, a pious gentleman who took an interest in the morals of his neighbors, came around and told me that I was going to spend two hours with him each week studying the Scriptures. I said in a pig's. And on the ninety-second day I went forth into the world. Age: 17; Condition: weather-beaten.

# visions of what used to be

Shortly after I became a newspaper reporter my mother took time away from her multitude of household duties to give me a little talk. She said I ought to try to be like Arthur Brisbane. She was a great admirer of Mr. Brisbane and read his column every day and told me that he was the greatest newspaper writer who ever lived. I didn't argue with her but I was more inclined to think that O. O. McIntyre was the greatest newspaper writer who ever lived.

My mother also told me that before long I would probably be getting my name above newspaper stories I composed and that I should give some serious thought to the by-line I would use. She reminded me that Smith is the commonest of American family names and that I would be justified if I fancied it up a little. She suggested that as a writer I call myself H. Allen Smith.

Since that day of yore I have known or heard about a great many Allen Smiths and some Allan Smiths and a few H. Allan Smiths and several H. Allen Smiths. Shortly after I got my first job in New York City an H. Allen Smith of the B.&O. railroad came to call on me in the old World building. Another turned up, years later, playing end for the Chicago Bears. This particular H. Allen Smith stood six feet two and weighed two hundred and twenty-five pounds. His arrival in professional football provoked some wry speculation on the part of William F. Fox, Jr., the Indianapolis sports writer. Mr. Fox announced one day in his column that George Halas had signed H. Allen Smith to play end for the Bears. Mr. Fox and I were old friends so he proceeded on the tongue-in-cheek assumption that Mr. Halas had signed *me*. He described my physical characteristics unflatteringly and at some length and suggested that while I might contribute certain novel touches to the game of football, I would consist of shredded flesh and shattered bone soon after my first appearance on the playing field. He concluded that Mr. Halas quite obviously had mislaid his marbles. I notified Mr. Fox that while I would be thrilled at the prospect of playing football for the Bears, I was not the H. Allen Smith who had been signed. I recommended that Mr. Halas hire me to play the opposite end, so that he would have an H. Allen Smith operating at either wing, just for laughs. Nothing ever came of it. Mr. Halas apparently was a man of limited imagination.

For years people have been sending me clippings about other H. Allen Smiths and once I got a tax bill, addressed to my home in New York but meant for another H. Allen Smith living in Huntington, Indiana. A great moment of my life came some years ago when a girl reporter for a college newspaper came to interview me. Right at the beginning she demanded: "Now, tell me what your *real* name is." She insisted throughout the interview that "H. Allen Smith" was clearly a nom de plume, a thing I had invented, and she went away convinced that I was lying. There are times when I think "H. Allen Smith" is a simpering and affected sort of name, somewhat faggoty-sounding, and I have even toyed with the idea of using a variation, maybe Harry Allen Smith. For another reason, there is a prominent citizen of our nation named H. Allen Smith, a three-term member of Congress. I am forever being confused with him and my old friend Harry Brand of Twentieth Century-Fox insists that I ought to compose a humorous essay on "My Double Life as H. Allen Smith" in which I would pretend that I was both writer and Congressman. I have not done it because there are certain things about the Congressman that lead me to believe that he lacks humor. Moreover, I suspect that he can stir up trouble for people who cross him. He is a former G-man and those guys have an organization, the Society of Former Special Agents of the F.B.I., and apparently they undertake little hatchet jobs for one another. I had one of them on my neck several years ago, and it was not a pleasant experience.

Congressman Smith is from Glendale, California, and his district includes the city of Pasadena. I have heard that politically he is conservative to the point where he makes Barry Goldwater look like a screeching anarchist. I have never met him and I feel that I can make it through life without that privilege. He is about three years younger than me and was born in my native state of Illinois. His home town is the same community that gave Louella Parsons to the world.

He got his education in California, became a lawyer, and then a G-man. He was sent to the California legislature for several terms and then landed in Congress. He gets my mail and I get his, and sometimes our telephone calls have been mixed up. Not long ago my wife got a bill from a store in Beverly Hills, meant for Mrs. H. Allen Smith of Glendale. And there was a time when our friends were telephoning to ask how Mrs. Smith was feeling—they had read in the papers that she had been hit in the head by a golf ball. If H. of Glendale goes much higher in the political world, I'm going to have to change my name. I recently heard of a girl who writes novels under the name of R. Prawer Jhabvala. I wouldn't mind something on that order.

Twelve years ago I produced a handsome and scholarly work called *People Named Smith*. It was a compendium of all the famous and infamous Smiths of today and yesterday; it included a history of the family and it had silver stampings on the binding and, with the able assistance of Leo Hershfield, I devised a beautiful coat of arms with daggers and a quill pen or two and a long-nosed knight in armor and a unicorn and a shidepoke and an anvil with mermaids whanging away at it. Mr. Hershfield, the artist, has known me for many years. He insisted on putting a *baton sinister* across the escutcheon and he made this *baton sinister* wide enough to show a dog running across it.

It was, in fact, a handbook that would be of sentimental value to everyone bearing the name of Smith. It was a shrewd and canny stroke on my part. I had ascertained that one out of every one hundred persons in the United States bore the name of Smith. If I could get a mere five per cent of these Smiths to buy my book, I would be able to rest on my oars for a few years. It was a sure thing. So I thought. But it turned out that almost everyone named Smith is either (1) stingy, or (2) illiterate, or (3) both.

In the course of long research for that book I found some unusual characters sharing my surname. I heard about a pig that won a blue ribbon in the International Livestock Show at Chicago—a pig named Light Green Smith. Bob Smith, the baseball historian, told me about an old-time ballplayer named Piano Legs Smith. There was a horse named George Smith that won the Kentucky Derby. And Grantland

Rice told me about a football star at Georgia who was known far and wide as Catfish Smith. I asked Mr. Rice if he got the name because he darted around in the manner of a catfish. "No," said Mr. Rice, "he got the name one day when he bit the head off a catfish for a dollah."

Only the most ignorant of all the inhabitants of this planet (possibly a Smith) would have to be told that we excel in numbers. Our lead is so commanding, our procreative instincts so well developed, that it is unlikely that any of the other family groups will ever catch up to us. There have been many times in the past when the Johnsons or the Browns or the Millers or the Joneses have taken to their mattresses and tried to make a fight of it, and some of these have actually shown slight gains, but in the end they faded and gave up.

We, the Smiths, are not only the largest family group in the United States; we also hold an easy lead in the British Isles. The Smiths are predominant in England and it is a fact that in Scotland there are many more Smiths than there are MacDonalds. In some sections of Scotland one out of every fifty persons is named Smith. Please keep in mind that we are dealing here with straightaway Smiths—people having the name Ess–Em–Eye–Tee–Aitch. Not Smythe, or Schmidt, or Smitt, or Smid, or Smed, or Kovacs, or Kowalski, or Gowan, or Taliaferro, or Haddad, or all the other versions and variations of the name.

No field of human endeavor is without its share of Smiths, from the arts and government down to highway robbery and indecent exposure. There is nothing we can't do and nothing we don't do. It could easily have been a Smith who kidnaped Charley Ross. A Smith, perhaps, was responsible for the presence of overalls in the chowder of Mrs. Murphy. A Smith very likely ate the first oyster. It may have been a Smith who wrote Shakespeare's plays and the first person to land on the moon could very well be a Smith.

We represent a perfect cross section of the population. A few years ago a New York City newspaper made a custom of telephoning Smiths at random whenever a symposium of public opinion was wanted. The answers of the Smiths were, generally speaking, just as wise as if the newspaper had called Browns or Johnsons or Cohens.

We are Black Republicans and Communists and Tories and Christian Socialists; we are Baptists and Catholics and Jews and Christian Scientists and Pillar of Fireites and Presbyterians and Jehovah's Witnesses and atheists. We are black and white and pink and red and brown and even yellow. We are rich and well off and just getting

by and starving to death. We are titled lords and honorable sirs and
we inhabit the hobo jungles. We are male and we are female and
some of us . . . well, you wouldn't quite be able to tell for sure.
We are bishops at the baptismal fonts and we are diggers of graves.
We have not as yet produced a President but one of ours, Abigail
Smith, married a man who became our first Vice-President and our
second President; and this same Abigail produced from her womb
another man who was to become the sixth President of the nation.

The greatest of all Smiths, to my way of thinking, was Sydney.
Hesketh Pearson wrote a biography of Sydney under the title, *The
Smith of Smiths*. I have read it, and I have also read an ancient
volume called *Wit and Wisdom of the Rev. Sydney Smith Being
Selections from His Writings and Passages of His Letters and Table-
Talk with a Biographical Memoir and Notes*. It is by Evert A.
Duyckinck. I mean the book is by Evert A. Duyckinck. It doesn't
say who wrote the title.

Sydney Smith was the fellow who first figured out about square
pegs in round holes and vice versa. Sydney is also famous as the man
who thought up the joke that first made Fred Allen famous—"It's so
hot tonight I'd like to take off my skin and sit around in my bones."
Once Sydney was asked to describe his family's coat of arms. He
replied: "The Smiths never had any arms, and have invariably sealed
their letters with their thumbs." That historic crack led me, a hundred
and fifty years later, to enlist the services of Leo Hershfield in the
job of devising an escutcheon for the Smiths.

Sydney had full realization, even in his ancient time, of the
difficulties confronting a Smith afflicted with a common Christian or
given name. When his daughter was born he named her Saba, after
a king mentioned in the 72nd Psalm. Anyone with the surname of
Smith, said Sydney, ought to have an uncommon Christian name
by way of compensation. My mother came up with the same notion
and so it was that as H. Allen Smith I hit the road out of Huntington.

I came into the business at the tail end of a great tradition—the
tradition of the itinerant newspaperman. A journeyman journalist
was just that, whether he worked as reporter, rewrite man, or copyreader. He never worried about getting fired because he never intended staying in one town for long. If things weren't run to suit
his fancy he had a pointed way of saying farewell. In those days one
of the busiest, most congested bottlenecks in the country was that

part of a managing editor's anatomy which served as a repository for unwanted jobs. I have often wondered if somewhere in our land there was not a managing editor who was eventually impelled to cry out, "There ain't any more room!"

Some months before my own departure from the Huntington *Press*, the redhead John Moynihan had accepted a job as city editor of a new daily paper in Jeffersonville, Indiana. He had been writing me, offering me twenty-five dollars a week if I'd come to Jeffersonville. He gave me a real chamber-of-commerce sales pitch on that part of Southern Indiana which lay across the Ohio River from Louisville. Every country lane, he said, had its sin-ridden roadhouses and there were gambling palaces everywhere and the land was aswarm with gorgeous whores. The very idea of living in such an atmosphere was most repugnant to me but I had no other offers so I accepted. As fast as I could get to the telegraph office.

The Jeffersonville *Bulletin* had been started by an upstate Hoosier named Claude G. Brodhecker and Mr. Brodhecker was the proud proprietor of the first teletype machine he had ever seen, I had ever seen, or the town had ever seen. In those days Mr. Brodhecker was somewhat country in his talk and mannerisms. He was so proud of that teletype machine that he had it installed in the front window of the *Bulletin* office and he put a notice in the paper about it, inviting citizens to stop by and see this marvel of the age of transmission. When they did come in he had a set speech which he used to explain its function, saying: "Now, this is the way it works. A man is setting at a typewriter up in Indynapluss and he typewrites on the typewriter up there and it typewrites on the typewriter down here at the very same instant he is typewriting on the typewriter up there . . . in Indynapluss."

Jeffersonville was about two hundred miles south of Huntington and so far as I was concerned I might as well have been in Tibet. I had traveled so far from home that there was a chance I might never see my family again. And the kind of life I now led was vastly different from life in Huntington. John Moynihan and I were Hoosier sybarites. We lived in a sumptuous hotel next door to the newspaper office. We ate most of our meals in the hotel dining room, surrounded by high-living, worldly wise drummers. The hotel occupied a fairly new building of glistening brick, was modern in every respect and I thought it both elegant and ornate. I remember that they once served *gigot of lamb* in the dining room and Moynihan and I

were so impressed by the word, which we and everyone else pronounced as *gigg-ut*, that we christened the blonde waitress Gigot and
she became Gigot to all her customers thereafter and may be called
Gigot to this day. I can still hear Monnie yelling at her, "Hey, Gigot,
snap it up with that peach pie!"

It's time I told you to keep an eye on John Moynihan. He and I
would go a long way together. What he had told me about the
Jeffersonville countryside was all true; there were gambling houses
up and down the river and prostitutes to suit every occasion and
gang killings and other lively doings. As city editor Monnie had a
staff consisting of me and Frank Rager, known as "Daddy"—a local
boy, short of stature but wiry enough to have been a star quarter-
back. We worked diligently in the daytime and played hard at night,
although I fell in love with a high school girl and defected from the
roadhouse run for a while. In fact Moynihan and Daddy Rager were
disgusted with the way I sat around soda parlors with the high school
crowd in preference to standing around crap tables with thugs and
practitioners of bawdry. They didn't seem to know, as I knew, that
many of the high school kids were almost as wild and untrammeled
as the people of the roadhouses.

Nevertheless I spent many a long evening with my two dissolute
friends, cruising the river roads in Moynihan's old automobile. I
have a vague notion that we drank quite a bit, and that such sex life
as existed took place in the back seats of automobiles—the worst place
on earth for it in the studied opinion of the same Mr. Mencken
who was touted so often by Moynihan. There were times when you
could step out the front door of a roadhouse and look at the flivvers
parked nearby and you'd swear that the drivers had left all the
engines running.

Living in Jeffersonville and commuting to Louisville where he
worked as star reporter on the *Post* was a tall, lean guy named
Howard Hartley. He sometimes joined us on our sinful expeditions
and one day he asked me if I would like to work in the big city,
meaning Louisville, pronounced Low-uh-vl. I said yes and within a
few weeks I was a rewrite man on the strangest daily I've ever seen.
A high-strung and sharp-witted man named King Foley was the
Number One rewrite man; I remember him mainly for the reason
that he could never get going in the morning until he had read every
word of O. O. McIntyre's column. I was the Number Two rewrite
man. Howard Hartley was the general assignment reporter—the only

one we had. There was a sports writer, a man at police headquarters and a Mawton Folks Kentucky Colonel who wrote editorials and was reputed to be a member of the Pendennis Club, which I was allowed to look at once from the outside.

There was one other—the foreman of this strange crew—Mr. George Newman. He bore the title of managing editor but he was much more than that. He was a short, baldish man with a black mustache and the beginnings of a strawberry nose. He sat at a big desk alongside a window that gave on the street and he ran the show. He hired and fired and, according to a rumor I once heard whispered in an alley back of the place, he had been known to give a man a raise. The *Post* had no copy desk—Mr. Newman handled that. He was city editor and slot man and telegraph editor and cable editor and copyreader and trouble-shooter and I suspected that he was always a little drunk.

One day I was standing at Mr. Newman's elbow, trying to get his attention, when a man walked into the newsroom and approached the throne.

"Mr. Newman," he said, "I'm George So-and-so from the Elks. We're having this big carnival thing next week and I got 'er all written up here, all the details, and we'd sure appreciate it if you'd run it in the paper for us."

"Thank you," said Mr. Newman, scarcely looking up, extending his hand for the copy. He quickly unfolded the sheets, counted the three or four pages and, without reading a single line, wrote a head over the story as follows:

## OH, LOOK WHAT THE ELKS ARE DOING!

He scribbled the type size, specified a three-column head, and tossed the whole thing into the copy basket. I looked at it later in the paper and found that the headline fitted the story exactly.

Mr. Newman never said much to anybody. The nearest he ever came to bawling me out was to beckon me up to his desk and hand me a story I had just written. "Don't write like that," he said, and turned back to his work. He didn't say *how* to write. But I took the offending copy back to my desk and studied it a while and finally recognized what was basically wrong with the writing. It stank.

As everyone knows newspapermen have always had a reputation for being hardboiled and cynical and lacking in sentiment. This reputation is not an invention of the motion pictures. By the time I hit

Louisville I had already been indoctrinated in the principles of free-press cynicism and callosity. Nothing was anywhere close to sacred. Misery and suffering was a matter of type-size. Shortly after I went to work on my first city newspaper a young man got the marathon hiccups in Louisville and after he had hiccuped a week or so, the story got out and the local papers began writing daily reports on the case. It was Howard Hartley's job to go out to the young man's house each morning and check on his condition and then phone in a report to me and I would compose a brief piece about it. Throughout the rest of the day Hartley would keep in touch with the situation by telephone. I remember those morning phone calls quite well. I'd slap on the earphones and hear our star reporter begin: "Hic . . . this is Hartley . . . yerp . . . hic . . . calling from . . . oghhk . . . erk . . . hic . . . yerp . . ." and so on. He'd hiccup all the way through his report and if I had any questions to ask I'd hiccup them at him and after the call was over I'd sing out to King Foley that hic the yerp hiccup hic story had erk just come in hic, and Mr. Foley would say yarp hic that's good gock. This went on for weeks until the poor guy got over his sickness. I see nothing comical about it now, in 1962, but I like to split a gut over it in 1925.

Now, what did I learn from our erudite sports writer, Henry Ewald? He was a big handsome footballish guy who quoted love poems by Kipling and these poems were not at all like other poems, such as *Hiawatha* and *The Cremation of Sam McGee* and *Casey at the Bat* and *Little Orphant Annie*. Henry Ewald loved to recite *Certain Maxims of Hafiz* and the part I enjoyed most was this:

> In public Her face turneth to thee, and
> pleasant Her smile when ye meet.
> It is ill. The cold rocks of El-Gidar
> smile thus on the waves at their feet.

Mr. Ewald typed out that part for me and I memorized it and one night over in Jeffersonville I recited it to the girl I loved and she said, "What the dickens does that crazy stuff mean, anyway?"

The thing I learned from Mr. Ewald, that had a more lasting effect, was physical rather than spiritual and involved the use of a straight pin. One day Henry and I were sitting talking and he took a straight pin out of his coat lapel. Then he picked up a one-column cut which was attached to a block of wood. He placed the point of the pin against his thigh, midway between knee and hip. Then he took the block of wood and began tapping on the pin and drove it straight through his trousers and into his own thigh meat. He hammered that pin until its head was down flush with the cloth. Being a cynic I said it was some kind of a trick. He did it over again, pulling the pin out of his leg and driving it in at another point. He said there was no trick to it, that the pin actually went into the thigh, that it didn't hurt, that he couldn't even feel it, and that it was a wonderful stunt because it always seemed to fascinate girls. It looked like a foolish thing to be doing but I was on the lookout for ways of fascinating girls and so I tried it and the pin went straight into my leg without a single sensation of pain. I spent the next couple of months driving pins into my leg and was the life of several parties. On my leg, however, it didn't seem to fascinate any girls. The only girl I ever did it for in private session told me she thought I had "a weakness in the coconut" and sheered away from me after that.

It was the spring of 1925 and life was real, not to mention earnest, and things were happening to me. The Kentucky Derby was coming up and one day on a hunch I approached the desk of my boss. I had learned that a Kentuckian looks upon his native state as God's country, whatever that means, and that there is an often-quoted statement: "Heaven is a Kentucky of a place."

"Mr. Newman," I said, "do you mind if I tell you something about myself?"

"Make it short," he said without looking up.

"I have never seen a Kentucky Derby."

Now he looked up. His eye examined me as if I were some prehistoric thing washed up on a lonely beach.

"Do you mean it?" he asked.

"I've never seen one," I assured him.

Within an hour I had a ticket and I saw the Derby. That is, I was present. I was on the property. I was at Churchill Downs. It came up storm clouds, as I recall, and hard rain, and the place got almost as black as night. After a while I learned that a horse named Flying Ebony had won and that Earl Sande was the jockey. The principal thing I recall about my first and only Derby was the presence of Damon Runyon, who began his story of the race with his famous poem. It ended:

> Maybe—but say, I doubt it,
> Never his like again—
> Never a handy
> Guy like Sande
> Bootin' them babies in!

Great balls of fire! I drank in the pure beauty of those lines and I almost sobbed and I was grateful to God for permitting me to be in the same town where they were written. After that all the rest of them—Longfellow and Greenleaf Whittier and J. Whitcomb Riley and maybe, but say, I doubt it, maybe even Robert W. Service—all of them could go soak their heads . . . in the cold waves at the feet of El-Gidar.

Shortly after that I wangled a press pass to the Memorial Day auto race at Indianapolis with the understanding that I pay my own transportation. The Ku-Kluxers of Indiana chose that week to stage a tremendous parade in Indianapolis, whose streets were already swarming with visitors. I stood on the curb and watched them march, and it seemed to me that there were millions of them, but I knew that underneath those scary robes were true-blue hunnert per cent Americans who wouldn't hurt nobody . . . unless of course they happened to be Catholics or Jews or Negroes or Bolshevickys.

Out at the speedway I grew bored with the race itself and wandered onto the lawn in front of the old press pagoda. I strolled down to the fence next to the track and stood there watching the racers shoot past and trying to figure out something I could write about.

Suddenly I heard a voice. "How do you like the Miller Specials?" a man asked. I turned and found an old geezer standing beside me, wearing a wrinkled overcoat and an old felt hat. I say he was an old geezer because, being around eighteen at the time, I considered anybody past thirty to be an old geezer and I had little use for geezers, not yet having achieved geezerhood myself. So I didn't answer him except to shrug my shoulders in a gesture that said go away. He rambled on about the weather and the crowd and the drivers and finally I just turned and walked off.

Returning to the pagoda I was immediately surrounded by other newspapermen, all demanding what I had got out of Henry Ford. For a moment I couldn't believe it—that I had been talking to, or, rather, talked to by, old Get-Out-and-Get-Under himself. They in turn refused to believe me when I said I didn't know it was Henry Ford. They pointed out that there was an agreement that all important news was to be shared. Some of them had approached Ford earlier and he had waved them off, saying this wasn't the right time for interviews. They wouldn't believe my story that I had closed my ears against his yammerings. They cursed me and then ostracized me for the remainder of the day.

There are many legends in the newspaper business about green reporters flubbing the big assignment. One of the most famous of these stories concerns the cub who was sent to cover the wedding of a famous heiress. When he returned to his office he made no move toward writing his piece and finally his boss approached him. "No story," said the cub. "The bride didn't show up." There's another about a Chicago reporter sent to cover a flood in Ohio. His first dispatch started off: "God sits on the Ohio hills tonight." His boss wired back: FORGET THE FLOOD AND INTERVIEW GOD. And not long ago I heard about a young man who was sent to Florida by the Associated Press to cover some speedboat races. The boy sent a dispatch back to Atlanta largely about the veteran racer, Gar Wood. The Atlanta office, noting that the speedboat king's age had not been mentioned, wired their boy: HOW OLD GAR WOOD? And the boy wired back: OLD GAR WOOD FINE. HOW YOU?

It seems to me that I was always getting myself into kindred situations and predicaments whenever I had anything to do with a big story. I turned out a straightaway story about the colorful crowd at the Indianapolis speedway, and how everyone ate fried chicken out of picnic baskets, and I said not a word about Henry Ford. Nor did I mention him when I got back to Louisville. If I had mentioned him, if I had confessed that I turned my back on Henry Ford when he was in a talkative mood, I would likely have been fired. By today's standards I had in my hands a far better story than if Henry Ford had picked the winner of the race, attacked the administration of Calvin Coolidge, called history a good thing and announced a drastic wage cut at his plant. I had a splendid story—how I, a lunkhead, had actually spurned Henry Ford out of ignorance whereas, had I been on my toes, I might have got all those sensational things out of him. The public, being lunkheaded itself, enjoys nothing so much as seeing another lunkhead in action. Look at Ed Sullivan.

Not long after the Indianapolis trip I heard about an opening on the Louisville *Times* involving a slight increase in salary, and I applied for the job and got it. The *Times* was the afternoon version of the *Courier-Journal* and the *Courier-Journal* was a very famous newspaper. For example, it once employed a columnist who could tell his readers whether a hen lays an egg because she wants to or because she has to. One of the young men I got to know in my new job was William Burke Miller, called "Skeets." He was the reporter who, a few months earlier, had crawled down into Sand Cave and reached the side of Floyd Collins, who was trapped down there and died before they could dig him out. Miller had been a sort of cub reporter but after the Floyd Collins thing they decided he ought to be given greater opportunities. The *Courier-Journal* and *Times* had a radio station called WHAS. The man who ran the station needed a voice that could handle the letter "W" correctly. Everybody he tried out for the job of station identification said, "This is Dubb-ya H–A–S." He found out that "Skeets" Miller had taken a couple of years of voice lessons and was, in fact, quite a singer. He auditioned Miller and gave forth a happy shout when he heard Skeets say Double-You instead of Dubb-ya. So Skeets became a sayer of Double-You for WHAS and later on was awarded the Pulitzer Prize for Reporting and went to New York and became an executive with the National Broadcasting Company. I say Dubb-ya.

The managing editor of the *Times* was A. Y. Aronson. Mr. Aronson called me aside one day after I had been on his staff for a month or two. He said he had a proposition that might interest me. He said that the publisher of a daily newspaper in the town of Bowling Green, Kentucky, had need of a bright young reporter and had asked him, A. Y. Aronson, to try to locate such a person. Mr. Aronson said this might be a great opportunity for me, standing as I was on the very threshold of my career. He said that Bowling Green was a splendid old town, a gem of the True South, and the newspaper itself was hoary with tradition. I resisted the urge to say that I had already worked on a hoary newspaper, in Jeffersonville. He told me that the pace was much slower in Bowling Green, that life was soft and gentle and lovely there and if you felt like it you could take a nap every afternoon. He said that the publisher of the paper was getting along, and that the history of American journalism was full of cases in which young men who had started as simple reporters on the smaller newspapers had ended up owning them. Mr. Aronson did a beautiful job of selling me on Bowling Green and it never once occurred to me that, in doing so, he was *un*selling me on *his* newspaper. He said that the Bowling Green publisher would pay my transportation down and back, and so I went.

The town, about a hundred miles south of Louisville twarge Nashville, was True South. There were trees here and there, and people moving listlessly through the streets, bowing to one another, and hound dawgs lying in the dust, yawning for the most part. It was hot but not halcyon in the downtown area. I felt certain that if I sauntered out to the plumb-nilly belt (plumb outa town and nilly in the country) I'd maybe come upon an old plantation, mortgaged, and on the lawn another Mawton Folks Kentucky Colonel* taking his leisure in the company of the most demurely beautiful young lady in all creation, and through the towering white columns of the manse would come Ole Shad, the grizzled family retainer, bearing the mint juleps and crooning fly away Kentucky Babe, and as he served the drinks he'd flash those white teeth in a happy grin and say, "Sho was nice, Cunnel, us a-winnin' de Dubby agin yestiddy."

But I didn't go out there where they had all that sort of thing. I went to the newspaper office and had my interview with the publisher. He asked me a good deal about my family. At that time I didn't know that one of my ancestors had been an imported gardener on the estate of Henry Clay up near Lexington. I'm not even sure if this information would have helped if I had known it. I was simply told that there was no great hurry about the matter and that I would be notified if they wanted me. So I went back to Louisville, having somehow fouled up a chance to become a julep-swiggin' Cunnel with a barn fulla Dubby winners and a grizzled retainer named Shad and that beautiful girl who, I forgot to mention, had a pretty little parasol and a pair of knockers that were about to jump out of her dress.

I continued on the staff of the *Times* and enjoyed one moment of triumph before I departed. National Guard units from Kentucky, Indiana, and West Virginia were in training at Camp Knox, a big military establishment thirty miles from Louisville, twarge Bowling Green. This is the same place that later changed its name to Fort Knox and got all that gold. Mr. Aronson sent me down to Camp

---

* Note for posterity: In the middle of the twentieth century, on television, there were frequent advertisements for chicken pie, and these advertising messages were spoken by a simulated Kentucky Colonel on behalf of someone he called "th' Mawton Folks"—Morton being the name of the folks who made the chicken pies.

Knox to represent both the *Times* and the *Courier-Journal*. I was given a comfortable room in a cottage occupied by two officers; I was permitted to eat at the officers' mess; and I had free run of the entire camp, possibly because I was the only reporter present.

During my stay in Camp Knox I was responsible for the biggest political story to break in recent Kentucky history—a scandal that had wide repercussions, reaching even to the floor of the United States Senate. It involved the Adjutant General of Kentucky and through him the Governor and a lot of other statesmen. To the best of my recollection there were two warring factions—the Governor and his adherents, and another group bent upon throwing the incumbent rascals out. Let me make it clear—I didn't know a single thing about this political war at the time the story broke. I don't know anything about it to this day. I was at Camp Knox writing long dispatches back to my paper about the sham warfare between the Red Forces and the Blue Forces and who was winning and what new units were coming in from Breathitt County and Lieutenant So-and-so from Paducah fell off a horse and broke his leg.

One day an orderly came to see me and said that General Such-and-such wanted to see me in his office. This General was a Louisville financier and politician, one of the leaders of the group opposed to the Governor. I walked into his office and he waved me into a seat and then gave me a sheet of paper with some chitchat regarding certain minor promotions in his command. I was glancing through it when he said:

"See this document right here?" He indicated a sheaf of papers lying on his desk. "This document involves a secret matter and if I should be called away from this office, you are not to look at it. Understand?"

"Oh, yes sir!" I assured him.

"It is a document," he went on, tapping on it with his forefinger, "of great political importance. If its contents became known to the public it would shake the State of Kentucky to its very foundations. Therefore, nobody must see it unless they are authorized to see it. Most of all, you newspaper reporters. I want it clearly understood, no newspaper reporter is to see this document. *IS THAT CLEAR?*"

"Oh, yes sir!" I exclaimed with great sincerity. Why should he doubt me, I wondered? My God, I was a trustworthy person, a person of integrity. I wouldn't have dreamed of . . .

"Every newspaper in the state," the General went on, "and

especially the newspapers in Louisville, and *most especially* the *Courier-Journal* and *Times*, those papers would give their eyeteeth to get their hands on this document. I tell you, it's a political bombshell. A po–littical buh–omb–shell! It's so . . . ."

The telephone on his desk rang, he answered it, listened a moment, then said he'd be right over. He got up from the desk, tapped his finger again on the forbidden document and once again uttered his warning.

"I have to leave this office," he said. "I'll be gone at least half an hour. Now, remember—you . . . are . . . not . . . to . . . look . . . at . . . this . . . document!"

"Don't you worry, General," I said, getting up. "I wouldn't dream of even touching it." I started briskly for the door. People don't have to say things twice to *me*.

"My God!" cried the General. "Wait a minute!" He slapped on his cap and made an end run and intercepted me before I could get to the door. He seized me by the shoulders.

"Don't leave," he told me. "You can loaf in here till I get back. There's some booze in that cabinet over there. Help yourself. But remember what I said—don't go reading that document! Don't read it!" Now there was a big grin on his face, and he was jerking his head in the direction of his desk, and then he contorted his face into a monstrous wink, and then he winked again, and then a third time. After that he left. I stood there a moment in deep thought. Suddenly it came to me. "Say!" I spoke aloud. "I do believe that he *wants* me to have a look at that document." I approached it nervously, cautiously, as if it were a venomous snake. I wasn't too sure of my ground and I wouldn't have been surprised if grim-visaged troopers with Lugers at the ready had come swarming through the windows. But I got hold of my apprehensions and read the beginning of the document and recognized what it was. They were bringing serious charges against the Adjutant General and making grave and nasty charges against the government in Frankfort. I decided to risk all, including my life, and made notes as fast as I could, and then hurried out and found a telephone and called Mr. Aronson at the *Times*. I told him that I wasn't sure about the General's intentions, that he might have been perfectly sincere in telling me not to touch the document, and I think that Mr. Aronson used the name of the Lord. He told me to read my notes to a rewrite man and then to stay where I was until reinforcements arrived.

Within an hour it began to *rain* reporters at Camp Knox. I remember that the old pro, Howard Hartley, arrived on the run and gave me a pat on the back and a big grin and said, "Quite a scoop, boy!" The important journalists from my own papers pushed me to one side, ignoring the fact that I was responsible for the whole thing. I had pictured myself in the role of hero, but to those guys I was just a jerk cub. I wasn't too unhappy about it when, a couple of days later, I was ordered back to Louisville.

That is the true story of my great journalistic coup at Camp Knox. It proves, once again, the enduring value of the tried-and-true principles. In the newspaper game it is necessary that a man be always alert; let him keep his mind ever clear, let him stand to the main chance, let him know the motives of men, and interpret them correctly. I know whereof I speak. I have been through the cauldron!

# orange blossoms and alligators

John Moynihan married a handsome Jeffersonville girl named Margaret Phipps and four out of five had pyorrhea and Claude Brodhecker gave up ownership of the Jeffersonville *Bulletin.* Frank Rager became an Indiana stringer for one of the Louisville papers and then, in that year of 1925, the girl who only carried the daisy chain took down with athlete's foot, and Thomas Beer used to write like this only not quite as good.

I continued at trivial jobs on the *Times* but I had tasted of glory in the Camp Knox adventure and I had a craving for banner-line action. Now and then one of the Louisville newspapers would undertake a crusade against the gambling joints along the Indiana shore and so I asked Mr. Aronson if I could try my hand at a one-shot exposé of these sinful places. He shrugged and told me to go ahead. I went over to Jeffersonville and rented a canoe and waited till dark to begin my investigations. The canoe wasn't at all necessary—I was simply glamorizing the assignment. I already knew all the joints along the river and most of them knew me and the simple way to have approached them would have been by automobile. That's the way I always had been doing it, but now I was engaged in a cloak-and-dagger operation. In a canoe I could glide stealthily through the night and, bending low over the paddle, creep silently upon my unsuspecting prey. I told myself that the roadhouses were skillfully camouflaged and guarded by lookouts armed with shotguns. And so I paddled the canoe from one establishment to another and some of the guys in some of the places would greet me with: "How come you out in a canoe without no dame in it?"

So I returned to Louisville and wrote a long story of my tour of these dives, and how it was obvious that they were operating with the full consent of the Indiana constabulary, and how they were aswarm with gangsters and fast women and how their purpose was to get the errant Kentuckian cockeyed drunk and turn a slinking female loose on him and take him for everything he had.

The story appeared on Page One the next day and my name was mud in Jeffersonville from that day on. The gamblers hadn't minded it much in the past when the Louisville papers crusaded against them; the reporters were strangers and nobody paid them any mind and as for the stuff they wrote, the gamblers just shrugged and said there were a lot of nuts in the world but newspaper guys were the nuttiest. But here was a local boy, one of their very own, a steady customer no less, coming around in a nutsy canoe and fouling his own nest, and the word went around that if they caught me in or near a dark alley they would fracture me up a trifle.

About this same time I had a telephone call from Claude Brod-hecker. He said that John Moynihan was in Florida and had written that everyone down there was rolling in money and that all of us should come down and get rich. Brodhecker said that he and Daddy Rager were going and that Moynihan had said I ought to come and that there was room in the car for me.

I accepted. I quit my job and we drove all the way non-stop and at last we arrived in the bustling town of Sebring. We located the office of the Sebring *American*, a daily newspaper, and telephoned Moynihan at the real estate office where he worked as a salesman. Brodhecker went into session with the newspaper's publishers; he had some thought in mind of investing money in the paper. Moyni-han and Rager and I were standing on the curb near the *American* office and our Irisher friend was telling us all about the boom. A plain-looking girl came along and Moynihan introduced her and said she was the society editor of the newspaper. She was a bit supercilious in her manner and looked down her nose at Rager and me and I said to myself, it is sure a good thing to travel all over the world like this, you certainly meet some screwy specimens, get to know human nature, sort of. Then Brodhecker came out and said there was only one job open on the *American*, that of general reporter, and that we'd have to decide between us. So we got out a coin and flipped it and I got the job.

I went to work immediately. Brodhecker and Rager hung around for a couple of days and then shoved off for Tampa. Within a few months both of them were back in Indiana and I was, much against my will, in love with that society editor who had snooted us on the street. Her name was Nelle Simpson and she was working at her first newspaper job. She came from a small town in middle Missouri and, apparently for social reasons, had put in four years attending the University of Missouri School of Journalism. After college she put an ad in a newspaper trade journal saying "will go anywhere" and soon she had an answer from a man named Rod Arkell, then owner of the Sebring paper, and off she went over the protests of her parents. Her father gave her a lecture before she left, about men.

The Great Real Estate Boom was still on, even when I arrived, and the town of Sebring was overrun by scores of dressy young men in fancy cars, with flasks on their hips and slickum on their hair. They were all selling real estate, or trying to sell it. The wall of the bubble was already weakening but nobody seemed to know that it would collapse very shortly. It was a wild and crazy time and a girl such as Nelle Simpson found herself in a pleasant position—there were two dozen young men for every passable girl in town. A sport had to have a Cadillac or a Lincoln or even a Rolls to get anywhere at all with the handful of good-lookers among the girls, and I didn't even have a bicycle.

Books have been written about the Florida boom and a million anecdotes told about it, so I'll not go into it here. My own favorite story concerns the late Wilson Mizner who was involved in real estate operations over at Boca Raton. A woman dragged Mizner into court and accused him of selling her a parcel of land sight unseen; when she finally saw it she found it was under water. On the witness stand she testified that Mizner had told her that she could grow nuts on that acreage. Mizner immediately interrupted. "You misunderstood me," he told the lady. "I didn't say you could grow nuts on that land. I said you could GO nuts on it."

There were bedrooms for rent in the Sebring *American* building and I took one of these and made my first acquaintance with the flying cockroach. They seemed to like the smell of printer's ink for they had established their own subdivisions around the newspaper building. Every night I would take a bag of oranges to bed with me, fruit I had picked from the trees back of the shop. Before turning off my light I would lie in bed and throw oranges at the huge roaches as they took their leisure on the whitewashed walls of my room. If I managed to kill three or four of them the others seemed to take the hint and they'd lie quiescent during the night. Once I thought of writing a book for little children, about a Yankee cockroach who traveled all the way to South Florida because he heard that when you got killed down there, it was with a fresh-picked orange.

I worked hard as a reporter, ate, threw oranges at cockroaches, and slept. Also I pined for Miss Nelle Simpson. It is disgusting to think how long it took her to get wise—how many weeks and months passed before she caught on to the fact that something special had crossed her path. She was real slow-witted in those days. I'd be walking along Lakeview Drive and she would pass me, usually riding in an expensive open car with some buck-toothed, silk-shirted, grinning hyena out of Georgia or the Carolinas, and she *might* nod in my direction, but usually she just ignored me. Treated me like I was dirt. This of course infuriated me, and I thought that I hated her, and the strange thing is that this girl, the girl I had thought at first to be plain-looking and a little dumpy, was beginning to take on an aura of beauty and grace and poise.

Her job was to traipse from hotel to hotel and copy the names of the guests off the registers. Back at the office she would type out these names, informing our readers who was staying at the Kenilworth and who was at Harder Hall and what visitors were stopping at the Nancessowee or the Hotel Sebring. Sometimes she would do little interviews, such as: "Mr. and Mrs. Wilmer Figg of Cleveland, O., are staying a few days at Kenilworth Lodge. They say Sebring is simply wonderful." It was required that every interview, whether a single paragraph or a full column, should include a variation of that last sentence—all visitors had to be entranced by the town, certain of its great future, convinced that its sheer beauty was unsurpassed by any other town in Florida.

The town of Sebring was tailor-made. A pottery manufacturer named George E. Sebring, who came from Sebring, Ohio, picked the site and had the town laid out after the design of an ancient place in Egypt called Heliopolis, city of the sun. The principal streets radiated outward from a circle, which represented the sun. A few blocks from the Sebring circle was Lake Jackson, a beautiful, sparkling body of water with fine homes along its shore and there were other lakes around town. Old George Sebring had his home on the shore of Lake Jackson and he was still alive and behind-the-scenes boss of the town during the time I lived there. It isn't often any more that one meets a man who has founded a town and so I was duly impressed by George E. Sebring, who knew the meaning of amortization and what an escrow was.

The original Heliopolis was dedicated to religion and so was its Florida copy. As I think back it seems to me that the town had as many preachers, active and retired, as it had real estate salesmen, and as many chiropractors as it had preachers. When the boom faded these chiropractors were sometimes seen adjusting one another's neck bones right out on the street. There was one who went around telling people, "I can cure any headache alive." He did this by seizing the patient's head with both hands and giving the chin a quick sideways jerk. He administered these headache jerks free of charge for quite a while, being naïve and idealistic. But when the traffic began to mount—there were a lot of headaches going around as the real estate market petered out—he began charging fifty cents a jerk. He knew nothing of the basic principles of the business world, else he would have given his headache cure a little better production, fussing with the spinal column, pulling on the legs, and charging a dollar. I never had one of his treatments although as a working journalist I imagine he would have given me jerks on the cuff. I never needed them; I am a human freak who never has had headaches. But I did have to go to a physician-type doctor. There in Sebring I began developing pains in my right hip and these came on during the nights and kept me from sleeping. There were moments when I came mighty near to reading a book. Instead, I would get up and dress and wander the streets of the sleeping town. The doctor told me that my trouble was sciatica and said it was unusual for a person of my years to be so afflicted and he guessed that the sciatic nerve had been injured in some way. He showed me where it was and then I got the answer. Those pins I had driven into my thigh back in Louisville. I told the doctor about them. He then made a peculiar observation. He said that I shouldn't be allowed to run loose. He said that if I were lucky the trouble would disappear eventually but that I might be afflicted the rest of my life, which wouldn't be long if there were any justice in the world because, in his studied opinion, any person who sat around driving pins into his leg deserved an early death, accompanied by much agony. He was a real interesting personality, this doctor. I think he had lost a lot of money in real estate.

The unhappy combination of unrequited love and sciatica still kept me awake and I began visiting with the policeman who was on duty at night. He was a chess nut and spent many hours trying to teach me the game. I never did catch on to it but I did learn the language of the game and in the future would be able to use such words as gambit and checkmate in my writing, which is the way with writers. The night cop was tolerant of my stupidity because he had long and lonesome hours and I was better than no chess player at all, and I didn't try to teach him how to drive pins into his leg.

After a while the pain vanished from my hip and somehow worked its way across-body and upward to my left shoulder. For several weeks I had these rheumatic twinges but I didn't go back to that doctor. Somehow his psychological approach didn't appeal to me— he had as much as told me that I ought to be dead. I don't like to have a man of that opinion prescribing drugs for me. This time I tried my own diagnosis. If I was too young for sciatica then I was too young for bursitis. If I acquired my sciatica from driving pins into my leg, then perhaps my shoulder pains could be traced back to some similar damaging activity. I applied my mind to it and I think I got it.

If memory serves, can spring be far behind . . . I mean, I think it was in Jeffersonville that I acquired my first wrist watch—a golden beauty which in time accumulated enough green mold to produce eight barrels of penicillin. For six months after getting that watch I all but tore my left arm off, thrusting it outward and then glancing at the glistering bracelet—always in public, of course, and whiplashing it most violently in the presence of pretty girls. I'm sure those lightning left jabs were responsible for my later shoulder trouble. Sometimes I think I have the same empirical type of mind that Benjamin Franklin had.

That myopic girl from Missouri continued giving me the cold stare and by now the staff of the *American* was dwindling fast. The real estate editor was fired, the sports editor moved on to some other town, and finally the editor himself—a man named Charlie Small who had been with Hearst in New York—took his departure. One morning I woke up in my little white room, fired a few oranges at the cockroaches, got dressed and went into the newsroom and learned that I had been appointed editor of the Sebring *Daily American*. My staff consisted of one person: Miss Nelle Simpson. I now began getting a little grim toward her. I gave her evening assignments, thus fouling up her dancing dates with those horse-toothed honyocks from the Georgia turpentine camps. I bawled her out for misspelling words. I lectured her on the finer points of journalism as I had been lectured in the past. I remembered the words that John Moynihan used to howl at Rager and me when we were his staff in Jeffersonville and when we would arrive in the office without any important news. "God damn it!" Moynihan would yell, "you can't have this many people living together without news breaking every minute of the day! Now, crack your ass and get outa here and *get me that news!*" I used the first part of that lecture on Miss Simpson, but not the last.

And what of John Moynihan now? There were no more customers for real estate and he and Margaret were living off grapefruit and trying to scrape together enough money to get out of Florida. One day he drove his green Studebaker to the *American* office and called me out, saying he had a couple of presents for me. He gave me the car.

"Take it," he said, gesturing as if he were a son of the Medici. "It's yours. You can keep it for almost a whole month before they come and get it. And in the back seat you'll find a set of the complete works of Joseph Conrad." A true patron of the arts, Moynihan. It turned out that the books hadn't been paid for either—there was something like twenty dollars due on them. I still have two volumes of the set, *Lord Jim* and *Victory*. The set was published by the same people who are publishing this book, Doubleday, and I assume that Doubleday was the firm to which Moynihan was indebted for them. If someone at Doubleday cares to come and reclaim *Lord Jim* and *Victory* I will yield them up without a fight, although after thirty-six years they are slightly travel-worn.

This was the first automobile I ever owned and I drove it everywhere. I took trips on weekends. I drove southward toward Lake Okeechobee looking for the haunts of a character I had heard about, a man named Alligator Ferguson. He is not to be confused with Alligator Platt, who worked the swamps and streams over toward Arcadia in an earlier period. In the business of capturing alligators, the first thing that needs to be done is to attract the attention of the alligator and lure him toward you. It is said that this Alligator Platt "stunk like a gopher turtle" though the figure means nothing to me. He would hide along the streams of De Soto County and let the vagrant breezes waft his personal odor into the swamps. An alligator, attracted by Platt's fetidity, would come seeking its origin. Platt must have really stunk because the alligator itself is one of the worst-smelling creatures on earth. The moment the alligator showed himself on the surface of the stream, Alligator Platt would leap in and seize the beast in his arms and down they'd go, threshing and splashing in a great swirl of muddy water, and after a while they'd break surface and there would be old Platt, astride his victim with his thumbs in the saurian's eyes. When people asked Platt why he went to all this trouble, all this great physical effort, he usually explained: "Saves ammynition."

Alligator Ferguson, whose hunting grounds lay south of Sebring, was more civilized in the conduct of his business. He used a gun. He was said to know more about alligators and their habits than any man alive and one account said he could "talk alligator talk." This alligator talk was somewhat like dog talk, consisting of a series of barks, and when Ferguson took to barking the alligators crawled or paddled in his direction. Sometimes there were cynical alligators who knew Ferguson for what he was, and lazy alligators who refused to respond to his barks. For these he carried a little pig in his arms. He'd twist the pig's tail and the pig would squeal and that would fetch any alligator on earth, alligators being, like me, partial to pork. Ferguson probably killed twenty alligators for every one that Platt rode to shore; Ferguson, in fact, captured so many that he didn't bother about marketing the hides—which were much sought after by French manufacturers of pocketbooks. He sold only the teeth, for which he was paid five dollars a pound. He often harvested five pounds of alligator teeth a week. I don't know how many alligators would be needed to make up five pounds of teeth; the books neglect to furnish us with this information, which would be of some importance to young people just starting out in the alligator business. Nor do I know who wanted those teeth.

I never did find Alligator Ferguson but down near the town of Hicoria I think I saw a fishfuddle tree. The Indians used to strip the foliage off this tree and drop it in a stream or a lake and it would fuddle the fish and make them easy to catch. I ate a few leaves.

Now that I was an auto owner I sometimes drove all the way to Tampa just to drink and eat at the Spanish restaurant, Las Novedades, in Ybor City. These being prohibition times, the liquor was always served in thick white coffee cups which made it taste better or, at least, more romantic. I sometimes suspect that I had another reason for going to Ybor City. I wanted to acquire the correct pronunciation of the colony's name which many Northerners call Eee-bore City or even Wy-bore City. It is Eee-bo City and I have had the pleasure, for more than thirty years, of correcting people who mispronounce it.

Driving to and from Tampa I sometimes stopped in a town near Mulberry to look at a tree for which the place was named. It was a big mulberry, ripped by lightning and spotted with bullet marks, for it was often used in the old days for legal hangings and Negro lynchings. Mulberry has an interesting history. It was once the center of a big mining boom—pebble phosphate mining. For a while the town was the same lawless type of community as the gold-mining boom towns of the Old West. There were saloons and gambling parlors and whorehouses and dance halls. Everyone carried a gun and there were Trampas Walks in the main street, and hangin's at the big mulberry tree every Monday morning. I've often thought of that period in Mulberry's history and visualized an old prospector, grizzled of course, half dead of thirst, weaving his way into town on foot, holding aloft a poke made of alligator hide, and crying out in a rasping voice:

"Pebble phosphate, men! Hull mountains of it!"

Howard Hartley came down to Sebring from Louisville and I informed the *American* publishers that he was the greatest reporter ever produced by the State of Kentucky and they hired him on a tentative basis. He didn't work out. Howard had never worked on a small-town newspaper and he applied big-town pyrotechnics to his job in Sebring. A girl who had been thrown over by her boy friend committed suicide and Howard pulled out all the stops on his type-writer. He made that thing into the god damndest most romantic tragedy since Mayerling, and sobbed and caterwauled in print, and slashed bitterly at the enormous cruelty pervading the world, and went on and on and produced a real journalistic masterpiece. I was so overcome by emotion that I gave his story a banner line and splashed it all over Page One. The next day the biggest committee in the history of Sebring called on us. Its members were in a state of shock as well as outrage. This sort of thing had never happened before in Sebring and would never happen again if they had any-thing to say about it. Such matters, if mentioned at all in the news-paper, should be mentioned in one plain and gently worded and *sorrowing* paragraph and that paragraph buried, as we used to say, back among the electric belt ads. The committee made such a fuss that the proprietors of the paper dismissed Hartley and he went on his way. Not long after that a committee at least as big as the Girl Suicide Committee called on me. This one was headed by the Mayor, a retired clergyman, and its members were in a sweat because I had written a Page One item about a five-foot rattlesnake being killed as it was crawling across Ridgewood Drive in the heart of town. Speaking for the committee the Mayor said that there were no rattlesnakes in Sebring and that even if there were, and ten thousand of them marched across Ridgewood Drive to the music of a rattlesnake brass band, such a matter should never appear in the local paper. I said I was sorry.

My younger brother Bill came to town without warning, thinking I might connive a job for him as a newspaperman so he could spend his days reclining in the Florida sun. I gave him an aptitude test and got him a job as a counterman in the town's lunch wagon. At this point I wrote and produced a night club act. Bill and I had several little routines which we would run through in the diner for the benefit of visiting crackers out of the swamps or the occasional tourists who stopped for sandwiches. I'd enter the lunch wagon in the role of customer and Bill would approach.

"What kinda pie you got?" I would ask.

"Pie?" he'd repeat. "Well, we got apple and pineapple and coconut cream and lemon meringue and cherry and mince . . . and as for berry we have . . . *razz, jazz, black, blue, goose and straw!*"

Or, I'd say:

"What kinda pie you got?"

"Pie? Well, we got apple and cherry and coconut cream and cherry and pineapple and cherry and mince and cherry and lemon meringue and cherry and chocolate and cherry and peach and cherry and . . ."

"I'll take cherry."

"Hell, we ain't got no cherry."

There must have been some bits in that routine other than pie bits, but I can't remember them. I do recall that cowpeas were a staple item on the menu as elsewhere in the South, and that soup was made from them, and this is the clever way a writer has of getting into a story that really has nothing to do with the matters under discussion. I know a couple who went traveling up and down the country sampling the best foods in the best restaurants of each region for the purpose of writing a magazine series on the subject.

They were in a famous restaurant in the South. They studied the menu and the wife spoke first.

"What is the soup du jour?"

"Cowpea soup, ma'am," said the waiter, sort of drawling it out. She stared at him a moment in disbelief and then said: "Well, I told my husband when we started this trip that I'd try anything once, so bring it on."

Sebring had but one resident celebrity—Rex Beach, the novelist. He was a big man with a bashed-in nose who was famous for his novels about Alaska. He was also famous for a comical saying that was current in the 1920s: "She was so dumb she thought Rex Beach was a pleasure resort."

Mr. Beach was, I believe, the first real book author I ever saw. The moment I met him I decided to do a history-making interview with him, a story that would begin on Page One and run into five or six columns inside. So I arranged for the meeting and sat down with this great literary genius and instead of asking him sensible questions I started playing the show-off. I had recently made a stab at reading a book called *The Americanization of Edward Bok,* so I started the conversation with Rex Beach by trying to demonstrate that I, too, was literary and bookish. I began this way:

"Well, well. How goes the battle with words?"

He grunted.

"Oh, by the way," I whirled onward, "I've just finished a corking good book. *Americanization of Edward Bok.* Wonderful piece of work. You've read it, of course."

"No," said Rex Beach.

Something in the way he spoke the word shriveled my brain and I never quite recovered. I came out of it with a story of sorts but it was far from the grandiose journalistic triumph I had planned.

Rex Beach spent the rest of his life as a Sebring resident. He bought up thousands of acres of muckland out toward Avon Park and busied himself growing celery and exotic flowers for the northern market. He had some kind of a connection with Fred Stone, the actor, and the Stone family visited him in Sebring. Also, the Colorado writer, Courtney Ryley Cooper, came to visit Mr. Beach and became a citizen of the town.

I hobnobbed with a couple of other famous visitors in Sebring. One was the celebrated lawyer, Samuel Untermeyer. His name turned up in Nelle Simpson's notes because he was a guest at Kenilworth Lodge. I went to call on him and he told me he had been vacationing in Palm Beach when he took down with a severe attack of asthma. He heard about the mountainous region in the middle of the state, he said, and so he came to Sebring in the Highlands and within twenty-four hours the rarefied atmosphere had done wonders for him. Sebring is 141 feet above sea level.

One evening I stopped at a drugstore in the middle of town and the soda jerk gestured toward a big open car at the curb and said, "Know who that is?" I said I didn't—there were two men sipping Cokes in the front seat. "Cornelius Vanderbilt Junior," said the soda jerk.

Now, here was something! The young man with the famous name had himself become the most famous member of the Vanderbilt clan; he had been making quite a splash in the newspaper business and owned a paper in Miami. I organized my swirling senses—I had a strong tendency to grow lightheaded and dizzy in the presence of fame—tried to put on an air of nonchalance and got ready to approach him. There was a vagrant notion knocking around in my head that he would recognize me for what I was—a real comer in the business—and hire me on the spot and maybe haul me right over to Miami that very night.

He was at the wheel of the car and I walked up beside him and introduced myself. A job in Miami! Maybe managing editor! Working for the famous Cornelius Vanderbilt Junior! Maybe become his right-hand man. I spoke in a loud, inane croak as follows:

"*Cornelius . . . Vanderbilt . . . Junior . . . as I live and breathe!*"

He smiled at me and then resumed sucking Coke through a straw.

"Imagine it!" I continued. "Imagine having such a famous and distinguished man as you right here in the middle of little old Sebring! What a story for my paper! Now, what do you think of Sebring?"

Mr. Vanderbilt knew the standard response to the standard question, and spoke it perfectly.

"You have a beautiful, I might say a spectacular, community here," he said. "There is every evidence that Sebring has a great future just ahead, just around the corner. I can sense that you have the makings of a great city here—possibly the greatest city of interior Florida. The people here *look good.* They are industrious and God-fearing and they will build well. Don't pay any attention to the dyspeptic calamity-howlers who are abroad in the land at this moment. The boom is not over. Conditions are sound. We've only seen the beginning of it. Excuse me now we've got to hurry along glad to have met you will you hand this tray to the young man give our best wishes to the people of Sebring so long" . . . and off he went. No invitation to call on him in Miami. No mention of a job. Oh, well. His mistake.

As editor of the local paper I was elected to membership in the Lions Club. The Lions met once a week for luncheon at the Hotel Nancessowee and I lasted one meeting. I arrived five minutes late and found that the club inflicted a penalty for tardiness. I was required to mount a chair and sing a little song that went:

> I'm a litt-tul prairie flower,
> I'm growing wilder evv-ree hour;
> Nobody cares to cultivate me,
> I'm as wi-yuld as I can be!

While singing this song I had to place my right hand above my head with the middle finger pointed downward, and then I had to revolve slowly on the chair until the song was finished. I did it.

Two days later the Lions baseball team played the Sebring Volunteer Fire Department for the town championship. Old George Sebring's son, Payne, was supposed to pitch for the Lions but when time came for the game to start he couldn't be found. Somebody asked me if I knew how to pitch and I said certainly and took the mound.

Those firemen hit every ball I threw. I'd try pitching ten feet out in front of the batters, but they'd simply run out of the box and hit them over the fence. All this time one of the head Lions was running back and forth in front of our bench. He was a man with a crippled back and he walked or ran in a bent-over posture. As he ran up and down the sidelines he kept crying out in an agonized voice:

"Pain! Pain! PAIN!"

For a while I was terribly distracted by his cries, thinking that the poor fellow was suffering great physical torment. Then it dawned on me that he was actually hollering:

"Payne! Payne! PAYNE!"

He was yelling for Payne Sebring, who still hadn't shown up. Naturally this continual crying for the Lions' regular pitcher didn't do my control any good. When the score reached nine to nothing with nobody out and the bases loaded, they yanked me. The short-stop, a chiropractor with an eccentric windup, took over the pitching job and the man with the bad back went to short. I went home. I didn't attend the next Lions Club meeting, or any after that, and I'm sure nobody minded.

By this time Miss Nelle Simpson had come to her senses and had fallen deeply in love with me, as was inevitable, all things considered, including the fact that the buck-toothed boys with the money and the big cars had all gone home. The boom was over. Starvation had set in.

Miss Simpson lived with a girl named Mary Gutman in a U-shaped Spanish-type apartment building called La Señorita. An unemployed real estate salesman named John McQuown was courting Mary Gutman and I was courting Nelle Simpson. The apartment had one room, a tiny bath and a kitchen no bigger than the bath. Along about this time I lost my job at the *American*; the owners were so broke that *they* had to go to work on their own paper. So Mac and Mary and Nelle and I did most of our cooking and eating at La Señorita—both girls were still working and kept the apartment stocked with groceries.

I went over to Tampa and got a job on a new paper, the *Telegraph*, which was being published in an old stone mansion. This didn't last long because the paper itself didn't last long. One of the things I did on the *Telegraph* was to interview a bull alligator. This beast lived at an alligator farm and was 160 years old. He was known to be 160 years old because his owner, an alligator man, said so. I went out and looked at this old bull and then went back and probed into some history books and wrote my interview, in which the alligator talked in Midwestern English, expressing his opinions of the younger Andrew Jackson and the Seminole chief Osceola, and ruminating, in the wandering manner that old alligators have, on the possibility that he may have met both George Washington and Abraham Lincoln, socially. This story was given a big spread by the *Telegraph* and for a while I was quite proud of it. I'm still glad I did it because I think it caused me, in after years, to develop a real substantial revulsion against any and all newspaper interviews with animals, and against any and all cute books in which animals talk and think just like big growed up human beings. I get the dry heaves from all of Kipling's critters, from Winnie-the-Pooh and Break Wind in the Willows and Uncle Remus and archy & mehitabel and Stuart

Little and all those idiot doings at Catfish Bend. It may be, too, that as far back as Tampa I learned that a man should not be overly opinionated.

I met a dog in Tampa and he didn't talk to me. Sometimes I went to the dog races with a sports writer whose name I've forgotten and one evening a trainer of hounds took us into a small room in back of the grandstand. There was a wooden box on the floor, with a lid on it, and the trainer went somewhere and returned with the dog he had going in the next race—due to be run in about ten minutes. The trainer got on his knees and wrapped both arms around the dog and then the sports writer lifted the lid from the little box. Out popped a live rabbit. He hopped around the room and the dog began to strain and slaver and jerk his head around and his eyes were about to leap out of his head. After about a minute the sports writer caught the rabbit and put him back in the box and we hurried to the betting windows and wagered everything we had on that dog. I would enjoy reporting that he lost, but he didn't. He won easily, and paid a big price, and I had winning tickets close to two hundred dollars. I refused to cash them, of course, because the thing didn't look to be quite honest. I just threw them away. Threw them on the ground.

There were rumors that the *Telegraph* was about to fold and somewhere I heard that there was a job open on a weekly newspaper in Lake Wales, a town much closer to Sebring, and so I went over there and was hired as a reporter. The publisher had a pup tent in his back yard and allowed me to sleep in it and I remember just one story I wrote in that town. It was an interview with a portrait photographer named Alexander who had become famous in his line and was now retired and took my picture, telling me that *one print* would have cost me seventy-five dollars if he had produced it in the usual course of business. I still have that picture. At that price I suppose it could be considered artistic. It shows me with my mouth slightly agape and this gives me an adenoidal look. That is, *I* always thought it was an adenoidal look. There have been others of differing views. Mr. Alexander put it in a nice folder and I presented it to Miss Simpson. Later on when she went back to Missouri she showed it to her father and told him that this was the young man she was going to marry. He studied that seventy-five-dollar picture a long while and then said, "He looks like a fella who would drink." He didn't know it, but he had extrasensory perception—at a time when it didn't even exist. His daughter, however, says she is certain he reached his conclusion from the fact that in the picture my mouth was open.

I didn't like sleeping in that pup tent and I didn't like being thirty-eight miles removed from Miss Simpson so I went back to Sebring and looked around for odd jobs such as caulking boats and washing cars. Mac and I continued to take our meals at La Señorita Apartments and, to put it bluntly, we were just plain living off those girls.

Parenthetically I would like to add that Mac and Mary were wed and made their way to Texas, sold real estate by day and studied law by night—both of them—were admitted to the bar, founded a mortgage company and an insurance company and some other companies, and as of this writing cruise around in air-conditioned Cadillacs and seem to have quite a bit of that Texas green.

The most dynamic real estate man in middle Florida during the boom was a former Texan named Jac Sheldun. He looked like Jack Holt of the movies and the girls all rolled their eyes when he was around. He was, I thought, a real cosmopolite, shrewd and intelligent and well-educated. He had the sportiest automobile I had ever seen, a beautiful Lincoln, and I knew it to be a fact that he sometimes spent as much as five dollars for a shirt.

Most of the other real estate people had long since dragged themselves out of Sebring but Jac stayed on, refusing to believe that the boom was over. He was some years older than me, and certainly I was unsuave, but he permitted me to associate with him from time to time. One of the things that made me admire him was the way he squinched up his eyes. He had a squint that gave him the look of a man who had found out all there is to know about Life. One day he and I were over at Avon Park watching the St. Louis Cardinals at practice. We were sitting in the bleachers and I noticed Jac go into his squint. He shoved his handsome profile forward a couple of inches, closed his eyes until they were slits, and peered at the ballplayers on the field. A moment later he spoke.

"Notice how I was squinting just then?" he asked.

"Yes."

"Know why I have a habit of squinting my eyes like that?"

"No. Why?"

"I come from Texas," he said. "Grew up on the Texas plains. Out there a man has to squint to look at the far distances. Any time you're in Texas you've got far distances to look at, and if you want to look far distances you've got to squint. It's a habit I've never been able to get over. Glad you asked about it."

Up to then I hadn't given much thought to squinting, but now it took on an aura of romantic significance, since Jac Sheldun was a romantic personality, and I began squinting at once. I never grew real convincing at it and people used to say, "Something the matter with your eyes?"

I had become a beachcomber on the shore of Lake Jackson, where nothing ever drifted ashore, when Jac Sheldun approached me with a proposition. He told me he had heard that a big real estate boom was shaping up in the city of Asheville, up in North Carolina, and that he was of a mind to go and have a look. He said that if I could scrape together a little cigarette money I could go along with him in his big Lincoln. I accepted. I would have gone to the ends of the earth with him. We took our time riding north and Jac seemed to have ample money and paid all the bills in the nice hotels along the way. He had a magnetic quality when it came to girls and I remember quite vividly an incident involving this quality in a South Carolina roadhouse where we spent a long rainy evening. It was a dim and shadowy place and we sat in a corner drinking corn and after a while Jac fastened his eyes on a girl who was sitting with a man at a nearby table. Jac just sat and stared at her and before long she was staring at him. She couldn't take her eyes off of him. She was a sweet-looking girl, about eighteen or twenty, and after a while the man with her began to get sore. He started fussing at her and then he came over and began picking a quarrel with Jac. Jac stood up, squinted Texas-style, and said, "One more word out of you and I'll spatter you all over this effing joint." The guy was convinced, and retreated, and had a few more angry words with the girl and then stomped out of the place. Immediately the girl came to our table. Jac pulled her onto his lap and poured her a drink out of our corn bottle and within five minutes, right in that public place, right in front of my very eyes, right square on his lap, he . . . My God I had never heard of such a thing. Later on when we were talking about it, he said, "So what was wrong about it?" and I exclaimed, "My God, what if the joint had caught on fire?"

We went on to Asheville and Jac checked us in at the Grove Park Inn, a famous and expensive resort. "We've got to bowl these people over with class," he said. "We'll take this town like Grant took Richmond. Now, this is what I want you to do."

He told me and I did it. I went to the office of the Asheville *Citizen*. I introduced myself to the city editor as a former newspaper-man of parts, now working as public relations man for one of the biggest real estate geniuses ever to operate in Florida. I named him. I told about the magnificent things he had done, dwarfing the achievements of Flagler and Fisher and D. P. Davis. I said that he had come to Asheville because he believed that Asheville was certain to become one of the great metropolitan centers of the South. Asheville would outshine Atlanta and New Orleans and Birmingham and Memphis and he, Jac Sheldun, was going to enter business here, make his permanent home here, cast his lot with the people of Asheville. He was, to be more specific, going to enter the real estate business here.

I had rehearsed it well and delivered it well and the city editor was impressed and asked me if I'd mind writing the story about Mr. Sheldun's arrival and his feelings about Asheville. I said I'd be happy to. It worked out just as Jac had said it would, and I wrote about a column, and even tacked on a couple of paragraphs about Mr. Sheldun's distinguished traveling companion, the well-known news-paperman, formerly of the Louisville *Courier-Journal*, H. Allen Smith.

The story was printed as I wrote it and the way Jac had it figured, this would throw the whole town open to us. They'd be standing in line at the Grove Park Inn, seeking interviews with the famous Mr. Sheldun, offering him vice presidencies in big corporations, and all that. Somehow it didn't work out. We sat and waited and nobody came and the phone stayed silent. I think perhaps that the Asheville real estate boom had petered out before we got there. Jac was bitterly disappointed and spoke harshly about the people of North Carolina, calling them effing hillbillies who were unable to recognize a good thing when it was shoved in their face. I returned to the *Citizen* and to my warm friend the city editor and asked him for a job and he said they weren't taking anybody on. So Jac and I parted company. I don't know where he went—possibly back to Texas to develop a new kind of squint. I went on to Washington where my Aunt Tyrrell Allen lived. Thomas Wolfe? He was just another guy at that time, an obscure English teacher in New York, living on canned beans.

I wasn't able to find a job in Washington. I called on Ulric Bell who was Washington correspondent for the *Courier-Journal* and a prominent member of the press corps in the capital. I reminded him that I was the lad who turned up the political scandal at Camp Knox—I didn't tell him the whole truth—and he said he remembered it well, and congratulated me. He sent me to a man named David Lawrence who had just started a paper called the *United States Daily* and in addition ran a big news syndicate. Mr. Lawrence questioned me briefly on my knowledge of politics. I had none. I lacked the ability to bluff in spite of my experience in Asheville; I have always been the world's most inept salesman, especially when the product has been me. Mr. Lawrence advised me that he felt I needed a bit more seasoning in the hinterland. So I told my aunt that I wanted to go back to Florida. I had never been on an ocean-going vessel so I decided to take a coastal steamer from Baltimore to Jacksonville. In Baltimore I made one last halfhearted try, visiting the offices of the *Sunpapers*. It was the tag-end of summer in 1926 and Baltimore was hotter than a witch's tit and I was almost pleased when the man told me they weren't taking anybody on at the moment. I got on the boat and went back to Florida where everyone was broke and miserable.

In Sebring the *American* was still struggling for life and I fell into conversation with two printers, a makeup man and a Linotype operator, who had a theory and a little money. They said the proper spot for a newspaper in Florida was in a town that had something back of it more substantial than phony real estate values. They said they had been cruising around and they had found a town called Bowling Green, over in Hardee County to the west of Sebring. It was a little town but it was surrounded by prosperous strawberry farms and other agricultural land. They had worked out a plan for founding a weekly newspaper in Bowling Green and all they needed was an editor. They said it might be rough going at first, and a lot of hard work, but that it was bound to pay out in the end and put all three of us on easy street. We rode over and looked at the town and the little wooden structure they had picked for their plant and I accepted the offer of a one-third partnership. At that point I would have accepted a job picking chickens. Moreover, I had a faint suspicion that Destiny was at work with me again. Remember Bowling Green in Kentucky, and how I almost became a potential future Kentucky Colonel Mawton Folks style? This little town of Bowling Green in central Florida got its name from a group of strawberry growers from Bowling Green, Kentucky, who settled the place in the 1880s. I would have been a fool to have turned my back on the obvious workings of Fate.

The two printers had acquired an old flatbed press which they moved into the building. All type was set in Sebring, placed in forms and hauled over to Bowling Green by automobile. All three of us worked day and night and Sundays—my two partners retained their salaried jobs in Sebring, but I devoted my full time to the Bowling Green enterprise. Being editor was more than just editing. I gathered and wrote the news and wrote the heads and sub-heads. I solicited advertising and wrote the ads. I went from house to house, getting subscribers, and on Saturdays if I could find time I'd range around among the visiting farmers, trying to interest them in our paper. When the boys arrived with the forms we really went to work. The old press broke down every ten or fifteen minutes. The papers had to be folded by hand and the pages cut, and then they had to be wrapped and labeled for the postoffice, and I did all that while my associates labored and sweated over the creaking flatbed.

It might have been worth all that effort if the town itself had shown any appreciation. I had a room in the musty home of the local bank president and it was his custom, whenever I hove in view, to put on a broad grin and then place his forefinger to his head and make circular motions. The other town merchants had much the same attitude. They were tactful toward me, considerate of my feelings, and usually greeted me with encouraging remarks like, "Ain't you folks gone bankrupt yit?" or "They's been some real nut-heads drift through here in my time but you birds take the cake."

The one merchant who showed any kindliness toward me was Mr. Chisholm, an old fellow who had a little grocery store next to the newspaper plant. He wore galluses and looked like Clarence Darrow. He was the only *nice* person in the whole Godforsaken town, and so what happened? Fate dealt him a backhand blow (actually a back*side* blow) right in my very presence. He had a privy out back of his store and one morning I was sitting behind the newspaper office, resting my bones, when I saw my elderly friend go into the outhouse. A few minutes went by and then I heard a maniacal screech. The door of the privy burst open and out came Mr. Chisholm. His pants were down around his ankles and he tried to run toward his store, but he was thrown to the ground. He was still screaming and I started for him but before I could reach him he was back on his feet and hopping in the manner of a participant in a sack race. He had one hand clasped to his bottom and now I could make out a single word he was yelling, the word "WASPS!" It was clear to me now that the wasps had got him in the crotch. He made it inside his store and I could hear his muffled howls, but they were diminishing in volume, and then suddenly they were as the stunning shriek of fire sirens—twice as loud and frenzied as before—and Mr. Chisholm came leaping from his store like a madman, his face contorted, tears streaming over his cheeks and roaring like a wounded animal. After a while I found out what had happened. He was in such pain from the wasp stabbing that when he got inside his store he seized the first palliative medicine that came to hand. It was a bottle of Sloan's Liniment. He poured some of it into his cupped hand and then sloshed it into the area of suffering. He had, in effect, turpentined himself and he told me afterward that the agony shot clean up through his body and made *even his hair hurt*. If a man has any perceptivity at all the time is bound to come when he recognizes the fact that justice doesn't always prevail in human affairs. It came for me there in Bowling Green. If anybody deserved to get it in the . . . to get it where Mr. Chisholm got it, that person was my landlord, the banker. Certainly not Mr. Chisholm.

The great Bowling Green newspaper venture collapsed, leaving the two printers as broke as I was, and I returned to Sebring. I had decided that it was time for me to get out of Florida but before I left I wanted to get my troth all plighted up. On a blustery September afternoon I borrowed an automobile (the finance company had long since repossessed the Moynihan Studebaker) and drove to Avon Park and bought an engagement ring. All right. I admit it. *She* paid for it.

We were on the road back toward Sebring and I was singing an Irving Berlin song, being quite a groaner in those days, and I began to notice that the car was swaying. It had been raining all day and a high wind was causing the car to drift toward the left side of the highway. We came into Sebring on Ridgewood Drive just in time to see the flat metal roof peel off of a two-story business building. It was quite windy.

We telephoned some friends and got up a party to celebrate our formal engagement. The party was held in a house near the lake, the home of a real estate dealer who hadn't been able to sober up long enough to make it back North. He was a man who had once taken a course in the Psychology of Habits and he loved to sit and lecture me on the subject. It had something to do with the fact that when I went into the bathroom in the morning to brush my teeth, I didn't say, "Now it is time for me to brush my teeth so I shall pick up this brush, this toothbrush, and I shall open the door of this cabinet, and I shall get out this tooth paste, and take the cap off of it, and squeeze out some paste, onto this toothbrush, and then put the cap back on this tube, and the tube back in the cabinet, and now I shall put the brush end of the toothbrush into my mouth, and jerk my hand back and forth . . ." No, he said, I didn't go through all that. I just walked into the bathroom and brushed my teeth without thinking about it. I have met some unusual people in my time.

So this party got to rolling and people brought liquor through the slashing rain and the girls made sandwiches and the phonograph was going with Gene Austin and Nick Lucas and Whispering Jack Smith and before long everybody was pie-eyed. Some time during the evening the phone rang and I answered it. Chief of Police Tom Worley, a handsome young ex-Hoosier, said that there had been a hell of a hurricane and that the town of Moore Haven, seventy miles south of us on the shore of Lake Okeechobee, was under water and the people needed help. Worley said he was trying to get enough able-bodied men together to start a rescue train out of Sebring at dawn. I told him who was present at the party and as I talked I glanced out the window. Somebody had turned on the headlights of a car and the beams were illuminating the lawn. There on the grass, with the rain coming at them in horizontal sheets, were two men busily turning drunken handsprings as if they made their living at it. I told the Chief of Police that we'd all be ready to go by daylight.

Four or five of us made it. Chief Worley and some others had loaded a couple of freight cars with groceries and medicines and tools and there were about twenty men making the trip. Some rode on top of the cars, some clung to various projections on the locomotive, and Tom Worley and I were on the cowcatcher. A hand-car went ahead of us scouting for washouts, of which there were plenty. We had to stop frequently and shore up the sagging rails. I was dying of a hangover and during those stops I'd go into the ditches beside the track and drink from the little streams of reddish, bitter, muddy water. Around noon we edged up to a place where the two steel rails rose in the air, turned over in a graceful arc, and then disappeared into the brackish water. No train would go beyond that point for a long time. Tom Worley and I looked off to the south and we could just barely see the Moore Haven water tower which had somehow survived the storm. Tom turned to me and said, "By god, I'm goin' in! You game?" I wasn't, not one bit, but I had to be. We stepped into the water and began wading. From then on we were wading about half the time and swimming when the water was over our heads. All the way in to Moore Haven we struggled past trees and bushes whose scraggy, stripped limbs were festooned with snakes—enough snakes to stretch all the way to Saturn.

The water was chest high in the main business street of Moore Haven. The hurricane had hit Lake Okeechobee and sort of shoved it over onto the town. Rowboats and motorboats were moving through the streets and most human life was confined to the upper floors of two-story buildings. I believe that Tom Worley and I were the first people to arrive from the outside world. So what? There was nothing we could do. We couldn't splash the water back toward Miami. We had made a heroic journey through jungle waters and venomous serpents and there had been moments when I heard the wing-flappings of the Angel of Death, and then we had made a triumphal entry in water up to our chests, and what came after that? We went and found a hotel that had been washed off its foundations and climbed up to the second floor and went to sleep. Later in the day a boat took us back to the railhead and we returned to Sebring. By now plenty of relief trains were moving southward toward the stricken town.

In Sebring the *Daily American* office had sprung to life, for the town was full of newspaper correspondents from Atlanta and more were coming in. The Associated Press sent a couple of telegraph operators to transmit copy, along with the best staff writer they had in the entire South. I remember what he looked like, how commanding his presence, how swiftly and smoothly he wrote. Most of all I remember the first line of the story he was composing when I first encountered him there in my old office. It was:

*The skies wept copiously.*

That was his lead, his first paragraph. I looked at it and read it over to myself several times and I thought, Oh God, if I could only some day write like that! If I could only put words together to evoke such realistic and yet lyrical pictures. But, no! I would never be able to produce such magnificent imagery. The skies wept copiously. The skies wept copiously. I walked around as if in a daze, repeating the words. I hadn't even known that there *was* such a beautiful word as *copiously*. The skies wept copiously! Jesus!

Thirty-three years later I sat on the terrace of the Royal Hawaiian Hotel in Waikiki and cursed that dashing AP man. I had been looking through a book about Hawaii, written by Charles Warren Stoddard and published in 1894. This Stoddard was a poet out of California but the book I was reading was prose, the kind of prose that comes out of a poet, especially the kind of a poet Stoddard was. Suddenly a line leaped at me from the book:

*The skies wept copiously.*

Exactly the same. Word for word. The line that had stirred my soul had been stolen by that sleazy Associated Press hack from the works of Charles Warren Stoddard and, for all I know, Charles Warren Stoddard may have stolen it from . . . well, from old Noah himself.

At that moment I, personally, almost wept copiously.

# CHAPTER 13

# I think you touch!

Working as an advertising solicitor for the Sebring *American* was a young Canadian whose name was Woodward or Woodford. He, too, had managed to hang on through thin and thinner but now the idea of eating regular meals was beginning to haunt his mind as a thing worth striving for. He and I put our heads together and organized a corporation. He had a Ford roadster and I had a portable typewriter and he said that with those two articles and our combined brain power, we could soon be rolling in wealth.

We were going on the road and produce city directories for towns that didn't have city directories. Woody said it was a cinch. We would drive into a town and go to the Chamber of Commerce or the Rotary or Lions or Kiwanis or, lacking any of these, summon a meeting of preachers. The preachers would be a last resort because Woody said that, in his experience, they were not as a class quite reliable. We would explain our project to the local people and get official or semi-official sponsorship. Then we would go to work. My job would be to take a census of the town, getting the names and addresses and occupations of all its citizens. These would be put together in alphabetical order. Meanwhile, Woody would be out selling ads to be printed in our city directory and he would also arrange for a printer to manufacture the little book. We'd pay the printer, give ten or twenty bucks to a local charity, and depart with the rest of the money, going on to the next town that would hold still for a city directory.

Nelle was by now working for the Red Cross which was trying to put the town of Moore Haven back together again. She was living in that same hotel where Tom Worley and I rested the day after the hurricane. Woody and I drove down to Moore Haven for a farewell visit and I assured my fiancee that I would send for her as soon as the money started pouring in from all those city directories.

And so we shoved off and I said good-by to Sebring, an ailing town at the moment. It continued in a sickly condition for years and then World War II brought an air base and later a race track for automobiles and nowadays the name of Sebring is known to racing-car nuts all around the world.

I told Woody that the Governor of Florida was a warm friend of mine and so we stopped in Tallahassee to visit him and ask a favor of him. This friendship dated back to an evening when he and some other politicians got together for an impromptu supper party in a suite at Kenilworth Lodge. I stopped in to interview the Governor and found him and his friends enjoying themselves immensely with bottled goods. The Governor clapped me on the back and urged me to join the party and I did and all evening he kept roaring at me that I was the best damn little ole newspaper editor he ever knew and I could have anything I wanted from the State of Florduh and any time I wanted anything at all, just to call on him. I was real flattered by all this gubernatorial attention, even though he had a tendency to call me Mr. Forepaugh throughout the evening.

At the State Capitol I told all this to his secretary and was ushered into the Governor's office. He was in a sour mood and couldn't remember me at first, so I went over the whole thing about the supper party at Kenilworth Lodge. He acted as if he didn't care to remember it, and that he would like to have me thrown bodily into the street, but I kept talking, reminding him about how much fun we had that night, and how drunk that Senator from Massachusetts got, and how drunk *everybody* got, and a few other things that went on, and finally the Chief Executive of Florida quit wincing for a moment and opened one eye and said, "What was it you wanted from me?" I told him, and we left Tallahassee with a letter recommending us to the world as honest and upright young men, worthy of trust in any quarter of the globe, and the letter was signed by the Governor of Florida. Class always tells. Woody said that the Governor's letter cinched it—we'd retire rich within a year.

And so we went lolloping along the Old Spanish Trail with its old Spanish moss swirling from the turpentine trees and we came to the Gulf Coast town of Biloxi where we took a room in a hotel. We walked around the streets for a bit and we seemed to notice a great abundance of young and pretty girls. After a while we talked to a local citizen who was sitting on a bench.

"You come to a mighty fine town," he told us. "The Number One product of this town is girls. Got more girls here per cappa-tye than any other town in the United States unless maybe Gulfport. Reason is, we got all these cannin' factories for cannin' shrimp and fish. And they's hunneds and hunneds of girls work in them factories. Fish is this town's Number Two product. So we got so many cannin' factories we need to keep a good crop of girls goin' all the time, so we got about forty high schools all fulla girls, turnin' them out for the cannin' factories, and that's the reason you see so many girls. It's a right good town."

Woody and I thought so too. Woody said he wouldn't mind staying in Biloxi a few days, sort of rest up for the great city directory campaigns that lay ahead. Just a few days, a week, maybe two weeks. Store up vigor. I said no. I said I was afraid we would get involved with some of these girls and after all I was an engaged man, and in love, and it wouldn't be right for me to have aught to do with these girls of Biloxi. Woody said he was happy that he had chosen such a forthright Christian man for a traveling companion and business associate, that I was a paragon of moral refinement, but why the hell didn't I think back to the days when all those buck-toothed guys were courting my girl friend in Sebring, when there were ten young men for every eligible girl? He pointed out that here in Biloxi the situation was reversed, that there were maybe a hundred lovely young things bobbing their chests at us for every young man there was to bob a chest at, and by god he, Woody, was gonna take advantage of it, even if it cost him his honor, and I could go somewhere and work crossword puzzles if I felt like it. I will sometimes go out of my way to avoid contention and argument, and this was one of those times. And I *did* remember about those jerks with the big cars in Sebring and how that crazy dame passed me by in favor of them, and here I was in this fabulous, fantastic town where the girls came swinging along three and four abreast, and they flirted outrageously and even called out endearments to complete strangers.

We stayed about a week. We'd have been there still, I think, if it hadn't been for an observation made by Woody one evening when we were getting dressed to go out. Woody was taking a shower.

"Hey," he called out to me, "have you noticed something unusual about these girls? I mean the way they all seem to smell like fish?"

Up to then I hadn't noticed it, but now I did—it became, in fact, almost overpowering. Consequently the city of Biloxi began to lose some of its moonglow and I convinced Woody that we were spending too much money and that it was time for us to move on and do some city directories. He complained, saying we might never again see such an opportunity as this anywhere on earth "or even in heaven." I told him: "You could stay here forever and you still wouldn't use them all up." And so we went on westward and skipped New Orleans and after a while entered Texas. This was to be our first field of operations. Woody said that to sell city directories it was necessary to go among people who thought well of themselves and who enjoyed seeing their names in print and that Texas was that kind of a place.

I had never been in Texas before, and I began squinting in the Jac Sheldun manner so I could see long distances when I encountered them. We chugged along for a while and then stopped in a dirty little town for our first job. We couldn't convince anybody that the town needed a city directory and a local preacher told us that he couldn't raise enough money to put some new wooden steps on the front of his church and we went on to another town. We tried half a dozen dust-covered communities, showing off that letter from the Governor of Florida, but those dumb, skinflint Texans wouldn't buy. We came to Beaumont and Woody decided this was a place where we'd make a killing and he set to work on the preliminary promotion. I wandered around looking at people and suddenly discovered that we were in a big place—that it would take me at least a year to get all the names and addresses. And then along came a glum-looking Woody with news that Beaumont already had a city directory.

We went on a while longer, a heavy smell of oil in our nostrils, and then one day we arrived in San Antonio with just enough money to last another couple of days. I pawned my typewriter and we turned north and drove to Tulsa, Oklahoma. Why Tulsa? Because old John Moynihan was there, working on the *Tribune*. And within an hour of my arrival he had me fixed up with a job on the *Tribune*. Woody telegraphed his folks in Canada and they sent enough money for him to make it home and I went to work for a pleasant man named Victor Barnett, who was managing editor of the *Tribune*.

A few days after I went to work for Mr. Barnett I advised Nelle to join me in Tulsa. Object: matrimony. Some years later it became quite a thing for a man to marry a girl named Simpson. The Duke of Windsor did it, and the Marquess of Milford-Haven did it, and even Bill O'Dwyer did it, and in each of these cases there was loud and vigorous journalistic activity. There was newspaper interest in my wedding, too, though I am able to recall that a freight train derailment in Pawhuska, Oklahoma, attracted more public attention than I did on the day I married a Simpson.

Women as a general thing are able to read the works of Mrs. Emily Post and retain their poise and serenity; some women even acquire a sturdy complacency from the pages of *The Blue Book of Social Usage*. On the other hand, I have known men who have said, quite flatly, that they wished the book were in the hot place. Personally, I have always tried to maintain a certain amount of emotional equilibrium whenever I pick up Mrs. Post's masterwork.

Not long ago I came upon the following provocative paragraph:

> Marriages are often performed in the clergyman's study or in another room at the parsonage. But such a ceremony is merely a marriage and not a wedding.

The first time I read that passage, especially the phrase "merely a marriage," I spoke harsh words into the atmosphere. Then I read it again, and reconsidered, and in the end I saw the subtle inner meaning of it. It is almost pure Truth.

At the time of my own prehistoric nuptials I was a rewrite man on the *Tribune* and while I was aware of my own intrinsic importance, I also knew better than to ask for a day off or even an afternoon off for the purpose of getting married. On my wedding day, then, I showed up for work at eight in the morning. At about eleven o'clock Nelle telephoned from the railroad station and said she had just got off the train. I told her to make herself comfortable and I'd pick her up soon after twelve.

When I arrived she was sitting on a bench looking a bit depot-haggard. I hurried her along to a cut-rate jewelry store and bought a shiny wedding band for seven dollars and fifty cents. Next we went to the courthouse and got the license and after that I put her on a bus that would take her to the Admiral Place apartment I had already rented. Now that I think of it, I didn't have any lunch that day.

Apparently I didn't miss it. I was back at my newspaper desk at five minutes past one.

I still didn't know where the ceremony was to take place but during the afternoon I found time to consult with the church editor of the *Tribune* and was advised that the town was loaded with reliable clergymen and that I couldn't do better, from a prestige point of view, than to choose a Dr. John Rice, pastor of the big Methodist church. "He is quite elderly," said the lady church editor, "but a nice man and he's in *Who's Who* and that's important and he does a damn good bang-up job with a wedding." I have known quite a few newspaper church editors over the years and they all have been people who seemed to think it was necessary in their city room surroundings to talk real slangy and employ the milder cusswords, such as hell and damn. This girl did it, and in addition had a peculiar history leading up to her job as church editor. The reason she was church editor was that she was being punished. Some time during the previous year, 1926, the grand opening of the Roxy Theatre was held in New York City. This was, up to then, the most ornately magnificent theater ever built and so key newspapers around the country were invited to send representatives to the opening, with travel expenses paid by the Roxy management. This girl got the job, and assembled a new wardrobe, and babbled endlessly about the topless towers of Gotham and Little Old Baghdad-on-the-Hudson and then off she went. She covered the opening of the Roxy and telegraphed some of the most vivid prose ever to pass through a Western Union office, sending back ten times as much copy as had been ordered. And then she refused to come home. She continued sending stories about New York and apparently was racing up and down Manhattan streets grabbing people indiscriminately and interviewing them. Victor Barnett finally notified her that unless she was back in Tulsa within twenty-four hours she could consider herself fired. She came back and Mr. Barnett appointed her church editor of the paper, a job which requires frequent association with people of questionable character.

I accepted her advice and telephoned the office of Dr. John Rice, and a girl said it would be all right for five-thirty. Nelle met me downtown soon after I got off work and we proceeded on foot to the church, attracting no attention. On arrival we found that Dr. Rice had an inner office and a large outer vestibule. I can't remember what all the excitement was about, except that it was some sort of dress rehearsal for Easter. The place was boiling with women, all apparently working at cross purposes and all talking in the language of the blue jay. We stood just inside the street door for a few minutes and nobody paid us any mind and then at last a woman came rushing up to me. About time!

"Could you help me with something?" she asked. "Take just a minute or two." She seemed short of breath.

"Be glad to," I said.

She escorted me over to a table where there was an outsize tray and crowded on the tray were about forty little glasses, the size of shot glasses or smaller. The woman thrust a half-gallon bottle of grape juice at me.

"Just fill up all these glasses," she said. "I'd do it myself but the man is here about the broken clarinet."

Up to that moment I was in fairly good physical and mental trim for a man on the very threshold of matrimony. Now, standing there with that big bottle in my hands, my composure vanished. I tried to hold myself under control, gritting my teeth, telling myself that I was a case-hardened newspaperman, wise about life, impervious to the stresses and strains that beset other people (I was nineteen). I began pouring grape juice into and around those little glasses. The more I poured the more that bottle shook, until it was wagging in my hands like a spaniel's tail. Eventually I got all the glasses filled, but I also got grape juice in the tray to a depth of perhaps a quarter inch, and I got it all over the table and on the floor and on my trousers and shoes.

Meanwhile my Simpson girl had grown impatient and decided that this was a ridiculous preliminary to a wedding. She began grabbing hold of various fluttering women and demanding action, and pretty soon the woman who was worried about the broken clarinet came back and surveyed the job I had done.

"Well," she said, testily, "I *suppose* that'll have to do."

She didn't thank me (I'm sure she thought I was an apprentice deacon available for odd jobs) and I moved away from the table, dabbing at grape juice spots on my clothing. By this time Nelle had succeeded in making herself understood, and another woman ushered us into the *sanctum sanctorum*. Dr. Rice was there at his desk, occupied with a lot of paper work.

"What's this? What's this?" he cried out, standing up and looking

at us as if we were bringers of bad tidings. The lady said that we were
the people who had come to get married.

"What people?" he wanted to know. "Nobody told *me* anything
about it! You would think I was the janitor here!"

He fussed around among the papers on his desk, looked up at us
a couple of times, then back down at the papers, and I had a feeling
that, *Who's Who* or no *Who's Who*, he had already forgotten what
we were there for. Then he addressed himself to the lady who had
brought us in.

"Well," he said, sternly, "you'd better go and get me two witnesses." She hurried out the door and returned in a moment dragging two other ladies, a Mrs. Brown and a Mrs. Landfair. One of
them, I don't know which, had her hands full of green crepe paper
and a pair of scissors, and her mouth was set in a straight, grim line
because she was holding a dozen or so pins in it.

Dr. Rice began opening desk drawers and finally came up with a
little book. He flipped it open quickly and began reading the words
at us. I didn't hear them because I had become fascinated by the
witness with the crepe paper. She hadn't realized that she was taking
part in a wedding until after it got started, and she still had all that
fluffy green paper in her hands, and the scissors, and she made some
tentative moves as if to take the pins out of her mouth, and dropped
the scissors on the floor, and in stooping to pick them up coughed
and spit pins all over the carpet, and she was straightening up just at
the moment the final words were being spoken.

The clergyman didn't kiss the bride. Neither did I. Somehow it
didn't seem appropriate. Dr. Rice opened some more desk drawers
and got out a marriage certificate and wrote our names and the date
and place and signed it. The legality of that document is questionable to this day because the good doctor's handwriting would con-
found the best cryptographers in the CIA. The two witnesses signed,
and Dr. Rice now shook hands with me and smiled rapidly; he was
in a hurry because the phone was ringing so I reached in my pocket
and got the five-dollar bill and handed it to him.

Outside on the steps we stood and looked at each other a bit and
grinned and said "Whew!" and I dug into my pocket and got out the
remainder of my worldly goods and counted up four dollars and
seventy-five cents.

"Wife," I said, "it's time for the honeymoon."

We walked down to a cafeteria and had what might be called a private wedding dinner, although I thought of it as a late lunch. Then we strolled over to the Orpheum Theatre where there was a movie and a vaudeville bill and I bought two tickets without noticing what was playing. When we got to our seats a comedian named Harry Burns was on the stage.

If you remember vaudeville you will remember Harry Burns. He was the dialect comic who always said, "I think you touch." Said it all the time, all through his act. He was real funny and we laughed every time he said, "I think you touch." For many years afterward that line had a sort of romantic significance for us—the way a song has a special meaning to other people.

Following the vaudeville acts the feature picture was shown. It was Virginia Valli—I have verified this by checking the Tulsa newspapers for that date—it was Virginia Valli in *Marriage*, described in the ads as "a photoplay based on H. G. Wells' story of unconquerable love." We sat through it, though I can't remember anything about it, unconquerable or otherwise, and finally went outside and caught a bus, saying occasionally to each other, "I think you touch," and laughing like crazy, and went on out to Admiral Place, and the next morning I was at my desk at eight o'clock. I sat opposite Joe Brandt, the city editor, who later became president of the University of Oklahoma, and he greeted me with:

"Morning. Call Eddie at headquarters and . . . oh, by the way, did you get married all right?"

"Sure."

"Congratulations. Write me a paragraph about it. Then call Eddie at headquarters. He's got a train wreck at Pawhuska."

One paragraph. And that one paragraph never got into the paper.

In retrospect I think I would say that it was a *simple* wedding. I'm not necessarily recommending it, in all its details, as the ideal type of ceremony. I'm even slightly apprehensive about trying to point a moral. It would be ridiculous for me to prescribe one witness with a mouthful of pins.

Yet I must, in all fairness, execute a slight bow in the direction of Mrs. Emily Post's famous book. She had it right. We were married in a clergyman's study. Amidst all that grape juice and crepe paper confusion, we actually had no wedding. We had only what we've got today—merely a marriage.

A month after our marriage Lindbergh took off from Long Island for Paris and there was great excitement around the *Tribune* office during all those suspenseful hours he was in the air. His flight dramatized aviation so vividly that when the notorious Kimes gang terrorized the town of Beggs, some distance south of Tulsa, robbing a bank and slaughtering some of the citizens, I was sent down in a flying machine to cover the story. It was my first flight and, as I remember, it was the first time an Oklahoma newspaper had ever covered a story by plane.

In Tulsa, too, I met a man who was to become a lifelong friend— Gene Austin. Gene was then at the peak of his fame, the nation's most prominent singer of popular songs. His records sold in the millions and Nelle and I had all of them long before we ever thought we'd meet Gene himself. He came to Tulsa to sing at our honeymoon resort—the Orpheum—and I begged Joe Brandt to let me do an interview with him, and got the assignment. I spent a lot of time with Gene backstage at the theater and we whiled away many hours drinking and talking in his suite at the Hotel Mayo. It was the beginning of a long and pleasant relationship that has survived for thirty-five years and which I intend to tell about in another book.

One day Victor Barnett called me into his office and said he had to let me go, that he had taken me on temporarily as a favor to John Moynihan, that my work had been altogether satisfactory but that his budget wouldn't permit him to keep me on. He said he could get me a job in Denver if I wanted it, and I said I did, and so he telegraphed a former *Tribune* man named Joe Alex Morris who had gone to work for the Denver *Post*. Morris wired back that there was room for me and for anybody else Mr. Barnett wanted to send.

# acrost the ocean to Idaho

When I was about twelve years old I knew a kid who was moderately half-witted and whose company I enjoyed because he had a funny way of saying things. One of the things he said many times was a statement of ambition and purpose, as follows: "By god when I grow up I'm gonna go clean acrost the ocean to Idaho." To this day whenever I hear something about Idaho, which is not often, I visualize it as a place somewhere east of Suez where the flying fishes play.

A train carried me from Tulsa to Denver and I had just as sound an idea of my destination as that boy had of Idaho. It's hard to believe that to move to Denver less than forty years ago was somewhat akin to leaving Earth.

As I shaped up, sitting on that train, I had half a year to go before my twentieth birthday, yet I had been employed on nine different newspapers, counting that thing we put out in Bowling Green and counting that pup-tent weekly in Lake Wales. I was pretty well seasoned, but not enough for the maelstrom that lay directly ahead of me. The whole city of Denver had been turned into one vast and incredible circus by a newspaper war involving a man named Bonfils and a man named Howard. As I approached the Continental Divide I knew nothing about that war; I had been told that "things are popping in Denver" but that was all. In spite of all that roving, I was still a fledgling, moist back of the ears, and I was heading right into the very center of a wild carnival described by Robert L. Perkin in *The First Hundred Years:*

Denver was treated to two years of such fantastic newspaper competition as taxes the credulity of anyone who was not an eyewitness. Those who survived it called the contest "The Battle of the Century," and although a relative peace now has reigned for some thirty years the commotion on the Western frontier evoked an amazed interest so general that it is still talked about with chuckles and headshakes whenever newsmen gather in press clubs or corner bars to relive lustier days.

On my arrival in Denver I registered at a cheap hotel and thought I heard bombs bursting in air and then found my way to Champa Street and the building which housed the Denver *Post*. Sirens began screaming somewhere overhead as I read the three gilt-lettered inscriptions across the façade of the building:

'TIS A PRIVILEGE TO LIVE IN COLORADO
YOU ARE NOW STANDING EXACTLY ONE MILE ABOVE SEA LEVEL
O JUSTICE, WHEN EXPELLED FROM OTHER HABITATIONS,
MAKE THIS THY DWELLING PLACE!

The story of the *Post* and its two fabulous publishers, Frederick G. Bonfils and Harry H. Tammen, has been told in great and lusty detail by Gene Fowler in *Timber Line*, which was published in 1933. Neither Tammen nor Bonfils had ever engaged in the newspaper business until they bought the sickly little *Post* for $12,500 in 1895. But nobody ever made a bigger or a louder splash with a newspaper than did these two buccaneers. They advertised themselves in their own paper as the most noble characters in the history of the world, the best friends that mankind ever had. The *Post* constantly described itself as *The Big Brother of the West* and *The Paper with a Heart and Soul*. Racks of special slug-lines were maintained in the composing room for use at the beginning of certain stories. Every story dealing with the weather started with the italicized line: *'Tis a Privilege to Live in Colorado*. If hailstones as big as baseballs were dropping in Champa Street, that line preceded the story of the storm. Even more nonsensical was the steady use of the slug-line, *Crime Never Pays*. It was stuck at the top of every story dealing with criminal activity and it had a foolish ring when used over an account of a bank holdup in which the bandit gang made a clean getaway with half a million dollars.

From stem to stern the *Post* was loaded with silliness posing as wisdom, broad inconsistencies that wouldn't fool a prairie dog and bold statements that a certified idiot wouldn't believe—yet the people of Denver either believed these things or simply enjoyed the colorful manner in which they were served up. I choose to think that the public believed in the vaunted integrity of *The Big Brother of the West*. But then I am slightly prejudiced—I happen to think that the average citizen is too stupid to drool.

Several months before I arrived on the scene Roy W. Howard had come in to Denver prepared to do battle with Bonfils and the powerful *Post* (Harry Tammen had recently died of cancer). Howard bought the historic Rocky Mountain *News*, a morning paper, and then started the *Evening News* with the announced intention of breaking the *Post's* stranglehold on the afternoon field. The war was on. Within a couple of months Bonfils had started the *Morning Post* with the announced intention of putting the Rocky Mountain *News* out of business, and now both sides began throwing great sums of money into the fight. No holds were barred. Ethics went out the window. A man stood in the street in front of the *Post* building with a table fork in his mouth and caught a potato thrown from the top of a skyscraper across the way. Bombs roared, sirens screamed, a flagpole sitter was perched high above the *News* building, and Harry Houdini extricated himself from his bonds while hanging Mussolini-like in front of the *Post*. No day went by without some new stunt, some fresh skulduggery.

On that summer day in 1927 I walked into the *Post* building and was directed up a flight of iron steps to the second-floor editorial rooms. I found Joe Alex Morris, late of Tulsa, functioning in the midst of a madhouse. Two big fat newspapers were being published in quarters designed for only one. Joe Morris took me by the hand and led me over to a swarthy, ruggedly handsome man named Bill Shanklin, who was managing editor of the new *Morning Post*.

"Here's that new guy from Tulsa," Joe Morris said to Shanklin.

"Read copy?" asked Shanklin, not even looking at me.

"No," I said. "I mean yes."

"Take off your coat," he said.

I was escorted to a chair on the rim of the copy desk. I told Morris I had never been a copyreader but that I knew what one was and he said not to worry, that nobody in the place knew what anybody else was doing. If a grizzly bear had come down from the mountains and walked into that big room wearing an eyeshade they'd have handed him a soft-lead pencil and put him on the copy desk. The two Scripps-

Howard papers up on Welton Street were hiring men away from the two Bonfils papers, and Bonfils was hiring men away from Scripps-Howard. *News* spies were known to be operating in the *Post* city room, and the *Post* planted a microphone in the hotel room used by *News* executives for strategy meetings. The *News* men discovered the hidden mike and then faked a conference in which they announced wholesale raises for everyone on their editorial staffs. The very same day Bonfils announced substantial raises for one and all. This must have happened before I got there. I don't remember it.

I didn't stay long on the copy desk, but asked for a transfer to the city side, and got it. I became a reporter and for a while my city editor was Sam H. Day, later managing editor of the New York *Journal*. He preached that no newspaper story should ever begin with the word "the."

Within a few months I somehow fell into the enviable role of Bon's Fair-Haired Boy. This meant that the great F. G. Bonfils had developed a strong personal liking for me and had designated me, quite unofficially, as the boy who would write things about F. G. Bonfils for the newspaper owned and edited by F. G. Bonfils; and the job also required that I scheme up some way, as often as possible, to get the handsome features of F. G. Bonfils reproduced in the pages of The Newspaper with a Heart and Soul.

Mr. Perkin described Mr. Bonfils well in his history: "Next after Buffalo Bill Cody, F. G. Bonfils was the handsomest man who ever walked the Denver streets. The eyes were blue and crackled with vitality. The hair was dark and curled in ringlets over a noble brow. Above a magnificently groomed and waxed mustache, the nose was patrician, ever so slightly aquiline. His chin and jaw were firm and prominent but subtly short of jutting. Although he stood only five feet ten, his erect, military bearing made him seem to tower over men much taller . . . Bonfils strode the earth like a conqueror."

During his lurid lifetime Bon was involved in more shady deals than any man of his time, if we are to believe the record as set down in Gene Fowler's book, as well as in Mr. Perkin's history. The stories told by Fowler and Perkin in print were common coin among the members of the *Post* staff and in the eccentric circles that made up the membership of the famous Denver Press Club.

Bonfils could engage himself in an incredibly ridiculous enterprise and still make it sound good. While I was in his employ he announced the establishment of The Frederick G. Bonfils Foundation for the

Betterment of Mankind and he made it appear to be far greater than all the big national foundations combined. I have heard that no one has ever been able to figure out the purpose of the Bonfils Foundation. There was a report given wide currency at the time that a large sum of money would be paid for the first round-the-world flight, nonstop, provided it started and ended on the pavement of Champa Street in front of the *Post* building. I suspect this report was a slight exaggeration, yet it sounds just like Bonfils.

He was one of the stingiest men who ever lived. After a three-day train trip from Denver to New York he would tip the Pullman porter a quarter and then likely give the man a solemn lecture about saving his money for the education of his children. Whenever Bon took a *Post* employee with him on a trip it was his custom to make the employee share traveling expenses. With all his money he once insisted that George Creel, then an important member of his staff, occupy a lower berth with him in order to save money. Creel got out of it by pretending that he was subject to conniption fits in the night.

On the staff of the *Morning Post* was a noodlehead who had been a professor at, I think, Harvard. I abhor the business of making a stereotyped noodlehead out of a college professor, but this one was a noodlehead. He was learned in the classics but he was junebug-daffy in all other directions. He was a distant relative of Bonfils, which explained his presence on the paper, and he was always referred to as The Professor.

Periodically this guy would walk into Bonfils' office and demand a ten-dollar pay cut. Now, you might think that a man of Bon's undisputed miserliness would be exultant in such a situation. Not so. To Bonfils, a man who would ask for a cut in salary was openly flouting one of Nature's first laws. He refused to consider it.

"But Mr. Bonfils," The Professor would plead, "I'm not worth what you're paying me. If you can't see your way clear to give me a ten-dollar reduction, *please* give me a five-dollar cut."

Bonfils would have nothing to do with such foolishness. Finally The Professor wrote a long and bitter note to Bonfils, declaring that he could no longer hold his head up in public while drawing a greater salary than he was worth, and left town.

He had good instincts, The Professor, and though he never seemed to fit into the staff's strange social life, he had a great yearning to *belong*. Once I invited him to a chili party at my house. I had a portable record-player and The Professor kept it going all evening

while he waltzed dreamily about the house with a straight-back chair
in his arms. He called the chair Xanthippe. Whenever the record-
player ran down he'd go to it and feed chili into the aperture where
the music came out.

"The poor little thing needs sustenance," he would say. He
jammed it full of chili and it was never of much use after that (my
chili was powerful even in the Denver days). And when the evening
was over I took The Professor to the door. He was a dignified man
and there was dignity and solemn good cheer in the arch of his neck
as he glanced back into the room for a final affectionate look at
Xanthippe. In parting he said:

"I want you to know that I have had the finest time of my life
tonight. And I want to compliment you on your chili. It was even
better than the chili at Childs'."

Bonfils was always seeking new ways to save money and once he
issued an order that in the future the middle names of people who
customarily used middle names were not to be used in the *Post*. Bon
had figured out on paper that if all middle names were eliminated the
annual saving to the *Post* would run to about a thousand dollars. I
was always expecting that he would order my by-line trimmed to
H. Smith.

At the time I worked for him Bonfils was approaching seventy and
he had a horror about old age. I remember that one of the first
stories I wrote for the *Morning Post* was about an "elderly" derelict
of seventy-three being found dead in an alley. A copyreader expunged
the word "elderly" and told me that it would have cost me my job if
it had got into the paper. Bonfils didn't permit use of the word on
anybody this side of a hundred.

I enjoyed being Bon's Fair-Haired Boy and did such an earnest
job of fair-hairing that I lasted longer than most. The important
thing was to get Bon's name into the paper, as legitimately as
possible, every day of the week; and even more important than that
was to find an excuse—legitimate, or fairly legitimate, or even
illegitimate—to get the boss's picture in the paper.

The sportsmen of Denver made this possible. They all knew the
proper course to follow. The moment a five-point buck was brought
down in the mountain forests, the slain animal was wrestled onto
the hunters' car, tied in place, and the car was driven at top speed
for Champa Street. Sometimes, I suspect, there were whole panzer
divisions of such cars racing down the mountain slopes headed for

the *Post* building. The moment one of them arrived a sentry in the business office would phone me. I'd alert a photographer and then go clattering down the iron stairs to make the arrangements. Then I'd dash back up and knock on Bon's office door and when he called me in I'd say, as if this was the first time it had ever happened, "Boss, there's a man down in the street got a beautiful five-point buck and he would like you to pose alongside of it." And Bon would say, "Why, I'd be happy to," and even if the President of the United States, or the *Post's* biggest advertiser, were in that room with him, he'd drop everything and head for the stairway and pose with the huntsman, shaking hands, the dead deer contemplating the classic scene with a glassy stare. And if it wasn't a deer it was a rainbow trout. The same procedure was followed by every fisherman who caught a sizable rainbow trout within a hundred miles of Denver. Once in a while there would be a deviation to break the monotony. I seem to recall a bear or two and I have a clear recollection of the time a cross-eyed lepidopterist arrived with a rare butterfly he had netted in the hills, and Bon posed holding it against his coat sleeve. My memory of this incident is distinct for two reasons. I had some difficulty writing the underlines for the picture because Bon's face did not appear. I called the butterfly by its Latin name and said, "it is shown being photographed while resting on the coat sleeve of Frederick G. Bonfils, publisher of the Denver *Post*." And I could never forget the conversation I had with Bonfils going back up the iron stairway after the picture had been taken. Suddenly he asked me why a butterfly is called a butterfly and I took a chance and said, "It's because they like to eat butter."

"Where do they get the butter to eat?" he asked, and I was in a momentary panic, but then I said, "Well, I suppose some people just leave butter out for them." I think I got away with it and I wouldn't be at all surprised to learn that Bonfils, a nature lover, took to setting out dishes of butter in Cheesman Park adjacent to his home.

My service as Fair-Haired Boy lasted until the *Morning Post* folded (the afternoon *Post* had its own Fair-Haired Boy) and it was after this event that Bonfils fell in love with the faun. A Denver hunter captured the faun somewhere in the mountains and brought the animal in alive for a photograph with Bon. He petted the animal and clucked and exclaimed over it so earnestly that the hunter made him a present of it. Bon sent out for a secondhand silver chain and a big dog-collar, secondhand. He brought that faun to work with him every morning and kept the unhappy creature in his office throughout the working day. The arrival of Bonfils and his deerlet each morning was a noisy affair because the animal had difficulty negotiating the iron stairway and made a tremendous clattering getting to the top. Sometimes Volney Hoggatt would get behind and give the faun a series of little boosts and when they finally made it, Bon would sweep into the city room triumphantly, sometimes dragging his reluctant pet, and then he would disappear into his office with the animal. Two or three times each day his door would open and Bon's handsome head would pop out. "George!" he'd cry, summoning the Negro janitor. "Oh, George! Hurry, George! Oh, George! *HURRY!*" And George would arrive on the run with broom and dustpan. This went on for several weeks and the atmosphere in Bon's office must have grown heavy, for he quit bringing the deer to work. I don't know what happened to it but I've always suspected that Volney Hoggatt may have poisoned it. Hoggatt was a genial, grinning man six feet and a half tall who apparently had been taking ugly pills all his life. He was Bon's bodyguard at home and abroad and he was jealous of any animal that captured the affection of his employer. Once when Bonfils was grieving over the death of his dog, Vol Hoggatt said to him, "But boss, you've still got *me!*" Whenever he found Bonfils in a depressed mood he had a way of bringing him out of it. He would spring into the air, turning a flipflop without ever touching his hands to the floor, and land on his feet with a big dumb grin across his face. The flipflop almost always brought a smile to Bon's countenance. Sometimes he even laughed, people said, but I doubt that. In all the time I was around him I never saw him laugh, never heard him laugh. He worshiped Calvin Coolidge.

Volney Hoggatt's job required that he sit in Bonfils' bedroom at night. In the last of many bitter court fights involving Bon, a document appeared which contained this paragraph:

> That because of the many and varied transactions in which he has been involved since 1881, he is subject to violent nightmares, and fears that in one of them he may reveal some of the shady transactions of his past, and requires a constant companion when asleep, so that he may be instantly awakened when seized by such spasms.

Our closest friends during the first part of our stay in Denver were the Joe Alex Morrises and the Morris Watsons. Watson was a good reporter and a swell writer. He had an enormous curiosity about the workings of the world and the nature of its inhabitants and he usually had a book in his pocket or under his arm wherever he went. Once he was assigned to the trial of a libel suit that had been brought against Bonfils. Bon insisted on having his paper's reporters sit beside him during a trial and it was his custom to whisper fiercely to them during the proceedings. It was said that this arrangement had a strong psychological effect on the enemy. In their view Bonfils was instructing his myrmidons in the violent language they were to use in their stories. Watson, who later got involved in a famous legal case as a result of his helping Heywood Broun start the Newspaper Guild, was sitting alongside Bon at this particular trial and the Governor of Colorado was in the witness chair, testifying against the *Post* publisher. Suddenly Bonfils turned to Watson and in a loud, clear voice, commanded: "Get up and hit that man! Go on! Hit him!" Watson was about to obey when the judge suggested in a kindly voice that he would appreciate it if Mr. Bonfils calmed down.

Morris Watson has told me that he got his job on the *Post* under a sort of contingency clause. They said he would have to prove himself, and his first assignment was a tough one. A Denver clergyman had absconded with church funds and one of his choir singers, and the local papers had been trying desperately to get an interview with the wife who had been left behind. She was interview-proof; she wouldn't let reporter or photographer get near her. And so Morris Watson was told to go get her side of the story.

He went to her house and knocked on the door a long time and then he heard her. She called out through the door that he should go away and then he heard a noise as if she were dropping to her knees and she began praying. "Oh, Father in Heaven," she pleaded, "must I be punished more and more?" She went on a bit and Morris realized that she was a deeply religious type of woman, and gabby religious to boot. He had, in his youth, held membership in seven different churches and he knew a thing or two about praying. So now he dropped to his knees and in a loud voice began imploring the Creator to interpose in his behalf. "Ask this God-fearing woman," Morris prayed, "to speak her mind about that husband who ran away with the money and Miss Crockett. Ask her to tell you, Lord, how it makes her feel!" And inside the door the deserted woman responded, "Oh, Lord, my husband is a dirty wretch. Who should know it better than I? From the day I first met him he was a sneak and a cheat and a dirty wretch. And as for that Crockett whore, if I could get my hands on her she would never look the same in this life."

And so Morris got his interview, through sort of supernatural means, and in the doing got his job on the *Post*.

Bonfils had a brother named Charlie who worked on the paper as a minor editor and who was as drab as his sibling was colorful. In 1928 the *Post* inaugurated a system of cash bonuses for the three best-written stories of the week. Charlie Bonfils was the judge. He was accustomed to do the judging each Monday immediately after lunch. His desk was in the middle of the city room and he would sit there with a pile of clippings, spending perhaps an hour reading them, scratching his head, holding a forefinger against his cheek, staring at the ceiling, debating the merits of the individual stories. It was probably the most important job they had ever given Charlie and he took it seriously. The prize for the best-written story was fifteen dollars, second prize was ten dollars, and third was five.

Fifteen dollars was a power of money and one Monday Morris Watson approached me and said there ought to be some lawful and ethical way of influencing Charlie Bonfils' judgment. He said he thought we ought to give mental telepathy a try. So as soon as Charlie went to work on the clippings, Morris and I took up a position where we could see which stories were under consideration. The moment Charlie picked up one of our own stories, we would close our eyes and concentrate hard and our lips would move in a sort of secular prayer:

"That's it, Charlie old boy! Pick that one, Charlie! Please pick that one! It's beautiful! Pick it for first, Charlie! Pick it! Pick it! Pick it!"

We kept this experiment going for two or three weeks and in that time Charlie awarded us just one five-dollar prize. The telepathy wasn't working too well so we abandoned it. Then one day Watson began a study of the winning stories which were always posted on the bulletin board. At last he came to me with a great discovery.

"I've got it!" he said. "I think I know how to get to Charlie. Use the word 'God' in your lead. Use it in the first sentence. I think it'll work."

A day or so later Morris was assigned to a story about a young lady who had killed herself in a cheap hotel room. She was broke and friendless and finished herself off with poison. Morris was there with the cops inspecting the body and the hotel room and a dreary rain had been falling for hours. He overheard one of the detectives say that in addition to all her other troubles, the girl had probably been depressed by the rain. Morris hurried back to the office and wrote his story. It began:

> Drip. Drip. Drip. Drip. Drip. Oh, God!
> If only the sun would shine!

Bang! Fifteen bucks. Charlie Bonfils awarded it first prize without a moment's hesitation.

Thereafter Morris and I went to astonishing lengths to work the word "God" into our leads. I can remember sitting at a typewriter and laboring almost an hour over an opening paragraph, trying to get God into it—stories about the price of a ton of coal, stories about the new airport, stories about lost dogs and weddings and distinguished visitors to our fair city. More often than not we arrived at ludicrous results and caught hell from the city desk, but whenever a story did get through with the word "God" in the first sentence, Charlie Bonfils never failed to give it a prize.

There was a related situation over at the *News* where Eddie Day, the managing editor, had a strange affection for any story that opened with the words, "Mystery surrounds . . ." There were no prizes involved but the boys on the *News* played their own little game, starting off their stories with those two words, knowing that Eddie Day would almost certainly schedule such stories for Page One. For a while in the columns of the *News* mystery surrounded quite a few things which were not surrounded by mystery at all.

All of this calls to mind the case of Edna Traylor. Edna was one of a whole battalion of girl reporters on the Bonfils papers. She was a pretty blonde girl on the smallish side and she always had a neat, scrubbed look which led some of us to refer to her as Edny, the 4-H Club Winner. Edna came out of Northwestern University and she had a predilection for certain words that were pure anathema to Bill Shanklin, the managing editor. Shanklin had a habit of standing up at his desk while reading proofs. Whenever he saw Edna's by-line over a story in proof he'd give that story a careful reading. It was almost a sure thing that somewhere in her story she would use "albeit" or "whilom" or "yclept." At first Shanklin talked to her quietly, like a father, asking her to forget such horrible words. But this did no good—Edna loved those words as devotedly as Shanklin hated them. I can remember seeing Shanklin standing there at his desk, reading proof, and suddenly he'd seize his head with both hands, turn his face toward the ceiling, and cry out:

"Oh, Jesus God! Oh God! That girl has done it to me again! She's used WYE-CLEPT again! Oh, God, please help me!"

He wasn't acting. And his abhorrence of certain words was not an uncommon trait. I have it myself as regards Edna's three words, plus "mulct." I once knew a copyreader who could not bear the sight of the word "ergo." Whenever "ergo" occurred in a piece of copy in his hands, he would scream like a water buffalo brought to childbed, rip the paper to shreds, hurl scissors and paste pot to the floor, knock over his chair, and start kicking the metal cabinet containing the world atlases. I used to put "ergo" into stories now and then simply because I enjoyed seeing him in one of his ergo rages. I must confess that he was eccentric in other directions and thought Mark Hellinger was a fine writer.

There were more girl reporters functioning in Champa Street than in any other newspaper shop I've ever seen. I have always had a strong prejudice against women reporters but it is a prejudice grounded in selfishness. I am speaking now of girls working off the city desk. A dame has certain advantages over a man in the reporting trade because of the mere fact that she is a girl, and that's not fair. She can easily wheedle her way past police lines at big fires and other disasters, whereas the cops might be inclined to tap male reporters lightly on the scalp with their billy clubs if the reporters got too frisky. Girls can gain entrance to houses and offices where gentlemen reporters might be thrown down the stairs. I have harbored this prejudice since Denver but I hasten to add that I have always been very fond of girl reporters *as girls*.

On the two *Post* papers we had Edna Traylor, albeiting and wye-clepting, and the brilliant Helen Strauss and frisky Cecelia Kelly who was killed in a plane crash while on assignment. There was Jessie Lamoreaux and Jessie Moffett and Wilda Vehlow, plus the most beautiful teen-age girl I believe I ever saw in my life, yclept Libbie Block, who grew up to become a successful fiction writer and who, yclept Mrs. Pat Duggan, is still my warm friend. She was sixteen when she came to work on the *Morning Post*. She was a bit naïve about some things and whenever she wanted to make a personal phone call she would walk across the room to Bill Shanklin's desk and pick up his phone and make her call. Shanklin was a strange man. He would get himself into a bursting rage over this girl's behavior, yet he could not bring himself to shriek at her to get the hell back over where she belonged. Instead, he would walk about ten feet away from his desk and then start striding around in a circle, uttering magnificent curses but only mouthing them, not letting the actual words come out. The veins would stand out on his forehead and he'd be clenching his fists and there were those of us who thought he would surely drop dead in his tracks. Yet he still couldn't bring himself to order that sweet little Libbie off his phone. Finally some of the other girls told her and she was surprised to learn that she had been an upsetting factor in Shanklin's life. "I only used his phone," she explained, "because I wanted a little privacy." Then there was the Wyoming cowgirl, Olga Moore, who later became a lobbyist in Washington and who turned out a book about her adventures hither and yon. The late Fred Allen once wrote a description of me which was somewhat less than flattering and, in fact, made it appear that I am as ugly as a Burmese gecko. I am, at last, able to contradict his blithesome libels with words written by Olga Moore. Recalling her Denver newspaper days, she said:

> Gene Fowler might be gone, but we had H. Allen Smith, who had not yet formed his famous preoccupation with totem poles and putty-knife factories. Allen was a slight, rather quiet youth about the office. He will hate me for revealing that his chiseled good looks caused some of the girls to call him "The Arrow Collar Man."

Hate you, Olga? I'll have you know I've had those words stenciled in gold on Pergamum parchment and hung in a worm-eaten frame above my bed.

The girls I have mentioned were all cityside reporters. There was also Frances Wayne, who was an institution at the *Post* and did a lot of private work for Bonfils. One Saturday Miss Wayne was leafing through a medical journal when she came upon an article discussing childbirth with special reference to the baby's own feelings and sensations at the very moment of being born. There was some speculation in the article over whether an infant suffers pain during the process of birth, and Miss Wayne thought this subject might be of interest to *Post* readers. She sat down and composed a small feature story and then certain doubts arose in her mind. Maybe the subject was too frank for treatment in a family newspaper. She took her story to Bonfils. He read it through with mounting excitement.

Then he dashed into the city room shouting for Bill Shepherd, one of his chief editors. On Sunday morning, with mighty political events occurring around the globe and horrible disasters reported in various localities, the *Post* hit the street with an eight-column bannerline in red ink, saying:

## DOES IT HURT TO BE BORN?

There were also assorted females engaged in departmental work, such as society and cooking and drama. There was one sweet young thing who served for a while as society editor of the *Morning Post* and who had a talent for malapropisms. She rarely let a day go by without creating some kind of fanciful and beautiful coinage. One day she wrote of how a local society leader had acquired "an expensive painting of Napoleon's son, La Leglong." And she once described a Denver family as being "famous for their longlivity." In her own little corner of the world this girl was a genius and I think she should have been given her head and told to write as she pleased. Longlivity is a much better word than longevity.

There was, too, one of my all-time favorite Denverites—the willowy and lovely Caroline Bancroft. Caroline was a Denver blueblood and was headed for leadership in Mile High society when she deliberately, while in full possession of all her faculties, talked Bonfils into letting her edit a book page in the *Post*. Up to that time, as I recall, book reviews and author gossip and all that high-toned crap had been confined to the pages of the *News*. But Miss Bancroft was acquainted with the world of literature and before she knew what was happening she was mixed up with the wild and irresponsible crowd of *Post* staffers who roared back and forth across town in those years.

By this time, as I shall relate in more detail shortly, I had emerged from my cocoon of abysmal ignorance and become book-crazy. So as soon as Miss Bancroft started her book page I began pestering her, pleading for the privilege of writing some reviews. Finally she gave me a war novel and I reviewed it. I said that it was the greatest war book ever written, not excluding *The Red Badge of Courage*. I made mention of *The Red Badge of Courage* to show that I had been around in the world of books; the fact is I had never read it but had only heard about it. The second book Caroline gave me was a collection of short stories and in my review I said that this was the greatest book of short stories ever published. Miss Bancroft spoke to me gently after that one, suggesting that I try to get control of myself, and gave me one more chance with a travel book called *The Desert Road to Turkestan*. This book, I wrote, was far and away the finest travel book ever put together by mortal man. I turned the review in and Miss Bancroft sadly struck me off the list of contributors to her book page. For what it's worth at this late date I would like to say that the war book I saluted was *All Quiet on the Western Front*. The book of short stories was *Round Up* by Ring Lardner. And *The Desert Road to Turkestan* was by Owen Lattimore, who hit the headlines many years later as one of Senator Joe McCarthy's chief adversaries.

I've forgotten which girl it was who did the Babe Ruth interview. Ruth and Lou Gehrig came to town on some kind of a barnstorming tour. As many already know, the Babe was a gross and vulgar man, much given to the steady employment of profanities and obscenities in his speech. He had grown up using such language and he never saw any reason for changing his habits. Nor could he ever understand why there was a double standard of dirty talk—why he could use certain words in the presence of men but never in the presence of women.

So it came about in Denver that the *Post* decided to send a girl around to interview the famous ballplayer and immediately there was alarm and apprehension in the Ruth-Gehrig camp. The Babe's managers and custodians were horrified at the thought of what might happen. So they sat down with him and had a long and serious talk. They explained that he should not use certain words in front of this girl who was coming to see him. They recited those words over and over to him, solemnly, speaking them the way a teacher says "cat" and "rat" to little children. They said he would have to be alert every instant, on guard against letting one of those words slip out. He growled and cursed and used some of the forbidden words now, saying he didn't see why the obscenity he had to change his ways for an obscenity broad from the obscenity newspapers. But they lectured and drilled him and then the girl arrived in the suite at the Brown Palace. Things went along swimmingly for a while and then the girl asked the Babe about the state of his health. He said he was in fine shape.

"Not a thing wrong with you physically?" she asked.

"Not a thing," said the Babe, "except I gotta get up in the night and go urinate."

His managers suppressed their groans, quietly seized their heads in their hands, closed their eyes, tried to force back the sobs. But the girl reporter breezed right along and in a few minutes departed.

"Good God!" they cried at the Babe. "After all we told you! After all your promises!"

Ruth had a look of perplexity on his face. What the obscenity had he done *now?*

"You had to go and tell her about getting up in the night!"

"Well, Jesus Christ," said the Babe, "I *said urinate*, didn't I?"

The top gal reporter over in Welton Street was Mary Coyle. She later married her boss, Bob Chase, and wrote the play *Harvey* which won her a Pulitzer prize, and other successful plays after that. She was a real rough-and-tumble fighter in the days of the Denver newspaper war. At that time the emphasis was more on getting pictures than on getting prose. All of us had to be accomplished picture-stealers because the rule in most cases was, first get the picture before the opposition gets it, and then worry about the story. We jimmied windows and crept up fire escapes and bribed apartment-house janitors in our quest for photographs of people who figured in the news, especially scandal-type news. I remember being in a semi-darkened room in the home of a woman who had committed suicide, and Mary Coyle was there. She was sitting on top of a bureau and we were awaiting the outcome of a family conference in another room and suddenly I noticed, in the dimness, that Mary was inching open the top drawer of that bureau and then her hand was creeping into it—she had seen someone slip some photographs into the drawer a bit earlier. I sidled over, nonchalantly smoking a cigarette, and suddenly gave the drawer a slam. It almost cut Mary's fingers off and she yelled like an asthmatic bobcat.

One of Mary's favorite stories about her newspaper years concerned her arrival at a Denver home after a wild, drunken family brawl in which three of the six people involved had been shot dead. Mary reached the house ahead of the police and identified herself to one of the surviving, blood-spattered men, and she has a vivid recollection of what he said to her: "Go on away. We've decided not to put anything about this in the papers."

# the pleasure of their company

One evening in November of 1928 a gang of us from the *Morning Post* staff went out to dinner. When we returned to the office we were greeted by a concatenation of hoots, catcalls, and bursts of demoniacal laughter from fellow employees and our attention was directed to the city room bulletin board. There it was: as of November 5th, meaning immediately, the *Morning Post* was suspending publication. Wham! Just like that.

Bonfils and Roy Howard had called off the war and now Denver had become a two-newspaper town. Most of us headed for the Press Club and there was a good deal of drinking. For the moment all was merriment and hilarity, as is the custom at wakes. For perhaps a week after that matters were confused. Nelle and I were now the parents of a son and our daughter would arrive in three months. During that bewildered week Walden Sweet and Josh Wilson and I organized the Young Newspapermen's Going Around and Cheering People Up Society. We, the dispossessed, were visited in our homes by laughing people bearing grog, and we in turn visited in the homes of others, bearing grog. Slowly people were making plans to head out for other climes. Most of us enjoyed the lunacy of youth and didn't worry much.

Then word came that Bill Shepherd, the grim and humorless managing editor of the evening *Post*, wanted to see a few of us. My name was on the list and I was offered a job on the afternoon paper. I took it. Robert Perkin says in his book: "Demobilization on Champa Street was abrupt. Virtually the entire staff on the *Morning Post* was summarily discharged, with neither thanks nor dismissal pay. H. Allen Smith, who had cannily acquired a skill in the highly specialized field of reporting Bonfils doings for Bonfils papers, was retained." Mr. Perkin is in error. I was kept on because of my Arrow Collar good looks.

Joe Alex Morris had already gone to New York where he joined the United Press. Morris Watson went to Chicago to work for the Associated Press. Some of the others, including Josh Wilson, settled in Wichita where the Levand brothers, old employees of Bonfils, had become publishers of their own paper.

Libbie Block says she remembers every detail of the Big Folding just as other people remember every detail of a great natural catastrophe, such as the election of a Republican. Libbie and I lived in the same part of town and eventually started for home on a streetcar together. I was somewhat drunk, and I began to grow a trifle maudlin about the plight of my little family, so Libbie—ever the fictioneer—quickly began inventing a story about how unhappy *she* was. Her parents, she said, had ordered her to marry a man much older than she, and he was ugly and smelled bad and she hated him, but she couldn't cross her parents because now she was jobless and no longer independent, and so she'd have to go ahead and marry him. I said, by god not as long as I drew breath. I went home with her and we rousted Dr. and Mrs. Block out of bed and I gave them a loud lacing down, told them they couldn't force Libbie into marrying that no-good smelly old bastard and pretty soon they were howling with laughter, and so was Libbie, and eventually so was I.

About the time that young Gene Fowler was working as a taxidermist's helper in Denver, a well-known local newspaperman named Arthur Chapman was writing the town's most famous poem, "Out Where the West Begins." For a time it was the most widely quoted verse in America and a framed version of it hung in the office of the Secretary of the Interior in Washington. The people loved it and I suppose some of them shed a sentimental tear as they throbbed it out, but in the eyes of the cynical Denver newspapermen of my generation the Chapman poem was unleavened corn. If you have never read it, here is how it began:

> Out where the handclasp's a little stronger,
> Out where the smile dwells a little longer,
>     That's where the West begins;

> Out where the sun is a little brighter,
> Where the snows that fall are a trifle whiter,
> Where the bonds of home are a wee bit tighter,
>     That's where the West begins.

Over the years outrageous parodies of the poem were written and the best of these, which I often heard recited in the Denver Press Club, began:

> Out where the handshake's a little freer,
> Out where the women have gonorrhear,
>     *That's* where the West begins.

The reason I bring up the Chapman poem is . . . but, hold! I haven't humored myself with a good digression for a while. Digressions are enjoyable affairs, especially since they irritate literary critics, and so I must tell a story about Arthur Chapman's son John, now drama critic of the New York *Daily News*. If you will permit me the brief pleasure of a digression from a digression, a tangent running off of a tangent, I might mention that the man John Chapman succeeded on the New York *News* was Burns Mantle, who started as a Linotype operator on a Denver paper. One evening, according to legend, the paper's drama critic got mulsified and couldn't write his review and Printer Mantle, who had seen the play in question, sat down at his Linotype and composed a masterful review out of his own head. Thus was born a drama critic. Now, back to John Chapman. He returned to Colorado for a visit in 1959. He was touring around the State and one evening stopped in a motel where the proprietor was a tall, slim-hipped, handsome, deep-voiced and clear-eyed gent, "every inch a Westerner." This noble-seeming character soon found out that John was from New York and then that John was connected with the theater in New York. What a coincidence! "Small world!" exclaimed the handsome frontiersman. Then he revealed that he himself had started life in New York and had worked for the famous Frank E. Campbell funeral establishment. And as for his connection with the legitimate theater, "I," he announced proudly, "embalmed Jeanne Eagels." Now, back to Arthur Chapman and his poem. I have always nursed a small resentment against the vulgar parodies of "Out Where the West Begins." These parodies were incited by the sentimentality contained in the original and if there is one thing a Voltairian newspaperman despises, it's sentiment. In this particular issue, however, I enter a dissenting opinion. I *like* Arthur Chapman's poem because I am sentimental about Denver. I can say in all honesty that never in my life have I enjoyed the company of men as much as I enjoyed those I worked with in Denver. And I loved the city itself. For all the hugger-mugger and skulduggery that went on in the town, I enjoyed living there. I'd go back and live there now if it were not for the winters. Oh, I know. They say it's a *dry* cold and therefore invigorating. That statement always reminds me of a cartoon I saw years ago, showing two workmen leaning on their shovels in front of a huge open door in a blast furnace. One was saying to the other: "Yeh, but it's a *dry* heat."

The people I worked with in Denver were, for the most part, highly competent in their jobs and some of them were brilliant. There was among them, in fact, a greater degree of excellence than in any comparable group of newspapermen I know about in New York City. They worked hard and they played hard and they were splendid company. There was a forthrightness and a sincerity about them in their relationships with one another that I've seldom encountered anywhere else. The best of them befriended me and treated me as their equal and put up with my ignorance. The important thing is, they made an unadvertised effort to guide me out of that ignorance. I got my education in Denver.

Back in Florida on my nineteenth birthday Nelle gave me a book—the complete stories of O. Henry. I read every one of them. I fairly gobbled them down. It was the first book I had read with relish since my days with Tom Swift and the Indians of the Joseph Altsheler books. I went mildly insane about O. Henry and was unhappy when I had finished the book because there were no more O. Henry stories to read.

In Tulsa and now in Denver the newspapermen I ran with talked about things that were not known to me. They talked about authors, and about the things that authors write, and I began to feel self-conscious about my lack of knowledge. One day I told Morris Watson, who seemingly had read everything, that I had the itch to read some books and I asked him what I should start with. He steered me immediately to H. L. Mencken and started me with *The American Language* and some of the *Prejudices*. Then I went out and bought a big, fat, one-volume edition of *The Outline of History*. I threw up my hands and quit half a dozen times in the first fifty pages of the H. G. Wells book. All that fossil stuff, all that universe and its mileages, all that Azoic and Proterozoic and Paleozoic and Mesozoic and Cainozoic and then those Carboniferous things and prehistoric monsters with their crazy names. What the hell did I care about all that? But I knew I had to get those things into my head, that I had to learn to spell pterodactyl, and so I laid in a supply of notebooks and began jotting things down as I read. Finally I made it to People. From then on I had no trouble. A single paragraph in Wells would lead me to other books and I began to accumulate a small library made up largely of history and biography. Morris Watson suggested more titles, and Josh Wilson set me onto Plutarch, and Lee Casey put me to work on Gibbon, and finally Sidney Beaumont Whipple took over my education, starting me off with *Pickwick Papers*.

Nelle and I rarely went out to the movies and we didn't roam the nearby mountains as we might have done. We stayed home. I spent almost all my spare hours reading and taking notes. Every week was cram week with me, and it was real hard work because I had almost no foundation to build on—keep in mind that I hadn't gone to high school or college. Many years later I found out that I was in fair company when I heard Jack O'Connell and Wolcott Gibbs discussing an article for *Cosmopolitan* magazine about people who had not enjoyed the benefits of a formal education. Gibbs said: "In my opinion the four most distinguished people who made it without a college education were Jesus Christ, Abraham Lincoln, Kid Chocolate and Eleanor Roosevelt."

Some years ago Dr. Bergen Evans, professor of English at Northwestern University (I feel sure he didn't teach *albeit* and *whilom* and *yclept* to Edny the 4-H Club Winner) took a strange notion into his head and edited a book of selections from my writings. Subsequently Dr. Evans wrote me a letter which is now one of my proudest possessions. If I had a grain of modesty in me I would not be sitting here writing my autobiography, so I present now a portion of the English professor's letter:

> The more I read of your stuff, the more favorably I was impressed and in going back to try to analyze why it took time, I realized that it was the cumulative effect of little things whose significance, in context, could easily escape first notice. Take one thing about your writing that impresses me very much— yet it is something that I am finding it hard to express except in a naked, dull statement—your courage. I just can't call to mind anywhere in the whole twelve or thirteen volumes a single place where you have pandered to vulgar prejudices, where you have

pulled a single punch or said a single thing in order to avoid offending some moron . . .

There's another thing about your writing—if you'll let me talk on and get it over with: I am fascinated at the correspondence of our ideas. I haven't found a single major thought or taste on which we disagree. Now, you quit school after the eighth grade which by modern U.S. standards is very little education. I went through High School, through College, through two graduate schools, and acquired, literally, more letters after my name than in it. What did I get for my time and money? If schools were what the ignorant believe they are, you and I ought not to speak the same language . . . It is silly, even to point an argument, for me to say that you are literate. I wish I were half so much so.

One of the choice annual assignments in Denver was that of covering the Cheyenne Frontier Days rodeo. I was given the job two years in a row, first as representative of the *Morning Post* and later as underwriter, so to speak, of Ray Humphreys, who was the star reporter of the afternoon *Post*. I got this prize assignment because I was facile with dialect, knew that Cheyenne was Ole Shy Ann, that a horse was a cayuse and a cow was a critter and a contestant was a cow waddy or a tophand or a saddle tramp. It was said that a Denver reporter once went to the Ole Shy Ann rodeo and wrote a story in which he called a horse a horse. His body was found next morning hanging from a cottonwood tree.

Ray Humphreys was a writer of Western fiction for the pulp magazines. It was his custom when he wrote his Western yarns—he turned out one short story every Sunday afternoon—to give his kookier characters and his nastiest villains the names of people on the *Post* staff. The real slobs in his stories were usually called Joe McMeel or Joe Cook or Hoss (for Horace) Stewart. Ray found it quite difficult to call a cow waddy by such a name as H. Allen Smith but eventually I made the grade and was immortalized in Western fiction as a wandering Englishman with bowler hat and monocle, an incredible bird-brain, a horse's behind in the cow country.

In Cheyenne we lived at the Plains Hotel and drank mountain rotgut and shot craps with bronc riders and bulldoggers and moved in the company of pleasant people. T. Joe Cahill, who has long been the foremost citizen of Cheyenne, was then press agenting the rodeo. Teejoe, as we called him in print, ranks right up there with Dexter

Fellows among the great popular press agents of our time. When I first arrived in New York the rodeo had just been installed as an Eastern attraction. It was organized and staged in Madison Square Garden and Teejoe was brought to New York to publicize it. Along came one of the radio networks with an idea—they wanted a girl bronc rider to broadcast from the leaping saddle. They hooked up a microphone and fastened it firmly under her chin and strung a mile of coiled wire away from it and then the gal came out of Chute Number Four. The cayuse was a real wild one. The girl was supposed to speak her feelings and fears as she went bobbing and jerking across the arena. What the radio audience heard was this: "Ooph. Ooph. Ooph. Ooph. Ooph." And so on until she was thrown to the ground.

Jack Foster covered the Cheyenne rodeo for the *News* and he and I became good friends and worked together later in New York. He is now editor of the Rocky Mountain *News* and I hear tell he's the best the paper ever had in its hundred years of existence.

In Cheyenne I met quite a few celebrities. One evening Ray Humphreys introduced me to Courtney Ryley Cooper, who had grown up as a newspaperman in Denver and then become a prosperous fiction writer. Subsequently he acquired a big house near the Rex Beach mansion in my Florida town, Sebring. Cooper was a top circus buff from his youth on and once worked for Buffalo Bill as well as Ringling Brothers and Barnum & Bailey. On his estate at Sebring his rose garden was shaped in the form of a circus ring with Roman chariots and other tanbark equipment scattered over the premises. Sounds a little nutty to me. I remember Cooper for a story he told that evening in Cheyenne. He had just recently attended a boxing match between two second-rate heavyweights. One of the fighters was punchdrunk to begin with and was out on his feet at the conclusion of the bout. A radio man got into the ring and thrust a mike into the beaten bum's face and yelled, "Say something to the radio audience!" The fighter blinked a couple of times, thrust his lower jaw forward so he'd look ferocious, and then announced: "I wanna fight Toooooo-ney!" Gene Toooooo-ney was champ at the moment.

In Cheyenne, too, I met Will Rogers. A statement that has become a reverential part of American folklore is the one attributed to Rogers: "I never met a man I didn't like." It is quoted constantly, it is engraved on the base of the Will Rogers monument in Oklahoma, and I have read that it was once printed on a United States postage stamp. In a book containing his fragmentary writings I have found a more likely version which goes: "I joked about every prominent man of my time, but I hardly ever met a man I didn't like." There is one hell of a heap of difference between the two. If he *did* say "I never met a man I didn't like" then, in my opinion, he was guilty of uttering one of the stupidest statements of all time. Further than that, if he did say it that way, he was telling a lie. He met *me* and he didn't like me.

One day I was sitting with other reporters in the press box at Cheyenne waiting for the show to start. A report reached us that Will Rogers had come to Cheyenne unannounced and was somewhere over in the arena. The assembled reporters decided that since Rogers was writing a daily newspaper piece, it would be nice to have him watch the rodeo from the press box and we would all get to dress up our stories with comical quotes from him, and so I was appointed a committee-of-one to go find him and extend the invitation. I crossed the track and wandered around the dusty arena and finally I located him. He had been talking to a couple of cowboy contestants but now he had turned and was walking toward the chutes. I intercepted him. I introduced myself and then told him how we would enjoy having him sit in the press box.

"No," he said, sharply and abruptly.

I decided that maybe he was being funny, such being his trade.

"Ah, come on," I said, grinning at him. "It's nice over there, out of the sun, and we'd all feel honored if you'd join us."

"Listen, kid," he said to me. "Go on back to your little press box and don't bother me. I don't wanna sit in your little press box. Now go away and leave me alone."

The pure nastiness of the Oklahoma lardhead nearly knocked me down. I wanted to speak a two-word expletive to him—an expletive that later became extremely popular in the armed forces of our land. But I stood there a moment in confusion and then I turned and made my way back and told the newspaper gang what he had said. They spoke the two-word expletive, changing the pronoun from "you" to "him."

I have read somewhere that when Irvin S. Cobb arrived in New York and got a job as a reporter he tried to interview a man he worshiped, Mark Twain, and Mark Twain was rude to him. This experience, I read, all but scarred Irvin Cobb for life—he never really got over it. I was not scarred for life by Will Rogers. I don't think I was scarred for more than maybe ten minutes.

I've met many a man I didn't like, and I've met many a man I liked tremendously and, as I've said, Denver harbored a good portion of the latter. So many names come back to me. There was old Otto Floto who gave his name to the Sells-Floto Circus and who was a sort of sports editor emeritus at the Denver *Post*. He was a celebrity and I used to hang around him in the sports department. Like many another man he enjoyed playing hero, and so he tolerated me.

Floto was one of Jack Dempsey's close friends and after Dempsey lost at Chicago he headed for California in a private railroad car, traveling over the Union Pacific. At Cheyenne the car was diverted and sent down to Denver so Dempsey could have an hour's visit with Floto. The old sports editor went to the city desk and asked that I be assigned to sit in on the meeting and so I went with him to the Union Station. Dempsey's car was shunted onto a siding in the yards and Otto Floto and I, with a photographer, went aboard. I sat off to one side and listened while the two old friends talked, and Dempsey was terrific, and self-deprecating, and I'd have consumed a bushel of nux-you-ated iron pills on the spot if I'd had them. As I remember Otto Floto was one of several big-name sports writers in Denver who couldn't write and who were reputed to be somewhat illiterate. They "talked" their sage opinions to sports writers who knew about commas and making paragraphs and starting sentences with capital letters and all that.

There was one sports writer on the *Morning Post* who could certainly write. He was Jack Hellman, brother of the Sam Hellman who in those days was widely popular for his humorous magazine stories. Jack later became a mainstay of V*ariety's* Hollywood edition and is there yet. One day he attended a Denver baseball game in which the score was something like 28 to 13. I'll never forget the lead Jack Hellman wrote on his story. It started off this way:

> Long years ago when I was a wee bit of a lad my sainted mother called me to one side and said, "My boy, I want you to promise me just one thing—don't ever, so long as you live, don't *ever* become a baseball scorekeeper." Yesterday her infinite wisdom was demonstrated when . . .

That opening paragraph made as profound an impression on me as the purloined description of the weeping Florida skies and Jack Hellman became another one of my heroes and remains so to this day.

I think I made it clear a while back that my attitude toward books and authors changed decidedly in Denver. One of the girl reporters on the *Post*, knowing of my new weakness, came to me one day with the exciting news that Dr. Will Durant had just come into town for a lecture. I made a telephone check of the hotels and located him at the Cosmopolitan. On the phone I assumed the nonchalant air of a knowing newspaperman and told Dr. Durant that I would like to pay him a visit. He set the hour and I went out and spent grocery money on a copy of his best seller, *The Story of Philosophy*. I then approached Johnny Day, my city editor, and asked if I might do an interview with the distinguished visitor and Mr. Day gave me his famous darkling look and said, "Listen, you idiot, don't you even know that Durant writes a column for the opposition?" Denver city editors were more gentlemanly to their reporters in my time than they were in the time of Gene Fowler.

Dr. Durant was writing something when I got to his room and he was a bit cool toward me. He took my copy of his book without saying anything profound or friendly and sat down and wrote at the top of the flyleaf, "Will Durant." I was right there, hanging over his shoulder, panting on his neck like a hot basset hound, and I uttered an impassioned protest: "Oh, please, Doctor! I wanted you to autograph it to me personally!" He sighed and asked me my name and then under his own name quickly scribbled, "to H. Allen Smith. Denver. 2–6–28." Then he slammed the front cover shut and thrust the book at me, almost violently. His actions were telling me to get the hell out of there and let him finish his work, but I was too stuperous with glory to know it. Instead of getting the hell out of there I planted myself in a chair, assumed what I thought to be an air of philosophic perspicacity, leaned forward just a bit, and said:

"Now. Tell me all about it."

Dr. Durant stared at me as if I had suddenly turned into an ill-disposed adder. Then he said:

"Young man, I am busy. Please go."

It was what you might call a strong hint, and I took it. The whole mortification of the thing didn't come down upon me for a while because I had that autographed book. I still have it and I get it out and look at the inscription now and again just to prove to myself that I am licensed to criticize the congenital wrongheadedness of the human race. I am licensed to do it because I am myself wrongheaded. It takes a schnook to know a schnook.

A newspaperman, if he wanted to retain his membership in the fraternity of amiable cynics, was supposed to embrace certain standard opinions. One of these was the belief that the greatest stuffed shirt in the United States, therefore in the world, was Dr. Nicholas Murray Butler, long president of Columbia University. I really don't know why this should have been. In the 1920s all you had to do to raise the hackles of the average newspaperman was to mention Dr. Butler's name. Even my old friend Hugh Troy used to think of Dr. Butler in terms of stuffiness. Hugh nursed the ambition to set up an ingenious and complicated practical joke, which required that he buy out the entire orchestra section of the Metropolitan Opera House on opening night. He would then issue the tickets for all of the seats and every person in those chairs would have thick black hair save only a certain number of bald men. These would be located in such a pattern that, viewed from the balconies and the Golden Horseshoe, their bald heads would spell out a four-letter word. The dot over the *i* would be provided by the bald head of no less a person than Dr. Nicholas Murray Butler.

I had absorbed enough of the cynical attitude to make me disrespectful toward Dr. Butler and then he passed through Denver on his way to make a speech somewhere. He was spending the night at the Brown Palace and I was assigned to interview him. It was a routine assignment, calculated to produce a half column of type at the most, and I approached it with routine enthusiasm, meaning none. I sat down with Dr. Butler and asked him a couple of dumb questions, such as "How do you like the invigorating Colorado climate?" and "What do you think of the glorious future of Denver?" He ignored my questions and began pouring words at me.

I came away with a story that was splashed all over Page One and tricked up with boxed excerpts of "Butlerisms" and a by-line that looked as big as a Buick. This performance enhanced both my income and my reputation; everyone thought my cleverness was responsible for the splendid story and I was given a raise. Chunks of the interview were even put on the press association wires and sent around the country because it was election time and Dr. Butler denounced prohibition and praised Al Smith. Yet my part in the thing was extremely minor. I had been no more than a stenographer recording the sentences of a man engaged in taking the world apart while happily in an eloquent mood. So far as Nicholas Murray Butler was concerned I, Smith of Denver, was a mere recording machine, a chunk of metal, a piece of wood, a nothing. I don't remember much of what Dr. Butler said there in the Brown Palace but I do recall that I came face to face with him several years later when I was on an assignment at Columbia University in New York. I looked up and there he was, crossing the sidewalk to get to his car. He looked at me and I looked at him. I recognized him instantly. And did he recognize me for the bright young man who had done such a magnificent job interviewing him in Denver? In a pig's behind. He brushed past me and said, addressing his chauffeur: "I've got to deliver a package."

CHAPTER 16

# youngest old reprobate
# on Earth

Yet in Denver all was not beer and skittles. There was more to
it than sugar moon and bottle pool. Every experience was not a
joyous and pleasant one. There came one of those bitter Colorado
mining strikes and Eddie Eisenhand, a handsome young photographer who later married Edna Traylor, the yclept-writer, went with
me into the mountains to get some interviews with strikers and
their families. I can't remember the town we visited but it was a
coal-mining community. Eddie and I somehow blundered into a
barn-like building on the edge of the town and found ourselves surrounded by a mob of menacing Wobblies—the name given to miners
who belonged to the International Workers of the World. I will take
oath that almost all of these Wobblies had black mustaches and
blacker scowls and spoke in heavy foreign accents. They didn't like
us. The Denver *Post* was the tool of the interests, the mouthpiece
of the capitalistic bosses, and those Wobblies said so in loud and
angry and accented voices. Some of them had two-by-four clubs in
their hands and they formed a circle around us and the circle kept
getting smaller and they kept snarling and shouting about the
dirty peeg Denver *Post* sonabitch. Then they got close enough to
begin spitting on us and I arrived at the reluctant conclusion that my
string had run out. It was clear that in the interests of the working
man and international solidarity they were going to kill us. Then a
man who had the biggest mustache and the loudest voice began
yelling at them to leave us alone, and the mob backed off enough
to let us get away. Those Colorado mountains are the home of the
quaking aspen, which is the thing that people always shake like.

Eddie Eisenhand and I shook like. It was a real frightening experience and turned me against organized labor and strikes, for a full twenty-four hours.

There was a reporter on our paper named Paxton Dent who, in conversation, frequently used the term "pseudo" in combination with other words, and he did an interesting job of mispronouncing it, always calling it suede-o. Along with other members of the *Post* staff I was a suede-o detective for a while. By this time I think it has been established that Mr. Bonfils was penurious. There was, as always, another libel suit and the trial was approaching so about half the reportorial staff was assigned to "jury duty." Mr. Bonfils was not one hundred per cent stingy in this particular operation. He let us rent automobiles for the work because it needed to be done in a hurry and it involved traveling all over the city of Denver. His attorneys had the complete jury panel list, with addresses. We had to visit all of these people who might be called as jurors in the libel trial and find out everything we could about their political beliefs, their religion, their income, their lodge affiliations, their past histories, and most important of all—what they thought of the Denver *Post* and its publisher. This sort of investigation was not too difficult and Mr. Bonfils thought it was altogether honest because when we called on these people we always told them that we worked for the Denver *Post*. We told them we were in the circulation department, interested in getting new subscribers and finding out how old subscribers liked the way the paper was going. We made our calls in the daytime when most husbands were at work or drunk in bed. It was best to talk with the wives because women are usually more courageous and more forthright in stating their opinions on controversial subjects. A man might say that in his opinion Mr. Bonfils had done many fine things for the city but there were a few other things that were, well, maybe just a mite questionable. His wife, however, would be more likely to say, "Why, they ought to take that Corsican bastard out and hang him!"

We made copious notes during these interviews and when the whole operation was finished Mr. Bonfils had a pretty complete dossier on every person who might appear in the jury box when his trial was called. The most interesting thing I learned on this assignment was that people, as a general rule, are consistent in their beliefs and their conduct. Time and again I sat and listened while sedate citizens of Denver cursed Bonfils and his newspaper, calling the *Post* a disgrace to humanity, a lying and thieving rag. So I'd ask them what paper they read. The Denver *Post*. And how long had they been reading it? As long as they could remember.

The final six or eight months of my life in Denver were spent covering the West Side Court. This was the building which housed the criminal courts and Johnnie Day assigned me to it permanently. Ray Humphreys had resigned from the *Post* to become chief investigator for the District Attorney's office, which was in the West Side Court building. He and his assistants conducted frequent raids on bootlegging establishments and there was always an adequate supply of sugar moon stashed around the building. One of the assistant district attorneys and I had dozens of bottles hidden behind the books in the law library which was in the basement of the building. My story wouldn't be complete if I failed to tell of my majestic performance in The Case of the Boy Bandits. One day I overstayed my lunch period down among the law books. Upstairs several teenage boys were on trial for sticking up a whole string of filling stations. The Case of the Boy Bandits was being given a big play in the papers because they had come close to killing a few people in their robberies. I sat in the basement for a long time, brooding over the fate of those nice, clean-cut lads, feeling sorry for them, knowing their lives were being blighted, that they'd probably go to the awful state pen for years and years. At last I got to my feet and mounted the spiral stairway leading to the main floor. I walked into the courtroom where the boys were on trial and where my friend, the co-owner of the booze, was at that moment addressing the jury, denouncing those hopeless boys, demanding that they be sent to prison. I walked up to the assistant district attorney, took him by the arm, pointed to his chair and said, "Go sit down!" He was so astonished that he obeyed me. Then I whirled and launched into a speech in defense of the Boy Bandits. I didn't get far because by this time the judge and everyone else had recovered from the unexpectedness of my take-over, and the judge was whamming with his gavel and a bailiff rushed up and seized me and a recess was called. Happily the judge and everyone else loved me for my good nature and my sterling character and my industry and wisdom and for the fact that I could put their names in the paper every day, and so I was not sent to jail and the whole matter was hushed up. The judge, a warm friend of mine, did preserve his own personal integrity and his judicial dignity by telling me that if anything similar ever happened in or near his courtroom he would horsewhip me in public.*

At this time the *News* was in money trouble and cutting down its staff and its reporter was withdrawn from the West Side Court. General assignment men were sent over only when big cases were breaking or important trials in session. Possibly the best reporter on the *News* at the time was a quiet, tall, slender character named Wallis Reef. Every time that guy came sauntering into the court building I knew I was in trouble. He'd walk in and loaf around a while, acting as if he'd just happened by and needed to rest his feet, and then the next morning the *News* would burst forth with a big exclusive story from the DA or some judge, and then Johnnie Day would eat my butt out, saying, "For Christ's sweet sake can't you learn to keep an eye on that goddam Wally Reef?" I never learned to do it.

Still, I couldn't have asked for a better assignment than I had, considering it from the standpoint of educational value. I covered various murder trials which were quite sensational locally, and I fraternized with prosecutors and jailers and judges and cops and even got to know some of them socially. I spent long days sitting in courtrooms until I could have performed the work of judge, prosecutor, or defense counsel quite adequately. I passed hundreds of hours listening to the business of jury selection. This was considered a dull and tedious procedure, but it wasn't to me. In theory a jury panel was made up of representative citizens. This was the average man, the man in the street. Well, not quite that. A juror ought to be a cut or two above the average man because he is a property owner. And these are the people, the so-called peers or equals, of those who are on trial. They render judgment. I have carefully refrained from all criminal activities throughout my adult life for the simple reason that I do not want such people passing judgment on me. And I have found that my opinion has not changed either with the passage of time or with geographical change. Several years ago I was called for jury duty in Westchester County, New York. There were a couple of hundred of us assembled on a Monday morning in a big room at White Plains. The jury clerks gave us each a card

---

* What ever happened to the good old American custom of horsewhipping an editor? I don't think an outraged citizen has ever walked into the Time & Life building and horsewhipped Henry Luce. The old customs vanish. Alas.

containing a simple questionnaire which we were to fill out. It called for such basic information as name, age, address, place of birth, occupation, criminal record, name of wife or husband if any, and a couple of other things no more complicated. It took all day to get those cards filled out properly. A majority of the men and women in that room were unable to understand what was meant by the words "occupation" and "place of birth" and "marriage status." They'd carry their cards up to the clerks and the clerks would look at them and with remarkable patience say, "No. You *still* don't understand. You'll have to try again." So they'd hand out another card and the "peer" would go back and start over, and foul it up once more. Those people were not competent to pass judgment on a bucket of hog livers. I'm keeping my nose clean.

One other thing I remember about the jury panels in Denver. I should have felt offended because those people made it clear that nobody ever reads the news stories that appear in the daily papers. Almost always, in every case, the prospective jurors would be asked:

"Have you read about this case in the newspapers?"

The most common answer was: "Only the headlines." Sometimes they only *glanced* at the headlines. But they never read all that stuff that was stuck on below the headlines. Never the stuff that I wrote, or the other reporters wrote. We were just wasting our time. Often the jurymen would say, "I don't read nothin' but the sports page," or, "I never read nothin' but the comics." Or even, "I don't never read nothin' but the sports page and the comics." Thinking back, I don't believe I ever heard a juror say he had ever read a single line of straight news in his daily paper.

One crime story I'll long remember fell into the hands of a friend of mine, Gene Lindberg, who was working at the time at the *News*. A cruddy little passion play came to town and opened a run in a crummy little theater. After the first performance the men who portrayed Jesus and Judas Iscariot went out and got drunk. They were weaving along Sixteenth Street and had reached Joslin's dry goods store when they got into a dispute. It culminated with one punching the other and knocking him through the store's show window. Gene Lindberg covered the arrests and then went to his office to write the story. An inspiration came to him and he asked if he might compose the head for the story, and was told he could. And so he wrote:

JESUS SETTLES 2000-YEAR-OLD GRUDGE:
KNOCKS JUDAS THROUGH PLATE GLASS WINDOW

Gene's story was used but his headline was killed. I feel almost certain that Bonfils would have given his approval to the head and the devil take anybody who complained.

Into Denver came a visitor named John P. Medbury, an authentic newspaper humorist. Medbury was of the Bugs Baer school, writing a daily syndicated column made up usually of humorous paragraphs. He was touring the West in a big automobile, accompanied by his first wife, his second wife, and his son. His first wife was the mother of the young boy and came along on the trip to look after him. His second wife came along because she was married to him. This arrangement seemed a little strange to me, but I was told that it worked out well and there was no fighting.

I attached myself to Mr. Medbury at once. His column was used in the *Post* and Mr. Bonfils asked him to stay around town for a week or so and write some special stories. The *Post* was, at that moment, engaged in a loud crusade against the location of the new airport. The *Post* said that political blackguards owned property in the very section where they were planning the big airport, and this was not nice. The political blackguards denied it, and said that the truth was, Bonfils owned a lot of acreage out in another section of town and that was where *he* wanted to have the airport built. So Bonfils asked Mr. Medbury to write some articles about the political blackguards and make them out to be ridiculous poops. Mr. Medbury did. It is my impression that the airport was built at the location where the political blackguards owned property, and not at the location where Bonfils owned property.

Mr. Medbury had a wide reputation as a spur-of-the-moment practical joker and I had an opportunity to see him in spontaneous and unrehearsed action. He and I walked down Champa Street one afternoon and stopped at the corner drugstore for cigarettes. Mr. Medbury had on a white shirt and no coat and yellow plus fours (so called because they were usually four inches longer than standard knickers) and in addition to all that, he had the general demeanor of a drug clerk. We were standing in the store when a man walked up to Mr. Medbury and said he would like to have a toothbrush. Mr. Medbury let his mouth fall open slightly and then stared at the man in disbelief and finally said:

"Did you say toothbrush?"

"Yes. A toothbrush."

"A toothbrush!" Mr. Medbury repeated. "You got hair growing on your teeth and you want to brush it?"

It was now the customer's turn to register shock. Then he exploded. He announced that he had been insulted and he demanded to see the manager.

"I am the manager, you miserable, hairy-toothed old goat," said Mr. Medbury firmly, "and if you don't get the hell out of my store I'll call the police."

The man hesitated, then turned and hurried for the door.

I have set down this little story not because I think it is screechingly funny but to show how far Mr. Medbury would go when a prankish mood was upon him. That customer was a good plus four taller than Mr. Medbury and might have killed him; moreover, if the real manager of the store had overheard the colloquy, *he* might very well have killed Mr. Medbury. It takes guts to be comical.

The Denver Press Club occupied its own two-story building, which had been erected and dedicated in the early 1920s. It stood off by itself and was not, as I remember, attached to any other structure. This isolation was thought necessary because of round-the-clock roarings and bellowings of the membership, and the occasional shattering of furniture. If they were nothing else, the members were considerate of their neighbors.

I have been in many press clubs in my life but this one was easily the best of them all. It had been laid out properly at the beginning. Upstairs, for example, there was a paneled library with shelves covering all four walls and easy chairs and divans. It was felt that a press club would not be complete without a library but it was also felt that if any member wanted to read a book the proper place for such a laudable pursuit was in his home; therefore there were no books on the shelves.

The true reason why the Denver Press Club was superior to others lay, of course, in the quality of its membership. No women were allowed across the threshold although I have heard that sometimes, late at night, some of the boys would smuggle a dame or two in, by way of the back door, and sneak them upstairs to the library where they had those easy chairs and divans. This was a serious breach of the regulations, however, and was severely punished whenever the offenders were caught at it. They were told they shouldn't oughta do such things and please don't do it any more.

There was a poker game that never seemed to end, going on week after week and month after month. There was a pool table. We spent many hours at Kelly pool or bottle pool and in one of these games a senseless but eloquent cry of despair was originated by Walden Sweet. Upon missing an easy shot Mr. Sweet, an erudite man of ponderous proportions, beat a furious tattoo on the floor with his cue stick and cried out in mortal agony, "Good Godley, Young Wadley!" Thereafter this ejaculation became as common among Denver newspapermen as the earlier Cleavely windbreak cry at the Huntington *Press*.

There is an apposite beauty surrounding certain incidents attending the grand opening of the Press Club. The day before the great event it was discovered that there was a shortage of drinkables. Keen minds went to work on the problem. It was learned that cops attached to the District Attorney's office had seized a truckload of bonded whisky and the contraband had been taken to the West Side Court.

Red Feeney, a reporter who knew the vanity of policemen, and Harry Rhoads, then a *News* photographer and still a *News* photographer, were sent to get the story and pictures. They had the officers lug the whisky outdoors and stack it under a tree and then they lined the heroic cops up for a picture. Harry Rhoads loaded his flash gun with enough powder to hole through the Moffat Tunnel and then he set it off. A vast cloud of acrid smoke spread over the scene and before it drifted away Red Feeney had transferred two cases of the vintage booze to his car. Harry Rhoads waited till the cops had quit coughing and their tears had ceased and then announced that he had neglected to insert a plate in his camera and would the boys please keep their places for just one more. He gave them another tunnel-opener and Feeney made it to the car with two more cases of bonded. When last I heard of him Harry Rhoads was in his seventies and still on the job and still telling that story, although through the years he has dressed it up a bit, saying that Red Feeney piled enough whisky into the car to service the Press Club for a year. I have used my customary honesty and restraint. I never exaggerate. I think four cases is aplenty. Well, maybe six.

I first got acquainted with Fred Othman of the United Press at the Denver Press Club, and the novelist Clyde Brion Davis who worked on the *News*. I frolicked there with Kaspar Monahan and Horace Stewart and Gene Cervi and Jean Bosquet and Ray Black. A steady customer was Frank White, a former drama critic whose father had been a drama critic before him. Mr. White was author of the finest play ever set to paper and if pressed would sometimes recite it. I don't remember its title but Mr. White used to say: "No matter what anybody else has accomplished, I can always lay claim to one distinction. I am the author of the shortest play ever written."

The drama has a single stage setting: the dreary living room of a New England farmhouse. As the curtain rises two characters are on stage. Lying in front of the fireplace is Eb, the son of the family. He is writing with chalk on the back of a shovel, doing his lessons. Seated in a rocking chair is the daughter of the family, Marybelle.

Suddenly the door is flung open, revealing at one and the same moment a raging blizzard and Paw, coming in from the chores. Paw holds the door open long enough for the audience to recognize the full fury of the storm outside. He is a tall guy with chin whiskers. He slams the door, stamps the snow from his feet, crosses the room and confronts Marybelle. He stares down at her for a moment, then lifts his arm, points to the door, and says:

"Git out!"

Eb looks up from his shovel-back and says:

"What's the matter, Paw? She ain't done nothin'."

And Paw replies:

"I know she ain't done nothin', but it's a-snowin' out an' out she goes!"

Curtain.

One of my tenderest memories of the Press Club is that of the great fist fight between Jean Bosquet and Sidney Whipple's proxy. Both Bosquet and Whipple were reporters on the *Post* and Whipple had become my closest friend. Sid was a little man and Bosquet was almost twice his size. One day in the *Post* city room Whipple was writing a story and Bosquet came along and picked up a sheet of the copy. He studied it a moment and then said:

"Listen, Sid, why don't you make your lead say that the . . ."

"Put that down!" said Sid.

That was the beginning. They quit speaking and pretty soon they were saying mean, gossipy things about each other and it was inevitable that the feud should reach a grand climax of some sort. Provocation followed upon provocation and at last Bosquet announced that he was going to maim Whipple. (Bosquet had a nice feel for language and refrained from saying he was going to cripple Whipple.) When word of this threat reached him, Whipple declared that if Bosquet ever laid a hand on him he, Whipple, would kick Bosquet in the crotch till he bled.

Bosquet sent a courier to Whipple, challenging him to a death grapple at the Press Club on the following evening. Whipple sent back word that he'd be there at nine o'clock and that Bosquet should write his will, wire his folks and get right with his Maker.

All these Arthurian negotiations were carried on with the aid of certain stimulants distilled from sugar beets, but when the next day dawned both men knew that there had to be a fight that night.

Obviously Whipple was no match for Bosquet and so he decided to engage a stand-in, or proxy. He approached Barney Cohen, a stalwart young man then employed in the *Post* morgue, or reference room. Barney was as big as Jean Bosquet if not bigger. Sid came to the point at once. He would be willing to engage Barney as a mercenary—pay him cash money to fight Bosquet. They haggled a bit, then settled on ten dollars, paid in advance, plus whatever medical expenses might be incurred. The compact was made.

Came ten o'clock that night at the Press Club. Most of the *Post* staff had assembled in the club lounge. Bosquet was there, slugging away at a bottle, brooding over the wrongs he had suffered at the hands of Sid Whipple, speaking of his sorrow that he should have to do this to Whipple's family.

Then the street door opened. In came Barney Cohen and behind him came Sid Whipple. They proceeded to the center of the room. The rest of us formed a big circle and inside the circle there took place a most unusual conference. It was all done with tremendous gravity and decorum. Sid announced that he had engaged Barney Cohen to fight for him, adding that if Bosquet had an ounce of manhood about him, he would accept the situation as being fair and equitable. Bosquet was in such a high fury that he did, in fact, accept it.

The entire company adjourned to the alley at the rear of the club. Automobiles were brought up to furnish the floodlights. Bosquet and Barney Cohen removed their shirts, then squared off and ripped into each other. It was a beautiful fight. They slugged and bled and grunted and cursed and all the while little Sid Whipple was scampering around the periphery of battle crying:

"Hit 'im, Barney! *Kill* the son of a bitch!"

They fought for a good twenty minutes and neither man gave evidence of yielding. By then, however, they were exhausted. Suddenly they stopped slugging and fell into each other's arms, sobbing. We led the gladiators back into the club and there were drinks all around, and then more drinks all around, and more after that, and pretty soon Bosquet and Whipple were hanging on each other and vowing eternal friendship.

"Jean, old friend," Sid Whipple was saying, "if you'll only do one thing for me. Sing 'The Rosary.' You sing it lovelier than anybody on earth."

So with Whipple at the piano, Bosquet sang "The Rosary," giving it everything he had. It was one of the most touching and heart-wrenching scenes I have ever witnessed, especially after all that juice of the sugar beet.

Sidney Beaumont Whipple had worked in Denver years earlier as editor of the *Express*. He had attained a certain local celebrity by conducting, almost by himself, a bold war against the Ku-Klux-Klan when that organization was at the peak of its power in Colorado. Then Sid left Denver and became editor of a paper in South Bend. He came back to Denver while I was there and joined the staff of the *Post* and before long he and I had become fast friends. He was one of the most companionable men I've ever met. He came originally from upstate New York and was a graduate of Dartmouth. He had lived and worked in Europe. He was a marvelous raconteur with a repertoire of cockney stories that he told, at my urging, over and over again. I remember most of them word for word and have gone over them in my mind but I don't think a single one of them can be repeated in these pages. Sid was a marvelous writer, and he could play *anything* on the piano, though he was at his best playing and singing bawdy ballads, such as "The Bastard King of England."

He was separated from his family and lived in a dump of a hotel midway between the *Post* and the Press Club. I think that he chose that hotel because of Mr. Nowatney. This was the man from whom Sid and I bought our sugar moon. Mr. Nowatney was a man with a flowing black mustache and a rich accent. He kept his battered old truck parked at a corner near the courthouse and dispensed his acidulated booze in pint bottles wrapped in old newspaper. His customers were mostly politicians from the courthouse and newspapermen from the Press Club. He and Sid were great friends and sometimes Mr. Nowatney would leave his truck and slip up to Sid's room for a couple of sociable nips of his own product. He did not smack his lips and exclaim over the bouquet of his nectar. He did not roll his eyes and speak of its exquisite taste. When he took a drink of it his face assumed the expression of a man being stretched on the rack while a hooded guardsman with a pair of pliers was pulling out his toenails. We liked Mr. Nowatney for his high business principles.

Wherever Sid Whipple lived or visited he had to have a rocking chair. For a small-bodied man he could incur Gargantuan hangovers and the only solace he could find for them was to rock in a rocking chair. One of the first pieces of furniture Nelle and I acquired was the chair known in our house for years as "Sidney Whipple's Rocker." Rocking calmed his nerves, and so did talking about books. I spent many hours with him in that little hotel room listening to the invigorating flow of his language. And I spent many more hours with him at our bungalow in South Denver.

We lived in a variety of furnished houses during our two and a half years in Denver. Once we had a nice brick house on East Colfax belonging to a dentist. He had gone traveling for six months and we took over his place while he was away. His office was in a room at the rear of the house and once I got to inspecting his equipment and decided to give my teeth a good cleaning. It took me quite a while to get organized, to find what I thought were the proper tools, and to get the machinery going, and to mix up a paste out of some stuff I found in a box. Then I went to work. While I was doing the cleaning I didn't notice that the little whirling things were whirling little threads of the sloppy paste in circles around the room, so that there were tiny crisscrossing streaks all over the walls and ceiling by the time I got through. Looked sort of spider-webby. I had to hire some people to come in and get it cleaned off properly before the dentist got back.

The house in South Denver was a pleasant bungalow with front and back yards and it became a sort of annex to the Press Club. There was a gathering of the gang every weekend and Sidney Whipple spent more time with us than he spent in his hotel room. In the summer months it was his custom to wander around the house in a pair of purple underpants and sometimes he got outdoors and scandalized the neighbors slightly. The neighbors were sometimes scandalized every hour on the hour but they never called the police. They usually, in fact, sat in their yards or on their porches and sought amusement in our doings. I remember one Sunday afternoon when a neighbor guy came to the back door and cautioning me to keep quiet, led me around the outside of the house and pointed to the financial editor of the *Post* who was sitting on the front lawn, in a child's express wagon, both feet up and both feet encased in jodhpurs, for the financial editor had been riding to hounds that morning. Sitting in the express wagon, he was stony-eyed drunk. He had the nozzle of my garden hose in his hands and he was moving the nozzle back and forth, watering down the dust in the street. The thing that made him look comical was the fact that no water was coming out of the hose. My neighbor said it was the funniest thing he and his wife had ever seen.

In the basement I usually had two big crocks of home brew going. One weekend, shortly after I had put down a new batch of brew, I missed Sid Whipple and went searching for him, hoping he had not gone wandering in the street wearing his purple underpants. I found him in the basement. He was sitting beside one of the crocks, a tin cup in his hand. He was already somewhat barreled but he was still thirsty. With his left hand he would push aside the scum on top of the green brew, dip the cup quickly, and then drink. At that stage of the brewing process the stuff was not fit to look at, let alone drink, but Sid justified his conduct by saying he had always favored home brew when it was real youthful.

R. E. Wilson, known universally as Josh, was another man of small stature and he had been the last editor of the Denver *Express*. Josh was a man of great talent and when the newspaper war was started in Denver he was with the *News*. He wrote blistering editorials about Bonfils and the *Post* and one day he told me of the conversation he had with Bon at the time he switched over to the *Post*. Bonfils had made it his business to find out who was writing those scathing, searing editorials and then he summoned Josh Wilson to his office. Josh had a handful of clippings as he sat across the desk from Bon.

"Now, Mr. Bonfils," he would say, "here is the one I did in which I called you blood brother to a rattlesnake."

"Oh, yes," said Mr. Bonfils. "I remember that one."

"And here's the one, Mr. Bonfils, where I said that if you died alone in the desert, the buzzards would turn up their beaks at your carcass."

"Yes," said Mr. Bonfils, pleased. "That was good."

"And this one," went on Josh, "you may have missed—I proved by Euclidian geometry that you are related to a female dog."

"Splendid!" said Mr. Bonfils. "I recall that one very well. Mr. Wilson, I think you and I will go a long way together."

But they didn't. Josh was hired to compose "So the People May Know" pieces for the *Morning Post*. He was taken on at a much bigger salary than the *News* had paid him and so he rented a big house. I spent a lot of time there and even lived there for a while when Nelle was visiting back in Missouri. Josh bought straight alcohol in gallon jugs and drank it without benefit of flavoring. He taught me to pour about an ounce of the alcohol into a glass, add an equal amount of water, and then drink it down. He had none of Mr. Nowatney's death-spasms on taking such a drink, and would exclaim, "Delicious! Better than those rare French wines!" I always noticed that my glass seemed to grow warm to the touch after the water had been added to the alcohol and years later a chemist told me why. He said that the alcohol underwent a chemical change when water was added and that this mutation continued for several minutes. I said that we always drank it down almost instantly after mixing it, which meant that the chemical change was taking place inside of us. The chemist said that by the rules of nature I should be dead.

When Josh Wilson got a bit of the churning mixture into his system he was inclined to grow flowery in his speech. As a writer he was given to great bursts of eloquent sentimentality. He grew flamboyantly poetical in his strophes on puppy dogs and harvest moons and mother love and Old Glory and Astral Planes and where at is Heaven. At home, staggering slightly, he would sometimes cry out: "Vengeance is mine, sayeth the Lord! God giveth and God taketh away! Hard work never hurt anybody!" He was a good companion and I missed him a lot after the *Morning Post* folded and he moved on to Wichita. He once referred to me as "the youngest old reprobate on earth."

The most popular and the most loved newspaperman in Denver history was unquestionably Lee Taylor Casey. Strangely, he was of a size with Sidney Whipple and Josh Wilson and the last time I saw him, two years before his death, he expressed a strong criticism of still another man of those general dimensions, namely, Ernie Pyle. Casey, himself a beautiful writer, was indignant over the fact that

Ernie Pyle had become famous as a writer during World War II. Lee had known Ernie for years and argued that the little war correspondent was actually a clumsy writer who deliberately turned out syrupy slop because he knew the public loves syrupy slop, especially in wartime. I didn't offer my own opinion; it was too controversial a subject for me and the great bulk of public opinion was already on the side of Ernie Pyle. So, I will hedge and merely say, I think Lee Casey was as right as rain.

For many years Lee wrote a daily column in the Rocky Mountain *News* and you could not live in Denver and pretend to be informed unless you read him. As a youth his mother had brought him to Denver to die of tuberculosis. He spent his first two Colorado years in bed and during that period he all but committed to memory Gibbon's *Decline and Fall of the Roman Empire*. All his life he read assiduously in Greek and Roman history. He was a true scholar and he managed always to remain so during a career of hard drinking and close-to-the-vest poker playing. He had a reputation for being somewhat near with a nickel and there was a time when he had an arrangement with Clyde Brion Davis through which Davis would write the Casey column if Casey grew "too tired" to do it himself. Casey coached Davis in his writing method, which involved frequent historical allusions, and Davis got so he could write the column so that only the most devoted of Casey readers would suspect the master wasn't feeling right on this particular day. Davis knew just when to throw in a reference to Marcus Aurelius or Pliny the Younger and after a while he began suggesting that Casey pay him for his job of back-stopping. He demanded two dollars for an editorial and five dollars for a Casey column and he got it, though Casey denounced him bitterly as a traitor to classical learning and a mercenary oaf.

Once again I must say in all sincerity that I have no idea why a man of Lee Casey's stature should ever have bothered with me, but he did, and was friendly, and talked to me about history and gave me tips on stud poker. Once a book peddler got to him when he was in a "tired" condition and sold him a set of the Harvard Classics. Casey later decided that he had no use for the books and he chose me as the deserving young man who would take them off his hands. He kept at me for a month, trying to sell those books to me, at a small profit to himself, but I didn't bite.

For several years before his death Lee wrote occasional columns telling how he had been shopping around among Denver morticians, trying to get a reasonable quotation on his own funeral. He asked for bids and went into long and amusing discussions of the mortuary art, and said that he was looking for something neat but not gaudy and having trouble finding it. He said that the best price he had been able to get was $127.50 and he thought that too high, and so he had reached a decision to keep on living a while longer.

In 1951 I was on a train passing through New Mexico when the Denver papers were put on board and I learned that Casey had died of a heart attack. I had an impulse to get off and fly up to Denver for the funeral—a very strange impulse for me because I hate funerals and stay away from them whenever possible. I didn't do it. I had seen Casey two years earlier and spent an afternoon with him in the Press Club where he arranged to have my membership card renewed after a lapse of nineteen years. The new card was dated nineteen years ahead. "We love you," said Casey, "and want to see you again, but only about once in nineteen years."

He was cremated and his ashes placed in the brick wall of the lobby in the *News* building. A small bronze plaque there says: HERE REST THE ASHES OF LEE TAYLOR CASEY—BELOVED BY HIS FELLOW WORKERS AND THE READERS OF THE ROCKY MOUNTAIN NEWS FOR FORTY YEARS. 1889–1951. It is a matter of pride to me that I knew him.

In the winter of 1928 the *News* began publishing daily feature stories by Sam Love, a staff writer for the United Press in New York. I thought they were superb stories and went about quoting them and reading them aloud when anyone would listen. I remember that I was particularly entranced by Sam Love's interview with a Japanese inventor who had built a new kind of parachute, mounted a railing of the Brooklyn Bridge, and leaped into the East River, where he was nearly drowned. When he was fished out of the water with the wreckage of his invention, all he would say was: "She achieve haywire." I thought this such a splendid piece of feature writing that I went around exclaiming, "Good Godley, Young Wadley!"

At last Sidney Whipple began telling me that I could write the kind of stuff that Sam Love wrote, maybe even better than Sam Love, and that I ought to pull up stakes and head for New York. I refused to even think about such a foolhardy procedure. Then Gene Austin came to town to fill a singing engagement. Mobs and banners and fireworks greeted his arrival, for he was tremendously popular. One evening he asked me to come up to his suite in the

Brown Palace for what he called A Drinkin'. Several other people were present, including the old movie actor, Lew Cody. Cody, once one of the top matinee idols of silent films, was drunk and in a bad mood and spent the evening abusing and cursing me because I was a newspaperman and he hated newspapermen and he told me over and over what I could do vis-à-vis a galloping goose. Gene Austin finally got a little embarrassed for me and he and I left and went to the Press Club and sat around the rest of the night and *he* told me I ought to be in New York—that if I'd agree to head East he would fix it with some people he knew so I would have a newspaper job on arrival. I thanked him, and rejected his offer of help, but now I had real hot palpitations for Gotham. I told Sid Whipple and he said he thought he would be able to steer me into a job with the United Press—the very organization for which Sam Love did all that lovely writing.

So I made my decision. One day in August of 1929 I walked up to Johnnie Day and said I was leaving. For ten days I had been telling everyone in town that I was going to New York, but when I told Johnnie Day I was leaving he said:

"Where you going?"

"New York," I said.

My city editor looked at me and deepened his habitual scowl.

"You better sew up your pockets," he finally said, and that was the official good-by I got from the Denver *Post*.

At the Press Club I spoke my farewells and Joe Diner, the club steward, said to me: "You'll be seeing Runyon. Tell him Joe Diner said hello."

I turned the new electric refrigerator back to the company, shipped my family off to Missouri to await the turn of events, bought two bottles of sugar moon from Mr. Nowatney, and got on a train.

I stopped off in Chicago to say hello to Morris Watson and was offered a job in the Associated Press bureau there. I rejected it. I was going to the Big Town.

# a literary tea for
# Lowell Thomas

It was Labor Day and depressingly hot and pterodactyls were flying back and forth in my stomach when I arrived at the bus station on Forty-Second Street. Now, what one person in all the world do you think would have been waiting to greet me? Right. John Moynihan. The same John Moynihan who had been waiting to greet me in Jeffersonville and in Sebring and in Tulsa. I got off that bus trembling with excitement and pure fright and Moynihan began talking about a kinkajou. He was working as an advertising copywriter for motion pictures and his current assignment was a production called *Rio Rita* in which there was an animal called a kinkajou. I looked at all the milling, sweating, unattractive people around me and was vaguely aware of the kinkajou talk; my first words spoken in New York City were: "Good God get me outa here!"

We took a ferry to Weehawken and a train to Ridgefield Park where Moynihan lived and where I was to live for the next two weeks. I remember Ridgefield Park for one thing alone. I was awakened each morning by a man crying out in a falsetto voice: "Doooooooo-gn!" When I finally asked Margaret Moynihan to go out and kill him, she said he was Dugan, the bread man.

On the day after my arrival I found myself back in Times Square. I saw a subway entrance. Here was the monster they had told me about in Denver—the horror that a lot of people had given as their reason for hating New York. Well, I thought, I've got to learn to ride on the thing and there's no time like the present. I went down the steps and into the swirling, suffocating mob. The temperature was close to a hundred. I was wrenched and yanked and shoved and finally found myself jammed into a car that was hurtling through the darkness. When at last I was able to claw my way free I was standing on the platform of the Park Place station. I stood there sweating and panting, noting that a button was missing from my coat and then watching the train pull out of the station. It was pretty bad, all right. Pretty rugged. But I'd just have to get used to it. I didn't realize that by chance I had started my lessons in subway riding at the very peak of the evening rush hour and at the busiest station in the city. Nor did I know that I was only a few steps from the building where I would go looking for a job the next day.

This was the Pulitzer building on Park Row, where the United Press had its offices. In that year of 1929 there were eighteen daily newspapers in New York City, not counting trade journals or foreign language papers. Today there are only eight. The Pulitzer building, commonly called the World building, stood on Park Row across the street from City Hall. Occupying a central and distinctive position on Park Row, it seemed to stand as a symbol of New York journalism. It was surmounted by a golden dome and when it was opened in 1890 the ceremonies lasted an entire day because it was the tallest building in the world. It was so high that people shuddered just looking at it, and some said the human race was getting out of hand. The New York *Times* in covering the opening reported: "From the terrifying height of sixteen stories men below lose stature and become crawling bugs." The assistant managing editor of the *World* was a veteran, hard-driving newspaperman named Ballard Smith. His office was on one of the top floors and for the first year he stayed at least eight feet away from the windows and confessed openly that he was afraid to look down from that altitude.

When I arrived in the UP offices on the third floor of this building I was carrying a letter from Sid Whipple to Karl A. Bickel, the president of UP. There was a switchboard girl in the hall and I asked for Mr. Bickel. She said he was in South America. I swallowed hard and blinked my eyes a couple of times and said thank you and turned away. I would go back to Denver, or maybe to Indiana. Then I remembered that Joe Alex Morris had gone from Denver to the UP and I asked the girl about him. She checked and he was inside and in a moment I was with him.

Joe Morris introduced me to a tall, dark, slouchy-looking man named Carl Groat who was one of the bosses and I mumbled something about having a letter from Sidney Whipple and Mr. Groat said they didn't have anything at the moment and I said thanks and then he said: "Hey. Wait a minute. Did you say Sidney Whipple?" He got quite excited about Whipple, and wanted to know where he was, and how he was getting along, and could he look at the letter. Then he gave me a job. There was a rewrite man, a well-known guy around New York newspaper shops, who had been flagrantly drunk for two weeks. He was lying on the floor in a speakeasy back on William Street. Two or three times a day someone would go over and shake him and say, "Harry, come on back to work." And Harry would use an army expression and go back to sleep. Twice Mr. Groat had been over himself and each time Harry had used the army expression and by now Mr. Groat had decided that the United Press might get along without Harry. This was the moment that I had walked in. Was it Fate? Was it Destiny? Or was it just Harry? I choose to believe it was just Harry. Half a dozen years later I went to work on the *World-Telegram* and was assigned to a desk on the rewrite bank. I started cleaning it out. It contained various possessions of the same Harry, who had just been fired for lying drunk on the floor of a Greenwich Street saloon and using the army expression.

Mr. Groat (now dead) walked me around the United Press office. First he introduced me to Bob Bender (dead) who was second in command under Karl Bickel. Then to Charlie McCann (dead) who would be my immediate boss. Then Paul White (dead), a staff writer who would go on to important accomplishments in network radio. And finally to Sam Love (dead), the man whose very existence was in a sense responsible for my being there. Sam turned out to be a good-looking, soft-spoken young man with prematurely gray hair. I spoke my great admiration for his writing and complimented him in particular on the story about the Japanese inventor who had jumped off the Brooklyn Bridge.

"It must have been fun," I said, "listening to him talk."

Sam laughed.

"Was he in the hospital when you saw him?" I asked. I was anxious to learn all about the modus operandi of this wonderful writer-reporter.

"Who?" Sam asked.

"The Jap inventor."

"Oh," said Sam. "I didn't see him at all. There wasn't any Jap inventor. I made it all up."

"Well!" I said. "Gee!" I added. "Whiz!" I concluded.

I went to work at once for Charlie McCann, who was boss of the night service, and on my second day I wrote my first "signer" for the United Press, a signer being a story with a by-line on it. The UP was addicted to the use of many code words and phrases, some being taken from cablese and the Phillips code. A well-handled, well-written story was called a bell-ringer. The rival Associated Press was always referred to in teletype messages as "Rocks." A story that had to be given special, "ahead-all" treatment for the reason that it involved Roy Howard or some other brassy individual, or a project that the big wheels might be for or against, such a story was called "moo." In earlier days it was referred to as a "sacred cow" but in the interests of speed and efficiency the term was reduced to "moo." When I first joined the UP it was a matter of fascination for me to watch such a story leave the hands of say, Carl Groat, to be taken by a copy editor, then passed along in flimsy sheets to the men filing the various national and regional wires. Mr. Groat would say "moo" to the copy editor, the copy editor would say "moo" when he handed it on to the first wire-filer, and each wire-filer would say "moo" as *he* passed it down the line. The "moo" was always spoken loudly so there could be no mistake about the importance of the story involved. A real, terribly important sacred-cow story was given a somewhat more elaborate send-off and the "moo" was bellowed all along the line. I once saw Carl Groat come out of Bickel's office with some copy in his hand, and the instant the door closed behind him he mooed a "moo" that Jimmie Walker probably heard across the street in City Hall, and he mooed like a small-town fire signal all the way to the main news desk.

For as long as I can remember there has been a legend in the newspaper business that the United Press is a Big Old Stingy Gut. Such an implication is laughable . . . because it is true. The most important codeword in the whole organization is "downhold" and the United Press alumni organization calls itself the Downhold Club, because "downhold" is the word that lingers longest in their memories when they think back to the days when they were Unipressers. Downhold means hold down and hold down means save money and save money means cut expenses to the bone if it means firing everybody in sight. I can't remember a time when there was not a downhold on; it was merely a matter of degree. There was a downhold on, or there was a *big* downhold on.

I was hired at close to a starvation wage, having neglected to tell anyone that I had a wife and two children. After a few weeks I felt that I had established a beachhead and so I went to Bob Bender and asked for a raise. He said there was a big downhold on at the moment but he'd let me know. Several days went by and then he called me in. What I had been hoping for was the standard type of raise for a man in my bracket—five bucks a week. I got fifteen. The United Press had a mail service which included a book-review column and this column was written by Paul White. Paul had just resigned to join the Columbia Broadcasting System and that's why I got the raise. Bob Bender said to me:

"On account of the downhold, I can't give you that raise, but I'll do better than that. I'll give you the book column. You sell most of the books you get from the publishers and I understand it strikes a year-round average of fifteen dollars a week. So, to all intents and purposes, you are getting a fifteen dollar raise. Oke?"

I said oke. In fact I was almost deliriously happy. Now I was a literary critic on a national scale. Little old me from Little Old Egypt! The books piled into my home and every two weeks a young man came around and carried away all volumes I didn't want to keep, paying me fifty cents each whether they were ten-dollar books or twenty-five-cent pamphlets. The young man had similar arrangements with other book reviewers including some of the top literary critics of the town. His name was Harry Shaul and he was the most superstitious man I've ever met outside of organized religion. He actually spent every Friday the Thirteenth in bed with the covers pulled over his head and refused to eat anything on that day or to answer calls or to talk with anyone beyond yelling, "Go away!"

Before this great cultural windfall, however, there was the small matter of the Wall Street Crash. It came less than two months after my arrival in town and for many people it was the end of the world. When it was going on it terrified me. Not because of any economic involvements. I was terrified because I knew it was a Big Story and I knew that I would be dragged into it and that I would make a fool of myself and probably lose my job. In addition to being dumb about grammar, I have a thing about high finance and the stock market and the theory of credit and what insurance policies say. To me the word "margin" means something at the side of a page. I mean *nothing* at the side of a page.

The story of how I covered the Wall Street Crash is still told around the UP offices and is included in the authorized history of the organization. Our office in the World building, as well as every news office everywhere, was in turmoil. Nobody had been able to find out what had happened, or what was happening, or what was going to happen. Then Bob Bender remembered an important Wall Street man, Frank Vanderlip, who had once been a newspaper reporter and was now Real Big in Money. Bender had known Vanderlip in the old days and so he got on the phone and arranged for the financier to be interviewed by a UP reporter.

Bender came bustling into the newsroom and looked around for somebody to send. Once again Fate was against me—all the competent men, all the men who knew the difference between a dibble and a debenture, were out of the office. Bender handed me a slip of paper with Vanderlip's name and address and told me to rush right down and interview him.

"But what should I ask him?" I said.

"Good Lord, man!" Bender exclaimed. "Ask him what all this *means.*"

I knew I could do that much, but what would happen after that? Suppose he *told* me what it all meant! My God, I wouldn't understand a word of it! I was in a highly nervous state when I was ushered into Vanderlip's elegant, paneled office. The famous banker was teetering back and forth in a chair behind his desk. I sat down opposite him and tried to say something but the words stuck in my throat.

"Well," said Vanderlip, "what can I do for you?"

I gulped. This was going to be earth-shakingly awful. I waved a quivering hand toward the window in a most clumsy gesture and said, "What does all this mean? I mean, what does it *mean?*"

"Young man," said Vanderlip, "I'm going to tell you what I think it means. But first I want you to tell me what *you* think it means."

He had me. Lord how he had me! He had me backed into a corner. I was a sick chicken, and for a few minutes I couldn't think, and then I decided to tell the truth.

"Mr. Vanderlip," I said, "I've only just arrived in New York from Colorado and I've got exactly ten dollars to my name at this moment. I not only don't know what it means—I don't even know what it *is.* I just supposed New York was like this *all* the time."

Vanderlip chuckled. "The fact of the matter is," he said at last, "that I don't know what it means either. My friends don't know what

it means. I don't think anybody knows what it means. But I told
Bob Bender that I'd give you a statement, so get your paper and
pencil ready."

And so he dictated a statement, and I didn't understand a single
sentence that was in it, and maybe he didn't either, and I took it
back to the office and they slapped it on all wires as if it were the
1918 Armistice and Bob Bender said to me, "Nice going."

That one had a mildly happy ending, but there was another
assignment growing out of the Wall Street Crash a couple of years
later in which, much to my personal satisfaction, I failed miserably.
Charles E. Mitchell, former multimillionaire head of the National
City Bank, got himself all snarled up in certain financial difficulties
and finally was indicted on charges of income tax evasion. Here was
one of the great How-the-Mighty-Have-Fallen stories of the period,
and I was told to go to Mr. Mitchell's house and interview him.

He lived in one of those marble-faced mansions on Fifth Avenue,
opposite Central Park, and when I got there a press photographer
was loafing around across the street. I asked him if Mr. Mitchell was
at home and he said he didn't know. I went to the front door hoping
to God that Mr. Mitchell was *not* at home.

I rang the bell and in a minute or two the door opened and a man
stood before me.

"Is Mr. Mitchell in?" I squeaked.

"No," said the man.

I knew it was Mr. Mitchell himself. Anybody would have known
it; his picture had been plastered over the front pages for days.

"Well," I fumbled, "that's too bad."

"Yes, it is," he agreed.

"Do you expect him?" I asked.

"Who are you?" demanded Mr. Mitchell.

"I'm a reporter, sir, from the United Press, and I'd like . . . I mean
. . . that is . . . I came up to try to interview Mr. Mitchell, but if he
isn't . . ."

"He's not home," said Mr. Mitchell, "and we don't expect him
home for weeks."

"Well, in that case, I guess I'll go back."

"While you're at it, you can tell that photographer across the street
that he's wasting his time."

"Yes, sir."

"You work for Karl Bickel, don't you?" asked Mr. Mitchell.

"That's right," I said.

"Well, when you see him tell him I said hello."

"Sure. I'll tell him. Tell him you said hello."

"Yes," he said. "Tell him Charlie said hello."

"Yes sir," I said. "Thank you."

He grinned and closed the door and I went out and told the photographer and then went on back to the office. Dumb? Well, not *too* dumb. I wasn't dumb enough to go back and tell Karl Bickel that Charlie said hello.

The reason I kept my job at the United Press was that almost always I chose my own assignments. My boss rarely knew what my daily "signer" was about until I had written it and handed it to him. Whenever I *did* get an assignment from him, I almost always found myself in trouble. One of the earlier jobs at the UP came on the birthday of John D. Rockefeller. I mean John D. Rockefeller the Nonpareil.

"Tomorrow," said Charlie McCann, "is old John D. Rockefeller's birthday. They've announced that he's not giving any interviews. So I want you to go up to Tarrytown tomorrow and interview him anyway."

Just like that. City editor type talk. Go interview the uninterviewable. Go find Livingstone. Don't come back without the story.

The next day I took a train to Tarrytown. At the station I talked to a taxi driver. He said that if I had the entire Chinese army back of me I wouldn't be able to get to Old John D. He said that if I had a trainload of what he called danna-mite I wouldn't be able to breach the barrier. I got on the phone and told Charlie McCann. I said there was a big steel fence around the whole estate. "Climb over it," he said. I told him that there were packs of enormous police dogs patrolling the fence on the inside, tear a leg off a man the instant he set foot on Rockefeller ground. "Kick the god damn dogs in the face," said McCann.

I ended up by having the cab driver haul me on a grand circle tour around the estate. The driver had grown up in the community and knew a lot of gossip about the Rockefeller family, and by quoting him extensively I came away with a pretty good story. At least it was enough to satisfy Charlie McCann.

There was one assignment in those beginning days in New York that I chose for myself and didn't enjoy too much. The Empire State Building had not yet been completed but even in its skeletal condition it was already the wonder of the modern world. One day I rode to the top in a makeshift elevator—I had a feeling that we were being jerked aloft on a cable made out of clothesline—and I crawled out on a girder to interview a steeplejack with a rivet gun in his hands. They told me just to look at Dominic, not to look down, and I'd be all right. I was supposed to crawl all the way out to Dominic but somehow I began to get nervous and I glanced at the girder and it was only an inch and a quarter wide, and it was swaying a little, and we were a full three miles above Fifth Avenue. So I only crawled partway out, looking at Dominic, and then I interviewed him with my eyes shut tight. It is possible that the germs of acrophobia got into me at that time. All the Rockefeller money and all the Joe Kennedy money, plus J. Paul Getty's spare cash, could not get me to do it again. I have to hire a boy to go up a ladder and clean the guck out of the gutters at my house. I have only two types of dreams. One is about lovely women, and the other is about falling out of airplanes, off the top of the Washington Monument and off the top of the Empire State Building. The dreams about lovely women predominate, about three to one, thank God.

There was a restaurant up in the dome of the World building and I often ate dinner there. Quite a few famous newspapermen worked in the building and I was always on the lookout for familiar faces. The first one I spotted in the restaurant was Harry Hansen, the book columnist. Once or twice I saw Heywood Broun up there, and FPA. Just recently I had a talk with Harry Hansen, now editor of the *World Almanac*, and he remembered the World restaurant, but not as well as I did. I could even remember that the Spanish waiter's name was Jean. Harry said that Walter Lippmann was a steady customer up there in those days but I wouldn't have known him if I'd seen him.

There was a little lunch counter back of the World building that was famous for its New York style beans, which came in individual boat-shaped casseroles and cost either a dime or fifteen cents. Each dish had a thick strip of crusty salt pork on top of the beans, and a touch of garlic was used in the cooking. Those were the best beans I've ever eaten and I learned how to cook them at home. I remember that little lunch counter for a reason other than beans. Several of us were beaning it up one evening when a bum came through the door and stood looking at us. We were only a few steps away from the Bowery and this guy must have been the official model for all other bums—a sort of gutter-drunk goal to shoot at. He was dirty beyond description and his clothes were in tatters and he hadn't shaved in the present century. We averted our eyes, pretending not to notice his obnoxious presence, that being the procedure for avoiding a panhandler. Then he spoke.

"Men," he said, "I ain't going to ast you for money to buy a cuppa coffee. I ain't gonna tell you that I ain't eat nothing in four days. Men, I am an old-fashion drunk. I got to have booze. I tell you, I *got* to have it! You would be doing me a great favor if you would help me out a little."

Every customer in the place kicked in. I gave a quarter. The bum must have gone out of there with close to two dollars. And I am not going to tack on the stereotyped ending: that the bum made much more money that I did, and never touched liquor. I believed and I still believe that he was what he said—an old-fashion drunk.

A press association writer works for hundreds of bosses and some of them are unreasonable. Every newspaper which subscribes to the service can order special stories or complain bitterly about the quality of the ones they are getting. In the early 1920s a report came out of Europe that Field Marshal Paul von Hindenburg had died suddenly in Berlin. An opposition news service, possibly Rocks, carried the story as being fact but the United Press waited, and checked Berlin, and found that Hindenburg was alive. A few days later the publisher of an important paper in Pennsylvania arrived in the UP offices in New York with fire in his eye. He was a client of the UP and he wanted to know why in pluperfect hell the UP hadn't carried the story of Hindenburg's death. He said the opposition paper in his city had sold fifty thousand extras and he was fit to be tied. He was shown the cable messages proving Hindenburg was alive. "I don't give a damn about that!" he roared. "I'm quitting your lousy service and joining up with one that knows its business!" And he did— signing up with the press association that had sent out the false report.

In my own time I remember lesser instances of client anger, one of which sent me exploring into the pig farming country of New Jersey. Some nut on another news service wrote a story about how water always whirls in the same direction when it's going down a drain, and how certain plants curl in that same direction. Now he had found out that a pig's tail always and forever takes the same direction when it curls. I cannot, at this late date, remember whether a pig's tail curls clockwise or counterclockwise. The fact remains that an important American newspaper publisher telegraphed the UP and demanded action on this matter. He wanted to know why his opposition had this information about the direction taken by a pig's tail, and *his* paper didn't have a word about it. He said in effect that we had better get the hell out and have a look at some pigs' tails if we wanted to keep *his* business. Such matters had to be taken seriously, for they involved money rather than intelligence, and so I went into darkest Jersey and examined the butt-ends of a number of pigs and wrote a story about them.

Within a very few months after my joining the United Press word got around among the confraternity of book press agents that I was a sucker for an author interview. All they had to do was show me a person's name on the binding of a book and I would almost break a leg getting to that person for an interview. Thus it came about in February of 1930 that I had a long session with the Illinois poet, Edgar Lee Masters. The subject was Abraham Lincoln. Mr. Masters had just written a book about Lincoln saying he was not a nice man, that he was ignorant and didn't bathe often enough and used coarse language and so on. I wrote the story and, to be sure, the protests came into the UP offices by the bushel basket. It was as if I had challenged the power of prayer. Abraham Lincoln was sacred, and the United Press had done a shameful thing by sending such slander over its wires. Some editors said that I should be fired. I protested to my employers that it hadn't been *me* talking against Lincoln—it had been Edgar Lee Masters. It is sometimes necessary to spell out such a simple thing to very important people. So, a decision was reached. I had to go find another authority on the life of Lincoln and do another interview, somewhat more complimentary to the shade of Lincoln. I located my man upstairs in the World building. He was Claude G. Bowers, then an editorial writer for the *World*. He had a new book called *The Tragic Era* which was about Lincoln and he gave me the story I wanted. He didn't want to criticize Edgar Lee Masters but instead blistered the German biographer, Emil Ludwig, for writing a new book about Lincoln that was "a superficial, pusillanimous piece of work which the American people should kick out of the country." I wrote my interview and the squawking clients were mollified and I had gained another friend. Claude Bowers was a quiet little guy who came out of Indiana and made the grade as a historian and biographer of commanding importance. Some people think his three-volume work on Jefferson is the best biography ever written about the Squire of Monticello. I didn't know that Mr. Bowers was all that important—I only knew that he was a genuine author and that was enough. I used to have dinner with him occasionally up there under the dome and mostly we talked about the Midwest. One of the interesting things about him was the fact that he spent his last twenty years as our ambassador in Spain and then in Chile without ever learning to speak Spanish. This is a difficult thing to believe, yet my authority for it is Hubert Herring, one of our nation's foremost commentators on the Latin-American scene. Says Mr. Herring: "I never heard him risk the simplest sentence in that language. He mispronounced the names of his Chilean friends, but this was of no importance; they understood him always, and respected him deeply."

The months I spent on Park Row coincided with the period of the literary tea. It was unthinkable that a book should be published without a party for its author on publication day, and all such parties were called literary teas. In 1930 I received my first invitation to one of these soirees and I accepted it eagerly. I sometimes felt like pinching myself to see if it were all true—me, a literary critic, and now being accepted into the cultural life of the greatest city in the world.

Jim Monahan, of the Century Company, invited me to attend a literary tea at the home of Lowell Thomas, whose latest book, *Land of the Black Pagoda*, was being published by Century. The Thomas apartment was a duplex, beautifully furnished, tastefully decorated, an altogether fitting residence for the famous explorer-author-lecturer who was even then beginning to branch out into radio. Mr. Thomas had never had a literary tea before, nor had he ever attended one. Jim Monahan knew about literary teas and suggested that this one be held in a hotel suite but Mr. Thomas said, "I should say not! We have this perfectly charming apartment and, after all, these are newspaper people, *my* kind of people, and I *want* them to be in my home."

By the time I got there both floors of the apartment were crowded with people. Mr. Monahan had provided an ample supply of Golden Wedding whisky and the crème de la crème of the literati were already belting it down as fast as they could. In the first hour the effects of the drinking began to show. Voices were raised. A couple of fist fights were broken up. I met a man named Harold Matson and had a couple of Golden Weddings with him while we talked about San Francisco, where he had been a newspaperman. I had a few

(20) Henry McLemore, the former actor. (INP PHOTO)
(21) Sam Love, inventor of a Jap inventor. (INP PHOTO)

(22) Paul White, always a friend in need. (INP PHOTO)

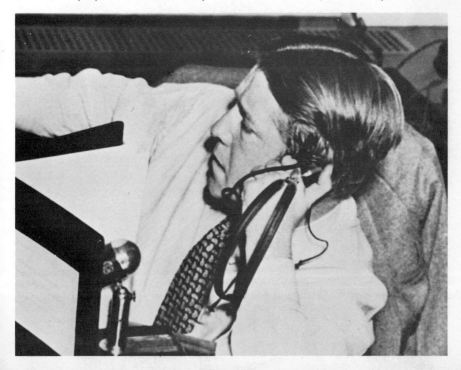

(23) Nelle and Morris Watson living it up in Jackson Heights.

(24) I become a world traveler. Grace Line junket to Panama in 1930. I forgot to tell about this in the book.

(25) The Arrow Collar Man attends his first literary tea (1930).

(26) Final night of the great contest. Henry McLemore takes on the Culbertsons while the dummy stands by, strangling back of that gates-ajar collar.

(27) Einstein looks for a Meter-Miser on the night he was kidnaped.
(PHOTO BY A. G. MICHAELSON)

(28) Doug Gilbert, who favored clam spaghetti.
(WORLD-TELEGRAM & SUN)

(29) Asa Bordages, a man with an urge for digging.
(WORLD-TELEGRAM & SUN)

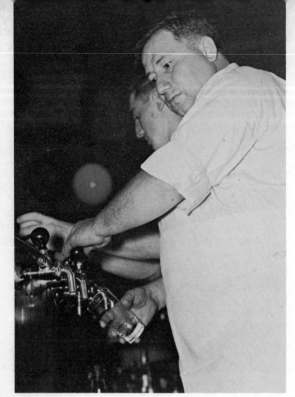

(30) There just *had* to be a saloonkeeper's picture in this book. The best of them all—Nick.

(31) Man with 35 cents in his pocket writing the weather story on a golden typewriter.
(WORLD-TELEGRAM & SUN)

(32) This is how it looks to be a rewrite man provided you look like me as I looked in the olden time. (WORLD-TELEGRAM & SUN)

(33) John Moynihan in California shortly before his death. (SAN JOSE NEWS)

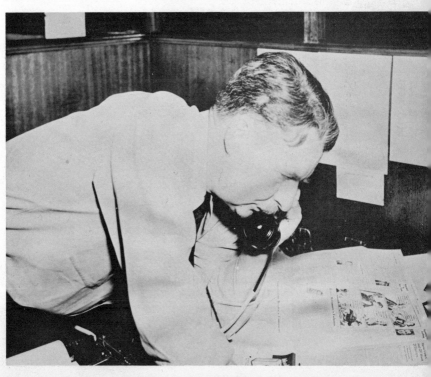

(34) Pop at seventy hard at work in a Virginia resort called Fidget's Retreat.
(PHOTO BY RITA CLARKE)

(35) . . . and so I became an author.

more drinks and met Burton Rascoe, one of the most widely known literary critics of the time. He had come out of Oklahoma, spent some time in Chicago, and I had heard a lot about him. I found him leaning against a door, his eyes half closed, a highball glass sagging in his hand. I approached him and introduced myself. He told me to go away and not bother him. Just like Will Rogers. I put on an air of terrible hurt and with a throb in my voice said: "I have looked forward to this moment for years—the achievement of my one flaming ambition—to meet the great Burton Rascoe. I am the founder and first president of the Burton Rascoe Literary Club of Tulsa. There are a hundred and eighty members and they meet every Tuesday evening and read aloud from the works of Burton Rascoe. And now . . . now . . . I meet him, and he tells me to go away. Oh, God!" I bowed my head and sobbed. Mr. Rascoe shook himself like a wet dog and put a hand on my shoulder. "Really," he said, "I didn't know. Great heavens, I didn't even know there *was* a Burton Rascoe Club in Tulsa. Please! Please have a drink with me."

"You can go straight to hell," I said to him. "I'm sorry I ever founded the stinking club. You can just kiss my foot."

I turned and walked away. He pursued me, and continued pursuing me, during the rest of the evening. He'd come up behind me and grab me by the arm and begin apologizing again and, of course, both he and I were getting more stimulated all the while. So I saw a pretty female standing by herself and someone told me she was Francine Larrimore, the actress, and I went up to her and tried to make like John Barrymore, and she spurned me, and so I went into the Burton Rascoe act again—I was the founder and first president of the Francine Larrimore Society, made up of people who simply worshiped the ground she walked on, and now at last my god look at how long this sentence is getting. Miss Larrimore reacted the same way Burton Rascoe had reacted, and now I had *two* important people trailing me around, trying to worm their way back into the good graces of the founder of their respective fan clubs. Harry Hansen was there for a while, and Carl Van Doren, and Lyle Saxon from New Orleans, and something over a hundred other people in varying stages of stimulation. Some of these, perhaps a fourth of all those present, were professional free-loaders, or gate-crashers. I would run into many such creatures later on—people who got most of their food supply and their drinks by walking into parties where they had not been invited. They were of two kinds—the garrulous, who could talk convincingly on almost any subject, and the strong, silent, mysterious type. They were real bums and chiselers, but they gave much thought and preparation to their profession. I think I have all the qualifications for their line of work save one: a passion for canapés.

In one room of the Thomas apartment a screen had been set up and Mr. Thomas was supposed to show slides of his travels in India. There were folding chairs and a projector and Mr. Thomas did get started on his illustrated lecture, but he never finished it. Drunks wandered in and out of the room and fell over the chairs and stayed a few minutes and some of them heckled Mr. Thomas, yelling, "Shut up fer krissakes!" and "Go straddle a camel!" Mr. Thomas finally gave up. I caught glimpses of him during the evening and he did not have the appearance of a happy and contented host. His wife, Frances, a person of gentility, wandered from room to room, watching people slopping drinks on her furniture and on her carpets, listening to the yelling and quarreling, looking at the people sprawled indecently on the stairway, kissing and hugging one another. Some said she wrung her hands a little.

I can remember that as the hour grew late someone was making an effort to get people to leave, and occasionally there would be the sound of splintering wood—God knows how much furniture was wrecked that night. I was wandering around trying to find somebody else to insult me, so that I could organize another fan club, and I noticed that my eyes had a tendency to close, and they must have closed, for the next thing I remember it was daylight and I was in the apartment of Harold Matson, the fellow from San Francisco. He has been my literary agent for twenty-odd years (*odd* is the word) and my close friend longer than that. Because of him I count it a blessing that I accepted the invitation to my first literary tea. I went to many of them after that and they were all just as charmingly cultural as the tea for *Land of the Black Pagoda.*

Long years afterward I was talking to Lowell Thomas and I reminded him of the party. He grabbed his head in his hands and said, almost in a whisper, "Please! Please don't say another word! I have traveled all over the world, I've been through hell, I've brushed elbows with death a dozen times, but that was my hour of true horror. I'd just as soon I never heard about it again as long as I live."

# the World's worst reporter

There were a great many nuts loose in the land in the year following the stock market collapse. It is not my intention to suggest that the depression produced a new breed of lunatics. They were present all along; the Wall Street Crash simply activated them. It may be that the spectacle of their betters caught in the act of stupendous and ridiculous failure led people of lesser quality to kick up their heels and play the goof. This was the time of the Dance Marathon, the epoch of the Tree Sitter. There were days, I do believe, when every tree in the metropolitan area had a sitter in it. Little children were doing it and octogenarian women were doing it. Many of these were endurance sitters, who patterned themselves on the people who perched on flagpoles. The idea was to climb up into a tree and sit there until you were dead or half dead. There was a great run on buckets, which were needed to haul stuff from sitter to ground and from ground to sitter. Hospitals reported a greater number of cases involving broken limbs than ever before in the annals of bone brokerage. Eminent clergymen passed the opinion in private that the human race was no longer entitled to salvation. Licensed philosophers standing in the shade of elm trees said that the animals would soon take over. The elm trees were occupied.

Over in New Jersey a young man who openly scoffed at tree sitters sought fame in the opposite direction. He stretched himself out in a coffin and had himself buried. In his coffin he had a telephone and a small electric light and there was an iron pipe through which food and crazy-people medicine could be lowered to him. Seemingly normal citizens were allowed to look down the pipe at his face for a fee of twenty-five cents and business was brisk during the afternoon and evening hours. The young man had an unlisted phone number— he said he didn't want crackpots calling him all hours of the day and night—but newspaper people are privileged and we were allowed to have it. I used to sit in the World building and call him and talk to him. I can't remember how long he stayed underground and I don't know what ever happened to him in later years. I feel quite sure that he made his mark in the world.

At this time, too, I first met Professor Alexander Meyer, undisputed rocking champion of the world and inventor of the Meyer Reversible Jiffy Bow Tie. Professor Meyer was a hawk-faced man of Russian descent who would sometimes sit down on a straight-backed chair and rock himself back and forth for weeks with only occasional rest periods. It might interest President Kennedy to know that the Professor was preaching the health benefits of rocking as far back as the middle 20s. But Professor Meyer was scornful of all rocking chairs. True health and strength and mental serenity came only from sitting in a non-rocker and rocking the body from the hips. The Professor invented the Meyer Rockometer-Swayoscope, a sort of antediluvian Univac. It was fastened to the back of his chair and registered each time his body banged against it. He needed to keep accurate account of the several million rocks he rocked during each engagement so that he could prove his right to the championship. The Professor always behaved as if the Kremlin and the Vatican and No. 10 Downing Street were all trying, through secret agents, to somehow steal away his title. From his conversations, one might have assumed that dozens of eager contenders, all in the pay of gangsters, were furiously and fraudulently rocking all over the land, bent on wresting his championship from him. Actually, so far as I could find out, there was not another rocker rocking anywhere in the world.

It was my custom to seek out and interview the Professor every six months or so because he was a man unafraid, a man with very strong opinions about the world and its inhabitants, and a man willing to state those opinions. He was angry at everybody and everything and sometimes he would just stand on a New York street corner and stare at the passing people, muttering to himself: "Crazy. All crazy but I'm."

Another type of nut quite active in those days, as always, was the spiritualistic nut. I attended my first séance within a month after my arrival in New York. The medium was a Negro woman and after she had brought back sundry kinfolks for the customers, she came through with a horse. No question about it. A man in the audience spoke up and said he'd like to communicate with a dear horse he had owned, a horse named Edna. Within thirty seconds there was a heavy clumping sound in the dark room and then the man who had asked for Edna's return let out a sharp cry. Edna had given him a sharp kick in the shin. If I were making this up, I would never give a horse such an improbable horse-name as Edna.

For a couple of years after that I spent a lot of time at séances, usually attending them with Joseph Dunninger. Dunninger had posted a small fortune in cash for any spiritualistic medium whose methods he was unable to unmask. He had been a leading magician for years and I always liked him because he never pulled a half dollar out of my nose. I have a nose that is large enough to hold perhaps $6.50 in half dollars and I have known other magicians who have embarrassed me in public by reaching up and pulling large objects out of it, including once a hard-boiled egg. Pardon me. A hard-*cooked* egg. Dunninger never pestered his friends with such stuff.

One of the chief ghost-conjurors then operating around New York was a little Italian named Nino Pecararo. He once brought back the spirit of Otto H. Kahn and the celebrated patron of the arts spoke in a strong Italian dialect. All of Nino's returnees spoke in dialect. Joe Dunninger and I attended a number of Nino's shows. The Italian boy enjoyed a large following because, some years earlier, he had helped convince Sir Arthur Conan Doyle that spiritualism is true.

We were in the elegant apartment of an architect one evening and Nino, concealed in his cabinet, was fetching back spirits as fast as he could talk. It was a lively and you might say populous show and when it was over I found myself standing against a wall between two middle-aged women Believers. One of these women turned to me and said:

"Wasn't it perfectly miraculous!"

"No," I said.

Both women came at me then, demanding to know what I meant by such a denial.

"Well," I said, "I'd never be convinced unless I could be inside that cabinet with him during one of his séances."

What a foolish thing to have said! Before I knew what was going on, another séance had been scheduled for a week later and Nino Pecararo had agreed that I could occupy the spooky cabinet with him. I tried to withdraw, but those women insisted that I go through with the bargain, since I was such a smart aleck, and of course Joe Dunninger egged me on.

This special séance was held in the office of a Broadway lawyer and Nino was quietly sullen when he arrived that night. A goodly crowd was there including Vincent Lopez, the orchestra leader, who has always been a walking encyclopedia of the black arts. Also present was the late Clara Belle Walsh, an incredibly wealthy woman who believed in all the things that Vincent Lopez believed in, and then some. All but Dunninger and me were Believers.

Nino's wrists and ankles were bound and his body was placed in a sack of heavy fishnet. Then he was roped securely to a straight-backed chair and lifted into the cabinet. Next they tied me to a chair and settled me alongside Nino, perhaps two feet away from him. The lights were turned off, the people in the audience formed themselves into a semicircle in front of the cabinet, and the séance began.

Nino and I sat in the darkest darkness I have ever known and faced a black curtain which separated us from the audience. The people outside made no sound, save for an occasional rustle of clothing or a slight movement of a chair. Nino scarcely moved a muscle for thirty minutes. During those thirty minutes my small store of courage began to flow out of me. I started thinking as follows: "This bastard is crazy. He's crazy and he's mad as hell at me for presuming to challenge his honesty. He's even crazy enough to kill me. I know already that he's able to wiggle himself out of those ropes and out of that sack. He's so furious that he's going to get loose and pick up that chair and brain me with it."

My thoughts raced along in that unpleasant vein and I started to sweat. Still no sound from Nino—no audible indication that he was escaping his bonds. Then, without warning, he let go with one of the most piercing shrieks ever heard on earth. It was enough to frighten a fence post. Coming as it did after that long, suspenseful, black silence, the shriek even frightened the members of the audience. I could hear their gasps and their exclamations. And me—I was too weak and limp to even shudder. All the strength had drained out of me. I just sat there and waited for him to strike, figuring myself as a sure thing for Out Yonder. He let half a minute go by after the shriek and then he spoke:

"That . . . was . . . Teeadore . . . Roosevelt."

I didn't believe in spiritualism then, and I don't now, but if that was Theodore Roosevelt, a violent pox on him. What a thing to do!

For a while I debated the advisability of getting out of that cabinet, but then I thought of the embarrassment of facing the people outside and resolved to stay a bit longer. What followed was another long period of silence. I could hear Nino uttering long sighs, and now and then a small grunt. The bastard was working himself free. This time he'd get me. This time it would be the chair on my head. Those were the longest minutes of my life—about forty of them—and at last it came again; another screech, worse than the first. I leaped a foot and a half off the floor, taking my chair with me. Then came Nino's voice again:

"That . . . was . . . King of . . . Italia."

And that was . . . enough . . . for . . . me. They hadn't tied me securely and I managed to get the ropes off. I didn't care any more about the shame of it. I simply got up and parted the curtains and got out of that place, away from Theodore Roosevelt and the King of Italia. The people outside understood and were silently sympathetic, and nobody chided me for leaving the cabinet. I took a chair in the rear and sat toying with the notion of killing that Italian devil.

The spirits that came into the room after that were less noisy and seemed, in fact, to have a certain jubilation in their voices. Nino began bringing back soft-spoken grandmothers and easy-mannered uncles and gentle-acting cousins. My departure from the cabinet had turned him into a spiritualistic ball of fire. Then Ed Wolf, a radio producer who was an old friend of mine from the Sebring days, spoke up and asked if he might have Napoleon Bonaparte on the line. There was a groaning and a grunting inside the cabinet and suddenly Nino came plunging through the curtains, carrying them with him. He was free of the chair but still in the fishnet and he began threshing about on the floor like—I've got to use the cliché because it fits so well—like a chicken with its head cut off. He had kicked the legs off two chairs and bruised up a few citizens before they got him pinned down. By this time the lights had been switched on and Miss Clara Belle Walsh was snorting away at a vial of smelling salts and someone threw a wastebasket full of water on the Italian medium. He quieted down and they cut the net and the ropes off him. Soon he opened his eyes, looked all around, and muttered:

"Whatta happen?"

I felt like showing him whatta happen. I even took a step forward and if I had been carrying a good stout club, I might have put him into the deepest of all trances.

The spiritualists now said that my experience in the cabinet disproved nothing. They contended that those shrieks had actually come from Teeadore Roosevelt and the King of Italia. I was too weak to argue with them. I went home.

Subsequently Nino Pecararo confessed himself a pure fraud. Dunninger got him to sign a confession in which he admitted he was nothing more than an escape artist, able to extricate himself from bonds. The spiritualists answered this by saying that Dunninger had hypnotized Nino into making such a confession. Sometimes I find it a little difficult to sustain my belief in the essential dignity of man.

That was the only séance I ever attended in any role other than that of observer. The truth is I was almost always a miserable failure on any assignment that called for employment of a forceful and dynamic approach. In this respect I differed from the really competent reporters I knew and worked with. Even Lucius Beebe, then with the *Herald Tribune*, was a better reporter than I. When Coste and Bellonte flew the Atlantic non-stop they said they were tired and so they were escorted to a big Manhattan hotel and hustled into a suite and allowed to go to bed. We valiants of the press soon located them but we were told that the heroic Frenchmen were asleep and we could not go to their rooms. To me this sounded quite reasonable and I was ready and willing to go back to my office. I did not believe, as all my colleagues clearly believed, that the end purpose of that transatlantic flight was a newspaper interview; that every major event in human history was ordained and organized in order that newspaper reporters could cover it and report on it. Lucius Beebe, the dude, was present in that hotel lobby when word came that we would not be permitted to see the French fliers. Mr. Beebe took off his expensive Homburg and hurled it to the floor and said hell and god damn and finally he took hold of the assistant hotel manager by the shoulders and was about to give him a good shaking when the rule was changed and we were permitted to go upstairs and awaken the fliers and get their story.

Then there was the time Jimmie Walker got into the mess that would culminate in his resignation. Word came that the Mayor, cornered and sore-beset, would talk to reporters in his office and so I crossed the street to City Hall. There the Mayor's secretary announced that only accredited city hall reporters would be permitted to attend the press conference. That left two of us out—Jimmie Kilgallen and me. Jimmie was a man of small stature and large energy and he was the top reporter for Hearst's International News Service. When the secretary said that we couldn't go in to see Jimmie Walker, I shrugged and said okay. Not Jimmie Kilgallen. He made such a commotion that the Mayor's secretary retreated in alarm and then Jimmie said to me, "Come on, we'll knock the god damn door down." He led the way to the Mayor's door and promptly flung himself against it, hammering on it with his fists, kicking it, and yelling all manner of epithets casting reflection on the honor of His Honor. It was a splendid performance, but I would never have done it. Unhappily it achieved nothing for us—we went away without ever talking to the Mayor. But when the big bosses of UP and INS heard about it, they went to work on the phones and raised such a ruction that Walker agreed to receive Jimmie Kilgallen and me in private audience.

I'm reminded, too, of a couple of additional performances on my part. One day Paul White called me from CBS.

"Hey," he said, "we got a fellow up here I think would make you a good interview."

"Who?"

"He's a singer from the coast. A real character."

"What's his name?"

"Crosby."

"Nah," I said. And that was that.

Then there was G. Edward Pendray. He was a young man with a pointy black beard and he had been a successful science writer and reporter. In 1930 he and a few friends organized the American Interplanetary Society at a meeting in the Pendray apartment. It was the stated purpose of this organization to experiment with rockets until they got one that would carry a man into space, and eventually to the moon. Along with other reporters I went to see Mr. Pendray on various occasions. We would sit and listen to him talk about the future of interplanetary travel, and we would manage to keep our faces straight, and then later on when we were outside—possibly in a speakeasy—we'd laugh and snigger about Pendray and his fool

Society. We looked upon him and his associates as screwballs, no more than a small cut above tea-leaf readers and Ouija (Weejee) board addicts and Imminent-End-of-the-World prophets. And there was an undertone of ridicule in the stories many of us wrote about Pendray and his rocketeering. His organization soon became the American Rocket Society and today is the leading technical group in the rocket and missile and space flight field. Mr. Pendray, now head of a prosperous public relations and industrial relations agency, holds Membership Card No. 1 in the Society. If any one man in the world could be called the father of space flight, Pendray is my personal nominee for the title.

I don't know if it is true any more but it used to be that a person who came to live in New York hated the town bitterly for the first six months. Then it began to take hold of him and within another half year he'd be hopelessly in thrall. It worked that way with me and after a while I began to feel myself a part of this incredible metropolis, and to love it for the aura of glamor and romance that always hovered over it. A young reporter was almost daily in the presence of fame. Those were the days of Grover Whalen's glad-handing and I sometimes had to step lively to avoid being trampled by the parades up Lower Broadway and the receptions in City Hall Park. One month I'd find myself trailing around after the Prime Minister of Great Britain, Ramsay MacDonald, and his dowdy daughter; the next month I'd be brushing shoulders with a man then looked upon as a great statesman, Pierre Laval.

My sister Lou came to town for her first visit to New York and I spent a day showing her around. I was the dashing young reporter, tough and knowledgeable about New York Town. "We'll see a lot of famous people, probably," I told Lou.

"Where?" she said, bursting with enthusiasm.

"Oh," I said with a casual air, "right on the street. We don't pay any attention to them."

She was thrilled at the prospect and privately I hoped we'd actually catch a glimpse of somebody passably famous. The Empire State Building was now open for business and the observation tower had become a great tourist attraction. I took Lou to the Little Church Around the Corner—the first choice of every Midwesterner I ever entertained in New York. Then we went to the Empire State. We entered an elevator on the ground floor and were alone in the car when two giggly girls came charging in. They were very attractive and one of them, in fact, looked a good deal like Norma Shearer. Then a man came to the door of our car and said, "Hey, you girls, you belong over here!" So the two gigglers departed, and now the door closed and up we went.

"Notice that girl in the white hat?" I said to Lou.

"Yes."

"Know who it was?"

"No."

"That," I said, "was Norma Shearer."

Well, Lou could scarcely contain herself. She rolled her eyes and sighed and exclaimed over it—being *in the same elevator* with Norma Shearer! I grinned, and acted blasé, and said to myself: "Quite neat. Got away with *that* one pretty slick!"

So we arrived at the observation tower and went outside and walked around a corner and there stood the two giggly girls, and the one in the white hat *was* Norma Shearer, and not only that— she was being shown the view by the Hon. Alfred E. Smith.

Served me right, for lying.

Aimee Semple McPherson came to town to appear on the stage of a Broadway theater and I was given the opportunity of "dating" her for an evening. The theater press agent, Irwin Zeltner, furnished us with a limousine and a bottle of whisky and mapped out a plan for the evening. I would take Sister Aimee on a tour of the Bowery missions, where she would appear suddenly like an angel out of a cloud and do some rousements and gather some bums into the fold. She complimented me for my ingenuity, saying it was a real good stunt, but she said she wanted it organized against any possibility of failure. She wanted the proprietors of the Bowery missions to know that she was coming and to promise that their halls would be full of derelicts. I had a secret, secondary plan—it was my intention to feed Sister Aimee from the bottle of whisky and get her a trifle tiddley and they pry some real juicy information out of her. I didn't succeed. I have an idea this had been tried with her before and she didn't co-operate. It did, however, become clear to me during the evening that there was more to Aimee Semple McPherson than simple spiritual beauty. She was in business. Her product was her own magnetic personality. And she knew how to sell it.

Gradually I made the acquaintance of well-known newspapermen such as Alva Johnston, Earl Sparling, Quentin Reynolds, Beverly Smith, Joel Sayre, and Meyer Berger. There was one, Howard

Cushman, who worked on the *Morning Telegraph* and then switched to the *World* and who was, I felt, destined to become one of the top humorists of the country. I have no idea what ever happened to him. He took to carrying a cane and then he disappeared from New York journalism.

One of the saddest moments in the history of American newspapers came the night the *World* died. I spent a part of that evening hanging around the *World* offices and I saw newspapermen openly weeping.

My oldest friends remained John Moynihan and Joe Alex Morris and Morris Watson. Then along came a new crony in the person of a boy sports writer from Georgia named Henry McLemore. He came to New York with the seat literally out of his pants and knowing even less than I did about grammar and punctuation. But he was a skillful bluffer; if he couldn't pronounce a word he pronounced it anyway. He referred to the composer of Symphonie Pathetique as Tatcherskowsky. He called a designer of ladies' dresses a coo-tooter-rooter. Henry was a real hungry-looking Secesh when he finally landed a job at the UP. He and I became good friends at once and lived near each other in Jackson Heights and eventually we worked more or less as a writing team.

One day I was walking across City Hall Park when I came face to face with Sidney B. Whipple. I was overjoyed at seeing my old friend again even though he was wearing a derby hat. He said he had quit his job in Denver, reunited with his family, and he was now looking for a job. He was even then on his way to the UP offices and within an hour he was hired, for they knew him well. So I ranged over the Big Town with Sid Whipple a part of the time, and with McLemore part of the time, and some evenings the three of us went adventuring together, often to the surprise and consternation of the citizenry. McLemore had not been married very long and his wife (first of a long line) had convinced him that it is the duty of a husband to come home after work. Sid Whipple and I had, of course, outgrown such plebian nonsense.

As working newspapermen we could go to almost any night club in town and eat and drink for hours and never even have to tip the waiter. I had done a couple of lively interviews with Texas Guinan and so I was usually given a great big glad-hand in her clubs. One night Sid Whipple and I went to Tex's place and took a table and in about sixty seconds the waiter installed a bottle of whisky (Golden

Wedding) beside the leg of my chair. It is time that I stated that I
was almost thirty years old before I learned that there were other
brands of whisky besides Golden Wedding.

Around midnight Texas came to work and stopped by our table
for a brief visit and ordered another bottle for us. Along about three
in the morning Sid and I, feeling the surge of adventure in our blood,
decided to go look for something a little more exciting. Stepping
high, we made it to the street and in a magnificent display of fool-
hardiness and ignorance entered a cab and told the driver to take us
to a nice lively drinking establishment. He drove us to an address
somewhere on the East Side and by happy chance I noted the name
of the dive as we entered. It was clearly a clip joint but Sid and I
were in such high spirits that we didn't notice many details. We saw
only an inviting bar and six or eight unattached girls, each appearing
lovelier than Dolores Del Rio or Mary Brian. And what's more, these
girls were *friendly*. They'd come right up alongside us and smile
and run their fingers up and down our arms and tweak our ears and
say hey big boy how 'bout buyin' baby a lil ole drink. Debutantes,
probably.

We bought them drinks—all they could hoist. For some reason my
body chemistry was out of balance and I remained aware of my
surroundings and was considerably more sober than Sid. I don't
know how long we had been in the place when the proprietor came
up to me and asked me if I'd like to take care of the bill. He handed
it to me. *L'addition* was somewhere in the vicinity of eighty-five
dollars. I sobered slightly, then tried a bit of bravado and said we'd
take care of it at once. I nudged Sid and got him away from a
couple of debutantes and took him into the gents' room and asked
him how much dough he had. He fumbled in his pockets and finally
came up with about three dollars. I had a dollar seventy-five. I told
Sid I thought we might be in trouble because of the bill. I reminded
him that there were several interesting-looking gentlemen lounging
around the place. With caps on. Yet I was still cocky about everything. After all, we were not tourists, we were not the fabled butter-
and-egg twerps; we were The Press. Yet I knew that something had
to be done about that bill. I told Sid to return to the bar and continue buying drinks for the girls. He did, without complaint, without
whining, like the soldier that he was. I got into a phone booth and
called the United Press.

On duty at that hour was one lone staff man, Sandor S. Klein, a

New York kid with plenty of moxie. It must have been around five o'clock in the morning.

"Sandy," I yelled into the phone, "drop whatever you're doing and rush right up here with a hundred dollars."

Sandy Klein had never *seen* a hundred dollars. He slowed me down and cross-questioned me about the nature of the place we were in, the kind of people who were there, the amount of the bill, and finally he got the name of the speakeasy out of me. Then he told me: "Get this straight, now. You and Sid stay put. Buy more drinks. Stall the guy about the bill. I'll see what I can do."

I went back to the bar. The proprietor came at me again and the gentlemen with caps on began moving a bit closer to us, but I laughed joyfully and said we had plenty of the old mazuma, and ordered a round of drinks for the house. In ten or fifteen minutes the front door swung open and in came two policemen. They brushed everyone aside and asked for Smith and Whipple. They seized hold of us and announced gruffly that they had been looking all over for us, that we were wanted at headquarters. They started jostling us out of the place. The proprietor now set up a howl. What about his money? The cops told him to shut his big fat face, that we were wanted men, and out to the street we went. They escorted us roughly around the corner where a taxi was waiting, its door standing open. They took Sid and aimed him through the door and then kicked him in. They aimed me, and kicked me in. Then they said, "Now, you bastards go on home and see if you can't stay out of joints like that."

I continued to interview authors right and left, from the imported British variety to the composers of cowboy novels. I went down the bay to meet Hugh Walpole and asked him the standard question about his opinion of contemporary American writers. He spoke of a new novelist.

"His name," said Walpole, "is Thomas Fox or Thomas Wolf or some animal creature of that sort. I have just read his book called something on the order of *Goodbye, My Darling*. Not at all sure of that title. Published by Scribners. You people should wake up to this young man. He has the makings of greatness."

I couldn't wake up to him unless I knew who he was and what he had written so I went back to my office and telephoned Scribners and they said the name of the book was *Look Homeward, Angel* and the author was Thomas Wolfe and that Mr. Walpole was correct about his greatness. They said they'd send me a copy of the novel if I'd give them a quotation from Walpole to use in their ads, and I did and they did. So a few days later this Walpole cove got up in public and announced that he had been misquoted, that he never said any such thing, and people began calling me, and I said that Mr. Walpole was an old foof, and here I was, right smack in the middle of a brisk literary controversy that might even have international repercussions. I figured that this Thomas Wolfe would probably call on me and thank me from the bottom of his heart for making him famous, but he didn't even phone me.

I got to know Theodore Dreiser and Sinclair Lewis and Carl Van Doren. Once I was walking along Fifth Avenue and I saw a man standing in the entrance to an office building and I recognized him as Henry L. Mencken. I was too overwhelmed with emotion to approach him, but later I arranged an interview with him and I saw him quite often all the rest of his life.

Actually in those days no celebrity outside the literary set made any great impression on me. One day, seeking a subject for my daily signed story, I read a note in one of the papers that Babe Ruth had become the proprietor of a hat store on Broadway and that there was to be a grand opening with the Babe presiding over the festivities. I telephoned Ruth's manager, Christy Walsh, and said I wanted to write a story about the opening and what time should I be there. Mr. Walsh asked me to come to his apartment on Riverside Drive at seven P.M. and he would take me down to the grand opening.

When I arrived at the apartment Mr. Walsh greeted me and said, "We're just finishing dinner. How about some coffee before we start?" I said that would be fine and he escorted me to the dining room. Some men were sitting around the table smoking cigars and drinking coffee and talking. Mr. Walsh called out their names for me and when he came to the Babe I was mildly impressed. I didn't even catch the names of the others. I sat down and had coffee and listened to the talk and gradually things began to come into focus. A big, quiet guy on my left finally said something to me and when I turned and looked at him I recognized Lou Gehrig. A minute later it dawned on me that the pudgy man on the other side of me was Knute Rockne. In another chair was Walter Johnson and next to him was Red Grange. All that was needed to complete the picture was Bobby Jones and Dempsey and maybe Man o' War. We all rode down to the hat store later in two cars behind a motorcycle escort and all I can recall of the trip was that Knute Rockne sat next to me and talked about the excellence of the knee-action principle embodied in the knees of the new Studebaker.

What a stupendous thing for a callow young man from the Midwest to stumble upon! Ruth, Gehrig, Rockne, Johnson, and Grange! If I had been a normal American boy I'd have wet my pants. But my worship of authors was so dominant that these sports characters had little appeal for me. This was an unreasonable state of affairs and it was necessary that something happen to end my one-track preoccupation with literary people. The instrument responsible for my disillusionment, I think, was a man known as The Mad Genius of the Bronx—Charles Fort. He had serious doubts that the earth revolves around the sun. He scoffed at medical science even on his deathbed. He subscribed to theories that a mud turtle would blush to believe.

I attended the first meeting of the Fortean Society in a suite at the Savoy Plaza on a cold, snowy night in 1931. Theodore Dreiser was there and Burton Rascoe and Ben Hecht. Tiffany Thayer, the novelist, was present as secretary of the Society but Dreiser did most of the talking. Fort himself, somewhat fishfuddled by it all, sat and puffed quietly at a cigar. I was told that Edgar Lee Masters, Booth Tarkington, John Cowper Powys, and Alexander Woollcott were among Charles Fort's followers.

Fort wrote books about weird natural phenomena, especially a force called teleportation—the reverse of gravitation. He cited scores of instances in which objects have been swished off the earth to vanish in space. Among these mysterious disappearances were not a few human beings who were standing in the middle of the road one moment and gone forever in the next. He called attention, for example, to the simultaneous disappearance of Ambrose Bierce in Mexico and Ambrose Small in Canada. Was someone Out There collecting Ambroses? Fort suspected as much.

Dreiser and the others at that little dinner made a tremendous fuss over Fort. A week or so later I went to visit the old boy in his grubby apartment up in the Bronx. I wanted to look at his files, the records which Dreiser had talked about so much. They consisted of thousands of newspaper clippings plus more thousands of penciled notes, written in a code known only to Fort, and these were pigeonholed around the apartment, many of them packed away in old shoe boxes.

Fort showed me a game of supercheckers he had invented, in which he employed one thousand men, moving them by battalions on a board containing some seven thousand squares. He told me that the stars were not actual bodies in space but that they were merely apertures in a gelatinous substance surrounding the earth. What we see is a light shining through these holes. Fort pursued this notion to such lengths that he once warned aviators against the gelatinous shell, declaring that if they were not careful they might find themselves stuck like currants in a blancmange.

He said there were fields of ice as big as those in the Arctic Ocean floating around in the sky. Hence, winter.

He went on and on, and I got to thinking about Dreiser and the others who were trumpeting his genius and I lost some of my blind enthusiasm for book authors. I began writing about movie actresses and strippers and athletes and . . . The Greatest Man in the World.

# the kidnaping of

# Albert Einstein

Several years ago Erwin D. Canham, editor of the *Christian Science Monitor*, made the following statement: "In an era of great technical changes, there have been less in the newspaper field than in almost any other." A real bum sentence, but the meaning is there.

Mr. Canham should have gone a step further and considered the editorial end of the newspaper field, thusly: there have been less changes in the gathering of news than in the technical department. There has been, in fact, a distinct deterioration in the whole field of newsgathering. Everyone is aware of this except one small group—the keen-minded, alert, energetic people of the press.

I have many things in mind but I'll be content to dwell on just one—the preposterous farce of the mass interview. The mob scenes of today are plainly a national scandal. I see them from time to time on television and then, once again, rush right out and apply for membership in the dogs. Scores and even hundreds of newspaper reporters, press photographers, radio and television reporters, technicians of one kind or another—all these and more converge on the airport or the railroad station or aboard ship to greet the arriving celebrity. The thing is pure senseless pandemonium from the word go. Nobody really gets anything in the way of news—save for an account of the obscene spectacle itself. The reporters screech questions and shove each other around, the photographers howl curses at one another and at the reporters, and if the person who is getting all this attention has anything important to say, he wouldn't be heard if he did say it. The entire operation defeats its own purpose and month by month it grows worse. The police can't do anything about it; a policeman who roughs up a newspaper reporter stands a good chance of being busted to stool pigeon. In fact not long ago in one of these journalistic mob scenes a policeman, trying to protect Marilyn Monroe from being hurt, got a television wire wrapped round his neck and was almost lynched in a sidewise direction; he had to be treated for his injuries in a hospital. I have not heard of any steps being taken by the sagacious overlords of the American press to do something about mass interviews. Only one thing *could* be done, barring whiffs of grapeshot. Such stories should be covered under an arrangement which we used to call "syndication." Let three or four reporters, representing different shades of opinion, be chosen for the assignment, along with one press photographer and one TV unit and one radio unit. Then let everybody share in the results. The way it is now nobody is likely to get any exclusive news— so why all the insane competitiveness over nothing? But do you think the press would ever hear of such syndication? They'd scream bloody murder, and wave the flag, and howl about freedom of the press.

Stop me, somebody. Don't let me go on. I may kill.

In my newspaper experience there was only one mass interview that bore any close resemblance to the insane, inane, frenzied things they put on today. That was the arrival of Dr. Albert Einstein in New York harbor on a December day in 1930, aboard the liner *Belgenland*. The usual small group of shipnews reporters attended but in addition there were more than a hundred others. Each newspaper and each press association sent several reporters, and quite a few magazines had writers present. Also there were advertising agency men who had wangled cutter passes and who hoped they could get the most famous man in the world to endorse hats, violins, shaving cream, a disinfectant, neckties, and hair oil. Deodorants weren't talked about much in those days.

Carl Groat, who spoke fluent German, led the United Press group which included Joe Alex Morris and me. The screaming and yelling began as we swarmed aboard the *Belgenland* in what one historian, covering a lot of territory, called "one of the zaniest performances in the history of the press."

The gentle, cow-eyed Einstein was brought into a lounge and was surrounded at once by this screaming, clawing, shoving mob. None of us, apparently, had any true notion of his achievement although there was one dedicated science writer who climbed onto a piano and at the top of his voice read off a two-hundred-word hypothetical question concerning the curvature of space. When he finished it, he cried out: "Dr. Einstein, do you agree?" The great physicist replied: "Agree? I don't even know what you are talking about."

Mr. Groat, the man who mooed his "moos" so mellifluously back in the office, was standing on a delicate little gold chair, crying out a question in German. Gott im Himmel couldn't have heard it over the din. Everyone seemed to be yelling at once. Some shouted in German, some in Yiddish, some in English, and a few whooped their questions in what may have been high Dutch of low quality. At one point Dr. Einstein turned to his wife and said in German: "They are like a pack of hungry wolves."

Above the roar of the mob it was still possible to distinguish some of the questions being yelped at the scientist. Many of the reporters had been instructed by their city editors to ask specific questions. Some of them had been told to demand of Einstein a brief and simple explanation of his theories. One young man kept yelling that he wanted relativity explained in ten words. Another was shouting over and over, "What is bent space?" And the benign Doctor finally spoke a mathematical truism. "A cow," he said, "can give only a certain quantity of milk at a stated time."

A momentary lull followed this remark, as if the eye of a hurricane were passing over, and then a reporter leveled a finger at Einstein and shouted: "Is space here?" The question was quickly translated, and only served to perplex the scientist more deeply, for he murmured, "In his finger does he mean?"

A few fist fights broke out between photographers and reporters. The photographers charged that the reporters were hogging Einstein, by crowding so closely around him. The reporters replied that relativity was one hell of an important thing, and getting the final, authoritative word on it was more imperative than getting a picture of a man.

When the ship finally reached its pier the press swarmed ashore, eager to get to telephones and typewriters. But not all of them. There were three or four reporters who were told to get answers to their questions if it took a week. So all afternoon and all evening they camped at the entrance to the Einstein stateroom. Whenever the door was opened an inch or two they would throw themselves against it and scream through the crack:

"Give us relativity in one sentence! What's the fourth dimension? Define space in five words! How do you split an atom?"

The good gray professor was unable to leave the ship until the following day. Whenever I have thought back to it, I have been just a little ashamed about our behavior that day because Albert Einstein was not the kind of man who should have been subjected to such indignities. He was a fine and dignified and wonderful old guy, as the people of Princeton came to know. They still talk about how they used to encounter him walking along the streets of the university town eating an icecream cone. Strawberry. And Jack Dempsey tells about the time he went into a Princeton drugstore to get something for an inflamed eye. He noticed a white-haired old man in the back of the store, trying earnestly to make a Yo-yo work. Dempsey thought for a moment he would go back and show the old guy how to operate the Yo-yo. Then he saw who it was. "Imagine *me*," said Dempsey, "trying to teach Einstein *anything!*"

Once in a syndicated column I wrote a short personality sketch of Einstein concluding with some observations about his childlike good nature and mentioning that I would enjoy understanding his theory. I got letters from two dozen different states written by people who said they understood it and were willing to tell me all about it. One man, a Mr. F. P. O'Hare of St. Louis, wrote nineteen pages, single-spaced. After discussing politics, religion, the Rock Island railroad and his own life story, Mr. O'Hare explained the Einstein theory. He said it had something to do with onion skins.

"Consider," he wrote, "the electric bulb burning over your desk. Consider this bulb surrounded by onion skins, each skin representing a surface around the bulb where the intensity of the light is equal. Now introduce another burning bulb into the room. The room has transparent, non-reflecting walls. There are now *TWO* onion skins . . ."

That's enough of it. I could go on quoting Mr. O'Hare indefinitely but I think the Einstein Onion Skin Theory is quite clear, or clear enough, at this point. Anyway, I prefer Joe Alex Morris's explanation. Mr. Morris wrote a book titled *What a Year!* which had to do with 1929 and in this book he gave the world a simplified analysis of relativity. The trouble seems to be that people don't realize that Einstein first had to formulate a *general* theory that included gravitation as determiner of the curvature of a space-time continuum and represented gravitation as a field rather than a force. It is necessary to have a clear understanding of *that* in order to appreciate what happened in 1929, when Dr. Einstein found a key to the formulation of a unified field theory, a group of equations applicable not only to gravitation but also to electromagnetic and subatomic phenomena. That's what Joe Alex Morris said. I remember once when he was going off on an assignment to Europe and some of us gave a small dinner for him in a Manhattan restaurant and everyone got to feeling real frisky and Joe decided to explain the Einstein theory to us. He stood up, holding a loaf of Italian bread in his hand as if it were a torch. He waggled the loaf of bread to get our attention and then cried out, "This, folks, is an imponderable object. God damn it, will you pay attention? This is an *imponderable* object!" I don't remember the rest of it, if there was any more.

At last I seem to be approaching the crux of this chapter—the story of the kidnaping of Albert Einstein. It occurred during a visit subsequent to the one in which we interviewed him on the *Belgenland*. In that period Dr. Einstein was, in the mind of almost everyone, far and away the greatest man in the world—perhaps even the greatest in the history of the world. He was so towering in his importance that many people stood in awe of him, as if he were some tremendous natural wonder (which indeed he was). Some people were actually afraid to touch him.

They gave a birthday dinner in his honor one evening in the grand ballroom of the Waldorf-Astoria and I attended it, sitting at the press table. It was not very exciting and after a while I remembered that my friend Jim Irwin had telephoned me and asked me to pay him a visit at the Waldorf.

James W. Irwin was a handsome public relations man whose clients were usually top-rung industrial corporations. Today he has his own company in Chicago. I first knew him when he arrived in Denver to work as assistant publisher of the *Post*, directly under Bonfils. He was and still is a brisk, vigorous, forceful personality and at the time of which I now write, he was head of public relations for the Frigidaire Division of General Motors. He had come in to New York to promote a thing called the Meter-Miser, which was attached to the new Frigidaire models. It mised meters. Jim had a dozen refrigerators set up in the Carpenter Suite at the Waldorf and he was alerting the New York press to the approaching miracle of the Meter-Miser.

Sitting that evening at the Einstein dinner I recalled the Irwin invitation and so I crept away from the press table and went to the Carpenter Suite where I found Mr. Irwin alone with his iceboxes.

He broke out a bottle and we had a couple of drinks. Then I went back to the banquet, just to check, and everything seemed to be in order, and so I returned to Mr. Irwin. We sat around a while longer and finally Jim said:

"What's that thing you said you were covering?"

"Einstein," I said. "Big blow-out for Einstein in the grand ballroom."

"Here," said Mr. Irwin. "Have another one. Now, I've got an idea. Why don't you go down there and get Einstein and bring him up here and let him have a look at our Meter-Miser."

I laughed. Evilly. Sneeringly.

"No," he said, "I'm serious. You could do it."

"Maybe," I said, "but I wouldn't be dope enough to try it."

"Why not?" he urged. "You'd have yourself a much better story than you'll ever get out of a banquet. Here, have another one."

I had another one, and Mr. Irwin kept talking, and he has always been a most persuasive gent. If he were not my friend I'd say he was unctuous. Anyway, he convinced me that it was worth a try. We synchronized our watches and he told me to return to the press table in the grand ballroom, wait one half hour, then try to snatch Albert Einstein away from a huge roomful of distinguished and influential New Yorkers.

We didn't have count-downs then, but we had zero hour, and when it came I got up from my chair and walked to one end of the speakers' table, which was a mile and a half long. I went behind the people sitting at that table and trudged along until I reached the center, and there sat The Greatest Man in the World. I leaned over his shoulder and said:

"Dr. Einstein, would you mind coming with me for just a minute?"

He jumped a little, in surprise, grunted, turned and looked at me with a startled expression, and then said something in German. He had not understood me. So I gave him a slow, tantalizing beckon. I simply held out my right hand and with my forefinger beckoned him out of his chair. He got up and nobody paid much attention as he padded along behind me, out of the big room, up a flight of stairs, and into the Carpenter Suite.

By this time Mr. Irwin had been joined by two associates. One was a photographer. The other was a Mr. Charlie Lawson, who was sales manager for Frigidaire. Mr. Irwin had quickly summoned Mr. Lawson to the scene for two reasons. The first and most important was, he wanted Mr. Lawson to see enterprise that was enterprise. And secondly, he knew that Mr. Lawson could sprecken zee doitch.

Dr. Einstein stood there near the doorway, looking around the room, a faint smile of friendliness on his face. He hadn't the faintest idea of what was going on. But Jim Irwin stepped forward, seized his hand, shook it, and said all in one breath:

"It is indeed a pleasure to make your acquaintance Professor Einstein Charlie tell him in German we want to show him the Meter-Miser and tell him what it is hey Mike get ready."

"I don't think," said Mr. Lawson, "that I can do it in German, but I'll try."

So he fired a long string of German at the Professor, who nodded occasionally, and continued looking around the room. Then they walked him up to one of the refrigerators and before long they had The Greatest Man in the World down on all fours. It's the truth. Dr. Einstein was down on the floor looking at machinery and Mr. Lawson was there with him trying to explain the Meter-Miser Theory in German, and the photographer was banging away.

I just stood off to one side, fascinated by the whole thing, astounded at what I had done, and then I began to get frightened. Those people downstairs. My God, they'd tear me limb from limb. I told Mr. Irwin that I had to get the Professor back to his people. I said right now. I said I didn't want any gott ver dammitee argument. I said I had done my part and he had got his man and he had got his pictures and that was enough. He said certainly, and I seized Dr. Einstein by the arm and hauled him out of there and took him back to the ballroom. I didn't go in with him. I just brought him up through the wings and gave him a little push into the alleyway back of the speakers' table. He started for his chair and then stopped, and turned back, and gave me a nice smile. After that he resumed his journey to the Seat of Honor.

There was a lively aftermath which I didn't know about until 1961. That night I telephoned a story in to the United Press about how Einstein had been lured away from his birthday dinner to look at the Meter-Miser, and how he had been photographed on his hands and knees. The story arrived late in the office and only a few paragraphs made the wires. These paragraphs appeared in the newspapers, however, and the next day there was trouble.

Mr. Irwin tells me that Bernard Baruch heard about the kidnaping and the picture-taking. Mr. Baruch was a warm friend of Einstein and telephoned him and found out it was all true. Then he called Alfred P. Sloan, Jr., at that time president of General Motors. Mr. Sloan called the president of Frigidaire. Those icebox pictures of Albert Einstein were not to be released. And now Mr. Irwin was called on the carpet. He had to ceremoniously, in person, destroy the negatives of those Einstein pictures in the presence of Frigidaire's big brass. And he would have been canned from his job except for one man—the same Alfred P. Sloan, Jr. Mr. Sloan never said so, but the chances are he was secretly pleased with the enterprise shown by Mr. Irwin, for a short time later he gave Mr. Irwin a big fat promotion.

As for me, I have but one faint consolation—one real pleasant remembrance out of those shameful proceedings. I have heard that Dr. Einstein hated banquets, and especially banquets given in his honor. When the invitations came he used to say to his wife, "It is feeding time at the zoo again." So I can only believe that the good-by smile he gave me that night was a smile of gratitude. For a mere ten or fifteen minutes I had taken him away from an unpleasant atmosphere. To his way of thinking, even looking at a Meter-Miser was more fun than looking at all those faces in the grand ballroom.

# *wild life on*

# *Forty-Second Street*

The United Press moved from Park Row to the *Daily News* building on East Forty-Second Street and a new boy joined our little group of madcap journalists: Johnnie Martyn from Philadelphia. Johnnie was a tall and personable young man who attracted beautiful women the way I always wanted to, and he brought with him to Forty-Second Street the word crock. Not in the sense that it was used later by the valiant men of our armed forces. As I have said the UP nurtured a code language of its own, including terms of fraternal affection, and now a new and meaningful expression came into Unipress usage: "Let's split a crock."

A crock was a bottle of cordial shop gin. A cordial shop was a shop with a sign over the entrance saying Cordial Shop. It sold nothing but gin and all the bottles were the same size and cost seventy-five cents each. There was a cordial shop a few steps away from the *News* building and this was the place we went when it came time to split a crock.

Crock-splitting involved two or three men, sometimes even four. Each man chipped in until the needed seventy-five cents had been assembled and then somebody went and got the crock. It was stashed in the locker room where, from time to time, the splitters of the crock took a belt out of it. The people on the dayside didn't split crocks, so far as I know; crock-splitting was a nightside institution. The nightside was, in fact, the sinful side of the United Press. A morning newspaper is usually a wilder and more depraved place then an afternoon paper. The splitting of crocks did not take place until the top brass had gone home for the day. Some time between five and six o'clock, almost every evening, somebody would lean over my shoulder and say, "Let's split a crock." Or I would lean over someone else's shoulder and say it.

I worked for a succession of nightside bosses in the *News* building, including Charlie McCann, Morris DeHaven Tracy, Earl J. Johnson, Boyd Lewis, Miles W. Vaughan, and one other. One day Johnnie Martyn and I arrived for work at two o'clock in the afternoon to find that Sidney Whipple had been installed as nightside chief—our boss. He was sitting at the executive desk, riffling busily through some papers, and when he saw us he called us to his side and had us sit down.

"Now," he said, "I want you fellows to know that I'm now the boss of this operation. We've had a lot of fun together, but that's all over. From now on, things are going to be different. *Get that straight.* I mean it. I'm not going to put up with any of your god damn juvenile foolishness. Is that clear? There'll be no drinking on the job. None. If I catch you guys drinking on the job, I'm firing you on the spot. Now. Do you understand?"

"Yes, Sid," I said.

"Sure, Sid," said Johnnie.

So Johnnie and I went about our afternoon duties, and I did an interview with a movie actor and came back to the office and about half past five was just winding up the writing job when I felt a presence behind me. Then a head came over my shoulder. "Let's split a crock," said the head. It was attached to the body of Sidney B. Whipple.

It would take twenty books the size of this one to encompass all the interviews I wrote during the dozen years I was a newspaperman in New York. I spent an evening with that king of the weirdies, Bernarr Macfadden. I was supposed to get a story out of him but I can't remember the topic because we never got to it. Macfadden spent two hours talking about stomachs, with special reference to the stomach of Karl A. Bickel, president of the UP. He told me what Bickel should eat for breakfast . . . on Monday. And then for lunch, and dinner, and breakfast on Tuesday, and so on through the week, with an occasional whack at some wheat germ, or a slug of sorghum molasses. I didn't write that story because I didn't think that Mr. Bickel would care to have his stomach publicized by way of his own trunk wires.

Periodically I would go down the bay to Quarantine and meet

the ocean liners for interviews with Texas Guinan or Henry L. Mencken or Henry Ford or visiting European authors. I missed one of the most charming incidents ever to occur in the history of ship-news reporting—the interview with Anna May Wong. I was on the ship but I had bypassed the actress to get at André Maurois. The other reporters all flocked into Miss Wong's quarters and she told them gay anecdotes about her travels in Europe. The interview was concluded and the gentlemen of the press departed in quest of other Big Names. One fellow, however, stayed behind and when he and Miss Wong were alone he said:

"Uh, Miss Wong, uh, well, you see, there was . . . I mean, uh, well, it's this way, Miss Wong . . . to be frank about it, well, uh, there was one other thing . . ."

Miss Wong smiled and didn't give him a chance to finish.

"It's not true," she said.

Such is the probity, the rectitude, the incorruptibility of the news-paper gentry that I personally have heard at least six of them tell that story as having happened to them. Each has solemnly said that *he* was the one. Yet I'm pretty sure that the Anna May Wong "exclusive" belongs to John McClain, and I've always suspected that John's friend, Robert Benchley, put him up to it.

Several times I went to see Lindbergh when he held press conferences in Juan Trippe's office. I sat in on a couple of Franklin D. Roosevelt's press sessions and once Louis Howe introduced me to the Governor. I met and interviewed both Edgar Wallace and Sax Rohmer, two British writing factories. I thought Edgar Wallace was one of the most remarkable men I'd ever met. He devised many fantastic methods of doing a man to death, and then *he* died of drinking too much tea. One day I sat beside Florenz Ziegfeld and observed him in the act of selecting showgirls for his next production. The famous showman and I were in the front row of the theater and there was a steady procession of young girls onto the stage. Each girl stepped into the spotlight, wearing next to nothing, and then obeyed the producer's directions to turn this way, turn that way, turn around. Every one of those girls was shooting for the moon. This was The Big Chance. And each of them was subjected to the cruelest kind of punishment—the sarcastic, lashing tongue of that old man at my side. "For God's sake who sent *you* here?" he'd exclaim. "Get her out of my sight!" he'd call out. "Jesus God, a mud fence!" he'd bellow. Many of those girls simply burst into tears and

ran off the stage. I didn't stay for it all. I couldn't. I've been told
I should not be too harsh with Ziegfeld in this matter—that his
conduct is the accepted practice among producers of girl shows.
That ain't the way I heard it.

Henry McLemore and I were assigned to many of the big sporting
events, such as heavyweight championship fights and the World
Series. The two of us contributed in many ways to the public mis-
conception of newspapermen. The *News* building had a circular
lobby (the last time I was in it I noticed that the lobby has absorbed
a bank, and is no longer circular) with a huge terrestrial globe in the
center. This lobby was usually crowded with tourists and Henry and
I, being young and gay, sometimes gave them a little show.

We'd come up Forty-Second Street and enter the lobby through
the main entrance. I'd slam through the revolving door, setting it
spinning like a top. I'd have the brim of my hat turned up in front,
a wad of paper in my left hand, a pencil in my right. As I charged
into the lobby I'd cry out:

"Gangway! Scoop! Scoop! Scoop!"

Then I'd rush through the throng of the bug-eyed tourists, toward
the elevators, and then into the lobby would come Henry, equipped
the same as I had been, and screaming:

"Stop the press! Stop the press! Stop the press!"

Henry had a sharper sense of dramatic values than I and instead
of dashing off-stage following his stop-the-press cries, he would come
to a standstill, put his pencil and paper in his pocket, adjust the
brim of his hat and stroll nonchalantly to the elevators. He had
been an actor in his youth, working with a stock company in Georgia.
Well, not exactly an actor—he was a sort of assistant prop man. The
only role he was ever given in a play was that of a bellboy, and he
had but a single line to speak. The leading man said he would like
to have a pitcher of ice water. Henry, as the bellhop, then declaimed:
"I will be happy to make water for you, sir."

Henry and I were what you might call writing primitives. We put
words together in patterns and formations that were new to the
world. Quite often they didn't make sense, but there was a *novelty*
about them. Once in Philadelphia, where we were covering the
classic that became known as the Pepper Martin World Series, we
climaxed a sequence of daffy adventures by writing a story of the
Big Game, a story that still ranks as unique in the annals of baseball
literature. Carl Groat was standing beside the news printer in the

New York office when our lead story began coming through from Philadelphia. Mind you, this was the biggest day of the most exciting sports spectacle in years. The first line of our story was: "Folks, have you ever been in Nokomis, Illinois?" The second line was: "You haven't?" The third line was: "Well, where *HAVE* you been?" (Man, that's sports writin'!)

Carl Groat read those lines, and then read them over again, and frowned in concentration, feeling somehow that as general news manager of a great worldwide press association he ought to bone up a bit on the game of baseball. Then along came Earl Johnson to stand beside him, and Earl read the lines and laughed, and Groat said to him, "Earl, do you suppose those two boys are drinking?" Earl laughed again. "Why, Carl!" he exclaimed. "How could you even *suggest* such a thing!" Earl Johnson was easily the most *understanding* boss I ever had at the UP.

I think the Nokomis, Illinois, reference in our story had something to do with a ballplayer named Jim Bottomley, but I'm not sure. This I do know—that insane, futuristic story was printed in newspapers all over the land, and the UP got many messages of congratulations for this fresh approach to sports reporting. Sort of Joycean. New Technique. Go to the wildest World Series in history and write about a little town in Illinois. Too, too dee-voon! (A saying of that period.)

Henry McLemore and I got so many compliments on the quality of our joint prose that we decided to get rich and famous. We set ourselves up as short story writers. It was our custom to meet at my apartment. I would send Nelle and the two children away. I'd roll a sheet of paper into the typewriter and then we'd forget it for a while. We'd sit down with a bottle of gin and "talk" our story until the gin was gone. Then we'd start to work. Within minutes we'd be quarreling, calling each other names and threatening each other with abrasions. Great artists are often difficult.

For a while we had a weekly radio program on CBS. Henry was the performer on "Professor McLemore's University of the Air." We wrote the scripts together. At each broadcast Professor McLemore taught a different subject, such as How to Write Popular Songs with Your Tongue Hanging Out, and What to Take with You When You Get Stranded on a Desert Island and Rules for Riding the Graf Zeppelin—on Top. I may be wrong but it seems to me that some of those scripts were quite funny and I would like to look at them again, but they don't exist. As quickly as he finished performing them, Henry threw them away, and we never gave the radio station any copies.

The radio program brought us in quite a bit of extra money but it didn't last—the public was not ready for Professor McLemore and would not be ready for him during the present geological era. We returned to the business of collaborating on short stories. It is Henry's recollection that we never got beyond the opening line of but one single story, and that line read:

> Mrs. Hester Van Primm walked out of the Hotel Plaza with twenty poodles on a leash.

Somehow we couldn't figure out what to do with Hester after that. The quarreling grew worse and finally resulted in our giving up writing as a team. We were in my apartment, shouting abuse at each other. I was in a chair and Henry was pacing the floor. He was in a South Georgia fury because I had said his sense of humor was dribbling out of his ears, that he couldn't write funny any more. Suddenly he whipped around, pointed a finger at me, and shouted:

"You (censored) (censored) (censored)! You don't deserve to live with that nanny-goat brain you got! I'm gonna throw your whole goddam apartment out the window!"

That's how mad he was. He needed physical action, violence.

"Go ahead and throw it, you (censored) (censored) (censored)!" I said.

He decided to start with the contents of the refrigerator. He opened one of the living-room windows, giving on an alleyway. Out went the eggs. Out went the bacon.

"Every stick of furniture in the place goes out!" he raged.

The bottles and the dishes made a frightful racket when they hit the concrete five floors below. Henry had finished with the contents of the refrigerator and was headed for the window with a floor lamp when the building superintendent came roaring into the apartment.

We had a time of it keeping the superintendent from calling the police, and we had to waste half a bottle of gin on him to get him pacified. When he had gone, Henry sat down across from me and grinned.

"You think I was bluffin'," he said. "You think I didn't mean it.

Well, I'd have done it. I'd have thrown everything out, and that includes *you*."

"Like hell you would've!" I said.

He leaped to his feet and was ready to resume the jettison job when I decided to temporize, yield, arbitrate, and surrender. I want no more collaborations. I get offers constantly from people with stupendous ideas who want me to collaborate with them. They get real prompt answers.

Henry McLemore was slightly off-beat. I remember the time he and I were sitting in one of our favorite hangouts, a German hofbrau on Long Island, with large steins of brew in front of us. The singing star of the floor show, Hans or Fritz or somesuch name, came and sat down with us. I got up to go see a man about a Dudelsackpfeifer. While I was gone Henry took a box containing a dozen aspirin tablets out of his pocket and dumped the tablets into my beer. Then he stirred up the mixture. "Watch him when he drinks it," Henry told Fritz. I came back from my errand and quaffed. In a short while my eyes began to roll around and my left cheek was twitching and then jerking. I felt that there might just possibly be something a bit wrong with me, and so I quickly gasped out a request for another stein of beer, and I drank it, and pretty soon my volcanic tics disappeared. The next day Henry paid me a high compliment. "Pal," he said, "I was sure you would fall on the floor unconscious, but you didn't. You got a real rugged constitution. Take care of it."

One morning around four o'clock he arrived in Jackson Heights from a party in Manhattan and he was walking along the street when he spotted a milk wagon. He remembered a bitter argument he and I had recently engaged in concerning our knowledge of farm life. He had told me that he could harness a horse blindfolded and I said he couldn't harness a horse if he had four large and sinewy arms. Here on the street before him was a horse, already harnessed. He reasoned that it was just as important to know how to *un*harness a horse as to harness one. He went to work quickly, and apparently he did know how to do it. He unharnessed that horse and led the animal up the street and entered the lobby of the apartment building where I lived, horse in hand. He was trying to get the horse up the first flight of stairs when the awakened tenants began assembling, and then the superintendent. The milkman, who had discovered that his horse had been rustled, heard the noises and arrived on the run to retrieve his rightful animal. Meanwhile Henry, recognizing the possibility of misunderstanding and trouble, had scampered up the stairs and found sanctuary in my apartment. Later in the morning he crept out and I could never again get him to set foot in that building.

I had occasional sports assignments outside our partnership. When Max Baer was heavyweight champion he had a reputation as an insatiable romantic. Alongside Mr. Baer, Errol Flynn was shy and virginal and frigid. I decided that Max Baer's views on girlhood, plus an account of some of his achievements in the field, would make an interesting story and Stuart Cameron, the UP sports editor, arranged for me to call on the handsome champ at the Park Central.

"Jesus Christ!" said Max, shaking hands with me, "you really got hold of a swell idea there. My experiences with ——. What a great idea! It'll make terrific readin'. My God, I got me two sets of lawyers. I got tax lawyers and I got —— lawyers. But listen, they're waitin' for me over at the Garden so come along and we'll talk about —— in the taxi.

He talked with great earnestness and becoming frankness all the way to Madison Square Garden. He told me about his first time, and he told it in vivid detail, and even gave me the name of the girl, and then he went on from there. He was burbling and bubbling and effervescing as he recited his sexual biography and whenever he'd arrive at a real exciting, real salacious point in his narrative, he'd say, "Now. Put this down on your notes. Put 'er down. This is the best part. She says to me . . ."

I never wrote a line of that interview. There wasn't a line of it that could be printed. I thought of doing a story saying just that, fumbling around with words and phrases in order to suggest the sheer unprintability of it, but even that would have been too "risky" for the UP wires. I didn't get a story but I did finally get to see Damon Runyon plain. When Baer and I arrived at the Garden we went into an office where Runyon and several other sports writers were waiting for the champ. Nobody introduced me to Runyon. I thought about introducing myself and telling him that Joe Diner of the Denver Press Club said hello. But I didn't. I just sat in a corner and listened to him as he talked with Max Baer.

On a December day in 1930 I paid my first visit to Harlem when I attended the funeral of the Angel Gabriel. The services were held at St. Mark's Methodist Church and De Lawd came, as did Marc Connelly, author of *The Green Pastures*, the play in which Wesley Hill had been Gabriel.

A few days earlier Hill had been killed by a taxicab and now he lay in his coffin in the crowded little church. Old Richard B. Harrison, De Lawd, sat on the dais and looked down at Gabe. The only weeping came from the wide balcony where now and again some Negro woman would rise from her seat and scream, then fall back into the arms of her friends.

The ceremony built itself toward a natural climax—the moment when De Lawd stood up and walked slowly to stage center, the white hair sweeping back from his benign face. De Lawd gazed down at Gabriel and a hush came over the auditorium. Then he spoke—spoke in the character of Harrison, the actor. But gradually Harrison the actor gave way to De Lawd, and De Lawd told of Gabe's impatience, how his lips were always itching to blow that "hawn" and summon man to judgment. Then the voice of De Lawd ceased, and his massive head dropped, and high in the balcony the voices of the Hall Johnson choir broke the stillness, singing, "I've Heard of a City Called Heaven and I'm Striving to Make It My Home." De Lawd stood there for a long moment, then his head came back up, and he raised his arms and cried out:

"Gangway! *Gangway for Gabe!*"

It was as dramatic as any scene I've ever witnessed.

De Lawd is dead now, but I saw him and talked to him a few months after Gabe's funeral. *The Green Pastures* company was finishing up an extended tour in a Pennsylvania town, and I wired Harrison asking if he could see me for an interview when he returned to Manhattan on the following Sunday. In the telegram I asked him to designate the hour and the place. He wired back:

SEE YOU AT YOUR OFFICE AT THREE P.M. SUNDAY.

So on that Sunday afternoon De Lawd walked Forty-Second Street like a natchel man. He came in and sat down at a desk and told me some amazing things about his tour. In almost every town where *The Green Pastures* played there were people, whites as well as Negroes, who fell beneath the mesmerism of Harrison's playing and reached the conclusion that he actually *was* God.

"A peculiar thing about it," said the old man, "is that nobody

ever got up from the audience and came across the footlights looking
for salvation. They always waited and came backstage to my dressing
room. Some of them would walk in and fall on their knees and get
hysterical, crying for their sins to be forgiven, reaching out to touch
me, and all that. What could I do? I could only try to soothe them
and tell them to be good."

When we finished our talk I escorted De Lawd to the elevator.
It being a Sunday afternoon, only one car was operating. I pressed
the button and we stood and talked for a while. I pressed the button
again and we waited and still no elevator. At last a sly grin came
over old Harrison's face. His back stiffened and he frowned as he
went into character.

"Son," he said, "it sho look like to me I'm gonna have to rare
back and pass a miracle and git dat ole elevator up here."

Whereupon the big door slid back and, with a wave of his hat,
he was gone.

My personal traffic with De Lawd had much the same effect on
me as it did on those people in his audiences. I founded a new
religion. It came to me in a vision that the world is going to end in
my lifetime. It was revealed to me that the end of the world will
arrive by stages, according to the earth's time belts. The people in
the Central Standard Time zone will get it first, then Eastern Standard, and then on across the Atlantic with Judgment Day arriving in
a sequence of waves, on around to the Pacific Ocean, heading toward California. There is a little uncertainty about what will happen
at the International Date Line—if there are any people out there
they will likely have to wait a full day for action, but by that time
everything will be so confused that nobody will give a damn. In this
revelation I was told that 145,000 of us will be allowed to enter
Heaven and I get to pick them. All the remaining people who
believe in my creed will be condemned to live on Earth throughout
Eternity, under the precise circumstances and conditions prevailing
at the moment Judgment Day hit them. Oh, yes, everybody else,
regardless of race, creed, color or political affiliations, goes to Hell.

Initiation fee, $1000. Dues per annum, $500.

I like to found religions.

# the bridge players, the nudists, and Gertrude Stein

It would not be truthful to say that the expression *snafu* was devised to describe my erratic progress through life. Yet I was always very expert at fouling up the detail, at doing the wrong thing. There was an incident back in the UP offices at the World building that seems almost typical. Along about the time that I was writing my first by-line stories, and those stories were appearing in newspapers all over the country, I began to develop an attitude of overweening cockiness. I was at my desk one day and looked up and saw a gawk standing nearby, a real rube with a large Adam's apple that was sliding up and down and giving an occasional little jerk. He was alone and gazing around the room at all the clattering machinery and I figured he was some chawbacon from the back pastures who had wandered into the place by mistake. I was feeling my oats about those coast-to-coast by-lines and so I got up and said to this rube: "Listen, mister, didn't you see that telephone operator out there? Don't come in here bothering people. Go on out there and tell her what you want for Christ's sake." His Adam's apple took a couple of extra jumps and he turned and walked out. Ten minutes later he was back, with Karl Bickel. I saw the chawbacon poke a thumb toward me and grin and then Bickel grinned and came over and introduced me to the guy, who was Eamon de Valera.

In spite of my genius for the bonehead play, there were some jobs where I acquitted myself adequately. Such as the Culbertson-Lenz contract bridge grapple which began on December 7, 1931, at the Hotel Chatham in New York. This was the most spectacular

and goofiest card game ever played in the history of man and I
advised my boss that I would enjoy covering it. He asked me if I
was a good bridge player and I said no, I didn't play bridge at all.

"Well," he said, "how come you want to cover it?"

"Because," I said, "it has the flavor of a fruit cake and also because
I consider bridge players to be daft."

This was adequate. I got the job and I think it was possibly the
most interesting newspaper assignment I ever had.

Weeks of fussing and fuming and name-calling preceded the actual
start of the match. Contract bridge, from its quiet beginnings around
1926, had by 1931 become a national rage. And into this situation
stepped a lean, suave, quick-witted superirritant named Ely Culbertson. He was then forty years old and possessed of a manner which
some people thought charming but which led others to cast their
eyes about in search of blunt instruments. His life in America up to
this time had been that of an obscure professional card player who
haunted the bridge clubs of New York City, sometimes prospering,
sometimes broke and in debt. He was certainly one of the ablest
card tacticians in the country and his handsome wife, Josephine,
was considered to be the best player of her sex.

Culbertson had a scheme. He spent hours and days and weeks
alone with a deck of cards, working out his own bidding system,
and when he was satisfied with it, scraped together enough money
to start a magazine called *The Bridge World*.

After a spectacular challenge match in England the fame of Ely
and Jo Culbertson was beginning to mount and as the Culbertson
system flourished, the book sales and prestige of the old established
masters, such as Work, Whitehead, and Lenz, declined. Culbertson
began to needle these older men. He wrote about them and he
talked about them on the radio. Eventually he drove them to the
wall and they turned to fight. Their anger was at white heat when
Culbertson picked out Sidney S. Lenz as the best card player in
the group and challenged him to a match of 150 rubbers, Lenz to
choose his own partner.

Sidney Lenz ignored the challenge and the wager of $5000
against $1000 that came with it but Culbertson kept hammering at
him, heckling him in the press and on the air. Culbertson's incredible
cockiness was paying off—his book sales continued to mount and
thousands of bridge teachers were signing up under his banner. The

old guard had to put up or shut up, and finally Lenz accepted the challenge.

Between the time when the rules were agreed upon and the match got under way, the nation's press discovered that it had something special on its hands—something similar to the World Series. In the week prior to December 7, twenty-four special cables were laid into the Culbertson apartment in the Hotel Chatham, where the first half of the contest was to be staged. A large press room, complete with rows of typewriters and telegraph keys, was established down the hall from the Culbertson drawing room to make reporters comfortable.

Lenz chose as his partner Oswald Jacoby, a handsome young fellow with dark hair and the build of a fullback, member of a championship bridge team. On the night the match started there was classic confusion in the various rooms and corridors of the hotel. The place swarmed with reporters and cameramen and society people and celebrities. Chosen to referee the contest was Lieutenant Alfred M. Gruenther, a thirty-two-year-old chemistry instructor at West Point. Everyone was most polite and after two rubbers, Lenz and Jacoby were 1715 points ahead.

The card table was at one end of the Culbertson drawing room. Across the center of the room were high, folding screens and there were six cracks, each about an inch wide, through which the reporters and favored guests could watch the contest. There was a chair at each crack and the rule said that no reporter or guest could look through a crack more than fifteen minutes at a time, and it was required that everyone walk on tiptoe. Signs ordering "Absolute Silence" hung throughout the apartment and on the door where the two Culbertson children were abed was a sign saying, "Quiet! Little Children Asleep and Dreaming."

An almost ghostly procession of reporters, columnists, and special guests tiptoed in and out of the playing room. Each New York newspaper assigned at least one reporter to stay with the match to the end. The Associated Press had two men present every evening, and one of them was my old friend Morris Watson. I was the sole representative of the UP, and the INS had a man present most of the time. Special writers such as Ring Lardner, Heywood Broun, Damon Runyon, Robert Benchley, Westbrook Pegler, Grantland Rice, Henry McLemore, Eddie Neil, and Lucius Beebe dropped in from time to time. Pegler spent one evening ranging through the halls asking the same question: "Who's pickin' up the tab?" Runyon insisted on challenging all the bridge experts to meet a team of Broadway characters at klab in a back room at Lindy's restaurant. McLemore came by frequently and once wrote a story about how it felt to be a "crack reporter."

Those of us who were present every night for five weeks might well have become bored with the proceedings if it hadn't been for Culbertson. He needed no press agent. In devising methods of irritating and enraging his opponents, he anticipated the Gamesmanship ploys which later appeared in books by Stephen Potter. He was consistently late getting to the card table and this infuriated Sidney Lenz, a man of little patience. Culbertson went into long periods of meditation before bidding or before playing a card, and Lenz soon grew bitter about the whole affair. Culbertson would sometimes have a juicy steak served on a corner of the table, eating as he played, and Lenz would complain: "My God, Ely, you're getting grease all over the cards! Why don't you eat at the proper time like the rest of us?" To which Ely would reply: "My vast public won't let me, Sidney."

At the end of the 27th rubber Lenz was ahead by more than 7000 points but on December 15 Culbertson took the lead for the first time. He never relinquished it after that and each evening as he arrived (late) at the table he'd smile sweetly at Lenz and in his rich Russian accent he'd say, "Well, Sidney, have you changed your system yet?"

Before long Lenz was accusing the Culbertsons of failure to adhere to the Culbertson system. There were many delaying arguments on this point and Lieutenant Gruenther, a much harassed young man, settled them as best he could. The lieutenant had to travel each afternoon from West Point to New York, supervise the evening's play, start back around one o'clock and be ready for an eight A.M. class. Mrs. Gruenther did most of the driving while her husband snoozed in the back seat.

The public took immense satisfaction out of the knowledge that these great stars of the game were frequently guilty of dumbhead plays. Once Jacoby quit, after a loud dispute with Lenz. Late on that particular evening Lenz suddenly turned on Jacoby.

"Why do you make such rotten bids?" he demanded.

Jacoby stared at him and didn't answer. Culbertson smiled, and said, "Shall we play another rubber?"

"Not with me," snapped Jacoby, rising to his feet.

Referee Gruenther intervened, saying that the rules required another rubber. Jacoby sat down again, then turned to Lenz and said: "Sidney, in a hand in the second rubber tonight you made an absolutely stupid defensive play, and then you criticized *me*. I'm resigning right now as your partner."

Lenz looked at him a moment in disbelief. "Well, well, sir; well, sir," he stammered, "all right, sir."

The next evening Lenz had a new partner, a rotund former Navy officer, Commander Winfield Liggett, Jr., who announced at the beginning that the outcome of the contest would prove nothing at all.

On the evening of December 30 came a new sensation. Several of us were sitting around the press room listening to Sir Derrick Wernher, a British-American bridge star, analyze the play. Into the room walked Culbertson. Sir Derrick asked him why he had not responded to a challenge he had issued the previous summer. Culbertson said he hadn't heard of any such challenge. Said Sir Derrick: "You liar. You're a slab-sided piece of beefsteak."

Sir Derrick was standing in a corner, a man of huge physical proportions. Culbertson strode up to him, fists clenched, glared up into his face and said:

"Why, you five-hundred-pound piece of English beefsteak, you, I consider you a cheap shark and not worth playing against. I wouldn't dirty my hands at the same table with you."

Sir Derrick responded in kind. Culbertson yelled that he'd bet $5000 to $2000 that he could pick a team from among the reporters present that would beat any team selected by Sir Derrick. "On second thought," Culbertson snarled, "I'll bet $500 you haven't got $2000 to bet." Sir Derrick then called Culbertson some more beefsteak and then called him a liar and Ely advanced on him just as Jo Culbertson came into the room and grabbed him. She dragged him away to the playing room but Culbertson refused to start the evening's contest until Sir Derrick had left the hotel. As the Englishman was leaving, Mrs. Culbertson called after him, "What a coward you are, Derrick!"

That was referred to, thereafter, as Beefsteak Night.

The second half of the match was played at the Waldorf-Astoria in quarters provided by Lenz. It all came to an end on January 8 with the Culbertsons victors by 8980 points. After the last card had dropped Lenz stood up and shook hands with Mrs. Culbertson. He then turned his back on Ely. Lieutenant Gruenther went back to West Point to pursue a career that would eventuate in his becoming Supreme Allied Commander in Europe.

After it was all over Ely Culbertson further cemented his personal relations with the American press by giving a stag dinner and brannigan for us in a private dining room at his hotel. Toward the end of the affair, after many bottles of Golden Wedding had been consumed, we played a crazy game of charades. In one of these Heywood Broun took the part of a race horse named Gallant Fox and I was his jockey. I rode Mr. Broun piggy-back while he galumphed around the long table two or three times, after which the others began throwing hard rolls and salt cellars at us. I believe I am the only person who ever so rode the great social critic. And so, as it had been for a month, the Culbertson-Lenz match ended on a dignified and cultural note. Almost everybody fell down.

Morris Watson was always getting himself involved in movements and causes, and some of these were pretty close to *avant-garde* crackpottery. In the summer of 1933, while still working for the AP and crusading with Broun on behalf of the fledgling Newspaper Guild, Morris decided to spend his vacation in a nudist camp.

He telephoned me at the UP and suggested that I bring my family up to visit him and his family in the camp, which was near the town of Highland, New York. He said that organized nudism was a real wonderful thing and made a lot of sense and that if I came up I could get a good feature story about it. I asked him if Nelle and I would have to go nude and he said we would be quite conspicuous if we didn't.

At this period I was proprietor of my own automobile, a Model A Ford, and so I loaded up my wife and two small children and we headed out one morning for Highland.

We drove over a long country road to get to the camp, which was perched above a splendid lake. There were about twenty-five naked people going about the normal business of resort life just as if they had clothes on. I think it worth noting that the girls who worked in the kitchen wore little aprons to protect themselves against hot grease and other splashings. My family and I stripped down to nothing and joined the unclad Watsons.

Before I left the city various gentlemen around the office, having heard that I was going to go naked in a nudist camp, came to me with a question. The same question, in every case. They all wanted to know one thing, and one thing only—what happened to a man, standing naked, when a naked girl of charm and shapeliness walks up to him and starts a conversation. So on this day, in the middle of the afternoon, I found myself sitting on a rock at the far side of the lake, my portable typewriter perched on my bare knees, writing a story about the things I had seen and done. It proved to be a most difficult matter to answer that universal question in a story which was meant for use in family newspapers across the nation. But I tried. My rock-written story began:

> HIGHLAND, N.Y., Aug. 17—(UP)—All arguments to the contrary, it is very embarrassing to have a young woman walk up to you stark naked and tell you that nudism is going to sweep the nation.

From that standing start I told how nakedness had seemed perfectly natural at the beginning of the adventure, and then a Miss Gronlin came round a corner, very blonde and handsome in all respects. And she didn't even have shoes on. Then:

> Your correspondent, a bird lover, became intensely interested in a thrush which was going into a power dive over Bear Mountain.
> She didn't go on about her business, this Miss Gronlin. She came right up and said: "Are you Mr. Smith?"
> I said I was.
> "I am Miss Gronlin," she said, and she laid a hand on my arm. "Please come and go swimming. The lake is wonderful."
> "Miss Gronlin," I told her firmly, "I am not used to this business."
> "Oh, that's all right," she burst forth, "the water isn't so deep in places."
> Well, the swim was great fun, and we rowed a boat, and . . . A Miss Emery, who was in charge of the dining room, came down to the pier and ripped off what little clothing she wore. She stretched her arms, yawned, and started off on a classical dance, one of those here-we-go-gathering-nuts-in-May dances.
> After completing it, Miss Emery did a sort of Immelman roll into the water and your correspondent, fearing for her life, swam rapidly toward her. She seemed, however, perfectly capa-

ble of swimming in deep water, and was exceptionally good at floating on her back.

And then, standing on the dock, still as naked as the day she was born, Miss Emery explained to me that the idea of a nudist camp is health. The sun, she said, is good for one.

That was the sort of story I wrote, with a little more about some of the characters in the camp. Finally I got my family together, we put our clothes on, said good-by and departed. We stopped in a nearby town where there was a telegraph office and I sent my story off to the United Press. I was positive that its total audience would be the men of the nightside in New York—that it would never be sent over the UP wires.

When I got to the office the next day I found that my nudist camp story had created a small sensation. The sort of thing I had written was looked upon as real daring in those days. The New York *Daily News* had given the story a prominent play and messages were coming from other newspapers all over the country, many of them demanding more copy on the nudist camp. I had enough material for a second-day story and wrote it, and it in turn got a big play. It was concerned with additional activities I had noted at the camp, with special reference to the peculiar aspect of a group of naked men pitching horseshoes.

The nudists were boiling mad because of my stories. Being daffy to start with, a bunch of them somehow made their way to Paterson, New Jersey, where there was a newspaperman named Allen Smith, and they closed in on him and threatened to punch his head off but he managed to talk them out of it. Then they consulted a lawyer and there was talk of a libel suit, but nothing ever came of it. And finally Morris Watson was offended because I had poked fun at the faddists he was favoring at the moment. I was given to understand that our friendship was ended, and then one day he called me up and said: "I'll forgive you for the dirty job you did on the nudist camp if you'll do one thing for me." I said for him to name it. "Join the Guild," he said. Up to that moment I had not become a member of the Newspaper Guild, possibly because there seemed to be almost no interest in it around the United Press. But after a while I did join and remained a member up to the end of my newspaper days.

One final note on the nudist camp assignment: Dean Frank Luther Mott of the University of Iowa School of Journalism included my first day story in a book containing the best news stories and features of 1933. My report on Miss Gronlin was saluted along with a story of the inauguration of Franklin D. Roosevelt by J. Frederick Essary and an interview with Stalin by Walter Duranty. That dumb little nudist story, which I was convinced would never see print anywhere, was later incorporated into A Treasury of Great Reporting, where I found myself traveling in the exalted company of many of the greatest writers of history—Samuel Johnson, Defoe, Dickens, Hugo, Greeley, Twain, Stanley, Jack London, Irvin S. Cobb, Richard Harding Davis, Swope, Kipling, Churchill, Woollcott, Mencken, Hecht, Runyon, Hemingway, Shirer, Murrow, Steinbeck, and so on.

Yet there was one big disappointment. If you can think back to the early pages of this book you may recall that I became a living legend in my own lifetime by acquiring a reputation as an eater of woolly worms. Now, in New York, I began to feel that I would enjoy being a living legend in a business that was almost overcrowded with living legends. One of the first essentials to becoming a living legend was to turn in a fabulously funny expense account. I set to work on one, covering the expenses attending my trip to Highland. The United Press (Big Old Stingy Gut) was usually very tough about expense accounts even when they were honest. The executive who checked them over and signed them before they could be cashed was famous for disallowing items that were at all questionable. So I worked out a long list of expenditures concerned with my adventure in nudity. I polished it for several days and then one afternoon approached the office of The Ogre. I had constructed the list so that the first few items would seem to be reasonable, then would come expenditures that would look a little irregular, and from then on the thing would grow outrageously funny.

So I walked in and stood beside his desk and put the long list down in front of him. He seized it and at the same time seized a pen. I saw at once what was wrong. For the first time in the memory of anyone in the shop, The Ogre had come back from lunch cockeyed drunk. He, the eternal quibbler, waved his pen above my masterpiece a couple of times, uttered a few loud obscenities, and *signed it.* Signed it without reading a single word. He couldn't have read it if he had tried. I was so upset, so disappointed, so frustrated, that I walked out of his office and tore the expense account to shreds and threw it away. I didn't even collect on the few legitimate expenditures I had made on the trip. And I abandoned all plans for becoming a living legend in my own lifetime.

Cultural affairs continued to occupy my attention. On a winter's night in 1934 I had the privilege of attending the Broadway première of Gertrude Stein's opera, *Four Saints in Three Acts*. The audience included many celebrities in the world of the arts, some wearing silk hats, and I was disgusted with them—ashamed of being a part of such a boorish group—for they looked upon Miss Stein's gripping words as comedy.

"Did he did we did," sang the Negro performers, "we and did he did he did did he did did did he did did he categorically and did he did he did he did he did he did he in interruption interruption interruptedly leave letting let it be all to me to me out and outer and this and this with in indeed deed and drawn and drawn work."

The audience simply went into spasms of ignorant laughter. Those oafish people made such a racket that I was scarcely able to follow the line of the story.

The opera was concerned mainly with Saint Theresa No. 1 and Saint Theresa No. 2 and St. Ignatius. These three performed with a variety of other saints, all portrayed by Negroes, and an assortment of angels. They did things about a telescope and a large fish net.

At one point the assembled cast began searching the horizon for an unnamed object. They sang:

"How many doors are there in it how many doors are there in it how many doors are there in it how many doors are there in it . . ." and so on, for a good long paragraph until someone, a contralto, got to demanding how many eggs there were in it, and one of the angels sang: "If it were possible to kill five thousand Chinamen by pressing a button would it be done Saint Theresa not interested."

With this Saint Ignatius brought out his telescope and sighted at the horizon, which resembled shiny, light blue oilcloth. Saint Theresa No. 1 then proceeded to beguile Saint Ignatius into letting her have the telescope, but instead of examining the horizon to find out how many floors, doors, windows and eggs were in it, she aimed it sweepingly over the audience itself, no doubt to determine how many paying customers there were in it.

There was a brief interlude in which the cast sang "My Country 'Tis of Thee" and then a voice asked how many nails there were in it. A clue came at once, in the following passage:

"Four saints are not born at one time although they knew each other. One of them had a birthday before the mother of the other one the father. Four saints later to be if to be if to be to be one to be. Might tingle."

Did tingle. I mean *I* tingled. Never, up to that evening, had I realized what remarkable things could be done with our language. I decided that if there was big money in that kind of writing, I was going to give it a try. I felt that I could write that way till the cows came home. Categorically, interruptedly, before the mother of the other one the father.

# CHAPTER 22

# Ben DeCasseres has a drink

During the early '30s professional wrestling was in a transitional period between honest dishonesty and dishonest dishonesty with bells on. The brotherhood of man being what it is, the promoters took advantage of racial hatreds in their matchmaking and there was more and more emphasis on sly comedy. Costuming entered the picture. It almost seemed as if the basic audience had been hand-picked. These Believers had to Believe so completely that they would be eager and willing to climb into the ring and clout a hated wrestler on the skull with a pop bottle. I stand today with Peter Ustinov who has said that the greatest acting and the finest comedy on American television are both provided by the wrestlers.

One evening I lugged a portable typewriter over to Madison Square Garden to do a feature story on the new fashions in wrestling. I arrived early and was walking down an aisle toward the press seats when I saw Saxe Commins, a book editor of my acquaintance. He was then with Covici Friede and he called me over and introduced me to a handsome man who was with him. It was Gene Fowler. Mr. Fowler was already a shining star in my little universe and now he made over me as if he and I had gone through college and a couple of wars together. He was possibly the most exuberant man I ever knew. He had a rich, deep, vibrant voice that hadn't a crack in it when he reached seventy. The most ordinary gestures became splendid and heroic when Fowler gestured them. When he asked a waitress for another slice of bread he was Alexander the Great rallying his legions at Helicarnassus. In his final book Gene said of James J. Walker: "Mr. Walker made everyone whom he met feel important and confident." There on the floor of Madison Square Garden Gene Fowler made me believe that meeting me was one of the rare great moments of his life. He continued doing so up to his final year.

We talked about Denver for a minute or so and then I went on down to the press seats to watch The Fabulous Frog, a pink-whiskered Frenchman, take on The Hairless Hun. Need I say that there was Hun blood an inch deep on the canvas before it was over?

There was another and closer friendship that began about the same time. A notice came in the mail that a Santa Claus convention was to be held in Grand Central Palace. This was the period of the NRA Blue Eagle codes and the department store Santa Clauses of New York City were assembling for the purpose of drawing up their own code of ethics. I was curious about this meeting because a department store Santa is basically a dishonest man in the same way that a politician is dishonest; a major requirement in each profession is a proficiency in telling lies.

At Grand Central Palace I wandered around in various exhibition halls, finding no Santa Claus convention, and at last I sat down near a bank of elevators to rest my feet. I was sitting there when an elevator door opened and a short, brisk young man stepped out. He darted glances all around and then approached me.

"Ah begya pahdon, suh," he said, "but Ah'm lookin' foh a buncha dad-blamed Santy Clauses."

I told him I had been doing the same and I figured from his looks and from his manner that he was a newspaperman, so I introduced myself. "Grrrr-eat day in the mawnin'!" he cried out. He was fresh up from Atlanta where he had been reading my UP stories for the last two or three years and now *he*, James H. Street of Mississippi, had been brought on to New York to write wire features for the AP. I would like to say, parenthetically, that while Mr. Street had a pronounced Secessionist accent, he doubled it and smeared ham fat on it and then tripled it whenever he was in the presence of Yankee strangers—a trait by no means uncommon among Southerners. In later years there were times when I heard Mr. Street almost speak plain English.

We sat down and swapped newspaper experiences for a while and made a date to see each other again and then went wandering and found the convention. The Santa Clauses were in a little room far off in one corner of the vast building. There were about a dozen of them and they had a keg of unethical beer on a table. They were dressed in their Santa costumes, save for the yak-wool beards which had been laid aside to facilitate the taking on of beer. If you have ever seen such an assemblage of Santa Clauses, minus their yak-wool whiskers, you have seen something. And if you have heard them talk, you have heard something. They came in all shapes and sizes and they quarreled a good deal among themselves and one of them fingered the inside of his nose more than seemed proper. It was all most disillusioning and since that day I have not believed in Santa Claus.

> [Please note that in the preceding paragraph I emphasized that the whiskers were made of yak wool. This is a piece of information I ran across eight or ten years ago. As is my custom, I jotted it down in one of my notebooks, figuring that some day I would have a chance to use it. I would be describing a department-store Santa Claus and I would say something about his yak-wool beard, and people would exclaim, "My God! How does he *know* so many things!" So, there it is, and I feel real good that I've finally got rid of the damn thing.]

Before long Jim Street and I would become fast friends. Our kids would grow up together and our wives would become as thick as women. For years Mr. Street and I were accustomed to go adventuring together and while our roamings occasionally proved a trial to organized society, sometimes even offending the body politic, we had fun. There will be more about Mr. Street at a later time.

A surprise phone call came one afternoon from Volney Hoggatt, who said that he and F. G. Bonfils were staying at the Hotel Commodore and that Mr. Bonfils would like to see me that evening. "*After* dinner," said Vol, pointedly. No free meals out of the Corsican. So I went over and found them in a small room and each man was stretched out on his bed reading. They were reading the Denver *Post*. Bonfils had sent Vol over to Times Square to pick up all available issues of the *Post*. "I can't make anything out of these crazy New York papers," said Bon. He got off the bed and motioned me into a chair and began asking me how I had been getting along.

"Son," he said, "you should never have left Denver. When you walked away from us, you walked away from the greatest opportunity Life has to offer. This . . ." and he gestured toward the window, "this is a terrible place to live and work."

I waited. It didn't come. He didn't offer me a partnership in the *Post,* or the job of managing editor, or city editor, or anything at all. So I started telling him about my work at the United Press and he acted as if he had never heard of it, even though he had been dealing with Roy Howard's press association for years. I told him that the main offices were just a block away and that I'd enjoy showing them to him. So he and Vol got into their coats, but before we left the room Bonfils said:

"Do your teeth for him, Vol."

I looked at the long, lanky Hoggatt, turner of no-hands flipflops. He suddenly maneuvered his jaws in some manner as to thrust his false teeth, upper and lower, a quarter of an inch or so out of his mouth, and this gave him a most forbidding appearance. Then, with the teeth still in that position, he began barking.

I turned to look at Bonfils. He was regarding Vol Hoggatt's performance closely but there was not a flicker of a smile, not a suggestion of a grin. Bon looked at me, to see how I was reacting, and I was grinning.

"It's Vol's new stunt," said the Little Napoleon of the West. "He's not a dog—he's a coyote. That's the bark of the coyote he did. Do it again, Vol."

Vol did it again. That was enough. It was not the kind of thing that would wear well. I heard later, from another Denver man, that this toothy impersonation of a coyote was Vol Hoggatt's latest device for cheering up his employer whenever his employer grew morose.

It was middle evening and we walked over to the *News* building and I took the two visitors around the office, showing them something about the mechanics of the over-all operation. Bonfils lingered longest beside the printer known as the West Wire, then being punched by Sol Davis. That was the wire that meant the West and Colorado and Denver and Champa Street. To Frederick G. Bonfils that was the *good* wire.

Though we were in the same building we saw very little of the newspapermen involved in the production of the tabloid *Daily News.* Even at that late stage of the game there was something not quite acceptable about the tabloids. I never liked the *Daily News* because it pandered, in a blatant and unashamed way, to the basic instincts and the vulgar tastes of the lower orders—the same as I do.

I did get to know a few of the *News* guys, including Sidney Skolsky, and when Sid was transferred from the Broadway beat to Hollywood, a big farewell party was thrown for him in a Times Square nightclub. I attended and I remember it best for the fact that I first met Helen Morgan there. If you didn't know it already, I am a fellow who has little regard for mystical matters. Yet there seemed to be something *extra* in this girl, an invisible vapor of feeling that came out of her. They had a small haystack on the dance floor and Miss Morgan, instead of sitting on a piano, lay back in the hay and they put a bluish spot on her and she sang. She was fully clothed and she lay perfectly still and sang about how she felt so lazy when she's lying in the hay. I've never listened to that song since that night without remembering her, and without that vague, ethereal something coming adrifting toward me, and enveloping me and . . . I believe what she had was a sex wallop.

There was much drinking at the Skolsky party. There was much drinking everywhere, all the time. I don't think I *knew* anybody who didn't drink and most of those I did know were the type who got so drunk they couldn't see through a ladder. These were days when the bitterness against Prohibition was growing stronger every day and people were all but drinking themselves to death just to make a point. I am offering no apology for the boozing in this book; it is merely the boozing that was in my life. And all of this leads us to another event that took place in the same year on the twelfth floor of the Waldorf-Astoria Hotel. The date was December 5, 1933.

A week prior to that day it came to my attention that Prohibition was approaching its end in the United States. I knew that I would be called upon to write some sort of an obit on the death of the Eighteenth Amendment, and so I dreamed up a stunt.

With the wire facilities of the United Press at my command, I decided to make it possible for a single individual, selected in advance, to take the first legal drink swallowed in the United States of America in thirteen years. I wanted to get H. L. Mencken for the enterprise but Mr. Mencken, who leaned to beer, was in Baltimore. Then I thought of Benjamin DeCasseres, whose Gramercy Park home I sometimes visited and who was always fond of talking about his skill with tankard, flagon, and shot glass. Mr. DeCasseres was an author of the iconoclastic school and had moved in a group that included Edgar Saltus, James Huneker, and the young Mencken. Now he fairly leaped at the chance to make history, get a free drink and get his name in the newspapers. I arranged for him to meet me at the Waldorf-Astoria immediately after lunch on December 5.

Before going to the hotel myself I had to check all the arrangements. The end of Prohibition was to be accomplished in Salt Lake City where the Utah Constitutional Convention was voting that day to ratify the Twenty-first Amendment. Ratification by three fourths of the states was necessary, and Utah was the thirty-sixth state to vote.

The United Press had, of course, a direct wire from the Salt Lake City convention hall into its offices in New York. I arranged to have another wire set up between the office on Forty-Second Street and a suite in the Waldorf-Astoria. The flash would come from Salt Lake City to New York and then would be swiftly relayed to us in the hotel suite and Mr. DeCasseres would hurl the first legal drink down his hatch. A telegraph operator was installed in the hotel suite and at the other end of the wire, in the United Press office, sat Alfred D. Greene, night wire chief of the UP. Mr. Greene was to relay the flash to the hotel the instant it bounced off the wire from Utah.

Al Greene was one of my close friends and before I left the office for the hotel I had a conspiratorial conversation with him.

Arriving at the Waldorf suite, I found Mr. DeCasseres with an illegal highball in his hand and an expression of beatific abandon on his face. The hotel management had agreed to furnish a bottle of liquor for the stunt but a disheartening mistake had been made somewhere along the line and an entire case of Vat 69 stood on the floor beside a divan.

Mr. DeCasseres and I, with two hours to go before the flash from Utah was due, began making inroads on that Scotch. After a while Mr. C. V. R. Thompson, New York correspondent for the London *Daily Express*, telephoned and said that there was strong European interest in our project and asked if he might chisel in just a bit. He wanted to have Mr. DeCasseres interviewed over the transatlantic telephone, a real big thing in those days, by one of the editors of his paper in London. I agreed to this, being already in an expansive frame of mind, and before long Mr. Thompson joined us and was assigned to a bottle of Scotch, at which he began taking heroic belts which he learned on the playing fields of England.

The telegraph operator was making a show of testing the hookup with Al Greene but I could see him casting parched glances at us so he was invited into the party. Mr. DeCasseres, who once described himself in print as an intellectual faun, was in good form, as he usually was, and was making an effort to remember how many times he had been hurled bodily out of Jack's restaurant in the old days.

Around four-thirty the brass sounder began chattering and Al Greene informed us that the Utah delegates had assembled and that the flash would be upon us within the next ten minutes. Having given us this warning Mr. Greene telegraphed an off-the-record query:

HAVE THEM BUMS STARTED DRINKING YET? WISH I WAS THERE.

The telegraph operator was in his place at the table and Mr. Thompson began putting his call through to London. Mr. DeCasseres sat across the room in an overstuffed chair and said:

"Columbia the Gem of the Ocean! You shall not crucify mankind upon a cross of needled beer! Fire when gridley, gredly! I'm half horse and half alligator! Fifty-four, forty or fidget! What hath God wrought! Whose house are we in?"

I directed Mr. DeCasseres to the chair he was to occupy during the historic ceremony. He was across the table from the telegraph operator. The London connection had been completed and a telephone was placed in Mr. DeCasseres' left hand. He began talking to the British editor as though the transatlantic telephone were a fake and a fraud, as though he were actually shouting across the bosom of the sea. I fixed him a fresh highball and another for myself.

We settled into our assigned places. Off to one side stood Ted Saucier, of the Waldorf staff, wondering if he hadn't made a horrible mistake by permitting such antics in these austere precincts. I stood directly behind Mr. DeCasseres. Mr. Thompson moved to his side and took the telephone away from him.

"In a few moments," Mr. Thompson said into the instrument, "we shall have the flawsh from Utah. Then Mr. DeCasseres shall take the first drink, and then I shall put Mr. DeCasseres on the wire for the interview. Stand firm."

It was 4:39 P.M. We were all tensely quiet, though weaving a little. Then the telegraph instrument sounded.

Click pause. Click pause. Click.

Unobtrusively I raised my glass to my lips and took a long swig. At once the instrument broke into a chatter.

"Flash!" yelled the operator. "Prohibition repealed!"

Mr. DeCasseres drank—drank fiercely, pouring part of the highball over his chin. He put down his glass and Mr. Thompson thrust the telephone at him.

"Hurrah for Tom Paine!" cried Mr. DeCasseres across the ocean. "This is the second Declaration of Independence. Bang the field-piece, twang the lyre! Whooooooopeeeeee! Gimmy another drink, boys, I'm thirsty!"

The man in London tried to get over some questions but Mr. DeCasseres wouldn't stop. He was bursting with patriotic fervor and international amity. He spoke feelingly of Thomas Jefferson, George Barnard Shaw, Wayne B. Wheeler, and the Gaekwar of Baroda. He declared his love for all the peoples of the world and Scotch whisky. He was still going when Mr. Thompson wrenched the phone away from him and rang off to save money.

After that I had to write a report on the affair for immediate use on the United Press wires. It was not the most intelligible piece ever written but it had words in it. When I had finished with it, we sat around and had some more Scotch, and then I had to return to the UP offices to write a story for the night wires.

I left Mr. DeCasseres trying to remember for Mr. Thompson and a couple of visitors—Lou Wedemar and Forrest Davis—the number of times he had been thrown out of Jack's in the old days.

So that is actually what happened on the afternoon of December 5, 1933, in the Waldorf-Astoria. Mr. DeCasseres never suspected that he had been double-crossed. He could not know that when the telegraph instrument clicked three times, those clicks were a signal to me. Al Greene was telling me that the flash had come in, that Utah had voted, that Prohibition was no more. Al Greene had given me the better part of a second to quietly take the first legal drink. And I took it.

If Al Greene's role in the foregoing episode seems secondary, that would be misleading. Mr. Greene seldom played a secondary role in anything. He was one of the rare characters of this earth and I had the privilege of working in the same room with him for five years. Three or four nights out of each week we had dinner together yet in all that time I never had a single luncheon with him. Al Greene did not eat lunch, and for an interesting reason.

"When I was about twenty," he once told me, "I worked in the depot at Wichita, Kansas. I was the telegraph operator. It was a pretty good job for a young fellow so I got married. Beautiful girl. What a shape! We took a little bungalow about a mile from the depot and I bought a bicycle. At noon each day I got forty-five minutes off for lunch. I'd rush out of the depot, jump on my bicycle, and pedal like mad for home, get there, jump off my bike, and run into the house. Then, with about five minutes to go, I'd come running out, get onto the bike, ride down to the depot, and go back to work. I didn't eat a bite of lunch for a whole year. Got out of the habit, I guess. From that day to this I've never been much of a lunch eater."

# narrow escape from wallpaper

Once upon a time in the city of Aguascalientes one of those crazy Mexican political conventions was roaring along and the quarrel over the presidential plum was between Pancho Villa and Venustiano Carranza. The convention appeared to be in a hopeless deadlock when Villa stepped forward with a constructive suggestion. He said he would be happy to commit suicide if Carranza would do the same, and this would surely break the deadlock. It seems to me that Villa's gesture contained a certain element of self-sacrifice. There is a great need for more of this nobility in the world, especially in the newspaper business. Over the years I have known quite a few men who could easily have improved the quality of American journalism by merely going out and drowning themselves.

The glittering, golden horizon that was New York City during my years in the provinces—the town that was Ultima Thule to almost every ambitious young reporter in the land—turned out to be at variance with the dream. There was always the unspoken thought in the mind of the outlander that a New York City newspaper was staffed with the very best journalistic minds that money could buy— that every member of a New York City newspaper staff was a star in his own right. This turned out to be a delusion.

New York City has more than its share of incompetent and mediocre puddinheads running around with press cards stuck in their hats. Some of the gentry in Manhattan have achieved the heights of riches and renown with less intelligence than was possessed by Charlie J. Kallikak. There are highly-paid people writing columns in New York today who would not be accepted by respectable mental institutions; there is a limit even to what an insane asylum can put up with. I have had enough years of working with them, and of sitting by and watching them function, to know what I'm talking about. There are newspaper writers in New York living in palatial duplex apartments, chugging around in Rolls-Royces, who could not have held a job on the Sebring *Daily American*. There are columnists functioning on metropolitan newspapers who could not possibly hold their positions if they didn't know where *eight* bodies are buried. Grab me, somebody. I may kill. I really may.

Now and then I toy with a fascinating notion: to move the whole staff of the Denver *Post* as it was in 1927 and 1928 to New York City and let it take over any one of the metropolitan dailies. If it could be done, the Big Town would have itself a real newspaper. Maybe even the best newspaper in its history. Even a cub reporter had to have a little talent to hold his job on the Denver *Post*.

I think I have it all fixed now for this book to get splendid reviews in the daily and Sunday newspapers, so let us proceed to the case of Miles W. (Peg) Vaughan, who was my last boss at the United Press. He was a short, chubby, florid-faced man who looked like a young W. C. Fields and he was for years one of the top American correspondents in the Far East. Then he was brought back to New York and made nightside manager and manager of me. When he was briefed on the nightside setup he was told that I was his feature writer and that I had possibilities.

He decided to do things with me, to mold me, to Henryhiggins me. After he got settled into his job he called me to his desk and asked me if I had ever read a short story called *Fifty Grand* by Ernest Hemingway. I said that I had. He then told me that it was the best short story in the English language, and contained the best writing on earth.

"I want you to get a copy of it," he said, "and take it home, and read it, and read it again, and keep reading it till you know every word by heart. I want you to learn to write exactly like that."

This is God's truth. Hang on—there's more to come.

I disobeyed my superior. In the first place I was not overly fond of the writings of Hemingway. I had read *Fifty Grand* and I thought the writing in it was herky-jerk. I still think so. And I would think so even if I did not have important opinion on my side. *Fifty Grand* was rejected by Ray Long when he was editor of *Cosmopolitan*; it was sent back by *The Saturday Evening Post*, turned down by both

*Collier's* and *Liberty,* and rejected by the famous editor Maxwell Perkins of Scribners. It was finally published by *Atlantic Monthly,* possibly when they weren't looking. I have just read it again. *Rien. Niente. Nichts. Nada.*

So I refused to become one of the most horrible of all worms infesting the writing trade—the Hemingway imitator. I just kept on writing the way I had been writing and Peg Vaughan didn't seem to notice that I wasn't writing in the rhythms of a donkey engine. After about two weeks he called me to his desk again and asked me if I read the "Talk of the Town" stuff in the front of the *New Yorker.* I said I did. He said that the "Talk of the Town" stuff was the best-written stuff in America and that I should now begin studying it carefully, reading it over and over, learning how to capture that style, no matter what kind of a story I might be working on. I said all right. And I went ahead as before.

Along about this time John Dillinger broke jail and was on the loose somewhere and the FBI was trying to find him. One afternoon I walked over to the New York Public Library and did a little research and then wrote an open letter to Dillinger. I addressed him in a friendly, fraternal tone, telling him to give himself up and save everybody a lot of trouble. I told him he couldn't get away with it, that it was only a matter of days and maybe hours till they grabbed him and maybe even killed him. I recited briefly the careers of other famous outlaws, from Jesse James on down, and how each one of them had tried to disappear, and each had failed and died violently.

It wasn't much of a piece and involved very little work and the moralistic overtones didn't disturb me too greatly. It went out to all nightside customers and the next day the messages were pouring in and copies of the papers with the Open Letter splashed handsomely on Page One. Peg Vaughan called me to his desk.

"We've hit it!" he exclaimed. "We've finally hit the formula I've been trying to find for you! From now on every god damn story you write is gonna be an *open letter to somebody!*"

I demurred. I resisted. I complained. I didn't want to spend the rest of my life as a writer of open letters. Anyway, I said, it wouldn't work. There were all manner of stories that simply would not lend themselves to the Open Letter treatment. I tried to kill the project in its tracks by saying I couldn't think of one for that very day. He thought of one. He rummaged around among the papers on his desk and came up with a letter from a woman in his home town in Nebraska or Kansas or acrost the ocean to Idaho. He showed me the letter. This woman reminded Peg that they had gone to school together and now she had heard that he had become a big important editor and she needed his advice. She said she had been writing poetry. Everybody told her it was good, just as good as the darn old poetry that was being published in the magazines and newspapers. She had tried to get the local paper to publish her poems but they wouldn't do it, the dirty old dumb twerps. Maybe her friend from yesteryear would get them published somewhere in New York because he probably hobnobbed with all the other great editors and ate lunch with them every day and so on. A woman who should have been strangled at birth.

She had enclosed several of her poems and Peg, the childhood chum, had read them. He confessed that he didn't think they were top-drawer.

"Now," he said, bristling with enthusiasm, "here's what I want you to do. Go find a poet. A good one. A poet that gets all his stuff published and makes dough out of it. Show him this letter and have him tell you how a woman should go about writing poetry. There must be rules you've got to follow, so find out what they are from this professional poet, and then write an Open Letter to this old friend of mine and tell her what he says. Man, that'll be another bell-ringer. I have an idea that there are people all over this country who want to write poetry but don't know how to go about it."

I thought about it a little while and then told him I didn't know any poets. He got sore. He knew I was trying to back out of the whole proposition. In the end his tone was beginning to grow a bit threatening and so I called up a girl named Lucy Goldthwaite who worked for a big book publisher and asked her if she could scare me up a competent poet. She soon had arranged a date for cocktails with Stephen Vincent Benét at the Biltmore. The three of us met and I told Mr. Benét that I was working for a man who had peculiar ideas and then I outlined this particular peculiar idea and Mr. Benét agreed that it was peculiar. He said it would be a little difficult for him to teach this Midwestern housewife all about writing poetry in just one Open Letter, written by a third party, meaning me. I said I understood all this but that I would appreciate his giving it a try, and he did. He also gave me an inscribed first edition copy of *John Brown's Body* but I didn't realize its value until much later—I was that upset about the god damned Open Letter business.

So I wrote the Open Letter to the lady versifier, and then I wrote another Open Letter the day following, and made it just as dull and senseless as my great talent would permit, and after that I heard no more on the subject. Because another idea was stirring in the fertile brain of Peg Vaughan. He called me to his desk. He asked me if I ever heard about the time Westbrook Pegler, occupying the very job I had now, betook himself to Brooklyn to attend the funeral of a prizefighter and had written a beautiful, beautiful story about that funeral—a classic of hearts-and-flowers writing. I said I had heard some vague report on the matter.

"Now," said Peg, "here's what I want you to do. Pegler wrote that piece a long time ago. Everybody's forgotten it. I want you to go into the files and find a copy of it. Then run over to Brooklyn and find a slum neighborhood to use as your background. Then make up a dead prizefighter and use Pegler's story, with the name changed and all. We won't put it on the city wire, so the New York papers won't know anything about it."

I protested loudly and vigorously.

"Hell," said Peg, "it was a beautiful story. Why let it lay there buried in the files? Git 'er out and let's go to town!"

I went back to my desk and sat down. I said to myself, this is getting serious. I had to do something. This guy might decide to ask me to write like Mark Hellinger. I shuddered, and went in and had a talk with the high command. They went to Peg and told him to leave me alone. But I don't think he liked me after that and before long we parted company on the issue of Bruno Hauptmann's trial in Flemington, New Jersey.

I had written the Lindbergh kidnaping for the nightside from the very beginning and now I was looking forward to covering the trial. All advance reports indicated it would be a real circus and I was making my plans when I heard that I was not to be sent to Flemington. I stormed down on Peg Vaughan. He said I had heard right. He said he needed me in the New York office to "tie things together" every night, that the UP was sending enough men to the trial. I could sit in the New York office and write the daily story under a Flemington dateline, and under my own by-line. I said I wouldn't do it. He said the hell I wouldn't. I said I was going to Flemington, or else. He said or else. And so I walked out of the News building and the next day Paul White gave me a job at the Columbia Broadcasting System. My first assignment was to go to Flemington, to the Hauptmann trial, with a newscaster of the time named Boake Carter. I helped Mr. Carter prepare his nightly broadcast on the trial and checked his copy for libel and, as it turned out, I was his announcer at the opening and closing of his broadcast. Also, as it turned out, there was very little work for me and I had a swell seat in the court-room and I fraternized at night with the wildest bunch of applejack drinkers in the history of mankind—the gentlemen of the New York press.

For a year I worked under Paul White and John G. Gude at CBS. I became acquainted with two marvelously funny men, Stoopnagle & Budd, and did some minor work for them, at the same time paying little attention to another funny man around the place—Fred Allen. I had long beer-drinking sessions with a pleasant guy named Bunny Berigan, never suspecting that he was already a legend in his own lifetime as a trumpet player. I got to know an antic little clarinetist named Pee Wee Russell, and a daffy musician out of New Orleans named Louis Prima. I ran around some with the old March of Time radio gang, including a roughneck announcer named Paul Douglas. A bunch of us from Madison Avenue went down to Washington to kick off a big radio series with a party, and a local guy named Godfrey, wearing a cowboy hat, tried to shoulder his way into our games; we told him to get lost. Then one day there was a playback of an old scene—the same scene that occurred years earlier in the boys' toilet at Huntington High School. This time it was a CBS elevator. I was telling Buck Curry what I thought of a certain CBS executive. There was only one other passenger in the elevator with us. I got my walking papers within the hour.

For a few weeks I worked at Transradio Press, a small organization that had been put together by former United Press people, hoping to capitalize on radio's increasing hunger for news. The head man of Transradio was Herb Moore, with whom I had worked at UP. In his role of executive, commanding the destinies of an office full of underlings, Herb had become an intensely serious man, deeply con-cerned over world and national affairs. He spoke prophetically about things. He was wise.

At this moment in history *Life* magazine burst on the scene. The first issue was preceded by weeks and months of pressurized pro-motion. The appearance of the first issue was to be such an earth-shaking event that, we were given to believe, if anything should happen to stop it the human race would not survive. And so the great day finally arrived. Herb Moore, along with everybody else in the country, was anxiously awaiting that first issue. He sent an office boy down to the corner newsstand to snatch up a copy and race back to the office with it. The boy arrived and placed the magazine on the desk in front of Herb. He stood up. The rest of us gathered around, saying nothing. Quiet reigned. Herb Moore carefully turned over the first sheet, let his eye rove over the pages, turned again, slowly, thoughtfully, examining every detail. We waited for his verdict. At last he reached the end. He turned the final page and looked at the back cover and then squinched up his eyes and stared a moment at the ceiling. Then, slapping his right hand on his desk, he announced:

"I give it six months!"

I worked a while for Paramount Pictures, in their Times Square offices, but ran afoul of a boss with whom I disagreed on a question of commas. I said the comma went inside the quotation marks. He said the comma went *outside*. We quarreled bitterly and he prevailed. The man who swallowed the first oyster had no more difficulty than I experienced in forcing myself to put commas outside of quotation marks, and finally I told this tyrant to take his job and insert it into some convenient orifice.

I now found a job with a man named Earl Newsom. Mr. Newsom was just getting started in the public relations business and had a small office on lower Broadway, south of the Woolworth tower. Somebody told me he was looking for a guy who could write persuasive copy and I went down and got the job. Earl Newsom went on to become one of the very top men in public relations and industrial counseling but when I worked for him he had but one or two clients and my pay check stirred memories of my newspaper days in Indiana. Nevertheless it was a job and Newsom was an intelligent and pleasant boss and my principal assignment was to try to sell the American public on drinking tea. Newsom was representing the Tea Bureau, which encompassed the whole industry, and tea people were in a steady sweat over the fact that Americans, and especially American men, lacked discrimination and taste and drank coffee all the time when they should have been drinking a more healthful and invigorating beverage, tea. The big stumbling block was the undislodgable feeling among men that tea was a sissy drink, a drink for ladies. A man by god wanted a strong cup of coffee. Newsom's job was to try to change this pattern of thought and I was supposed to dream up ways of effectuating that change. For example, I thought of having real rough guys stop their real rough work for a tea break. I remember going down to the docks near the Battery on a cold winter's day and taking along some tea-making equipment and setting it up on the deck of a tugboat. The men of the tugboat, with snow on their shoulders and icy winds blowing through their whiskers, posed for pictures drinking hot tea. I've forgotten how we talked them into it—probably gave them a few bottles of booze. Anyway, the idea was to get such pictures taken, and then talk the newspapers into running them and the further idea was that if you kept this sort of thing going, say for a couple of hundred years, you might change the habits of the American male and get him to drink tea.

One day I was sitting in my little cubbyhole in the Newsom office feeling depressed about the kind of work I was doing and the low estate to which my fortunes had fallen. Earl Newsom had just taken on a new account, something called the Wallpaper Institute. In a few days, I thought, I'd be put to work trying to think up ways of convincing the American public that interior paint was somehow poisonous, and not one-tenth as handsome and serviceable as good old wallpaper, and I'd still be on the damned tea thing, and then my eye fell on the projecting corner of an office building a few blocks away, over on West Street at the river. It was the building housing the New York *World-Telegram*. I had been in the *World-Telegram* city room quite a few times in the past and now I closed my eyes and thought of how it looked over there. What the hell was I doing sitting in Earl Newsom's office worrying about wallpaper? The place where I belonged was over there—working on a newspaper.

The United Press kept a man on duty every day at the *World-Telegram* and I knew that man. His name was Bob Musel and he was a friend of mine. I got him on the phone. I asked him if he thought Bo McAnney, the city editor, would consider giving me a job. Bob said he thought he would, and went and asked, and then said that Bo McAnney wanted to talk to me. Within an hour I was hired as a rewrite man, to report for work as quickly as Earl Newsom would let me go. Earl grinned when I told him. He said that from the beginning he had known that public relations was not my . . . well . . . dish of tea. He said that I belonged on the *World-Telegram* and that I could leave the tea and the wallpaper any time I wanted.

Before we proceed to the *World-Telegram*, however, there are two incidents out of this miserable period which I would enjoy recounting. One involved Edgar A. Guest. Mr. Guest had been signed on to do recitations on the radio and Bob Taplinger, of CBS press, got up a small luncheon party to celebrate this mighty event. For some reason Bob invited me and I leaped at the chance to meet this towering figure of the American literary scene. There were about a dozen of us in a private dining room at the Hotel New Yorker. Mr. Guest was cheerful and friendly and, being in the company of newspapermen and press agents, he said hell and damn frequently. Things were going along smoothly and we were all engaged in a heap o' livin' when a door at the end of the room opened and Bob Taplinger let out a cry.

"Oh my God!" he yelled. "How wonderful! Look who's where! Nick Kenny! Oh my God! History's being made! The two most popular poets in the United States—in the whole world—right here in the same room!"

Well, sir, it turned out that this was the first meeting of the two most popular poets on earth. I must explain that Bob Taplinger was always an effervescent guy, capable of wrenching great excitement out of very small matters; he made this meeting out to be the greatest confrontation since Stanley looked at Livingstone. The behavior of the two bards themselves, however, was the thing that impressed me, the thing that will always stay green in my memory.

Edgar Guest shook hands with Nick Kenny, who had once described snow as God's dandruff, and Mr. Guest said:

"Nick, I have been reading your stuff and loving it for years."

Nick blushed clear to his ankles, and hung his head, and pawed the floor.

"Aw, fuh Christ's sake, Mr. Guest!" he protested. "Aw, fuh Christ's sake!"

"It's the truth," said Mr. Guest, sincerity ringing in his voice.

"Awwww," said Nick. "I don't bleeve one god damn word of it. You're just bein' nice. My God I ain't even in the same *league* with you!"

"Don't you ever believe it," said Mr. Guest. "You take my word for it—you're tops!"

It went on like that for quite a while and then Bob Taplinger had an idea—why not have these two great men recite their own poems at one another? Mr. Guest was willing to reel off a couple of verses but Nick refused. He insisted in his foghorn voice and his longshoreman's vocabulary that he was not in the same class with Mr. Guest, that he would be a fool to pretend that he was.

"My God," he cried, "you want me to carry some coal to New-castle?"

Personally I was eager to hear Nick recite one of his greatest poems, the one about the football player who was killed during a game and which concluded with the heart-rending lines describing how, behind angel interference, he swept through that Maroon eleven, and plunged between the goal posts, which in this case led to Heaven.

But I was bashful and sensitive about my own unimportance in the presence of these two giants of the literary scene. I simply went away happy that it had fallen to my lot to be present.

And then . . . the case of *Fortune* magazine.

There was a long period when I couldn't find a job of any kind. During my years at the United Press I had made the acquaintance of one of the Chrysler boys who had set himself up as a publisher of fine books. He was turning out classics in superb bindings and some of these books were worth better than a hundred dollars apiece. He put me on his free list for a while and so I had a couple of shelves of valuable books in my home. Now I began selling them, two or three at a time, in order to buy navy beans for my family, stave off the landlord, and get subway fare for my job-hunting. I had no friends, now that I was unemployed. People who had been my blood brothers when I was a working newspaperman now crossed the street when they saw me approaching. This was especially true in the Broadway sector, where sentiment overflows in song and story, where friendship is towering and eternal and where they'll slit your throat for twenty-five cents in cash. So, I was carrying my precious books to a store on Fifty-Ninth Street, operated by a reptilian creature who had recognized my condition at once. He gave me a dollar apiece for those leather-bound beauties and when I all but wept, pointing out how luminously and luxuriously handsome they were, he snarled at me, "Take it or leave it." I took it.

After one such transaction I was walking along Fifth Avenue feeling somewhat bitter toward the biological species in which I held tenuous membership when I saw Paul White approaching. I almost started across the street myself, to save him the trouble, but he came straight ahead and hailed me in a friendly way as of yore and said he had been trying to get me on the phone. He said that a few days earlier he had run into a man named Eric Hodgins, an editor at *Fortune*, and that Mr. Hodgins was on the prowl for a good writer-reporter. Would I care to see Mr. Hodgins? I said I certainly would, and we went into a store and Paul telephoned and made an appointment for me.

I made my way to the Chrysler tower—the same building where those expensive Chrysler books had been given to me—and to a big paneled office where I faced Eric Hodgins across his desk. He ran over my journalistic past with me briefly and asked me if I knew anything about the *Fortune* techniques and I said I thought I did. Actually I didn't.

"I'll tell you how we go about doing a job," he said, and my hopes brightened for I thought he was inducting me into the organization. "When we have settled on a subject for an article, we organize a staff for that single project—a staff almost as big as a newspaper staff—with editors and writers and researchers and legmen and photographers and maybe even some specialists, such as economists, architects, engineers—depending on the nature of the job at hand. This staff sets to work and sometimes it takes months to finish its project but when it *is* finished we know that we've done a thorough job."

"It sounds interesting," I said, trying not to show my eagerness. I had a feeling that I was in—that I had finally stumbled into my destined place in the journalistic scheme, that my fortunes and the fortunes of *Fortune* were, as of that moment forward, inextricably as they say intermingled.

"Now," said Mr. Hodgins, exuding the fraternal warmth and friendliness of one journalist to another, "now I'll tell you what I want you to do. It's a big job, and I don't want you to underestimate it."

I smiled back at him and began mentally rolling up my sleeves, and said, "I'm all ears."

"I want you to go out," he said, "and do a *Fortune* article . . . *on your own*. Choose your own subject. Do every bit of the leg work. Write it the way you think it should be written for *Fortune*. Gather your own photographs, or arrange to have them shot. This is the way you can prove to us what you can do."

"Yes," I said, a little uneasily, "but I'm not quite sure what you mean when you say I should pick my own subject. Could you give me a little idea?"

"Certainly," he boomed. "Take the steel industry. Go out to Pittsburgh and do the steel industry for us, from top to bottom and

back again. And when you get it all finished, bring in your copy
and your pictures. Then we'll know what you've got to offer us. *Then*
we'll know if you belong on the staff of *Fortune*."

I could feel my gizzard beginning to crisp and curl at the edges.
What was this man saying to me? Was he suggesting that . . . I had
trouble getting the next question out of my mouth.

"How long," I said, "do you think it ought to take me to do the
steel industry?"

"Six months," he said. "Maybe eight . . . maybe even longer."

"And about expenses . . ." I said, my voice grown weak.

"That," he said with a hearty smile, "is *your* worry. *Fortune*
will forget all about you when you walk out of this building, and
until you come back with your job finished. I have a hunch you can
do it. I have a feeling that you're going to do it, and that your
future lies here with *Fortune*. Let me assure you that once you're in
here, once you've made the grade with us, you'll have a job that
means something."

I sat there a few moments, swallowing hard, a sort of dizziness
in my head, and the inside of my mouth was dry. I wanted to tell
this man that my lean and hungry ass was dragging, that I had no
more than subway fare in my pocket and that I had cashed in milk
bottles to get that; I wanted to show him that the soles of my shoes
were paper-thin, and take him to the crummy little apartment where
I was living on Long Island; I wanted to tell him that the thing he
had suggested was as preposterous as if he had assigned me to go
down to the Battery, jump in the water and swim around the world
non-stop. Somehow I didn't tell him any of these things. I nodded
to him and got up and walked to the door and as I went through it
I heard him call out, "Good luck with the blast furnaces!" At that
moment I'd have enjoyed shoving him into one; nor, when I finally
got squared around, did I forget him. Once I sat down and tried to
figure out what it would have cost me, out of my own empty pocket,
to have spent six or eight months in Pittsburgh doing the steel
industry up brown for his magazine. The nearest figure I could get
was something over five thousand dollars. But time eventually healed
my wound and I was able to tell about my near-miss at *Fortune*
and laugh about it. Anyway, the joke was on the magazine—I never
did show up with that Pittsburgh stuff. I even came to realize that
Eric Hodgins had actually not been at fault—he could not have
known that I was destitute when I sat across from him. Later on he

wrote about Mr. Blandings in a novel. This Mr. Blandings bought an old New England farmhouse and did things with it in a stupid and witless sort of way. The book had a wide audience and there were some among its readers, I'm sure, who felt that nobody outside a mental ward could have been as impractical and fumbling as Mr. Blandings. And it was whispered along the literary grapevine that Mr. Blandings was actually Eric Hodgins. If that were so—if Mr. Hodgins was as bewildered by the economic facts of life as Mr. Blandings—then my own experience with him was understandable. And if you say to me, "So what was he doing editing a big magazine like *Fortune?*" I can offer in his defense, "That's a purty good question."

# relations between organisms

# at Nick's

On the morning that I reported for work on the New York World-Telegram I had both the aspect and the manner of a scarecrow. I was somewhat aciform and my clothes did not fit me. Bo McAnney escorted me flappingly past the copy desk, past the Bell Tower (a pillar with a fire-gong at the top) and to a desk in the middle of the rewrite bank.

Toward the rear of the room Douglas Gilbert, an acidulous and acrimonious man in thought, word, and deed, took a long look at me and turned to Elliott Arnold and said:

"Where in the name of God is Bo getting his rewrite men these days? You suppose he's got traps set off Staten Island?"

A very pretty compliment on my first day at the Telly.

Doug Gilbert was a man of considerable talent, one of the top reporters in New York, and he was my friend for a long time. Well, not exactly my friend. He was nobody's friend. Let us say that he tolerated me. Off and on. Once I had the agreeable task of interviewing a disagreeable man, Alexander Woollcott. Mr. Woollcott sat with a yard and a half of his belly hanging out of his Oriental pajamas and abused me and abused my newspaper. "Do you," he asked in his clipped, precise manner, "do you have a shred of excrement by the name of Douglas Gilbert attached to the staff of your bilious sheet?" I said we had. Mr. Woollcott then cursed Mr. Gilbert at some length for having once written something about him without asking his permission to so write. Back in the office I told Doug what Mr. Woollcott had called him.

"Get him on the phone," said Doug, "and tell him I said he is a jar of Vaseline, hospital size."

After I wrote my story about the amiable Alec, I was told that he spoke of me as "a tiny smear on a microscopic slide." Mr. Woollcott didn't waste much love on people and neither did Doug Gilbert. I once heard Doug say of Cecil B. DeMille: "He has a magnificent grasp of the obvious." I spent many hours standing at the bar of Dominic Settiducatti's tavern with Doug, listening to him talk on the theater, music, New York newspapermen, religion, Fowler's *English Usage*, art, medicine, and so forth. He had a theory that American women are ruining their stomachs by overpoliteness in holding back wind when they are in the presence of other people; he said that if you study the faces of women in public you will see the evidence. I got the impression that Doug went around New York looking at the faces of women for this reason and this reason alone. Interesting pursuit, but not very aesthetic. Not even very romantic.

During one of our conversations Doug came up with the idea that he would enjoy having a pillow stuffed with belly-button lint. He said he would like to acquire the pickings from thousands of belly buttons and have them put into a pillow and then he'd sleep with his head on that pillow.

Standing at Mr. Settiducatti's bar we developed the idea further and at one point Nick himself came along and listened for a while and then departed, wagging his head from side to side and saying: "God, what people I got coming into my place."

Doug said he would want to hire an agent to go around collecting the belly-button lint. This agent would have to probe the belly buttons of many shy and recalcitrant people; his first job would be to gain the confidence of the owners of the belly buttons. That in itself would be quite a feat. I said I wasn't at all sure how I would treat that agent if he came to me and asked for the lint out of my belly button. I don't need it. It would be good for me to get rid of it. But I might be inclined to consider my belly-button lint to be property of such an intimate nature that I wouldn't be willing to have it fished out and stuffed into a pillow.

Doug Gilbert said he would have to be careful about the character of the agent he engaged. He couldn't take a chance on hiring some guy who would cheat—who would disappear for a couple of years and then come around with a gunny sack full of stuff which he *claimed* was prime belly-button lint but which in fact was stuff taken out of the hot boxes of railroad freight cars. Doug pointed out that the agent would have his own problems. He could never permit a prospect, or holder, to go out of the room and then come back with the lint from his or her belly button. The extraction would have to be performed right there on the spot, with the agent removing the lint, or the owner of the belly button removing it before the agent's eyes and handing it over. You can readily see how it would take a long time to collect enough belly-button lint to stuff a pillow.

Later on I worked out an advertising campaign which could be used to facilitate the search for lint. Startle and delight the public with the information that their belly-button lint is worth money. Splash display ads around, in this manner:

DON'T THROW IT AWAY!
THE BELLY-BUTTON LINT MAN
WILL BE AROUND TO SEE YOU!
HAVE YOUR WHOLE FAMILY
SAVE BELLY-BUTTON LINT
AND ENJOY A VACATION
IN BEAUTIFUL VERMONT!

Years ago I wrote some speculations on this project in one of my books and people began sending *me* belly-button lint from all over the country. A group of stenographers in the RCA building even organized the Rockefeller Center Belly-Button Lint Club and sent word that they were collecting for me. I had to explain to all these people that I was not personally after the contents of their navels. Nor did I suggest that they send their lint to Doug Gilbert. In fact I concealed his identity when I wrote that earlier account of his project. He was an irascible and unpredictable man and people who knew him took no chances on arousing his ire.

For example, he kept his own son-of-a-bitch list. This was a memorandum book containing the names of people and institutions he hated for one reason or another. He was always afraid he would forget one or another of them and so he kept a record of them. The entire New York subway system was on that list, and so was the New York Telephone Company. Whenever he was writing a story for the paper, almost any story, he would get out his little book and run through it and see if he could find an enemy who could be attacked in some manner during the unfolding of that story. His story might be an interview with an actor. Doug and the actor would be talking in the latter's apartment and the phone would ring and the actor would answer it. Wrong number. More talk. Another ring. Another wrong number. Doug's idea was subtle—he would ruin the telephone people by attrition, wearing them down with little snipings of this nature.

He served for several years as drama critic of the *World-Telegram*. Being a man of surpassing acerbity, he was sour on almost everything but orange juice, whisky, and the legitimate theater. He hated his newspaper job and yearned for an opportunity to work in the production end of the theater.

One day a man who was famous in theatrical production called Doug and said he wanted to see him about a job. It was an important job, and the producer was a man who almost had principles, and the salary would be twice what Doug was getting on the paper. The two men arranged to meet for dinner in a quiet restaurant just off Times Square.

This was Doug's splendid opportunity, the thing he had been dreaming about. He sat in a booth, opposite the Great Man. They had a couple of drinks and then ordered dinner. Doug got a plate of clam spaghetti. They talked along as they ate and things were progressing favorably. Then tragedy struck, in its nasty little way, without warning. Doug had his mouth full of clam spaghetti. Before he could stop himself, before he could even turn his head, a tremendous paroxysm seized him, his mouth flew open and he sneezed a mighty sneeze, splattering that theatrical gentleman from chest to scalp with clam spaghetti. The Savior himself wouldn't have hired Doug after that.

Doug had an active dislike for a majority of the people he worked with. When one of these outcasts approached him at Nick's bar, he'd turn his head and move quickly away. He had no qualms about being rude; sometimes he seemed to glory in it. For some reason not clear to me, I got along with him as well as anyone on the staff and sometimes we went uptown together and played the big time saloons and I even got to know his family.

One afternoon I was walking down the hallway that led to the locker room. I saw him approaching and as we neared each other I said, "Hi, Doug." He glared straight ahead and hurried past me. At first I thought he was merely in the grip of a horrifying hangover. A few minutes later I walked over to his desk. He didn't look up from his typewriter and I asked him if he wanted to duck out and have a couple at Nick's. He still didn't look up. "What's eating you?" I demanded. No answer. I went back to my desk and thought about it for a while and then wrote him a note, asking for an explanation. A copy boy handed the note to him and, without reading it, he tore it into bits.

He never spoke to me again. I spent hours trying to think back, trying to figure it out. I had not done a single thing I could think of that would cause him to quit speaking. I had a mutual friend approach him and ask what was troubling him. He said, "Don't mention that scum's name in my presence."

Not long after that I left the paper, still unspoken to, and then one day Doug was sitting in the Hotel Gotham with a double martini in his hand when he slumped over and died. Now I'll never know. Or maybe I will. It could be that I'll see him at his place of residence in the hereafter, in which event I intend to say to him, "Hey, why did you quit speaking to me?" The chances are he won't even look up from his shoveling.

There has been a trend in recent decades to minimize the depravity of newspapermen. By depravity I mean, for the most part, the thing that Frank Ward O'Malley meant when he called up his friends and said, "Let's play saloon." I have in my files an article written by a prominent member of the Los Angeles Newspaper Guild, pleading with Hollywood screen writers to quit libeling newspapermen. This is an old, sad song that I've heard before and seen in print before, many times. Newspapermen, they say, are not at all like they have been pictured in movies.

We are now approaching the end of a long book and I think that any reader who has stayed with me this far will recognize the fact that carousing has taken up a lot of my time in the past. Right down to the end of my newspaper work in 1942 I ran with hard-drinking people in every job I had. If a newspaperman was not a hearty drinker, then he was very likely a nut in some other direction. There was one teetotaler on the *World-Telegram* who collected horse manure off the pavement of West Street before going home to suburbia each evening. This old guy carried a suitcase to and from work and each evening he'd go into West Street and scoop up horse-droppings and lug them home for his flower garden. He thought those of us who drank were peculiar.

Half the staff of the *World-Telegram* headed for Nick's as soon as the day's work was finished. Some would stay at the bar for thirty minutes or so, then go on home. Others would still be there at midnight. If their wives telephoned during the evening, there was a standard response given to them by the help: "No ma'am, he ain't been in here since Labor Day." The executives of every city newspaper I ever worked on were extremely tolerant of drunks. I would not be able to count the number of men I have seen arrive for work almost too drunk to stand. Few of them were ever fired; more likely than not, they'd be gentled into a taxicab and the driver paid to take them home. Perhaps the next day they would be spoken to sharply; in the offices of other businesses, insurance companies and railroads and mail order houses and oil corporations, they would have been canned on the spot.

Most of the things that men do when they are sober are, to me, quite comical. This is especially true when they are trying to prove out the altogether untenable notion that man has dignity. Men in their cups often tend to exaggerate this posture of dignity and thereby become, in my view, even funnier than sober men. I have always enjoyed observing and writing about drunks.

Jim Howard was one of the best rewrite men on the *World-Telegram*. There were occasions when, like the rest of us, he would arrive at work in the throes of the collywobbles and the clammy-damps. I don't think I've ever seen a man who could put so much into a hangover as Jim. It was his custom to walk from the subway to the office along Barclay Street, and there was one block of Barclay Street lined with stores dealing in religious equipment and ornaments. The show windows of these stores were usually crowded with bleeding statues of one kind or another. Jim could not bear the sight of these things on his bad mornings. He would take another route if he could remember, otherwise when he came down Barclay Street he'd walk with his face turned away from those store windows. Doug Gilbert knew about Jim's phobia and one day planned a somewhat grisly joke. Doug went to one of the stores and bought a bleeding statue, a cheap one about four feet long with a lot of red paint on it. He carried it to the office and waited patiently for the day when Jim Howard would arrive with a twee-whilliger. This could be accurately foretold by noting Jim's condition in Nick's the night before. And so the morning came and Jim entered the office with a hangover that could have won a Pulitzer prize. Doug had placed the bleeding statue, wounds uppermost, across the top of

Jim's desk. Jim came down the long approach, all but feeling his way from pillar to pillar, and at last arrived at his desk. The entire office paused, waiting for the explosion. Jim looked down. He seemed to study the statue for a moment. Then he picked it up, almost gently, and turned and tossed it across the aisle and into the sports department. After which he pulled out his typewriter, sat down, and glanced at the city desk as a signal that he was ready for work.

Once in a great while, moon phases being what they are, a Wave of Reform would hit us. I remember the time when several of us, grown tired of the night-after-night-after-night routine, held an impromptu meeting and decided to cut down on the foolishness. For months we had been spending every night in Nick's and this was beginning to tell on our health, our work, and our home life. We reached a firm decision. From now on, we said, we would not go to Nick's unless there was something important to celebrate, unless a special occasion of some kind demanded it. The day after that there was no special occasion, nothing to celebrate, and we all stuck to our resolution and went straight home. On the following day Asa Bordages and I sat at adjoining desks and spoke of how wonderful we felt, and how clear our minds were, and what a fine thing it was to live in this way, and Asa wanted to know if by any chance it was my birthday and I said no and I thought perhaps it was his wedding anniversary and he said no and he asked me if I knew the date of Roy Howard's birthday and I said no and we sat moodily for a while and I said my god this is awful and called an office boy and asked him to bring me, from the reference room, *The Book of Days* in two volumes and *A Dictionary of Dates* and *Cyclopedia of Classified Dates* and *American Book of Days* and *When Did It Happen?* It was the 24th day of July and I began looking for that date in these books.

"Here is Henry Shaw," I said to Asa. "It is Henry Shaw's birthday."

"Read on," said Asa.

"Henry Shaw," I said, "founded the Missouri Botanical Garden in St. Louis. That's about all."

"Doesn't seem quite strong enough," said Asa.

I checked through the other books and found that this was the date on which Dr. Nathaniel Lardner died in 1768. I told Asa that if it turned out that this guy was related in any way to Ring Lardner we had our man, and could hold a delayed wake for him. But Dr. Nathaniel Lardner merely wrote *Credibility of the Gospel History* and there was no suggestion that he had any connection with Ring.

So I moved on to Simon Bolivar, whose birthday it was, and we held him in reserve while we considered the Feast of St. Eloi, the patron saint of mules. July 24th is the Feast Day for mules and I thought this was a splendid thing to celebrate, but Asa grew up with a lot of mules and burros in Texas and had some kind of a fixation on the subject, and then I discovered that it was Pioneer Day in Utah—the anniversary of the day Brigham Young looked at the basin and the lake and said, "Enough. This is the place." So Asa and I went around the office telling people about it and got a bunch together and headed over for Greenwich Street and arriving at Nick's door Asa cried out, "Enough! This is the place!" And in we went. We used those date books a great deal from then on, celebrating the birthday of Phineas P. Quimby, the invention of the unwinding paper pencil, and the wedding anniversary of William Randolph Hearst.

Asa Bordages was tall with black hair and he always seemed to be in a hurry. He is a living legend in his own lifetime, at least in the neighborhood of West and Barclay. He was an energetic reporter, one of the best; he was a good enough writer to produce novels that evoked high praise from the critics; he was a star on rewrite, a genius at research, a whiz with the girls and the worst pinball player I ever encountered.

At Nick's we shook dice for drinks and played the pinball machine for money. The most famous pinball game in the history of the resort was the one which ended with my winning two thousand eight hundred and fifty dollars from Asa. It started as an innocent social game, shortly after dinner on a Wednesday night, and it continued until four A.M. In the first hour we reached a point where Asa owed me thirty-five dollars. Neither of us had any money and were signing tabs for the drinks. So at this point I began to get uneasy. Asa wanted to shoot double-or-nothing.

"All right," I said, "but Asa, I want it understood—you pay me Friday. Right?"

"Of course!" cried Asa, as if there could be any question about it.

So he shot and owed me seventy dollars. He talked me into double-or-nothing again and then he owed me a hundred and forty. He asked for another double-or-nothing and I said no.

"Damn it!" he exclaimed. "I *told* you I'd pay you Friday!"

"Well, all right," I said. "But just be sure you do!"

It went on that way the rest of the night. I got cagey and refused to let him shoot double-or-nothing but I would allow him to shoot for fifty or a hundred dollars a game. And even after we had passed the point where he owed me two thousand dollars, he would repeat, in solemn pledge, that he would pay me when he got his salary check on Friday and I, in equally solemn manner, would advise him not to forget it.

And so, out of exhaustion, we finally quit and went home to get an hour or two of sleep and when we met later in the city room Asa said to me: "Hey, do you remember anything about last night?" And I said: "Not a thing, except we were at Nick's."

I was sitting beside Asa on the rewrite bank one day when he decided to send a telegram to a girl in Chicago, saying "I love you" one hundred times. The Western Union man was his friend and when Asa explained how he wanted the message to be sent, the telegrapher gave him an argument.

"Listen, Asa," he said, "all you got to do is say 'I love you one hundred times.' If you do it the other way, my God look at the money it will cost you."

"No," said Asa, "I want you to send 'I love you' and send it over and over until you've got one hundred of them."

"But, Asa," said the Western Union man, "can't you see how much money that's gonna cost? You can get the same effect by saying it . . ."

"I . . . said . . . one . . . hundred . . . times!" said Asa, and that's the way the telegram went off.

One method of punishing an incorrigible sinner was to put him on lobster rewrite for a few weeks. Both Asa and I served long stretches in this gray Siberia, where the customary hour of starting work was three in the morning. Day or night, Asa was a fellow with an immense talent for arriving late. Some said he did it just to have an excuse for dramatizing the *reason* for his tardiness. He could make a subway delay sound like the end of the world. At one period when he was working the lobster trick he was arriving late so often that steps had to be taken, and George Lyon gave him a final warning. If Asa was late again, by so much as one minute, he was finished.

The rest of the staff figured that it was pure fantasy to suppose that Asa would ever get to work on time, especially when ordered to do so, and on that fatal morning every eye was on the clock. At precisely three o'clock Asa came bursting through the door. It was summertime but he had on an overcoat. Behind him came a taxicab driver carrying a large laundry bag.

"Made it!" cried Asa, glancing at the clock on the wall.

He then removed his overcoat and stood naked as a Texas jaybird. He had awakened late, phoned for a cab, thrown his clothes into the bag, got into the overcoat and raced for the office. There are still some who insist he sat up all night planning it that way.

I have mentioned that he was good at research. He was actually unexcelled in that type of work. He was never happier than when he had an assignment that required him to spend long hours in the Public Library. They knew him there as one of their best customers. Sometimes, even when he had no specific job to do, he'd go to the library and work at some research just for kicks.

I have not seen Asa for years but a friend tells me of the satisfying kind of life he leads. He lives in a small town in New Jersey in a house that is jammed with books. After a notable career in the Marine Corps during War II he settled down in this house and began enjoying a life of scholarly research. He became interested in the career of an obscure American politician—let us call him Walter Ravetto Harris. Asa decided that Walter Ravetto Harris was a great man, that history had not done right by him, and that he, Asa Bordages, would rectify this terrible blunder. Asa went to work on a biography of Walter Ravetto Harris. Almost all of his research could be accomplished among the books in his own library. He worked long hours, digging for detail and color, filling notebook after notebook, and then one day, after about a year of this joyous labor, he came across the name of John Sutherland Fox, another obscure American politician.

"Great Scott!" exclaimed Asa. "Here is a MAN! To think that I never even heard of him! John Sutherland Fox!"

He put his Walter Ravetto Harris notes aside and went to work researching the life of John Sutherland Fox. He went to New York and Philadelphia and had more books shipped out to his Jersey home. He dug and dug, reveling in his research, and in the end he came upon a man named James Mackey McMahon, a far more fascinating character than the other two, and so he . . .

That's Asa.

# plush wings at ease

When I first joined his fraternity Nick's saloon was a foul trap across the street from his present location. Joe Mitchell once wrote two memorable pieces for the *New Yorker* about a downtown bar and grill, frequented by newspapermen, and I suspect that many of the stories in those articles had their origin at Nick's, both the old place and the new.

Nick's was an establishment where we went to observe the social amenities and it was also a place where we sometimes went to get staggering drunk. You are shocked at such an honest declaration? It was John Barrymore's father who said that staggering is a sign of strength—the weak ones have to be carried home.

The actual bar in Nick's old place was an antique in the sense that it was old and sway-backed and unsteady. It was unsteady because of Sutherland Denlinger, a large lusty citizen who was on the staff of the *World-Telegram* and whose nickname was Speed. Whenever he was feeling a bit gay Speed liked to sing in a powerful baritone voice. He sang "Miss Brady's Piano Fortay" and "Tiddly Winks God Damn" and a ballad about a little English boy with a chorus that went:

> Wing, wang, waddle, to my ding dong doodle,
> O my fim, fum foodle, it's a long ways home.

Many men have enjoyed singing in bars but Speed Denlinger was unique among them because of his knack for punctuating his lines with action. Whenever a punctuation mark was suggested in the lyrics, he would pause and roar, "Charge!" and hurl his two hundred odd pounds against the bar, tipping the whole rickety structure inward a couple of feet, sending glasses and bottles flying through the air, and giving nervous prostration to brooding drunks as well as to Nick. From a safe distance it was a great thing to watch Speed singing that song about the little English boy, for in his arrangement it would go something like this:

Wing . . . CHARGE! . . . *Crash!* . . . wang . . . CHARGE!
. . . *Boom!* . . . waddle . . . CHARGE! . . . *Wham!* . . . to
my ding dong doodle . . . CHARGE! . . . *Cuh-rasssh!* . . .

We didn't realize it at the time but Speed was preparing us for the future; his style was a precursor of things to come in the singing line.

Jimmie Street, yet to become famous as chronicler of the Dabney clan, telephoned me one day and asked if I thought he had a chance of getting a job on the *World-Telegram.* He had quit a job with Hearst to try his hand at free-lancing but he said he missed getting that regular check every week and he wanted to get back into newspaper work. Bo McAnney already knew about Jimmie and agreed that his rightful place was in our Barclay Street Zoo. So Jimmie came to work and stayed less than a year and nothing, not even the furniture and fixtures, was the same after his departure.

Jimmie was one of the kindliest and most sentimental men who ever lived and yet he had a Cal Coolidge type of face that made him look as if he smelled something bad. Sometimes he looked mean even when his face was in repose and when his thoughts were of violets. I intend to write at length about him in a later book for he was one of the closest friends I ever had. For the moment let us be satisfied with the story of the mirror. When he got to rolling real good Jimmie was a brandy drinker. A *chain* brandy drinker. And there usually came a period in his brandy drinking when he grew mean. I think perhaps that at this stage his mind got to dwelling on the all-pervading justice in the world, and the inherent honesty of man, and the dignity of the race to which he belonged—and he'd get himself into a statuesque rage.

One afternoon Jimmie was standing alone at Nick's bar, drinking brandy. He had arrived at his mean stage. He was hunched down in his overcoat and had his hat pulled low over his eyes. He was awash in a sea of animus when suddenly he saw a face. It was the face of a man he instinctively disliked. Hated, in fact. Jimmie glared at this man. The man glared back, boldly and insolently and hatefully. Jimmie growled a couple of times, tightened his jaw muscles, squinted up his eyes and then picked up his shot glass and threw it with all his strength at the hateful stranger. There was an ear-splitting crash. Jimmie had shattered the big mirror over the back bar. He had thrown the shot glass at a reflection of himself. Cost him seventy-five dollars.

In his youth Jimmie had been a Baptist minister, known as "The Boy Preacher of the South," and he could deliver an old-time evangelistic sermon. One evening some of us were in Nick's listening to Jimmie tell about how he could fetch a man to Jesus in a matter of a few minutes, and there was talk of a bet. The next thing anybody knew Jimmie had accepted a challenge. Standing at the far end of the bar was Joe Brady, a former *World* man, now an assistant city editor of the *World-Telegram*. Jimmie made a bet that he could jerk Joe Brady down the sawdust trail within ten minutes of going to work on him.

"I won't try it though," said Jimmie, "till he's had a couple more drinks. He's a Catholic and it won't be easy."

Nobody told Joe he was on the very doorstep of salvation. Jimmie got onto a bar stool and started out slowly, and pretty soon he was yelling and whooping and waving his arms, and directing his appeals straight at Joe, and Joe just grinned and moved in closer, and in less than the stipulated ten minutes Joe Brady was down on the floor groveling in peanut hulls, tears streaking down his face, crying out that he was a terrible sinner and begging forgiveness.

We always got our pay checks at noontime on Fridays and the custom was to cross the street to a bank and get them cashed on our way to lunch. Many of the staff members, especially the regulars at Nick's, were somewhat irresponsible about money matters, and the wives of these men had a habit of gathering on the corner in front of the bank each Friday noon. Sometimes there would be a dozen of them and their weekly meetings were looked upon as social affairs—a sort of West Street hen-party and ambuscade. They got to visit with each other briefly while waiting for their dirty bum husbands to emerge from the bank with the money. Of course my own wife never had to go through such a humiliating routine, at least no more than occasionally, say once a week. It was always an interesting thing to observe the actions of the individual couples once the husband had arrived with the cash. His wife would detach herself from the hen-group and the two of them would stroll casually along the sidewalk a few yards, getting out of earshot. Their lips would be moving, and there would be pleasant little smiles, but the language they spoke to each other did not somehow fit these facial expressions.

The husband would place a courtly hand on his wife's arm and flash a smile at her and his lips would move as if he were asking about the welfare of their dear children. What he would be saying, however, was this:

"You god damn dirty bitch." Smile. "I told you to quit coming down here and embarrassing me like this." Loving pat on arm. "One of these days I'm gonna let you have it, sure as Christ, right in the puss." Glow of deep devotion.

His wife would toss her lovely shimmering hair, raise her soft eyes to his, smile ever so sweetly as if she were about to throw herself into his arms for a long and lingering kiss. And her lips would be moving and at a distance it would appear that she was thanking him for the nice things he had just said, and expressing her happiness at being married to such an admirable man, but what she was really saying was this:

"Why, you drunken bastard." Short giggle of pure delight. "If I didn't come down here and get this money there wouldn't be a bottle of milk in the house all week." Simper. "I ought to take you to court, you worthless bum." Slow sensuous smile. "In fact I ought to take a butcher knife and put you out of your lousy drunken god damn misery."

These unfortunate men, geniuses in their way, would hand over most of their money to their wives, always trying to retain enough to pay their tabs at Nick's, though very few ever got out of the debit swamp. I often heard that some guys had tabs running back as far as six months and still Nick would give them food and drink on the cuff.

Friday night was usually known as Cabaret Night simply because the crowd was greater and noisier than on other nights. More money was spent, or more tabs signed, and Cabaret Night could sometimes grow into a pretty wild affair. I remember quite a few such nights but the one that stands out above others is the one that starred Helen Morgan.

I had become a friend of the singer. A Broadway acquaintance mentioned to me one day that Helen Morgan was sitting alone, day after day and night after night, in a little room in the Park Central

Hotel. She had few friends left, or maybe she just didn't want to see anybody. She had a reputation as a boozer, but at this time she was not drinking herself stuperous—at least she never did in my presence. I went to see her and we sat for several hours in that little room, just talking about former times—my former times as well as hers—and she asked me to come back, and I did.

So, one Cabaret Night at Nick's things were beginning to heat up and a goodly crowd was there and along came Mel Heimer, euphoric and frisky, and he says hey you're so damn smart you're so buddy-buddy with ole Helen Morgan why don't you go get Helen Morgan to come down here and sing for us and I says why not and I got on the phone and she said sure. So I hopped a cab and picked her up at the hotel and hauled her down to Nick's. She was still a very beautiful woman and she was, of course, a living legend in her own lifetime. I must say the boys really put it on for her. Such old world courtliness from such a bunch of bums! Even Doug Gilbert. Doug volunteered to play piano if she'd sing some of her old songs, and we hoisted her on top of the old beat-up Steinway and she sang for an hour. And then she got down and Nick gave her a big wet kiss and told her she could have all the brandy in the house now and forevermore. I remember glancing up at one point and seeing Joe Mitchell behind the bar with an enormous carving knife in his hands, raised aloft, the point of the blade aimed downward at the chest of Vinnie, who was Nick's partner. Vinnie had hold of Joe's wrists and Joe was straining mightily, trying to bring the knife down and kill Vinnie. And across the bar stood Joe's wife Therese, watching the scene. She did not cry out for Joe to stop, nor did she cry out for Joe to kill Vinnie—she just stared, fascinated by it all. Then along came Nick and took the knife away from Joe and a bit later I asked Joe what the trouble had been and he said what trouble. And then a distant roar of "CHARGE!" and the bar tipped halfway over as two hundred and fifty pounds of Speed Denlinger hit it.

The dear, sweet memories of days gone by are, with many people, concerned with crinoline and old lace, gliding canoes and parasols and weeping willow trees and a full moon set above the curve of a palm tree. My sweetest memories are of Cabaret Night at Nick's.

Readers of the *World-Telegram* may recall seeing, from time to time, the by-line of Weston Barclay. This was a made-up name, from the address of the paper, West and Barclay. It was used sometimes on policy stories, on stories where the actual writer didn't want his real name used, and on stories written by guys who already had a by-line in that day's paper. I dedicated a book, *Low Man on a Totem Pole*, to Weston Barclay; in so doing I was dedicating it to all my former associates on the paper. And once again I salute old Weston, for it would be impossible for me to mention all the people who were my friends there. Almost everybody has forgotten about Red Starr. He was hired as a rewrite man on the same day I reported for work and he lasted a month or so and then vanished. He was strange. Not because he drank, but because of the excuses he gave the office for not being able to come to work. Instead of calling up and saying he had a terrible case of the trots, which was the standard excuse, Red Starr would have a friend do the telephoning. He would wait until the hour when Bo McAnney was at his desk, then he'd have his friend call Bo, and the friend would make a big production out of tendering Red's excuses. "Mr. Starr," he would say, "has contracted double pneumonia and won't be able to come to work for two days." Or, "Are you acquainted, Mr. McAnney, with the Prime Chateaubriand Boquetiere with Sauce Bearnaise as served at O'Reilly's Chop House? Well, our friend Starr tried it last night and . . ." For a while Mr. McAnney enjoyed these inventions so much that he took no action. Then one morning a strange voice got through to Bo and said: "This is Red Starr's attorney calling. I want to advise you that Mr. Starr will not be able to come to work today on account of illness. There is no law that says he must tell you the nature of that illness, and if you try to make anything out of it he will haul you into court." To which Mr. McAnney, a tough man in a corner, responded: "In your capacity as counsel for the defendant, I want you to advise Mr. Starr that if he shows his face around here just once I will commit a capital crime upon his person." And so we saw nothing further of Red Starr. He was an original.

His chair was taken by a recruit from the south, a young man who weighed three hundred pounds. His name was Joe Carroll and when he fell off a bar stool he shook the entire neighborhood and it required the labor of four strong men to pry him loose from the floor. He drank double Scotches, claiming that a psychiatrist had told him he had a split personality, and he had to keep those two personalities in balance by feeding a Scotch to one, a Scotch to the other and then taking one for himself. Sometimes all three hundred pounds of him got drunk at once and then there was likely to be trouble. He had been hired because his mother was big in politics in the Shallow South and he was kept on the job for that same reason, even though he was barely capable of putting together a two-paragraph obituary. He rarely went to Nick's but did his drinking in a waterfront saloon near the office. He was cured of drinking by a miracle. Or so I heard. One summer afternoon he was throwing his blubber around in the saloon and his eye fell on the pinball machine. He lurched over to it, managed to fumble a nickel into it, and started a game. His body-english must have been at fault for he lost his balance and fell on top of the machine. One elbow crashed through the glass cover and struck one of the bumpers. This created some sort of a crazy short circuit in the house and set off a burglar alarm on the front of the building. The burglar alarm added its shrill voice to the banging and shrieking of the pinball machine itself. In Joe's fuzzy mind he had hit the greatest jackpot of them all. Beyond that he couldn't reason. It was clearly a miracle. He staggered out of the place and went home and the story goes that he never took another drink from that day on. That's how the story goes. It goes that way.

There was a tramp reporter around for a couple of months, a skinny guy from Pennsylvania who used to blurt out, "Hemingway is my god." He had a vaporous brain and fancied himself as a genius and imitated Hemingway in his horrible prose. He was a lone drinker and when he said, "Hemingway is my god," or, "I worship Hemingway," he was not talking to anyone other than himself. We used to hear him speak these lines and we got into the habit of responding with such remarks as, "Go shoot a water buffalo!" or "Why don't you go somewhere and veronica a bull?" One night this guy went to Nick's and was standing with his foot on the brass rail and drinking rye and saying Hemingway is my god and the rain was slashing at the window and roiling on down Greenwich Street and somebody was saying why don't you go pit some cocks or something but he was paying us no mind and then he began mumbling curses against the copy desk because those lugs knew nothing whatever about the English language and the placing of words in a beautiful beautiful sentence the way he did. So he staggered out of the place and made it to the paper and poured a quart of glue into the pneumatic tube which served to transport copy to the composing room. Quite a mess. Man was not made for defeat but the old man of the city desk didn't know that and so our boy got himself fired.

In those days Nick's was almost a private club for *World-Telegram* people and their friends. Occasionally an outsider would push his way in, plainly intent upon a fool's project: glamorizing himself through association with a crowd of colorful newspapermen. Among these was a Scandinavian salesman named Christiansen, usually called Chris. One day he wasn't there and the next day he was everybody's pal and he bought more than his share of drinks and at first he was not too much of a nuisance, so he was tolerated. He got so he knew everybody and everybody knew him and then before long everybody was sick of him. He was a talker. What he talked about was himself. He had been in World War One and he never tired of describing his heroic adventures in the trenches. He told about killing Huns with his bare hands, about wiping out enemy machine gun nests with grenades, about slaughtering whole battalions with his rifle. These gasconades grew untenable. Being outspoken men, we parfit gentil knights of the *World-Telegram* began telling Chris to shut his god damn face. It got so he could scarcely open his mouth without being called a fake and a liar. We taunted him mercilessly, calling him a coward, saying he would turn tail at the first sign of a fight. Eventually he became almost a symbol of cowardice. He was that kind—a blowhard and yellow to the core.

Then one day a man walked into Nick's and ordered a drink from Louie, the bartender. Louie set the drink in front of the stranger who promptly pulled out a pistol and shot Louie through the tripes. He then turned his gun on Nick and let go a couple of wild shots. Chris, the braggart, had been sitting on a stool at the back end of the bar when the first shot sounded. He climbed off the stool as calmly as if he were going to the men's room. He walked down the bar toward the gunman. His fists were clenched and he crouched slightly as he walked toward the thug.

"Why," said Chris, "you sniveling little son-of-a-bitch punk, I'm gonna bust you in two."

The guy pulled the trigger and Chris died there on the floor. The gunman ran out and disappeared toward the Hudson River and was never seen again. Louie recovered. And all of us went to Chris's funeral.

Nick himself had been foremost among those who derided Chris and his boasting. But now Nick too recognized his wrong and after the funeral he sat down at a back table and in a fit of self-abasement wrote a poem. I still have a copy of it. Here it is:

A soldier boy was he
Fear he knew not
He saw Flanders Field out afar
Returned with a wound or so
With all the glory a doughboy could get.
He set foot on American soil
To live a few years in the past.
And then to wander in a bar room
That was to be his last
'Tis God's will who is our Master
And our Judge Supreme who said
Chris, you did your last for your fellow humans
You tried hard to conquer a menace to life here on earth
But met with his maker
But a soldier to the end.

It is rather unusual for poetry to keep leaping into my pages but I must tell about Joe Mitchell's poem. I was still deeply taken with the literary life and I talked the desk into letting me do a series of articles about it. In this series I used a fictional young man named Tertius K. Hack and had him write a novel, and then had him go through all the procedures involved in having his book published. I had to give Mr. Hack's novel a title. I thought of the many book titles I had seen that seemed to make no sense at all, that apparently had no slightest connection with the books they were on. So I reached into the deep recesses of my brain and came out with a meaningless phrase, *Plush Wings at Ease*. That was the title I gave Mr. Hack's novel. But every author who fastens a senseless title on his book is quick to defend it and explain it. Quite often it is a senseless line taken out of a poem. So now I decided that Mr. Tertius K. Hack's title should have had its origin in poetry. In other words I needed a poem in which the phrase appeared. I was giving this matter some thought when I noticed that Joe Mitchell was sitting at the desk in front of me. I typed out the words "Plush wings at ease" on a sheet of paper and handed it to him.

"Joe," I said, "suppose you had to write a poem containing that line. Think you could do it?"

He read it.

"What's it mean?" he asked.

I explained that it meant nothing, and told him what I was doing and that I wanted a short poem with that line included in it, so Mr.

Hack could pluck it out and use it for his book title. Joe turned back to his typewriter and in a couple of minutes handed me the poem, which I used in my story. Here it is—one of the few poetical works of the many-sided genius, Joseph Mitchell:

> When I hear those wings flap,
> They make me sneeze.
> Please go and set those
> Plush wings at ease.

I've always thought it had the smell of immortality.

# the light touch

A rewrite man seldom goes outside the office on a job. His work keeps him close beside the city desk where he may write two or three dozen stories, of varying length, in the course of a single day. This fellow, the rewrite man, is the unsung hero of the newspaper trade. I say so because at the *World-Telegram* I was hired as a rewrite man and I was a rewrite man the day I left.

It is a rare thing for a rewrite man ever to attract any public attention, although a few members of the fraternity spend their off hours quietly working on scholarly books, like I done. The feature writers in the back of the room and the people who write columns are the ones who get the letters from book publishers and the bids from the magazine editors. The rewrite man sits at his desk and grinds out copy all day long and he has to be fast and accurate and smooth and knowledgeable. Yet he remains anonymous. As my wife and I so often say: the wrong people got the money.

During most of those years I reported for work at seven A.M. I wrote the stories of murder trials and muggings and subway wrecks and hurricanes and divorce cases and suicides and strawberry festivals and cats trapped in walls and starving recluses found with sixty thousand bucks pinned to their underpants and night club brawls and building collapses and the weather. For better or for worse I had what is known around newspaper shops as The Light Touch. Guys with The Light Touch are scarce and when one comes along he gets a lot of Light Touch work thrown at him. All week long I used to get stories tossed at me with the abrupt order, "Make it funny." The routine assignments that come to a newspaperman who has a reputation for writing funny stuff are endless. Every Friday the 13th means that he must be hilarious for a half column or so. Each time daylight saving time begins or ends he must write about the confusion of it all. Ground-hog day and April Fool's Day and New Year's Day and maybe even the anniversary of Dr. Nathaniel Lardner's death—these are all occasions for making-it-funny. Each time a new telephone directory comes out it is plunked on the desk of the Light Touch guy. Make it funny!

For the reason that I had the Light Touch I began getting most of the "get-rid-of-a-nut-at-the-door" jobs. A steady procession of lunatics moves through the reception room of a metropolitan newspaper and it is common practice to have a staff man talk to them in order to keep them from growing violent and heaving furniture around. Phil Stong worked on the World before he became a novelist and one day he went to the reception clerk and said: "Whenever you get an inventor of a perpetual-motion machine, send him to me." They came almost daily, and Mr. Stong accumulated a remarkable collection of blueprints, crude drawings, scale models, and scientific essays, all dealing with perpetual-motion machines.

Messiahs in sandals came to the World-Telegram reception desk, and people who had worked out new forms of government for the United States, and ladies seeking husbands or trying to get rid of them, and quacks with cures for cancer, and people who had roller-skated or crawled or walked backward or ridden a mule all the way from Yucca Valley, California, plus countless individuals with cosmic grudges against other individuals or groups.

The city desk would say, "Go get rid of a nut at the door." In the course of getting rid of many such nuts, I listened to them, and I began writing stories about them. For example, one day I went out and found a dumpy woman from Brooklyn who had a scheme for doing away with press correspondents in Washington—really a quite admirable notion. She carried a bundle of dirty documents under her arm and had a wild look in her eyes.

She told me that years earlier she had been working in the kitchen of her home. She was looking into a pan of stewing tomatoes when she *saw a voice*. She didn't hear it, she saw it. It was a message that told her the President would two days later at fifteen minutes before eleven o'clock in the morning sign a certain bill into law.

"It heppening!" she cried, banging a fist against my chest. "It heppening like I see the woices!"

Since that day, she said, she had been able to look into other kitchen utensils and determine exactly what would happen in Washington two days later. Never in any other city—just Washington. She could tell in advance what Congress would do; she knew when Cabinet members would marry or resign or drop dead; her double boiler never failed to tip her off about reciprocal trade agreements and filibusters.

She had decided to commercialize this great talent which she said God had given her. She pointed out to me that our newspaper spent large sums of money for Washington news and after spending all this money didn't get the news until after it had happened. How crezzy! How dawpey! She proposed that we discontinue all dealings with Washington correspondents and let her provide us with red-hot items from the nation's capital—two days ahead of all other newspapers. For this service she wanted fifteen dollars a week.

When I began easing her toward the elevators she grew a trifle hysterical, reading skepticism in my manner. She announced to me that her work had been fully endorsed by the White House—by both Presidents Coolidge and Hoover. In proof of this she produced a couple of dirty letters. They were written, true enough, on White House stationery. One was signed by a secretary to Coolidge, the other by a secretary to Hoover. They were worded exactly the same:

"The President has received your letter and thanks you for it."

I wrote a story about this clairvoyant lady. Another time I wrote about a nut at the desk who could write upside down and backwards using both hands toward the middle. He gave me a demonstration on a slate and I chronicled his achievement in one paragraph:

Into the World-Telegram office today came Mr. Frederick D. Anderson who said that he could write upside down and backwards using both hands toward the middle. He did it, too.

That was all. I kept it that short because I wanted to try a typographical stunt and have it printed in the paper upside down and backwards. After some discussion, the city desk agreed. The type was set in the regular way and then I went to the composing room and supervised the business of turning it upside down in the column. The printers had some difficulty understanding what I was doing. They were accustomed to being bawled out for turning items upside down in the forms, and here was a knothead from upstairs demanding a deliberate commission of the sin. We finally got it fixed and that edition of the paper came out and there it was, right in the middle of Page One. Lee Wood took one look at it and notified the copy desk that a foulup needed fixing on Page One. I went to Mr. Wood and told him it was upside down deliberately, that it was meant to be funny. He said it would only confuse the readers. I said that the readers would turn their papers upside down and they would get the point at once and it would cause them to laugh. He said he didn't think so. He was an old-time newspaper-man and he couldn't stand the sight of *anything* upside down on Page One or any other page, and when I continued pressing the point, he grew a little irritated. He said, think of all the people in the subway, reading the paper, and everybody turning it upside down, might even cause a panic. I argued that it was a good item and ought to have some special kind of typographical treatment and he said well, try it some other way. So I went back to my type-writer and wrote it backwards, beginning with the final period, this way:

.oot ,ti did eH .elddim eht drawot sdnah htob gnisu sdrawkcab
dna nwod edispu . . . and so on.

I rode this one down to the composing room and had it set and said to the printer on makeup that I wanted *it* turned upside down. He peered at the type and tried to read it and then gave me a long searching look. Printers always know everything. They know so much, they are so wise, that sometimes they don't even have to talk. This one didn't open his mouth. He just turned the item upside down and put it into the form and I went back upstairs. I wish I could have heard that man's report on the day's events when he got home that night. Well . . . Lee Wood took one look at the item when the next edition hit his desk. He walked at his usual breakneck pace to the city desk and said all right, there's a limit to all things, throw the god damn thing out.

Writing newspapermen often complain about the copyreaders —the men who read their stories for grammatical flaws and who often blue-pencil whole paragraphs and whole pages of stuff which, to the mind of the man who wrote it, was sheer deathless prose. Copyreaders are usually older men than the reporters and they usu-ally know ten times as much, and they know *that*, too. Their chief deficiency lies in a peccant humor that creeps upon them with age, withering their wits and quite often arousing in them a bitterness toward the world and its people. They are nervous irritables. They are responsible for the tradition that no one shall ever whistle in a newspaper office though some people claim this interdiction originated with nervous telegraph operators. Let a stranger walk in, whistling ever so softly, and before he has taken ten steps he is likely to get a paste pot against his head. I have seen a copyreader, driven momentarily out of his mind by a passing fire engine, rush to a window and scream curses at the Mayor of New York and all his Commissioners. Beyond this irritability, however, copyreaders are occasionally very nice guys.

I remember a young man who had a brief career as a Broadway columnist on the *World-Telegram*, during which he had the misfortune to challenge a copyreader old enough to be his grandfather. He'd turn in his copy at night and the next day it would appear in the paper with copydesk alterations and deletions. The young man grew furious over the manner in which his prose was being butchered. He found out that a certain lobster-trick copyreader, a man past sixty, was responsible and one night he telephoned this copyreader.

"Mr. Doyle," he said, "I don't want you to get sore now but I'm damned well fed up with the way you've been trimming my stuff."

Mr. Doyle held his peace.

"After all," went on the columnist, "this is Broadway stuff I'm writing. You don't know anything about Broadway. You never get around the hot spots. You're not qualified to pass on Broadway topics. Now, admit it, Mr. Doyle."

Mr. Doyle cleared his throat. Then he spoke.

"Yes, Jimmie," he said, "you're right. I'm just a country boy. I don't know a thing about Broadway and the night spots. I never been in one of those night clubs. I don't see Times Square once a year. I'm a country boy, brought up on a farm, spent most of my life on a farm, and consequently there's only one thing I know. I know horse shit when I see it."

Copyreaders are the only people in the world who, as a class, when they are casually asked how they are, respond in detail. When you salute an ordinary person with a "How ya?" he is likely to say "Fine," even though he's dying on his feet. Not a copyreader.

"How ya?" you say to a copyreader as you pass him in a corridor. Forthwith he seizes hold of you and goes into a long discussion of his bodily ills. He tells you about his liver and his kidneys and his palpitations and how he can't sleep nights and how the doctors have ordered him off whisky and how he is nothing more than a perambulating corpse.

One of the most colorful copyreaders ever to ride the rim at the *World-Telegram* was a dashing fellow named Gordon Cummings. He had a jaunty mustache and liked checkered shirts and wore a porkpie hat at his work. A copyreader will sometimes lose control of himself and cry out in agony against some horrible condition that is preying on his mind. Gordon Cummings was no exception. There were times when he would drop his tools and turn his face to the ceiling and cry out in the manner of a soul in torment: "Oh, Lord, deliver me from William Philip Simms!" Or, "Take him, Lord, take Westbrook!"

Mr. Cummings figured prominently in a drama of wartime America which I think should be adapted for television production. When the draft boards of War Two cleaned most of the young men out of the city rooms, an experiment was undertaken. The copy boys went off to war and there were no replacements, so for the first time in the history of journalism copy girls were hired. This placed a terrible strain on the conversational habits of rewrite men and assistant city editors and especially on copyreaders. All hands had been accustomed, since the time of Joe Piltdown, to the use of profanity and obscenity, both industrially and socially. For years there had been women around, writing society and fashions and cookery, but these were accustomed to strong language and, in fact, could sometimes purple up the air a bit on their own. Now all these teen-age girls were frisking about the big room, carrying copy, doing little errands, smelling fresh and full of sweet innocence. And this was the time when Errol Flynn went on trial for rape in California. The trial was a major story and yards and yards of copy poured off the tickers. Gordon Cummings was handling the Flynn story and a situation arose which led some to believe that he would grab up his shears and kill a young girl. One of the copy girls found out that she could get all the details of the Flynn trial ahead of everybody else— by simply leaning over Gordon Cummings' shoulder and reading the copy as he worked on it. My God, I shake all over just thinking about it. There is no sin known to any religion, no crime known to any court, as heinous as that of reading over a copyreader's shoulder. And here was this sweet and innocent young thing spending all her time at it, with the fiery Gordon Cummings as her victim.

It was only a matter of time until he killed her. Yet he took it for a while with cavalier patience. He had gentlemanly instincts, but they were beginning to evaporate. He mentioned in the men's room that the hour for killing the girl was not far off. Up to that time the girl had unconsciously saved her own life by never speaking to him. But the breathing on him was getting him. Everybody watched, and then the moment came when the girl spoke to him.

"Tell me something," she said. Gordon's head swung around. This meant death. "Tell me," said the girl, "does statutory rape mean doing it standing up?"

Gordon stared at her a moment, then his face twisted into a big grin, and he burst into a great howl of laughter. Everybody else roared. The tension lifted. That girl's question had solved a delicate wartime problem, a near crisis on the home front. From that moment on everyone spoke in the language he was accustomed to use at his work. And if a copy girl whistled, or leaned over a copyreader's shoulder, she was addressed in prose that was forceful and strong.

# *no sense of shame*

A bibliopolical engineer named Henry Castor informed me by mail not long ago that there is such a thing as an H. Allen Smith type of story. Mr. Castor said that a woman in California came to him with such an anecdote and . . .

> She said it had to be true, like your stories, because nobody could think up such things. She has a friend in New York, a guitarist whose hobby is collecting ancestors of the guitar. He had just recently added a cistern to his collection (it sounded like cistern, and I know it wasn't a zittern, with which I am familiar, being a cool ornithologist) and he was prowling the city for new prey. He found it in a community of Armenians— a genuine oud. An oud is something like a guitar but five feet long. Made him conspicuous hauling it home, and nowhere more conspicuous than in the subway shuttle at Grand Central. It was around three in the morning when he hit the shuttle, and only two or three other people were about, but he still felt conspicuous. Especially when one of the early birds came over to him and said, "That a mighty nice oud you've got there, mister."
>
> A rictus is a gaping orifice.

Mr. Castor is brilliant and slovenly. That man didn't have a cistern. Nor was it a sistrum. Very likely it was a cittern, a medieval instrument, offspring of the rotta, the rebab, and the rebec. Furthermore, oud is not spelled oud and I haven't been able to find out how it *is* spelled. And as for a rictus, it is the throat of a personate corolla.

It may be that the oud man story is my type of story because of my years of dealing with those nuts who came to the *World-Telegram* reception desk, though I do not wish to imply that a collector of ouds and citterns is a nut. He might be, though.

Mr. Castor somehow knew that the oud story was the type of story that would appeal to my particular sense of humor. I heard recently from Dick Bradford of New Orleans that he had experimented with growing a beard, and that it had come out scraggly and hedgehoggy and that Joe Shields had said, "It looks like the formal gardens at the House of Usher." I thought that was a very funny remark but I'm sure there are vast ethnic groups who would find nothing amusing in it.

Morris Gilbert once wrote that the greatest piece of literature ever to appear in the *World-Telegram* was a poem that came from my typewriter. It follows:

> If you should chance to meet
> A stranger on the highway,
> And for a match he asks you sweet,
> Do not turn and fly away—
> It may be your cousin.

I did not realize that it was imperishable at the time I wrote it but Mr. Gilbert, a dilettante member of the Lost Generation, said that there was a clean beauty to its lines, a rhythmic sweetness that was almost sickening.

Alton Cook, being a Midwesterner, remembers the story of the swarm of bees. Word reached the office that these bees had assembled on Sixth Avenue, covering the entire front of a saloon. The city desk assigned a young man to rush to the scene and gather a report on this natural phenomenon. He was a native New Yorker and a swarm of bees was something completely outside his experience. At last he phoned in and I got the job of taking the story from him. He covered it as he would have covered a three-alarm fire.

"I'm phoning from across the street," he said. "I can see these bastards all over the front of the saloon. There must be a couple million of them and they're all bunched up."

"What's the name of the saloon?" I asked him.

"Can't tell you that. These bees have got the name covered up so I can't read it and I don't want to go over there and ask."

"Why not?"

"Hell," he said, "I understand they bite!"

Then there were the weather stories. In the mind of every rewrite man the job of turning out a weather story was forever and always a minor irritation. Then one day Floyd Taylor, being told to do a paragraph about the weather, glanced out the window at the golden sunshine and wrote: *Weather Story: This would be a nice day to have off.* He tossed it over to Elmer Roessner on the city desk and Elmer chuckled and said hell let's use it and they did and that was the beginning. In a very short while, for the reason that I had the Light Touch, I became the author of daffy weather pieces. An artist named Bill Pause dreamed up a chicken character to illustrate these pieces, and I gave the chicken the name of Arpad. For a few years Arpad was the most famous character connected with the paper, attracting considerably more attention than Heywood Broun or Westbrook Pegler.

Most of the time I dreamed up the weather stories on the subway. The trick was to turn out a weather story that had little or no mention of the weather in it. Or, if the story did have some actual weather information in it, that information was wholly secondary and not meant especially for human consumption. Here is one with an actual forecast in it:

### THROUGH THE YEARS TO THE WEATHER

One fine, springy day in 1850 a gentleman named James Liddy, of Watertown, N.Y., went to a county fair in his surrey. It was a lousy fair and Mr. Liddy curled himself up on the seat of his surrey and went to sleep. When he awoke he felt remarkably refreshed, and he was smitten with an idea. He went home and forthwith invented the first bedsprings known to man.

Today is a nice but cloudy day—nice to go to a county fair and sleep on a surrey seat. Tomorrow it will likely rain—a good day to stay home and commune with Mr. Liddy's invention.

I remember one morning when I was feeling fierce and they told me to whip out a weather story and I picked up a newspaper and happened to glance at the latest quotations from the Fulton Fish Market. The price of dabs was given. I didn't know what a dab was. I simply wrote that dabs were bringing X-cents per pound and that you better get 'em fast because today would be warm. The next day I quoted the price of dabs again. There had been a slight rise and

I suggested that these were truly great days for the dab. Partly cloudy. After that, the weather story read, "Dabs doing okay." And finally there appeared on Page One:

Weather Story
Dabs.

I am not one to go around making hasty claims, but I do believe that is possibly the shortest weather story ever written. The most profitable weather story ever written, profitable that is to the writer thereof, was composed on a gold typewriter. It read:

> This is the only weather story ever written on a gold type-writer in the history of journalism or the history of anything else. The typewriter is called the Gold Royal and has been on display in the window of Cartier's at Fifth Ave. and 52nd St. This weather story is being composed with white gloves on in a base-ment room at Cartier's. The typewriter would cost something over $5,000 and everything on it but the space bar is heavily plated with 24-carat gold by Cartier artisans. The ribbon depos-its gold leaf on the paper and the magic margin works perfectly. The typewriter belongs to M. V. Miller, vice president of Royal. It spells fairly well and the weather for today will be much colder with rain.

The gold-leaf letters were typed on black paper and then photo-graphed and used in the paper, spread over three columns, with a picture of the author wearing white gloves and sitting at the gold typewriter. Well, the Royal people were so happy about the whole thing that they sent me one of their typewriters. This book is being written on it just as twenty-some other books have been written on it, and countless articles and stories for the magazines, and thou-sands of letters.

There was meaning behind all that foolishness, for both those who wrote the weather stories and those who read them. They repre-sented an unconscious revolt against the stiff and formalized and long-winded and unintelligible weather reports that had been ap-pearing in the newspapers for ages. Previously we had been accus-tomed to writing meteorological bilge about occluded fronts which nobody understood and dry adiabatic lapse rate which nobody un-derstood and upside down isobars which nobody gave a damn about. Even we who wrote the stuff didn't know what we were saying. Two or three words would do it—the rest was all dressing and ornament. And so it is today on television. All that is needed is for Miss Have-a-Happy to poke her head in view and holler, "Umbrellas tonight!" or "Head for the beach!" or "Sticky."

The weather stories finally attracted the molasses-slow, rhinoceros-heavy attention of *Time* magazine. They did a story and in one single column of type there were only about eight errors of fact—a splendid sort of showing for *Time*. The magazine story was responsible for the fact that I'm inclined to wince when people say to me: "I remember your stuff a long time back—when you were writing those weather stories." The *Time* piece was largely about me and I became aware at once of a whole series of small, petty jealousies around the office. People got real upset, and worked themselves into swivets, like girls. One man on the staff came forward and said that hell, he originated the funny weather story ten years earlier, and he got to believing it, and went out and tried to drink himself to death. The whole business of the weather story became unpleasant to me, and I tried to get out of ever writing any more of them. I sometimes think that there are a thousand incidents in my life that would drive a psychiatrist off his rocker. And one of these would be the fact that I was rendered unhappy by a weather story. Maybe containing a single word: dabs.

The United States Weather Bureau never decorated me for my work. I've won no Pulitzer prize. The French Government has never pinned a ribbon on me. I have no medals. But I must make mention of the one single stroke of recognition I've had in a long career as a writer. Occasionally the trade papers print the lists of the awards that have been made to writers. These lists run into pages and pages of type. It takes hard and earnest effort to *avoid* getting one of these medals, cash awards, fellowships, loving cups, scrolls. I have done it. Through sheer perseverance I have succeeded in writing a whole shelf full of books without receiving so much as a Cub Scout salute. Once, however, I had My Moment. I got My Award. It was a scroll declaring me to be the outstanding feature writer of the metropolitan press. I was so voted by the vast student body of New York University. Well, not exactly the entire student body. Just the junior class. That is, the junior class of the School of Commerce. Not the *whole* School of Commerce—just the Washington Square branch. The scroll was presented to me at the Junior Prom and the award was such a citywide sensation that my own newspaper reported all the facts the next day and then said:

Mr. Smith arrived at work this morning only ten minutes late. A reporter was immediately assigned to interview him. He said:

"In my tempestuous career as a newspaperman I have met many college people and I have attended perhaps 422 Junior Proms, or what appeared to be Junior Proms. I can say, however, that never before have I seen such an intelligent bunch of young people. There before me last night was a sea of faces. Beautiful young womanhood. Handsome young manhood. And intelligence was writ in every countenance.

"Up until then I had always felt that college people were sort of dopey. But these people, these New York University Juniors, are unquestionably the most brilliant people I have ever met."

Mr. Smith will be required to work his full eight hours today. No time off for scroll-staring.

All this while I had been doing interviews. On slow afternoons the desk would let me go uptown and see famous visitors and write about them. I developed a frightening technique in this direction for Ben Crisler, himself an interviewer for the New York *Times*, wrote about me one Sunday as "the man whom film actresses dream about after eating too much Welsh rabbit, lobster thermidor, etc. Mr. Smith is the cold-bloodedly empirical interviewer who tickled Simone Simon to test the theory that she was ticklish, and who is generally regarded in select Hollywood circles very much as the goblins are regarded in the poem by James Whitcomb Riley."

I would fain point to one small error in Mr. Crisler's glowing tribute. I did not tickle Miss Simon to test the theory that she was ticklish; I goosed her to test the theory that she was goosey. But in those archaic days one didn't say such things in print; one didn't even goose young women. Often.

I think I must have interviewed every Hollywood star of any consequence in those years and I enjoyed myself doing it. For one thing, that kind of work gave me an opportunity to meet such a man as John Barrymore. And such a woman as Joan Crawford. Then there were interviews with the Sally Rands and the Faith Bacons and the Mae Wests and the Gypsy Rose Lees and the Lois DaFees. I wrote about a remarkable girl named Marian Miller who came out of my native state of Illinois and who worked in a New York burlesque house. She could hold her body perfectly still and make her breasts jump. She could make them jump from side to side, in unison.

Then they would jump away from each other and back together again. After that they jumped up and down, and finally she made them rotate. She did it for me. "Do it again," I said, for I thought it an incredible performance. She did it again. Then she talked a bit about how it was all a matter of muscular control. After that, just to make sure, I had her do it again. It was a real pleasure to interview that girl.

Dozens of the interviews I wrote have been reproduced in earlier books and I don't intend to repeat them here, save for one. That was my meeting with Miss Kathleen Fears. She belongs in the story of my life for she represents, once again, the interposition of Fate.

If you can remember back to the account of my days in Tulsa and my marriage there, you may recall that the church editor of the Tulsa *Tribune* was instrumental in lining up a clergyman for me. She was the one who fell in love with the Roxy Theatre. Years later a press agent walked into the office of the *World-Telegram* and offered me the opportunity of interviewing a girl who also had been church editor of the Tulsa *Tribune*. She had given up religious writing and was now impersonating Anna Held in a night club tableau by entering a bathtub full of milk while naked.

At the night club I found Miss Fears in a dressing room that was being used during the evenings by Ozzie Nelson, then a band leader. She was six feet tall and had dark red hair and looked something like Loretta Young. She had a certain aura about her which, for want of a better term, I have given the name "sex appeal." She took her ease on a wicker chair and we talked of Tulsa.

"I finished high school," she said, "and one day just walked into the *Tribune* office and said I wanted to be a reporter. They made me the church editor right away, but what I really wanted to do was go out with the cops and do murders and rapes. They said if I worked hard I might lead up to something like that. From what I had always heard a newspaper office was a tough sort of place so I always smoked cigarettes around the city room. I liked to sit with my feet cocked up on a desk because my legs are so darn long. Then the boss came around and said that it was all right with him personally but I would have to keep my skirts down and my feet on the floor and quit smoking because the reverends were always dropping in with news items. I have no sense of shame, you know."

This last observation was followed by an interruption from Eddie Lynch, the photographer who had come along.

"Would you," he said, "please take off your clothes now so we can get some pictures?"

"Why, certainly," said Miss Fears. She went on talking while she removed her hat, coat, shoes, stockings, dress, and other random items of raiment. She had no sense of shame. Eventually she was down to a G string. A G string, if you didn't know it, is what is left after an H-bomb scores a direct hit on a bikini. Miss Fears lit a cigarette and crossed her legs.

"Sally Rand," she said, "came to Tulsa and she had a group of girls who were six feet tall or over. She happened to see me one day when she was in the *Tribune* office and the next thing you know I'm touring with her show. We didn't have to do nudes—the tall girls. We had one act where at the end we turned our backs to the audience and the seat of our pants fell out. That was the nearest we ever got to it. For me that was a sort of warming up for later things to come."

Miss Fears later left the employ of Miss Rand and by 1935 she was exhibiting her charms on Broadway.

"One year at the Casa Manana," she said, "I did the main nude. They had me in a glass house that came up on an elevator through the floor of the stage. I thought up the idea of painting my bosoms red for that act. You should have seen it. It went over big. I looked like a couple of stop lights coming out of the basement."

Eddie Lynch was getting jumpy, and broke in again to say we had better get started on the pictures. All this while he had been staring at Miss Fears, cocking his head to one side, standing in different parts of the room and sighting at her with one eye and then the other and behaving in a most professional manner. Finally he opened a door that led into a bathroom and suggested that we shoot Miss Fears standing in the shower. The room was cold but she didn't seem to mind. She said she gloried in going naked and believed that it made her healthy. She said she never felt the cold and in all that expanse of flesh I couldn't detect a single goose pimple. If there had been one, I'd have seen it. As she got off the wicker chair I noticed that the pattern of the weave had been transmitted to her skin, giving her a most enticing appearance. Newspaper work can be rugged.

Eddie took a dozen shots of her, none of which ever saw an

engraving room. Then Miss Fears returned to the wicker. I asked her about G strings. They had become a significant part of the contemporary American scene; Sally Rand even had a practice of autographing old used G strings for her close friends. I asked Miss Fears where the G string got its name.

"I really couldn't say for sure," she said, "but I've always been told that it comes from the G string of a violin, which is very low and at the same time first class."

She said she hoped to be a fashion designer and then I asked her about romance. She said she would marry a millionaire if he was nice-looking and kept his mouth shut and stayed home while she went on trips around the world. It is a peculiar thing how much stronger the flood of romantic feeling surges in the hearts of women than in the hearts of men. As I write this chapter of my book Miss Bette Davis is quoted in the public prints as feeling much the same as Miss Fears felt more than twenty years ago. Miss Davis said yes, she would gladly marry again if she could find a man who had fifteen million dollars, would agree to sign over half of it to her before the marriage, and would guarantee that he would be dead within a year.

Miss Fears mentioned an additional stipulation in regard to romance.

"I wouldn't even marry a millionaire," she said, "if he was fat. I hate fat people. A fat man ran up to me once and bit me on the chest and I have never liked fat men since then."

I wanted to ask her if she minded it very much if lean men bit her on the chest, but then I thought this might sound flippant. Anyway she said she had another appointment, and so she put her clothes back on and shook hands warmly and said it had been quite a coincidence—a former Tulsa reporter being interviewed by another Tulsa reporter.

I don't forget my old newspaper friends. I have never forgotten Miss Kathleen Fears. I still have her picture, posed gracefully in the shower. Very low and first class.

# ... and nobody else is either

In the hallway of my office are two tall green cabinets that are crammed with memorabilia and organic fertilizer, all relating to my sparkling and spectacular career in the world of letters. Plus a bushel or two of notes on which I have set down my rollicking opinions of the literary life.

These files must stand fallow for a while. I need to live a little longer. I have reached the age where I bump into things; where I was once accustomed to walking around the corner of a building, now there's a good chance I'll hit it. Still, I intend to go banging and blundering around and within a couple of years or so I may be able to get at Volume Two of these reminiscences. I have a strong suspicion that the nuclear bombs will be falling before then but they will clean out the readers as well as the writers and it will be a sort of Mexican standoff.

My newspaper years and my years as a free-lance litterateur overlap slightly. While I was on the *World-Telegram* I started two different books and threw them away. Then I wrote two books that were published without anyone much noticing the fact. Finally, against my will, I wrote one that became a big hit. The details of all these events and my subsequent doings at home and abroad all belong in Volume Two.

As I finish this one, the autobiography of Virgilia Peterson has been making quite a stir. It is her second book of memoirs. I have had traffic with her in the past and if I were not already bespoken and took, I would enjoy marrying her—she'd be ready to write

Volume Three in ten days time. Her book has been described in the following terms:

"In this unique document, Virgilia Peterson has probed herself and her time with a fierce and shining integrity . . . Fascinating, superbly and subtly intelligent, *and* intelligently written . . . It is a sensitive, generous, compelling and compassionate book . . . A high-spirited, disciplined and honorable book, intensely personal and passionately honest . . . unsparing, dramatic and most beautifully written . . . I have rarely found such poignant honesty nor so much hard-earned dignity in self-revelation."

Coincidence again! Sounds almost exactly like *this* book, doesn't it? Well, maybe not quite. But one thing I can tell you: my second volume will stand up under that description. And it will be better than this first volume because in it I intend to state my opinion of things. I'm going to speak my mind in Volume Two.

One last thing remains to be reported here. I still had to deliver a message entrusted to me on the day I left Denver in 1929. It took twelve years to do it. In the final months of my newspaper work an invitation came from a movie company. A new producer had been hired in New York and before he departed for Hollywood a party was being given in his honor. I attended and at a propitious moment walked up to . . . but let Damon Runyon tell it himself:

> When Mr. Smith first came to New York some years ago he brought a verbal note of introduction to us from an old acquaintance in Denver, a Mr. Joe Diner, long the steward of the Denver Press Club and known to hundreds of newspapermen between the Coasts. We have not seen Mr. Diner in years but our recollection of him is undimmed by time. Mr. Smith did not deliver his note of introduction until recently. He stepped up to us one evening and without any preamble remarked: "Joe Diner says hello."
>
> We understood at once. It was Mr. Diner's way of letting us know that Mr. Smith was all right. We do not know if Mr. Smith ever fully appreciated the compliment to himself in the cryptic message but Mr. Diner never lightly put his okay on an individual.
>
> H. Allen Smith is slugging up there with the leaders in the literary department. We judge he is belting in that league at about the pace Joe DiMaggio is maintaining in the American . . .
>
> Mr. Joe Diner would feel proud of Mr. Smith.

One thing you can depend on about me. I'll deliver a message.

And so at the finish I find myself indulging in a change of heart; I have decided to accept the designation of *humorist*. I do so with a low obeisance in the direction of a man named Homer McLin. A few years ago there was a discussion in a national magazine concerning the proper definition of a humorist. Mr. McLin wrote in from New Albany, Indiana, as follows:

> A humorist is a fellow who realizes, first, that he is no better than anybody else and, second, that nobody else is either.

I am a humorist:

# Index